HOW INDIA LOST HER FREEDOM

HOW INDIA LOST HER FREEDOM

Pandit
SUNDERLAL

Popular Prakashan
www.popularprakashan.com

Published by
Asmita Mohite for
POPULAR PRAKASHAN PVT. LTD.
301, Mahalaxmi Chambers
22, Bhulabhai Desai Road
Mumbai - 400 026
info@popularprakashan.com

First published in Hindi, in March 1929
2nd Edition published in November 1937
3rd Edition published in 1960 by Publications Division, Government of India
4th edition published in 1963
First published in English by Popular Prakashan in 1970
Reprinted in 2018
Reprinted in 2023

(4551)
ISBN: 978-81-7154-490-5

PRINTED IN INDIA
by Trinity Academy For Corporate Training Ltd.
Pune

CONTENTS

HISTORY OF THIS BOOK

While this book was being written, it created such a stir that a decision to ban the book was already taken by the British Government. The first edition of 2,000 copies appeared on 18 March 1929, and the book was banned on 22 March 1929. Between this gap of four days, 1,700 copies were sold. Mahatma Gandhi described this proscription as "Daylight Robbery" and advised the people to break the law and to face imprisonment rather than submit the book to the authorities. After persistent efforts the ban was at last lifted on 13 November 1937. The second edition of 10,000 copies appeared soon after and was sold outright against orders received for 14,000 copies. The third edition was brought out by Publications Division, Government of India, in 1960 which was soon followed by fourth edition in 1963.

FOREWORD

I consider it a great privilege and an overwhelming honour to write a foreword for this book by late Pandit Sunderlal. Pandit ji was the rarest of the rare combination of spiritual, intellectual and human qualities. He was a multifaceted person. Perhaps his most unique aspect was his unconditional and complete belief in humanism in its most complete sense, which he practised like a true *Karamyogi*.

My connection with Pandit ji goes back three generations. My late grandfather, Mr Abdul Majid Khwaja (1885–1962), and Pandit ji were close friends; they participated in the Freedom Movement and made enormous personal sacrifices in winning independence for our country from the British rule. My first memories of Pandit ji are his coming to our house in Aligarh during the 1960s when I was just entering my teenage years. My father, Professor Jamal Khwaja, former Lok Sabha MP from Aligarh (1957–62) and an eminent philosopher who taught at the Aligarh Muslim University (AMU), treated Pandit ji like his uncle. Pandit ji treated me and my siblings like his grandchildren. Indeed, I consider myself utterly blessed to have met towering personalities like Pandit Sunderlal, Raja Mahendra Pratap and Dr B. N. Pande, three eminent nationalist freedom fighters and statesmen. I can say in all humility that my interaction with these personalities in my formative years played a great role in the evolution of my philosophical, intellectual and spiritual growth. One cannot overstate the great inspirational impact of meeting noble human beings, who by their mere presence and their actions, silently but irrevocably, transform for the better all who come in contact with them.

Late Mr A. M. Khwaja and Pandit ji shared many common values. One of the most powerful was the study of different religious thought systems and a commitment to promoting peace and harmony among the followers of all religions in India. My father played a key role in imparting to his children the values of humanism, tolerance and empathy. He encouraged us to shun narrow-minded prejudices which blight one's personality and promote intolerance and negativism in society.

I recall meeting Pandit ji many times in our ancestral house, Sami Manzil in Aligarh, from the 1960s onwards. One event which deeply influenced me was when my father invited Pandit ji in 1973 to give the main discourse when our newly constructed house (called Al-hamd) was inaugurated. The traditional practice in the Muslim community is to have a *Milad* in which verses from the Holy Quran are recited and a talk on the Prophet of Islam is given. It shocked many people when my father invited Pandit ji to give the main talk for the *Milad*. Being a great scholar of Islam, Pandit ji gave a scholarly, powerful and compelling discourse which included recitation of the verses from the Holy Quran in Arabic and their translation in simple Hindustani. He also spoke fluently on the life and preaching of Prophet Mohammed (PBUH). This was a transformational event for the audience present. Many of them later profusely thanked my father for exposing them to the great knowledge of Quran and Islam which Pandit ji had. Some of them confessed that this was an eye-opening event in their life. They realized that if one is born into a particular religion, it does not mean that he/she should not deeply study and respect other religions.

Another important event which I recall is my father inviting Pandit ji to give a lecture in the famous Kennedy Hall of AMU somewhere around 1970. If I remember correctly, the basic theme of this lecture was 'Pluralism and Tolerance as Civilizational Values'. I vividly recall the audience being spellbound by Pandit ji's deep and erudite knowledge and the breadth of his vision. Moist eyes were common when Pandit ji used to speak—he was so powerful in his oratory. The genuineness and authenticity of his thoughts and actions used to trigger powerful waves in the audience who used to instantly connect with him. Both these events are as fresh as yesterday in my memory and continue to be an abiding source of strength and inspiration to me.

I studied BA (Hons) History at St. Stephen's College, Delhi, as an undergraduate from 1971 to 1974. In 1973, I came across Pandit ji's book *How India Lost Her Freedom* in the college library. Having been already exposed to Pandit ji, I read the book page to page with great diligence. This book changed the way I looked at history. The book followed the fundamental principles of historiography, that is, whatever you record should be based on authentic sources and not on hearsay, conjectures and assumptions. The famous historian E. H. Carr has most lucidly and with great clarity expounded on the broad principles of historiography in his famous book *What Is History*. Taken together, these books of E. H. Carr and Pandit ji help in understanding why history is an important discipline. It inspired me to pursue my MA in history from AMU after completion of my graduation.

The great contribution of Pandit ji is in his original work of four volumes titled *Bharat Mein Angrezi Raj*, published in the 1929, proscribed by the British and later republished when the ban on the book was lifted. It was in the 1970 that Pandit ji's monumental work in Hindi was translated into English and published by Popular Prakashan, Mumbai. Pandit ji has irrevocably exposed the deep, sinister and unfortunate prejudices of British historians who have distorted original sources through selective misquotations and false translations of some original texts. Their basic objective was the splitting of Hindus and Muslims, promoting hatred among them, dividing the Indian society and thereby establishing their colonial rule.

Without being emotional, Pandit ji has quoted extensively from the original sources, exposing in particular the translations of Elliot and Dowson among others. I consider it a great tragedy of our times that most Indians are unaware of the true facts. Many serious controversies currently prevalent in our society can be understood in the correct light when we read this book. We will then discover shocking untruths and totally false so-called facts, which are accepted today by society, to be the creation of fertile minds intent on dividing the Indian society and weakening it.

The recent book by Shashi Tharoor *An Era of Darkness: The British Empire in India*, which has received well-deserved recognition and appreciation, is, in many ways, a continuation of

Pandit ji's work in *How India Lost Her Freedom*. The approach of Mr Tharoor is similar to Pandit ji's monumental work. I am not sure whether Mr Tharoor had read Pandit ji's book before writing his extremely compelling and intellectually sound history on the impact of colonialism in India.

Pandit ji launched the publication *Karamyogi* in 1909. He was also the editor of *Swarajya*, a Hindi weekly in the early part of the 20th century. He was President of the All India Peace Council between 1950 and 1962. I understand that he has authored more than 40 books. He was President of the India–China Friendship Association. He established the Hindustani Culture Society in 1941 as its Founder Secretary. The Presidents of the Hindustani Culture Society included eminent personalities such as Dr Sir Tej Bahadur Sapru, Bharat Ratna Dr Bhagwan Das, Mr A. M. Khwaja, Dr Syed Mahmud and Padma Vibhushan Dr Tara Chand.

It is fascinating to note that Pandit ji was originally a revolutionary freedom fighter and a member of the famous Ghadar Party. His comrades included Lala Hardayal and Sachindranath Sanyal who were involved in a conspiracy against Lord Curzon, the then Viceroy of India. After coming into close contact with Mahatma Gandhi in the early 1920s, Pandit ji became a Gandhian and a true practitioner of non-violence or Ahimsa. He was jailed seven times for his participation in the freedom movement of our country. In many ways, Pandit ji represents a holistic evolution of a revolutionary freedom fighter to a Gandhian believing in non-violence. Indeed, it would be difficult to find many among his contemporaries who can match Pandit ji's multifaceted qualities as a practitioner of peace and non-violence in its widest sense.

The three key life missions of Pandit ji included: promoting essential unity of all religions; promoting communal harmony between Hindus and Muslims; and promoting and practising the composite culture of India. In 1944, Pandit ji published his famous book *Gita Aur Quran* simultaneously in Hindi and Urdu. Later, the book was translated to Gujarati, Marathi, Bengali and Arabic. Its English version was published in 1957. After being out of print for many decades, it was recently republished in 2016. This book is one of the most powerful books which one can ever hope to read as it conveys the message of the Bhagavad Gita and the Holy Quran, emphasizing the commonality of their universal message. In today's turbulent times, the need for reading *Gita Aur Quran* cannot be overemphasized. The two books of Pandit ji available now in English should be essential reading for all Indians to understand our '*Bharatiyata*' and the greatness of our Indo-Vedic civilization.

I must record my highest gratitude for SAGE Publications for taking this seminal initiative of publishing *How India Lost Her Freedom*. SAGE is doing a great service to humanity and to our country by printing Pandit ji's work which had gone into oblivion.

It is my sincere and fervent hope that all readers of this book will start understanding that it is only through peace, empathy, tolerance and compassion that a nation and its people can develop. The seeds of bigotry and violence cannot blossom into fragrant flowers of peaceful coexistence. I feel a strong personal and spiritual connection with Pandit ji in penning these few thoughts.

R. H. KHWAJA, IAS (Retd)
Former Secretary to the Government of India

INTRODUCTION

The Art of Writing History

The present-day art of writing history is very much a product of modern European civilization. The art existed more or less in ancient China, India, Iran and Egypt also. In each one of these countries we have got some written records of that country's ancient civilization. This art further developed in ancient Greece and in ancient Rome. Some of the works of history written by Greek and Roman writers of that period are still regarded as authoritative. Then came the period of Arab supremacy. Probably no ancient people laboured so much on giving a scientific form to the art of writing history as the Arabs. The Arabs made special efforts to preserve historical truth in their historical writings. In the 11th century A.D., the famous Arab historian Al-Berouni wrote a very beautiful scientific treatise on the art of writing history. He warns all students of history that it is very difficult for any writer of history to avoid misstatements born of his own natural prejudices and proclivities. The Arabs also produced a number of other critical writers on the art of history-writing, men whose scientific analysis of the subject is still regarded as valuable. Still we must admit that no historical events were recorded in such detail in ancient times as is the case today. In ancient times, and specially in ancient India, the task of writing a history of one's own country or of one's people was not given so much importance as it is given now. That is the reason why we find no connected history of ancient India today. That is why in order to study the history of most of the ancient civilizations we have to take help from their classics and mythological stories, their popular legends, their stone inscriptions, their general literature, their coins and similar other sources.

As a matter of fact, the reason for our attaching so much importance to the art of history-writing in modern times is to be found in the peculiar mental outlook of present-day nations. The fact also appears to be that history-writing is not considered so important for the true development of man as it is considered today. Our works of history mostly deal with the political conditions prevailing at a particular period. Probably no man can be absolutely unbiased in matters concerning contemporary politics. Consciously or unconsciously, every writer has his or her own prejudices and preconceptions. No two writers give equal importance to any particular event of their time or look at any event from the same point of view. Besides one's personal prejudices and proclivities, every writer suffers from his social, communal or national prejudices also, and these prejudices cannot but lend their own colour to his writing. Therefore, it is almost impossible to get an absolutely unbiased record of historical events. Again, such biased historical narratives themselves become instrumental in infecting their readers with the same bias. The mischief goes on from generation to generation. Moreover, why should human memory be burdened with an infinite number of dates and an equal number of names of individuals and their doings and characters? Our mental capacities, after all, are limited. May it not be better if, instead of remembering all the evil deeds and the good deeds of those who have gone before us, we concentrate only on the good in all, and on the results of our collective human experience from age to age? We know that in politics particularly, mutual hatred and the conflicts of real or supposed self-interests play a much greater part than love of humanity or sacrifice for other's good. That is why Indian, Greek or other writers of old, the writers of *puranas* or mythological stories, instead of writing detailed accounts of their own time or a detailed history of their own country, preferred to leave for posterity a record of the highest moral, social and religious ideals till then reached by humanity in their mythological narrations. That is also why in some of the noblest books in ancient literature even the author's name is not mentioned. That is why it is almost impossible to know the actual dates of events mentioned in ancient Indian history or in our literature. It is in this sense that books like the *Ramayana* and the *Mahabharata* are much more helpful and of much greater benefit to mankind than the usual works of history.

Difficulties Facing Writing of History

The difficulties which face a writer of contemporary history increase considerably in the case of a writer of past history. The latter too has to depend upon similarly biased and, therefore, coloured accounts of those times. On account of the distance in time and lack of authentic knowledge of conditions then prevailing, the writer has to grope through even greater darkness. Such difficulties multiply in the case of a writer of the history of India, especially of the British period of Indian history. The writer has to draw mainly on available records by British writers of the period. No continuous historical record of that period written by any Indian writer of those times is available. The few incomplete records of current events that are available contain internal evidence of the sad fact that at least some of the Indian writers of those days were in the pay of the British.

Wherever and whenever a nation has been ruled by another nation, writers belonging to the ruling nation have naturally tried, on the one hand, to write up and so encourage the patriotism, the self-confidence, the self-respect and the courage of their own nationals, *i.e.,* the rulers, and, on the other, to write down and so discourage the growth of these very qualities among the ruled. Almost all "Indian history books" of the period written by British writers are saturated with this proclivity of their authors. Perhaps, the history of no other country in the world has been so deeply coloured and even distorted as that of India of those days, as presented by contemporary writers. The nature of the relationship between India and England at the time had made it almost impossible for history-writers generally to produce an impartial "historical" record of contemporary events. The Imperialist outlook of British writers, on the one hand, and British influence on the minds of the English-educated Indians who had to earn a living under their British masters, on the other, led to an inevitable distortion of facts and events. Thus it is that the available material on the history of India relating to the British period is full of

(i) emphasis on comparatively trivial and meaningless events and things,
(ii) suppression or minimisation of the importance of really important historical records,
(iii) misrepresentation of important historical events and even of their sequence,
(iv) Falsely blackening the character and the deeds of Indian personalities and similarly white-washing the character and the deeds of British personalities of the period, and even
(v) complete omission of many a real and true fact and event and at the same time presentation as true of purely imaginary happenings.

With isolated exceptions, even the "histories" written by Indians, particularly by Indian professors of British-dominated Indian universities, are also infected with this sort of poison. It may be admitted, to our shame, that sometimes the infection is even more virulent in the case of Indian writers. It could not be otherwise in view of the unnatural position of India at that time.

In support of our contention, we reproduce below some excerpts from the writings of only a few European scholars.

The famous French scholar, M. Herve writes:

> "History, so far, has been the most immoral and perverting branch of literature. It exalts greed and wholesale murder when greedy and murderous lusts are satisfied in the names of nations. Fraud is taken as evidence of clever diplomacy. What is counted immoral down below is held admirable in courts and on thrones."

The well-known historian, Lecky, writes:

> "The object of the politician is expediency ... a disinterested love of truth can hardly co-exist with a strong political spirit. In all countries where the habits of thought have been mainly formed by political life, we may discover a disposition to make expediency the test of truth." *(Rationalism in Europe)*

The distinguished British philosopher, Herbert Spencer, relates that a particular king of France, whenever he wished to read a book on history, used to say to his librarian "Bring me my liar." Spencer writes that the above remark of the French king was not far from truth concerning books of history written during his time. Spencer says:

> "Beyond accounts of kings' reigns, of battles, and of incidents named in the chronicles of all the nations concerned, we have nothing to depend on but treaties made to be broken, despatches of corrupt and lying officials, gossiping letters of courtiers and so forth. How from these materials shall we distil the truth?" *(Facts and Comments)*

Lies in State Papers

The early history of British rule in India has perforce to be gathered mostly from the published reports and other papers of the East India Company. About the authenticity of these, James Mill, who was at one time the head in England of the correspondence branch of the East India Company, and whose *History of British India* is considered to be most authentic, warns us of

> "the skill which the Court of Directors have all along displayed in suppressing such information as they wished not to appear."

In the advertisement to the second edition of Captain J. D. Cunningham's well-known book, *History of the Sikhs,* 1853, P. Cunningham writes:

> "The printed materials for the recent History of India are not of that character on which historians can rely. State papers, presented to the people by both Houses of (British) Parliament, have been altered to suit the temporary views of political warfare, or abridged out of mistaken regard to the tender feelings of survivors."

The well-known historian, Sir John Kaye, who had once been the Secretary of the Political & Secret Department of the India Office in England, has this to say at one place in relation to the Afghan War:

> "The character and career of Alexander Burnes have both been misrepresented in those collections of State papers which are supposed to furnish the best materials of history, but which are often only one-sided compilations of garbled documents, counterfeits which the ministerial stamp forces into currency, defrauding a present generation, and handing down to posterity a chain of dangerous lies." (*History of the Afghan War,* Vol. II p. 13)

The reader will know more about these "one-sided compilations of garbled documents" in the pages of this book, especially in the chapter on the Afghan War and in several other places. If such is the reliability of the records of the British Parliament, then to what extent can the statements of ordinary history-writers be depended upon?

The historian Freeman concedes that the British Government's proclamations, dispatches and other political documents constitute "the very chosen region of lies". He goes on to say:

> "Here we are in the very chosen region of lies ... yet they are instructive lies; they are lies told by people who knew the truth; truth may even, by various processes, be got out of the lies; but it will not be got out of them by the process of believing them. He is of childlike simplicity indeed who believes every royal proclamation or the preamble of every Act of Parliament as telling us, not only what certain

august persons did, but the motives which led them to do it."

Some Instances of Lies in "Histories"

Till about 1924 A.D., the writer of this book could not imagine the number and the fearfulness of the lies that had, in fact, found a place in most of the books of the history of India written by Englishmen.

Of all books in English about Sindh, *The Conquest of Sindh* by Major-General William Napier (the brother of Sir Charles Napier, the "conqueror" of Sindh) is considered to be the most authentic! To prove that the conquest of Sindh by the British was a boon conferred by them on mankind, William Napier has in numerous ways blackened the character of the people and the Muslim rulers of Sindh of the time by falsely accusing both of unheard of inhumanities. One of the accusations was of "infanticide", about which Napier writes:

> "And how did these monsters destroy their own children? First they gave potions, called *odalisques,* to procure abortion; if these failed, they sometimes chopped the children to pieces with their own hands immediately after birth; but more frequently placed them under cushions and sat down on them, smoking and drinking and jesting with each other about their hellish work, while their, children were being suffocated beneath them." (*The Conquest of Sindh,* Part II, p. 384)

The atrocious lie has been exposed by Captain Eastwick who had lived in Sindh and had ample opportunities of mixing with the people of Sindh and their rulers for a number of years during the period. He also knew the Sindhi language and was well acquainted with the prevailing customs of the Sindhis. In support of his exposure of this scandalous lie, Captain East wick has given the following quotation from the *History of Netherlands* (Vol. II, p. 242) by another European scholar, Frattan.

> "There are many statements of history which it is immaterial to substantiate or disprove. Splendid pictures of public virtue have often produced their good if once received as fact. But when private character is at stake, every conscientious writer or reader will cherish his 'historic doubts'; when he reflects on the facility with which calumny is sent abroad, the avidity with which it is received, and the careless ease with which men credit what it costs little to invent and propagate, but required an age of trouble and an almost impossible conjunction of opportunities effectually to refute."

It is needless to repeat that according to the evidence of Englishmen themselves, the statement of William Napier is a pure concoction. Till 1843 when the East India Company occupied Sindh, the moral standard and the private character of the people and the rulers of Sindh, collectively and individually, were far higher and purer than those of Napier and his countrymen of those days. Not only have the people of Sindh been falsely and baselessly defamed by Napier in his book, but he has also tried his hardest to tar with the same brush the Amirs (rulers) of Sindh too. Those Amirs, who had never in their life touched anything intoxicating, who had religiously avoided even smoking and who took extraordinary precautions for the protection of the honour and chastity of women, have been painted by Napier as drunkards and libertines. We are making these affirmations on the basis of what has been written by dependable and responsible British writers of that period. Further details about this affair will be found in our chapter on Sindh in this book.

False Accusations Against Indian Rulers

In exactly the same way, Siraj-ud-daula has been described in English history books as a licentious profligate and drunkard of the worst type. Siraj-ud-daula, in deference to the death-bed advice of his maternal grandfather, Alivardi Khan, never touched liquor since the day of his ascending the throne up to the last day of his life. (Scrafton's *Reflections,* as quoted in *Banglarltihas, Nawabi Amal* by Kali Prasanna Bandyopadhyaya.) His private life was unblemished except possibly for such weaknesses as were common to the lives of 99% of Indian or British rulers of that day. Similarly, grave injustice has been done to the character and private lives of Mir Kassim, Haidar Ali, Tipu Sultan, Nand Coomar, and other Indian heroes and heroines.

The English historian, Sir John Kaye, plainly avers:

> "… It is a custom amongst us … to take a native ruler's kingdom and then to revile the deposed ruler or his would be successor." (*History of the Sepoy War,* Vol. III, pp. 361–62)

Fictitious Pictures

Important incidents and events have been similarly dealt with. Even the pictures of Indian rulers in several books are entirely fictitious. Haider Ali's picture in several English history books depicts him with moustache and beard. The fact is that he had discarded both since his adolescence. In Cassell's *History of India,* which is considered to be authentic, we find a picture of Emperor Bahadur Shah with his beard dressed up in the Rajput style, with a *dhoti* round his loins like that of a Marwari and with a pair of Rajput shoes on his feet!

As a matter of fact, at least 90% of the books on the history of India prescribed in the curriculums of our schools and colleges, particularly till the end of the first half of the 20th century and to an extent even now, have no greater factual value than ordinary fiction. The only correct statements in them generally are the dates of certain events, the names of rulers and such other things. Such works of history are extremely harmful and have exerted and are exerting an extremely poisonous influence on the developing mind of Indian youth.

Hired Writers

The historical narratives of a few Indian scholars of that period are, no doubt, truthful and dependable to a certain extent. But their number is very small. Besides, we are faced with another great difficulty with regard to them.

See-arul Mutakhareen, written in Persian, is considered to be and is in fact a fairly reliable history of the last days of the Mughal Empire in India. Even so, Syed Ghulam Hussain, its learned author, admits in the book itself that he had been won over by the British during the war between the British and Emperor Shah Alam. Thus, whatever he wrote about the incidents of that period is a narrative by one who had been hired by the British for writing in a particular way.

There were several other writers (amongst them Indians too) of history books in Persian and other languages who were paid by the East India Company, from time to time, for recording fictitious events in their writings. As an instance, we might mention Abbe Dubois. He wrote in French his famous book about the manners and customs of the Hindus of his time. Lord William Bentinck paid Dubois eight thousand rupees for it and got the book published in English under the sponsorship of the East India Company and the latter gave a life-pension to Dubois for that service.

For writing a life of Haider Ali in Persian, Mirza Iqbal, its author, was paid by the East India Company. The book, from beginning to end, is full of bias, prejudices and baseless vilification of Haider Ali's character.

Col. Miles has written a *Life of Haider Ali* in English, which he claims is a translation from the Persian book, *Nishan-Hyideri* by Mir Hussain Ali Khan, whose original manuscript was supposed to be in the private library of Queen Victoria. We have read Col. Miles' book and were amazed to find page after page containing phrases and expressions quite identical with those which are to be found in the English edition of a French writer's book, *History of Haidar Shah.* The French book had been written during the life-time of Haider Ali. Mir Hussain Ali Khan's Persian book was written thereafter. If the Persian writer had lifted these phrases and expressions from the French book or from its English translation, then it would be impossible to believe that in translating these from Persian into English Col. Miles just happened to use whole phrases and expressions which occur in the English translation of the French book. It is obvious, therefore, that either the alleged Persian manuscript does not exist anywhere or Col. Miles' book is not a translation, as claimed by him, of any such Persian manuscript.

Other similar instances can be quoted about the "histories" of India of the British period. It is true that, then as now, honesty or truth had no place in Western political life. It is also a fact that, to a very large extent, the Western art of history-writing is but a part of and as such is guided and controlled by Western political activities. European scholars like Professor Seeley, Professor Goldwin Smith, and historians like Freeman have admitted it to be so. "Politics have no conscience" is a well-known English adage.

Propaganda Technique in World War is the title of a book by H.D. Liaswell published in 1927. It has been plainly stated therein that, as a preparation for a future global war, all political leaders, rulers and military commanders should not only study the science of warfare and of armaments but should also make the art of telling lies scientifically a regular item of the curriculum of their studies. According to the same writer, in the Great War of 1914–18, the first to succeed most in telling lies was England. America was the next and did even better than England. "The mastery of this art displayed by President Wilson," he writes, "is unparalleled in the history of the world." He has further given instances of several notorious lies circulated by the British during the Great War of 1914–18. One such lie published in the papers of the world was that the German soldiers had cut off the hands of many Belgian children. It was entirely false. The then Prime Minister of Italy, Signor Niti, wrote about this piece of news after the end of the war:

> "After the War, a wealthy American sent his representative to Belgium with the object of arranging for the livelihood of the poor children whose small hands had been cut off. The representative could not find a single mutilated

> child anywhere in Belgium. When I was Prime Minister of Italy, I and Mr. Lloyd George together carried out a thorough investigation into the truth of the allegations of these inhuman atrocities. We had been given even the names of the places and of people relating to several of these accusations, but our investigations proved all these stories to be fictitious." (Translated from the Hindi *Vishal Bharat,* August 1928)

Another story that went round in those days was that a factory had been established in Germany which manufactured soap and glycerine by boiling the dead bodies of soldiers. Even photographs of the factory were published in English newspapers. The falsehood of this "news" was exposed in 1925, when the German Government publicly declared it to be entirely false without a grain of truth in it. Ultimately, the British Foreign Minister, Sir Austen Chamberlain, had officially to accept the German Government's declaration and to express the hope that "this false report will not again be revived".

Innumerable lies of this nature were continually published during World War I by or on behalf of England and her Allies.

Another book on the subject entitled *Falsehood in Wartime* was published by Arthur Ponsonby, a Member of the British Parliament. Ponsonby had been at one time Deputy Secretary in the Foreign Department of the British Cabinet. In commenting on this book, another well-known Member of Parliament, Wilfred Belloc, wrote:

> "The book irrefutably proves that falsehood and fraud were pressed into service in the conduct of the 1914–18 World War and the people of the world were deliberately deceived as regards the real aims and objectives of the war from beginning to end. If there has ever been a war which seemed to be motivated apparently by righteousness, it was this World War. At least the Allies proclaimed that they were fighting only for the freedom of small and weak nations and for the protection of the sanctity of international treaties. They claimed that their aim was to destroy

militarism. What fraud, what a hypocrisy and what a lie." (Translated from the Hindi *Vishal Bharat*, August 1928)

The effect of such an untruthful and fictitious narration of "history" penetrated so deep into our national life and exercised such a baneful influence, particularly on the minds of our intelligentsia, that it has been one of the greatest obstacles in the way of our national development. This evil effect was deliberately intended and sought to be achieved and intensified by propaganda carried on in diverse ways and forms. Books prescribed for our schools were filled with fearful incidents which were purely imaginary. As a result, most of the educated people of our country were caught into such an intricate maze of historical misrepresentations that they were absolutely unable to think out right methods of safeguarding the best interests of their country and their people.

A Few Examples of Misrepresentation in Our History

Our books of history tell us that from time immemorial India has always been an object of invasion by foreign people through its north-western frontiers; that India was never able to repel such invasions and that she had almost continuously been subject to the rule of one foreign people or another. Of all such invasions, the one by Muslims is averred to have been the most formidable. The Muslim invaders of India are described as a barbarous and fanatical people who had, for a thousand years before the advent of the British, subjected India to their tyrannical rule, had destroyed the ancient Hindu religion and culture and forcibly converted to Islam crores of Indians. We are told that our Muslim rulers were by nature only licentious and fanatical pillagers. Even the greatest and best of the Moghul Emperors are painted as hypocritical and hostile to Hindus, Hinduism and to Hindustan. We are assured that the Muslims did no good to India and that the period of their rule had absolutely nothing to its credit. The incoming Muslims are accused of having in every way destroyed the real national life of India. Hindus and Muslims, we are told, have never had a friendly and harmonious relationship with each other in this country, nor was it ever possible for them to have such a relationship. The books of history prescribed for students in schools and colleges are still devoted mostly to the propagation of the theme that misrule and anarchy were rampant in the country and internecine fighting broke out almost every other day before the advent of the British who for the first time in many centuries established peace and good government in the country. On the basis of such assertions which concealed the uglier aspects of British domination, we were made to believe that British rule was a blessing for India. We were even warned that if, unfortunately, British rule ever ended, then one of two consequences would inevitably follow: Either another foreign power would invade the country from the north-west and conquer it, or the Hindus and Muslims would again start fighting with each other and push the country towards ruin.

We propose to clear these misstatements and misrepresentations by describing in detail all foreign invasions of India previous to the coming of the British. We shall also show the extent to which the country succeeded in resisting and repelling those invasions. We shall describe too how far such invasions were common to other countries in those days and how far the other countries repelled or resisted them. In short, we shall try to answer the following questions:

(i) Whether England herself and also other European countries have ever been invaded by foreigners,

(ii) Whether the invaded European countries defended themselves more successfully than India,

(iii) Whether there had been Muslim invasions of several European countries before the Muslim invasion of India took place, and

(iv) If there were such invasions then, how the invaded European countries, as compared to India, faced them.

We would analyse the nature of the Muslim invasions of India and their effect on the life of the country. We would look closely into the actual ways and means adopted for the propagation of Islam in India and into the kind of treatment meted out to the Hindus by the Muslim rulers of the day.

The questions which we propose to deal with in the following pages are:

What kind of relationship resulted and has continued between the Hindus and the Muslims from the thousand-year-old contact between the two religious faiths.

How far Muslim rule in India led to India's progress or otherwise in the spheres of arts, science, education, agriculture, trade, industries, administration and material prosperity.

We shall also describe the conditions in England at that time. We shall describe the causes of and the means adopted for the establishment of British rule in India and, lastly, its consequences for India.

COMPARISON BETWEEN INDIA AND ENGLAND OF THOSE DAYS

England in the Seventeenth Century

The contact of India with England was in reality a clash between two entirely different sets of ideals, cultures and civilizations. Let us see what was the picture of England at the time of her first contacts with India.

William Draper, the well-known historian, writes as follows:

> "The peasant's cabin was made of reeds or sticks plastered over with mud. His fire was chimneyless—often it was made of peat. In the objects and manner of his existence, he was but a step above the industrious beaver who was building his dam in the adjacent stream. There were highwaymen on the roads, pirates on the rivers, vermin in

abundance in the clothing and beds. The common food was peas, vetches, fern roots and even the bark of trees. There was no commerce to put off famine. Man was altogether at the mercy of the season. The population, sparse as it was, was perpetually thinned by pestilence and want. Nor was the state of the townsman better than that of the rustic; his bed was a bag of straw, with a hard round log for his pillow. If he was in easy circumstances, his clothing was of leather; if poor, a wisp of straw wrapped round his limbs kept off the cold ... As to the mechanic, how was it possible that he could exist where there were no windows made of glass, not even of oiled paper, no workshop warmed by a fire? For the poor there was no physician ... Sanitary provisions there were none."

Describing the moral conditions of the people of England in those days, Draper continues:

"The rapidity of its (syphilis) spread all over England is a significant illustration of the fearful immorality of the times. If contemporary authors are to be trusted, there was not a class, married or unmarried, clergy or laity, from the Holy Father, Leo X, to the beggar by the wayside, free from it ... Its (England's) population hardly reached five million ... It was a system of organized labour, the possession of land being a trust, not a property. But now commerce was beginning to disturb the foundations on which all these arrangements had been sustained, and to compel a new distribution of population, trading companies were being established; men were unsettled by the rumours or realities of immense fortunes rapidly gained in foreign adventure ... A nation so illiterate that many of its peers in Parliament could neither read nor write ... to so great an extent had these immoralities gone that it was openly asserted that there were one hundred thousand women in England made dissolute by the clergy ... The vilest crime in an ecclesiastic might be commuted for money, six shillings and eight pence being sufficient in the case of mortal sin ... the close-of-the-seventeenth-century ... London ... was dirty, ill-built, without sanitary provisions ... Wild animals roamed here and there ... In the rainy season the roads were all but impassable ... it was no uncommon thing for persons to lose their way, and have to spend the night out in the air. Between places of considerable importance the roads were sometimes very little known, and such was the difficulty for wheeled carriages that a principal mode of transport was by packhorses, of which passengers took advantage, shoving themselves always between the packs ... Towards the close of the century what were termed "flying coaches" could move at the rate of from thirty to fifty miles in a day ... near the sources of the Tyne, there were people scarcely less savage than American Indians, their half-naked women chanting a wild measure, while the men, with brandished dirks, danced a war-dance ... It might be expected that the women were ignorant enough when very few men knew how to write correctly ... Social discipline was very far from being of that kind which we call moral ... the husband whipped his wife ... A culprit was set in the pillory to be pelted with brickbats ... women were fastened by the legs in the stocks at the market-place ... Such a hardening of heart ... The houses of the rural population were huts covered with strawthatch ... In London the houses were mostly of wood and plaster, the streets filthy beyond expression. After nightfall a passenger went at his peril, for chamber windows were opened and slop pails unceremoniously emptied down. There were no lamps in the streets ... Hardly any personage died who was not popularly suspected to have been made away with by poison, an indication of the morality generally supposed to prevail among the higher classes ... flood of immorality."

As for the freedom of thought in the England of those days, Draper goes on to say:

"The University of Oxford had ordered the political works of Buchanan, Milton, and Baxter to be publicly burnt in the court of the schools ... In administering the law, whether in relation to political or religious offences, there was an incredible atrocity. In London, the crazy old bridge over the Thames was decorated with grinning and mouldering heads of criminals, under an idea that these ghastly spectacles would fortify the common people in their resolve to act according to law. The toleration of the times may be understood from a law enacted by the Scotch Parliament, May 8, 1685, that whoever preached or heard in a conventicle should be punished with death and the confiscation of his goods. That such an infamous spirit did not content itself with mere deadletter laws there is too much practical evidence to permit anyone to doubt ... Shrieking Scotch Covenanters were submitted to tortures by crushing their knees flat in the boot; women were tied to stakes on the sea-sands and drowned by the slowly advancing tide because they would not attend Episcopal worship, or branded on their cheeks and then shipped to America .... The court ladies, and even the Queen of England herself, were so utterly forgetful of womanly mercy and common humanity as to join in this infernal traffick." (*The Intellectual Development of Europe* by John William Draper, Vol. II, pp. 230–44)

Comparison with the India of Those Days

The above lengthy quotation gives a vivid description of the conditions prevailing in British towns and villages of that period. Out of the above quotations also emerges a picture of the way of life then led by the British people, their occupations and industries, their law-courts and their offices, their education, and their religious and social behaviour, etc. We must remember that it was exactly the time when travellers to India from all over the world were amazed at the religious broadmindedness of Kabir and Dadoo, the universal love and the cosmopolitanism of Akbar, the administration of justice by and under Jehangir, the prosperity of the country during Shahjehan's reign and the wonderful arts and crafts of the time. Dozens of Indian towns were at that time thickly populated and were adorned with grand and beautiful buildings. The Forts at Delhi and Agra and the Taj Mahal had already been constructed. The reign of Aurangzeb saw the acme of prosperity, contentment, and good administration throughout the length and breadth of the country.

Conditions similar to those in England prevailed in most of the other European countries too. We must not also forget that these conditions persisted in England right up to the beginning of the 18th century. Draper's description clearly indicates that halfstarved and semi-civilized Englishmen of those days were attracted by the wealth and prosperity of countries like India to which they went as traders. Trading companies like the East India Company were formed for the purpose.

The fact is that the England of those days had never had such a period of refinement and civilization, of peace, progress and prosperity as had then been obtaining in India for thousands of years. We shall revert to this subject later.

Efforts in History to Civilize England

In the historical period about the time of the birth of Jesus Christ, the first outsiders to reach the British Isles to try to civilize the backward inhabitants of the country and to instil in them the ideas of good and evil, right and wrong, were the preachers of Mithraism from Iran. It was the same ancient religion which first gave the idea of morals to the Romans. There was a time when the Mithraic religion greatly influenced the lives and thoughts of people throughout England. In various parts of England, temples were erected to the great Vedic God Mitra from whom the religion of Mithraism derived its name. The remnants of those temples can still be seen in various museums of that country. But this healthy civilizing influence on the British people could not last very long, partly on account of the difficulties of travel and partly on account of the low state of civilization in England at the time.

The next in history to undertake the task of civilizing England were the Romans. For four hundred years the Romans ruled over England. But England was situated on the distant border of the Roman Empire, and the main purpose for which the Romans used England during the four centuries of their rule was to ship thousands of English boys and girls every year to other parts of their Empire to be sold as slaves in the market. At one time, slaves from no other country were as much in demand in the markets of the Roman Empire as slaves from England.

The third wave of civilization which touched the shores of England during the historic period was the preaching of Christianity to the people in or about the 7th century A. D. But on account of their own backwardness, the people of England could then learn little from the noble teachings of Jesus Christ except the prevailing idol-worship, a few superstitious beliefs, and useless sectarian conflicts.

Then comes the period of Arab domination of Europe. For several centuries, the Arabs ruled over the greater part of Europe, from the Black Sea to the Atlantic. Europe had never seen better days in culture, in civilization, in the advancement of science, in medicine, in education, in arts and industry. But England remained outside the pale of the Arab Empire of those days. The centres of education throughout Europe were, at that time full of Arab professors. Arabic was the medium of highest education throughout Europe even upto the 10th and 11th centuries A. D. No man was regarded as educated in England unless he knew Arabic well. But after a few centuries, narrow sectarian tendencies destroyed this Arab influence. This was followed by nearly a thousand years of what are called the "Dark Ages" of Europe which at least for full five centuries plunged England into "darkness".

In short, ideas of good and evil, of right and wrong, *i.e.,* moral ideals which had been rooted in India for thousands of years, because of the ancient Vedic, Buddhist and Jain religions and which had become the legacy of every Indian, could not take root on the soil of England.

Till the beginning of the 18th century, the common man in England was sunk deep in poverty. With the exception of a few wealthy people or landlords, the condition in which 90% of Englishmen lived in those days was in several respects no better than that of slaves. The much-boosted Parliamentary system of Government had its origin in mutual conflicts, rivalries and hostility of the people in England, for which there never had been any reason or place in the much more civilized, well-organised and prosperous India. Englishmen could not imagine the extent to which the village people in India enjoyed real self-government through their well-organised village panchayats armed with all authority and power. Nor could that wonderful and sacred relationship between the king and his subjects, which had obtained in India during the Hindu and Muslim regimes for about 2000 years, ever be established in England.

It cannot be disputed that moral ideals are established only after centuries of civilized social life—a life which the British had not till then had the good fortune to live.

Contact Between England and India

In the beginning of the 17th century, an ancient country like India came into contact for the first time with a country like England. For about a hundred years Englishmen in India, by carrying on some sort of trade, made profits on a rather modest scale. After the death of Aurangzeb, the dawn of the 18th century witnessed the decline of the power and prestige of the Mughal Empire. During the preceding one hundred years, the avarice and ambitions of these foreigners had increased beyond reasonable limits. No question of foulness or otherwise of the means adopted could be an obstacle in their way. Under the guise of establishing commercial houses, they started constructing fortresses and military bases. Inexperienced and liberal-minded Indian rulers did not care to interfere in their activities. Permission to trade and for other facilities had already been granted to these so-called British traders. The foreigners went on increasing their power and influence. There was no limit to the amount of wealth they amassed by fair means or foul. The wealth thus acquired was used for maintaining armies.

Naturally, there were occasional conflicts and even fights among different Indian rulers. In Madras as well as in Bengal, the Britishers, with their newly-formed armies, gradually began to take part in such conflicts, sometimes on the side of one Indian ruler and sometimes on the side of another. This gradually led to an increase in the Britishers' power and influence. The increasing weakness of the Mughal *Durbar* at Delhi left no central power capable of understanding the situation and meeting it effectively. Territory after territory was brought under their own administration by these foreigners by pitting one Indian ruler against another. We will now let English historians give a description of the ways and means adopted by Englishmen gradually to establish a far-flung Empire in India, thereby putting an end to the independence as well as the peace and prosperity of the country.

Ways and Means by Which British Empire Was Founded in India

An English historian writes:

> "Some native sage has compared the Europeans in India to *dimaks* or white ants, which from dark or scarcely visible beginnings pursue their determined objects insidiously and silently, destroying green forest trees and in their excavated trunks building edifices, communicating by numerous galleries with the hardened clay pyramids, far and near, that denote where formerly flourished the far-spreading cedars. Attacking everything, devouring everything, they undermine and sap and desolate. The simile is not a very flattering one, though it is not in some measure without its aptness either ... After all, however, there can be no question that in our early connection with

India, there was much from the contemplation of which the moralist will shrink, and the Christian protest against, with abhorrence." (*The Calcutta Review,* Vol. VII (1847), p. 226)

Another English writer says:

"How did the Company acquire Bengal, but by perjury and forgery? Or Arcot or any other principality?" (*The British Friend of India,* March, 1843)

William Howitt, the well-known historian, observes:

"........ the mode by which the East India Company has possessed itself of Hindustan, is the most revolting and unchristian that can possibly be conceived ...... if ever there was one system more Machiavellian, more appropriative of the show of justice where the basest injustice was attempted, more cold, cruel, haughty and unrelenting than another, it is the system by which the Government of the different states of India has been wrested from the hands of their respective princes and collected into the grasp of the British power ...... Whenever we talk to other nations of British faith and integrity, they may well point to India in derisive scorn .... The system, which for more than a century was steadily at work to strip the native princes of their dominions, and that too under the most sacred pleas of right and expediency, is a system of torture more exquisite than regal or spiritual tyranny ever before discovered, such as the world has nothing similar to show." (*The English in India—System of Territorial Acquisition* by William Howitt)

The Verdict of Herbert Spencer

Giving a bird's-eye view of about a hundred years of British rule in India, the famous British philosopher, Herbert Spencer, wrote in 1851:

"The Anglo-Indians of the last century whom Burke described as 'birds of prey and passage in India' showed themselves only a shade less cruel than their prototypes of Peru and Mexico. Imagine how black must have been their deeds when even the Directors of the Company admitted that the vast fortunes acquired in the inland trade have been obtained by a scene of the most tyrannical and oppressive conduct that was ever known in any age or country. Conceive the atrocious state of society described by Vansittart, who tells us that the English compelled the natives to buy or sell at just what rates they pleased on pain of flogging or confinement. Judge to what a pass things must have come when, in describing a journey, Warren Hastings says: 'Most of the petty towns and serais were deserted at our approach.' Cold-blooded treachery was the established policy of the authorities. Princes were betrayed into war with each other; and one of them having been helped to overcome his antagonist, was then himself dethroned for some alleged misdemeanour. Always some muddled stream was at hand as a pretext for official wolves. Dependent chiefs possessing coveted lands were impoverished by exorbitant demands for tribute and their ultimate inability to meet these demands was construed into a treasonable offence, punished by deposition. Even down to our own day (1851), kindred iniquities are continued. Down to our own day, too, are continued the grievous salt monopoly and the pitiless taxation that wring from the poor ryots nearly half the produce of the soil. Down to our own day continues the cunning despotism which uses native soldiers to maintain and extend native subjection, a despotism under which, not many years since, a regiment of sepoys was deliberately massacred for refusing to march without proper clothing. Down to our own day, the police authorities league with wealthy scamps, and allow the machinery of the law to be used for the purposes of extortion. Down to our own day, so called gentlemen (Englishmen) will ride their elephants through the crops of impoverished peasants and will supply themselves without paying for them. And down to our own day, it is common with the people in the interior to run into the woods at the sight of a European." (*Social Statics* by Herbert Spencer)

Sins of East India Company

Another English writer states:

"… the Government of the East India Company in India was trained from the very first with mighty vices … for generation after generation, the great aim and object of the servants of the Company, from the high civil and military functionaries downwards, was to squeeze as large as possible a fortune out of the country as quickly as might be, and turn their backs upon it for ever, so soon as that object had been attained … In perfect truth has it been said … that the subjugated race found the little finger of the Company thicker than the loins of the worst and most dissolute of their native princes." (Dr. Russell)

A Resume of This Book

It is not necessary to give any more extracts on the subject from British writers.

The intensely tragic story of the hundred years' (1757–1857) rule over India by the English East India Company will unfold itself in the pages of this book;

(i) How loyal Indian soldiers in obedience to their English officers sacrificed their own lives in fighting against their own countrymen;

(ii) How faithful Indian rulers observed their treaties with the English;

(iii) How deliberately the English broke their treaties and their sacred undertakings with Indian rulers times out of number;

(iv) How the European employees of Indian rulers betrayed their employers at every step;

(v) How English Residents accredited to Indian *Durbars* sowed seeds of internal dissensions and resorted to bribery, secret intrigues, assassinations and forgeries while at those *Durbars*;

(vi) How Indian rulers, lured into the snares of treaties and friendship with the English, were so inextricably entrapped that they could not get out except at the cost and loss of everything they held dear;

(vii) How the East India Company following its deliberate policy put an end to the Village Panchayats and their administration and to the indigenous educational system by closing down hundreds of thousands of *pathshalas* and *maktabs* and also destroyed the trade, industries, crafts and other means of livelihood of the people that had flourished for a thousand years; and

(viii) How by all these means the country was brought down from the position of one of the most progressive and prosperous countries of the world to that of one of the weakest and poorest countries in the world.

Earlier Invasions of India—Pre-British Invasions

For a correct understanding of the causes of the establishment of British rule in India, we must have before us a complete picture of India, as it was prior to British rule; in other words, of India during the Mughal period. Also a cursory glance at the invasions of India preceding the Muslim invasions, right from the earliest times, is necessary. We would further like to find answers to the following questions:

(i) Whether or not several European countries were similarly invaded by foreigners;

(ii) If they were, then how far the European countries, as compared with India, succeeded in resisting those invasions.

Our brief narration of these will show that India was not subjected to such invasions any more than other countries and that the invaders did not meet with greater success in India than elsewhere. Instead of being unable to defend herself, India was far more successful in resisting the invaders than similarly invaded European countries and was often successful and victorious, both materially and morally, over the invaders.

The Aryan Invasion

The invasion of India by Aryans is said to have been the first invasion of India and, according to European scholars, it took place some 2,500 years before Christ (*The Cambridge History of India*, Vol. I, p. 697).

All historians agree that modern Indians, Iranians and Europeans are all descended from one and the same ancient Aryan stock. It is said that some five thousand years ago, the Aryans migrated in different directions from the Central Asian region and conquered and populated India, Iran and the whole of Europe. Thus if it was a matter of disgrace for any country to have been conquered by the ancient Aryans, then it was so not only for India alone, but was equally so for Iran, Russia, Germany, France, England, Greece and so many other countries. The impress of the ancient Aryan language and culture is as deep on the language and culture of these countries as on the language and culture of India. Then, again, it is a fact of history that while the Aryans, who migrated from their Central-Asian homeland towards Europe and occupied most of that continent, lived a semi-civilized life for thousands of years, those who arrived in India laid the foundations, according to European scholars themselves, of a great, glorious and mighty civilization at least thousands of years before the birth of Christ. One of the reasons for this phenomenon was that when the Aryans came, India was not uncivilized. We find ample proof of the cultural heights attained by the original inhabitants of India in ancient Sanskrit literature. Indeed, it is not open to doubt that in several respects, the culture and civilization of the indigenous people were higher than those of the newcomers. Incontrovertible support is lent to this statement by the researches made in connection with Mohanjodaro and Harappa.

The North-Western Boundary of India

Another point has to be borne in mind in order to assess the real nature of the various listed foreign invasions of India, from about 1000 B.C. up to the death of Aurangzeb in 1707. The region comprising the present Afghanistan, Baluchistan and some adjoining territory has been the bone of contention between India, Iran and also some other countries to the west of Iran. Several Hindu and Muslim emperors of India ruled over Sheistan, Herat and Afghanistan. Many ancient Iranian as well as Greek writers have described India's boundary as situated on the west of Afghanistan and Baluchistan and have held all that hilly region to be a part of India. After the Aryan invasion, the India invaded subsequently by several invaders has been taken to mean India inclusive of all this region, so that even those invaders who never reached the Sindhu river have been called "invaders of India". For instance, it is stated that the famous Iranian Emperor Darius (522–486 B.C.) ruled over a vast Empire which included some part of India too. But the stone inscriptions of Darius clearly show that he never advanced beyond the Sindhu river.

Pre-Alexander Invasions

Some mention about two other invasions of India before that of Alexander which advanced up to the nearest bank of the

Sindhu river is to be found in history. One was about 800 B.C. by the world-famed Assyrian Empress Semiramis, who crossed Baluchistan in an attempt to conquer India. About this invasion the Greek historian, Niarcus, states that Semiramis had to run back for her life from the Sindhu river with only 20 survivors of her army. The second invasion was by the famous conqueror of Iran, Kuru. The name "Kuru" is written as "Cyrus" in English. But the real Irani name was Kuru. He is counted amongst the greatest conquerors of Asia. Kuru is believed to have been the grandfather of Dara (Darius) and is regarded as the builder of the vast Iranian Empire. Kabul, Iraq, Syria, Turkey, Babylon, Egypt and also a part of Greece had accepted this Iranian conqueror as their suzerain. After Semiramis, Kuru invaded India. But he too had to flee for his life with only seven men from the Sindhu river, and in the end succumbed to the wounds inflicted by some unknown Indian (*Ibid,* Vol. I, pp. 330–31).

Alexander's Invasion

We now come to the invasion of India by the world-famous Greek conqueror, Alexander the Great, in 326 B. C. Not a country, from Eastern Europe to Afghanistan and Baluchistan, could withstand the army of this invincible conqueror. He invaded India from the north-west, and crossed the Sindhu and the Jhelum rivers. He was confident of annexing to his Empire the green fields and the prosperous plains of northern India and of reaching the sea on the eastern coast of the sub-continent, and fortunately for him, political conditions in India had already deteriorated. For a long time enmity had persisted between the ruler of Taxila, on the border of India across the Jhelum, and Paurav (called Porus by the Greeks) the ruler of the Punjab, on the Indian side of the river. The ruler of Taxila joined Alexander against his rival Paurav. Alexander sent emissaries to Paurav demanding his surrender. Paurav's answer was that he and his army would talk to Alexander and his army on the battlefield! The army of Alexander which had crossed the Jhelum, included Indian soldiers of Taxila's army (*Ibid,* p. 361).

The invading army far out-numbered the defenders under Paurav. Paurav's two sons fell in the battle. Alexander was victorious. Paurav was wounded, taken prisoner and produced before Alexander. Greek writers unanimously testify that Alexander was so enchanted by the dignified bearing of the handsome Paurav, his courage and bravery, that he publicly expressed his unbounded admiration for Paurav and restored to Paurav what the latter had lost to Alexander on the battlefield.

After entering into a treaty with Paurav, Alexander advanced further. Chief amongst the ruling powers in the India of that period was the Kingdom of Magadh. Alexander planned to attack Magadh. But his soldiers, who had had enough of fighting with Indians in the battle with Paurav, refused point-blank to cross the river Bias. Greek writers describe how hard Alexander tried to infuse into his army his own love of adventure and his indomitable courage. But it was no use, and the matchless world conqueror was forced to abandon his dream of the conquest of India and to retire from the banks of the Bias river.

Megasthenes, the Greek historian, clearly states that no invader of India before Alexander had succeeded in conquering India (*Ibid,* p. 331).

Other Greek Invasions

After Alexander and before the Muslim invasion of India, there were several other invasions, but only a few of them could be called successful and the successful invaders broke off all relations or contacts with their own countries and settled down in that part of India which they had somehow conquered. They made India their home and thereafter identified their own interests with the interests of the Indian people. In a short time, they completely merged into and became one with the indigenous people of India.

The first two unsuccessful invasions after Alexander were by the Greek military commanders, Selucus and Antiocus.

Some 20 years after Alexander, his General and successor, Selucus I, also invaded India. At that time, Emperor Chandragupta, the founder of the Maurya dynasty, had already established his rule over the whole of Northern India. It has been stated that Chandragupta had, in his boyhood, met Alexander. Chandragupta opposed Selucus with an army of five hundred thousand men and nine thousand elephants. Selucus lost heart and entered into a treaty with Chandragupta whereby Selucus acknowledged the sovereignty of Chandragupta over the whole of India east of the Sindhu river and, in addition, ceded to Chandragupta Kabul, Kandahar, Herat and Baluchistan. Thus both Afghanistan and Baluchistan, which had till then been ruled by Governors appointed by Alexander, were now merged into Chandragupta's Indian Empire.

In some books by Greek writers, it is stated that Chandragupta married a daughter of Selucus. In return for all this Chandragupta presented Selucus with 500 elephants and Selucus went back to his own country across Afghanistan.

After the death of Chandragupta's grandson, the world-famous Emperor Ashoka, there came a partial decline in the power and influence of the Maurya dynasty. For the second time after Alexander, the Greeks again invaded India. The Greek Military Commander, Antiocus, crossed the Hindukush mountains and entered the territory of some small Indian principality on the border. Antiocus could not, however, achieve anything beyond collecting some provisions for his troops and a few elephants. Thus Antiocus too had to turn back unsuccessfully from the banks of the Sindhu river.

Certain invasions after that by Antiocus are, however, mentioned, only a few of which could be truthfully termed as successful. These invasions were of two types, namely,

(i) those by the Bakhtiyari Greeks, and
(ii) those by Shakas (Sidiyans), Huns and other semi-civilized Tribes.

The Greeks Settle in India

Some of those who had accompanied Alexander had settled down in Western Asia. Originally, their leaders had been appointed Governors of some Asian provinces by Alexander himself. Some time after Alexander's death, they established a dominion of their own in Iraq which was later known as the Bakhtiyari Kingdom. The Bakhtiyaris, in order to white-wash the blot of Selucus's defeat, reconquered Herat, Afghanistan and Baluchistan as a first step. Thereafter, they began to invade the country across the river Sindhu and advanced up to the Punjab, Sindh and Saurashtra (Kathiawar). In Kalidas's Sanskrit drama *Malavikagnimitra,* mention is made of a battle on the banks of the river Sindhu, in which Vasumitra, the grandson of Raja Pushpamitra, defeated and repulsed the *Yavan, i.e.,* the Greek army. In Sanskrit books of the period, the word *Yavan* was always used for the Greeks. Subsequently, the Greeks settled down in India and made India their home. Milind, the Raja of Shaka (Sialkot), who is mentioned in the Buddhist work *Milind Punh,* was a Greek.

No contact or relationship of any kind whatsoever subsisted between these Greek settlers in India and the countries of their origin like Greece and Iraq. They became a part and parcel of the Indian people and adopted as their own the Indian languages, literature, religions and culture. The famous Buddhist teacher, Nag Sen, converted to Buddhism Raja Milind, who later came to be counted amongst the most righteous and justice-loving monarchs of India and a true benefactor of his people. His subjects were all very happy and prosperous.

Another instance is that of the Greek royal emissary, Heliodorus, who journeyed from Takshashila (Taxila) to distant Vidisha (Bhilsa) and there became a convert to Vaishnavism. At Vidisha he erected a pillar in memory of Shri Krishna (*The Cambridge History of India,* p. 558). In the inscription on the pillar, Heliodorus has described himself as "Heliodor Bhagwat". "Heliodor" means a sun-worshipper, and "Bhagwat" means a follower of Bhugwat, *i.e.,* Shri Krishna.

The Greek settlers in India, with the help of the Indian art of painting, considerably improved the ancient Greek art of painting which they had brought with them from Greece. In the same way, the Buddhist painters of India, too, learned a good deal from Greek art. In astronomy, science and metaphysics, too, the Greeks learned a good deal from Indians and *vice versa*. The Greek settlers began freely to inter-marry Indians. These great new-comers got so completely mixed up with the Indians of those days that today no trace has been left of their former separate ethnic identity.

Invasions by Shakas and Huns

As mentioned earlier, the Greek invasions of India were followed by the invasions of the Shakas, the Pahlavs and the Huns. These invasions, too, like the Bakhtiyari-Greek invasions, can be said to have been successful only in a limited sense. Like the *Yavanas*, these invaders too ultimately settled down in India in exactly the same way.

During the century of the birth of Christ, Gandhar (Kandahar) and Pushakalavati on the west of the river Sindhu, as also Takshashila on its east, came under the sway of the Shakas (Scythians). For some time, parts of the western Punjab and of Sindh were also ruled by the Shakas. In the same century, Pahlavs (Parthians) conquered Sindh. Thereafter these people began advancing towards the south. But the Andhra Emperors gave them battle and successfully checked their advance towards the south. Consequently, the Shaka domination of the country went no further than the Vindhyas.

The Settling Down of These Indians and India

History shows clearly that the Shakas and the Pahlavs who ruled parts of Northern India settled down completely in the country and instead of continuing to live as foreigners, they were so deeply impressed and influenced by the higher culture of India that they became Indians in every sense. They adopted the Indian way of life, Indian names, Indian moral concepts, Indian religions, Indian languages and Indian culture. For instance, the most famous of the Shaka Emperors was Kanishka, who laid the foundations of the Kushan Empire in India, and who ruled over Afghanistan and even beyond. He became a convert to Buddhism. The Shaka era, at present prevalent in India, was started in his memory with the date of his accession to the throne. The dominion of Kanishka extended to the Vindhyas in the south and to the Altai mountains of Central Asia in the north. His capital was Purushpur (Peshawar). He played a great part in propagating Buddhism and ultimately rose to be the Convener of the Highest Sangat (Assembly) of Buddhism. He laid the foundations of the Mahayana sect of Buddhism. He also took a leading part in the promotion of the Sanskrit language. Buddhism was taken to and propagated in China, Tatar, Tibet and Northern Asia mostly by his missionaries.

The Shakas called themselves Hindu Kshatriyas and were accepted as such. Most of their names ended with the suffix "varman" or "dutt". By degrees the Shakas too, like the Greeks, merged into Indians and became absolutely indistinguishable from the rest of the Indian people.

Mention may now be made of the only other invasion of India— that by the Huns during the period intervening between the Shaka Pahlav invasions and the first Muslim invasion of India. In fact, the Huns' invasion of India was the most ferocious ever on this country. Practically no country in Asia or Europe escaped their savage onslaughts. To protect themselves against these very Huns, the then Chinese Emperors got constructed the famous 2,000-mile-long "Great Wall" of extraordinary thickness and height on the border of their country. It was the Huns who, about 150 to 200 years before Christ, ransacked and completely destroyed the Bakhtiyari Kingdom. Russia and the rest of Europe also were devastated for a thousand years by the ravages of these Huns. Naturally it was impossible for India to escape their invasions. Before the birth of Christ, the entire region from Iraq to the North-West Frontier of India was under the sway of the Huns.

The Huns invaded India in the middle of the fifth century A.D. At one time their rule was firmly established over the Punjab and Central India right up to Malwa. The Hun chief, Turaman, defeated the then Indian Emperor, Buddha Gupta.

Soon afterwards, however, Hun domination in India was obliterated by the defeat of Turaman's son, Mihirkul, at Koroor near Multan in 573 A.D. by the Indian Emperor Yashodharma Dev, whose capital was at Ujjaini and whose Empire extended over the whole of India from the Himalayas to the Eastern Ghats and from the Brahmaputra to the Arabian Sea. After that Rajya Vardhan completely swept away the remnants of the Huns from Northern India.

We have, so far, described one by one all invasions of India preceding the Muslim invasion. Our entire description is based on the writings of European historians. This will give a clear idea of the number of invasions of India during that period, of their nature, of the successes of Indian resistance and of the resulting losses or gains to India. Finally, the magnitude of the difference between these invasions and the coming of the English would also be clear from what we have narrated above.

Invasions of Other Countries

The fact is that invasions from outside are, more or less, a common factor in the history of all countries. Even so, India was not invaded so often as other countries of the world, particularly those of Europe. We shall now narrate the foreign invasions of various European countries. Our narration is based on the writings of European historians themselves. It will thus become evident that the devastation of India resulting from such invasions did not amount even to a fraction of that which spread over the whole of Europe for more than a thousand years as a result of such invasions.

Invasions of Europe by Asians

Many European writers of history admit that the Asiatic peoples had begun invading Europe thousands of years before Christ. We have already mentioned the Aryan invasion of Europe. European historians mention other invasions too by other Asiatic peoples.

Round about 800 B.C. such invasions occurred from time to time. But leaving all these alone, we would like to deal briefly with only those invasions which took place after the birth of Christ.

From the second century onwards, many East and Middle-Asian peoples like the Huns, the Avars, the Bulgars, the Khazas, the Patzenaks, the Magyars and the Mongols were, from time to time, marching out of Asia and invading various parts of Europe. The European countries which were thus invaded and ransacked for a thousand years included Russia, Germany, Italy, England and Spain. The early invaders established their own settlements all over Eastern and Central Europe. The invaders who followed defeated and dispersed the earlier settlers northwards and eastwards and settled themselves in their places.

So many European countries were being invaded continuously and so often that it is unnecessary here to deal with each of such invasions. We would, therefore, summarise all these invasions of Europe covering about a thousand years in the very words of European historians.

The Romans ruled over England for 400 years. After this an Asiatic people, the Saxons, pouring out of their original homeland, somewhere in Central Asia, drove away the Romans and brought under their own rule the Britons, the original inhabitants of England. The English people of today, who are in every respect free in their own country, are thus a mixed race descended from these very Britons, Saxons and other peoples of those days.

Devastation of Europe Through These Invasions

The fact that even the mighty Roman Empire could not withstand these repeated invasions is indication enough of the straits to which the rest of Europe must have been reduced by them. In the fifth century A D., the Huns, who have already been mentioned in connection with India, had established an independent empire of their own between the Caspian Sea and the river Danube. The then enfeebled Roman Emperors paid regular tribute to these

Hun Emperors. Another similar Hun empire was established in Western Europe also in the 5th and 6th centuries A.D.

Describing the devastation of European society caused by these invasions, the well-known French historian, Boissonade, writes:

> "The upper and the middle classes of the people of the Old Roman Society either disappeared in that storm or the invading barbarians looted and finished them. Such of them as escaped somehow merged themselves into the invaders ... In Britain the invading Anglo-Saxons utterly destroyed the Britons ... These cruel invaders not only took away the lands of all big landlords and began to live upon them themselves with their families but they also killed those landlords and destroyed their churches ... They took into their slavery all those Britons who escaped the devastation ... There was so much misery all around that many Britons in despair found some sort of shelter only in slavery. In the districts of the Danube and the Rhine, in Gaul (France), in Belgium and in Italy, these conquerors kept as their slaves all those people of the Roman population whose lives they had spared ... In Britain, these people committed such atrocities that persons of old high families there left for Armenia in North-Western France in order to save their lives and a very large number of Britons were actually put to the sword ... In Aquiton and in Spain, believing Christians and their clergy were beaten, put in chains and then burnt alive. Everywhere when the cities and the towns were plundered, the womenfolk had to put up with extreme indignity. After conquering Rome, the Visigodsh under Aleric reclined under the shadow of trees and compelled the sons and daughters of the senators of Rome whom they had imprisoned in their harems to serve wine in cups of gold to the reclining conquerors. After every invasion, the number of women increased in the camp of the invaders ... In Macedonia, Thessali, in Greece, in Illyria, in Epirus and in the provinces of the Danube, the invading Turanians, Germans and Slavs killed all men and made women and children their prisoners!

Prosper, the Christian priest of Acquiton, in one of his poems, laments thus —"The temples of God were burnt and the monasteries were looted. If the waves of the ocean had swept over the entire land of Gaul (France), our loss would not have been so great." ...... The Huns ruined everything and made barren the entire country through which they passed ...... The historian Idantius writes that in the fifth century "only the name" of Spain remained. Both in the east (of Europe) as well as in the west innumerable flourishing cities disappeared and could never rise again. The Huns alone ruined seventy cities in the east .... In Britain prosperous small towns like Londinium (London), Eboracum (York), Camelodonum (Colchester), Dorovernum (Canterbury), Ventise-norum (Norwich) and Aquasalis (Bath), which had been founded by the Romans, were reduced to ruins and debris ...... Pope Gregory I cried out—"It appears that the end of the world is approaching!" ... Penonia, Naricum, Ratia, Helvasia (Switzerland), Gaul (France), Belgium, Britain, Spain and North and Middle Italy had specially to suffer great hardships. The people of the Balkan Peninsula had probably to suffer even greater hardships. All historians of that period declare with one voice that the same desolation and devastation spread over Greece and other East-European countries as upon Italy and other West-European countries and that a similar feeling of all-round desolation and devastation was left upon the minds of historians themselves. Some had even begun to believe that the end of creation, predicted in Christian scriptures, was really about to come." (*Life and Work in Medieval Europe* by P. Boissonade, Book I, Chapter II.)

The above description deals with the invasions of Europe during the fifth, sixth and seventh centuries A.D. About similar invasions of Europe during the eighth, the ninth and tenth centuries, the same historian writes:

"In the 9th and 10th centuries new invasions spread desolation all over Western Europe. The freebooters of

Scandinavia, who were called the "Northmen", continued evil deeds similar to those of the Germans for about a century from 830 to 911 A.D. They massacred the masses, enslaved people, burnt cities and plundered or destroyed Christian Germany, the Low countries (Holland and Belgium), Western France, Scotland, Ireland and England. In Eastern Europe, the Maghyars, who were the kinsmen of the Huns and the Avars, spread desolation in the plains of the Danube, in Central Europe, in north Italy and in Eastern France. In Southern Europe, the Saracens, the Berbers and the Arabs continued their depredations on the sea-coast of Italy and in the adjoining islands, in Provence and in Dophine (South-eastern France)." (*ibid*, Chapter X, p. 115).

Describing the results of the invasions of nearly one thousand years, Boissonade in the end writes:

"The barbarian invasions created a real calamity. Within two hundred years that splendid and well-organised edifice of the Christian Roman Empire, under whose shade workers and artisans had flourished, had made great progress and attained great prosperity, turned upside down from the foundations to the pinnacle and in eastern Europe too its foundations became absolutely hollow. One could see ruins all around. Disorganisation and anarchy prevailed in place of organised society. The place of law had been taken by the principle of might was right. The production of wealth had ceased in every form. The treasures which the previous generations had accumulated had been scattered and all economic and social progress had come to a standstill." (*Life and Work in Medieval Europe* by P. Boissonade, Conclusion, p. 233)

We have briefly described above the results of these Asian invasions of various European countries in the words of European historians themselves. On reading this description, one can easily see whose frontiers had been weaker or more vulnerable, those of India or of Europe, or which of these two defended more successfully its frontiers against such foreign invasions. After this it remains for us only to describe the Muslim invasions of both India and Europe.

ISLAM AND INDIA

Muslim Invasions of India

Now we come to the Muslim invasions of India. We were told and are sometimes still told that the invasion of India by the Muslims was the last and most destructive of all invasion, that it destroyed the entire social, religious, moral, economic and political life of the country for an indefinite period and that it divided the country permanently into two opposite camps. The Muslim invasion of this country is often described as the greatest calamity that ever befell this country. Muslim rule over India is presented as a proof of the weakness of the people of the country. On the basis of the above premises, attempts were made to prove that the British by coming to India saved the country from the evil effects of that great calamity.

What is more unfortunate is that even today, long after the disappearance of foreign rule from India, such wrong notions still exist in the minds of a considerable number of our countrymen and are proving a great obstacle in the way of India's genuine national integration.

Undoubtedly, no outside invasion can be a matter of pride for any country whatsoever. Even then, as in the case of other previous invasions, so in the case of the Muslim invasions, we shall have to see if only India had to face them or if other countries of the world also had to face similar invasions in those days. We shall also have to see if the Muslims of those days first of all invaded India or if they invaded some other countries also even before invading India. We shall have to see if India faced such invasions more successfully than other countries. We shall have to see how far the ultimate results of the Muslim invasions of India proved beneficial or otherwise to the country.

The Prophet Mohammed

The Prophet Mohammed was born in 569 A.D. In 609 A.D. he began to preach his new religion. The main features of this religion were as under:

(1) The Arab people were then divided into hundreds of small tribes and clans. Each tribe worshipped its own god or goddess in the form of an idol made of stone or clay or some other material. The Arabs as a people had no idea of one Universal Formless God of all. Prophet Mohammed taught them to give up worship of all their separate tribal gods and goddesses and in their place to worship only the One Formless Universal God of all.

(2) The Prophet tried to demolish the barriers which separated the people of one tribe or clan from another and unite the entire Arab people into one compact nation.

(3) He tried to abolish numberless social and religious customs, ceremonies and superstitions of the Arab people and to raise their social and moral status.

(4) The Prophet emphasised the equality and universal brotherhood of men and the need of leading a moral life for the good of all.

The teachings of Mohammed equally concerned the religious, social and political aspects of life. His teachings inspired the Arabs with a new life and a new spirit. They came out of their desert homes and spread out over the world for religious and political conquest. Within a hundred years of the death of the Prophet, they established their rule over a very large part of the then civilised world.

Muslim Rule

In 629 A.D. the city of Mecca acknowledged Mohammed as its ruler. Within two years, from 629 to 631 A.D. the whole of Arabia accepted him as its leader and ruler. Mohammed died in 632 A.D. In 636 A.D. the Arabs conquered Iraq (Mesopotamia) and Sham (Syria). In 637 A.D. Jerusalem came under the sway of the Arabs. Between 637 and 651 the whole of Iran acknowledged the Arabs as its rulers. Between 701 and 715 the Arabs reached the frontiers of China in the East and established their Empire over the whole of Tatar and Turkistan.

At the same time, the newly-awakened and adventurous Arabs looked towards the West also. Between 638 and 641 the whole of Egypt became a part of the growing Arab Empire. Between 647 and 709 the whole of North Africa including Carthage became a part of the Arab Empire.

Even the mighty Roman Empire in Europe could not escape the Arab invasion. Spain came under Arab rule during 700–713 A.D.

All this is the story of Muslim conquests in the first century of Islam. Conquests by the Arabs and other Muslim nations continued. Gradually, the whole of Russia, Greece, the Balkans, Poland, more than a half of Europe, came under Arab rule and remained under that rule for several centuries.

An Incident

It was in 636 A.D., during the time of Khaleefa Omar, that some units of the Arab navy were, for the first time, sighted off the Indian coast. They appeared at Thana, near the island which is now called Bombay. They had been sent under the orders of Sakaifi, the Muslim Governor of Bahrain (Iraq), without permission having been obtained from Khaleefa Omar. It is recorded that when Khaleefa Omar came to know of this expedition, he became angry with the Governor of Bahrain and the naval units were ordered back without touching the shores of India and without any armed conflict whatsoever. The Khaleefa further issued orders that if any expedition was again sent against India, those responsible for it would be severely punished.

This minor incident is indicative of the degree of mutual regard and respect that existed at that time between Muslim Arabs and Indians. We shall deal in more detail with this relationship between the Arabs and the Indians of those days later on. But before we do that, we would like to describe here the first regular invasion of India by the Muslims, its causes and consequences.

First Muslim Invasion of India

In the beginning of the 8th century A.D. some Arab traders died in Singhal Dweep (Ceylon). They had come from Iraq. The Raja of Singhal Dweep sent a few orphan daughters of the deceased Arab traders in a special ship to Hajjaj, the then Muslim Governor of Iraq. On the way, some Kutch pirates, called Bavarij, attacked the ship and took away the girls. Hajjaj came to know of it and demanded the girls from Dahir, the Hindu Raja of Kathiawar. Dahir was unable to comply with the demand. Thereupon Hajjaj in 712 A.D. sent an expeditionary force under the leadership of Muhammad Bin Qasim to invade India by land through Baluchistan (Elliot's *History of India*, Vol. I, p. 118). This was the first Muslim invasion of India. India was at that time politically in a somewhat weak state, about which we shall say more later. Muhammad Bin Qasim conquered Sindh and Multan and established his rule over both.

Muslim Rule Over Sindh

With reference to the invasion of Sindh by Muslims, four things have to be kept in mind, namely:

(i) That the first Muslim invasion of India took place after Muslim rule had been well established from Tatar in the east to Spain in the West.

(ii) That according to the historian Vilks, Hajjaj, the Governor of Iraq, was notorious in his own country for his harshness to his subjects and a good many Iraqi Muslims had sought protection from the resulting hardships by escaping to Konkan, Kanya Kumari (Cape Comorin) and other places in southern India.

Yet after the conquest of Sindh, its conqueror, Muhammad Bin Qasim, wrote to Hajjaj and asked for his instructions about the treatment to be meted out to the people of Sindh. Hajjaj replied as under:

> "When those people have submitted and have agreed to pay taxes to the Khaleefa, it is not proper to make any further demands on them. We have taken them under our protection and we cannot in any way touch their person or property. They have the liberty to worship their own gods. In no case should anyone be forbidden to follow his own religion or be prevented from doing so. They should be permitted to live in their homes as they like." (*The History of Medieval India* by Ishwari Prasad, pp. 52, 53)

(iii) That testifies, as history very clearly shows, that Muhammad Bin Qasim impartially treated his Hindu and Muslim subjects and exactly in the same way. Dr. Beni Prasad in his book the *History of Jehangir* (p. 89), says "Mohammed-Bin-Quasim's administration of Sindh in the 8th century was a shining example of moderation and tolerance", and

(iv) That for the next three hundred years, that is, before Mahmud Ghazni's invasion of India, there was no other invasion of India by the Muslims, nor did Muslim rule advance beyond Sindh or Multan during that period.

Relations between Ancient Arabs and India

We shall now describe at some length the relations which then subsisted between the Arabs and the Indians. The two had first come into contact with each other, at least 500 years before the birth of Prophet Mohammed, that is, long before the Arabs became Muslims. Since the time of the birth of Christ, thousands of Arab traders used to come to the eastern as well as western

India and set up several small kingdoms of their own in North-Western and Central India. Several new tribes also began to call themselves Rajputs. So much so that before the first Muslim invasion, almost the entire country from the Punjab to the Deccan and from Bengal to the Arabian Sea had split up into a number of separate independent states, each ruled by its own Rajput chieftain. There was no power strong enough to keep together all these big and small states under one central administration. Every now and then, these states fought with one another, spurred by the desire to extend their respective territories. In other words, instead of one powerful Central Government for the whole of India, the entire country was under the rule of a number of rival kings, each independent of the others. National or political unity of the country had become only a dream. The capitals of old all-India Empires like Magadha, Pataliputra and Gaya were lying in ruins and so were Vaishali, Kushinagar, Kedia, Ramgram, Kapilavastu and Shravasti, names famous in Buddhist history. Their places had been taken by other much smaller and less important centres of the country's political and economic life.

It was also a period of decadence in the religious life of the country. Within 250 years of the Buddha's death, that is 250 years before the birth of Christ, Buddhism had driven the then decadent Hinduism from India and had itself taken its place. But the hostility of the Brahmin priests and of the upper castes, whose prerogatives had been taken away by Buddhism, still smouldered. Gradually and insidiously idol-worship and old Hindu religious ritualism crept into Buddhism also. Foundations of the Mahayan sect of Buddhism were thus laid in northern India. In the temples of this new sect, besides the worship of Lord Buddha, the worship of a large number of images of smaller deities, called Boddhisatvas, Amitabh being the principal among them, was also introduced. The entire ritualism of Hindu temples crept into the Buddhist temples also.

Original Buddhism had dethroned the then dead language Sanskrit from its place of honour and had given it to the spoken languages of the people, like Prakrit and Pali, in all religious ceremonies as well as in literature. Now in the new Mahayan sect of Buddhism, Sanskrit was again given the place of honour in place of Prakrit and Pali. The path of knowledge called the *Gyan Marg* was again largely replaced by old-type ceremonies and rituals, collectively called the *Bhakti Marg.*

The result was that the various sects of Hinduism then existing, like the Vaishnava sect, the Shaiva sect and the Tantrik sect, all gradually united to turn out Buddhism from India and once more give its place back to ancient Hinduism. Buddhism had practically abolished the Hindu caste-system and raised the status of the lower classes of people, specially the women and the *Shudras* in society. Now, with the revival of Hinduism, the old caste system with its superiority of the Brahmins and the degradation of women and *Shudras* once more came into vogue. Indian society once more tended to become stagnant and unprogressive under the priestly and ruling classes with their renewed special privileges. For the vast masses of people, religion once more meant little more than the observance of intricate and degrading caste rules such as untouchability, idol worship, the worship of innumerable gods and goddesses including the fearful Rudras and the ferocious Shakti, long journeys to places of pilgrimage and performing a hundred superstitious customs and ceremonies, all necessitating payments to and maintenance of the priestly class.

Buddhism had laid emphasis on the acquirement of knowledge, both temporal and spiritual, *i.e.,* on *Gyan Marg.* Its place was once more taken by complicated ritualism called *Bhakti Marg* and *Karmkand;* even the study of spiritual literature was reserved for the few at the top. The Indian literature of those days, the recorded accounts of Chinese and Arab travellers, as well as the coins and the inscriptions of those days all bear witness to this state of affairs in India about the eighth century A.D.

At the time of the coming to India of the Chinese traveller, Fa Hi Yan, in the 5th century A.D., Buddhism had already disappeared from India except in the north-west, from Kabul to Mathura where it still existed in its original form called "Hinyani". Two hundred years later when Huen Tsang, the famous Chinese traveller, visited India, he found that in the north also the "Heenyan" sect had been replaced by the "Mahayana" sect of which we have spoken earlier. His narrative shows that the worship of the Hindu god Shiva particularly was then prevalent throughout India in full force. In the vicinity of Ayodhya, he came across people who offered human sacrifices to the idol of Durga every year. Shashank, the Shaiva King of Bengal, had started the demolition of Buddhist temples in his kingdom and the replacement of the image of Buddha in Buddhist temples by the image of Shiva. He had also begun the persecution of the Buddhists and their expulsion from his dominions. Huen Tsang also met at several places people of a sect called the "Kapalikas", who wore garlands of human skulls. He writes that the followers of both Buddhism and Shaivism could be found simultaneously in Afghanistan, Iran and in the adjoining region up to Central Asia. Subsequent Arab travellers like Mohammad-Bin-Ishaque, Al Nadeen, Al Shahrastani and others have in their books confirmed the Chinese traveller's account in this connection. Their writings further show that by the time of the arrival of the Muslims in India, Buddhism had practically disappeared from this country and had been replaced by the Shaiva and other Hindu sects. Al Berouni writes that the worship of Shakti, Soorva, Chandrama, Indra, Brahma, Agni, Skanda, Ganesh, Yama, Kuber and other Hindu gods and goddesses had restarted and separate sects in honour of each of them had again sprung up, in addition to the Shaiva and Vaishnava sects. Buddhism and Jainism had stopped the use of meat and wine as food, but both these again became a part and parcel of religious worship through the influence of the followers of Shakti worship and Shiva worship.

To sum up, India in its political, religious as well as social life was then in a state of progressive decay, deterioration and darkness. Politically, it had split up into numerous small states, each hostile to the other. Hundreds of sects divided its religious life. Numberless anti-social customs and superstitions throttled its social life.

Advent of Islam in India

Just about this time, Islam entered India. As mentioned above, there were already a number of Arab settlements in India, particularly in the south, even long before the birth of Islam. The sea-ports of India and disembark there every year. The history of that period mentions several big Arab habitations or settlements, particularly along the western coast of India, especially at Chal, Kalyan, Sopara and Malabar. Even before the birth of Christ, there were many Irani and Arab settlements in southern India and in Lanka (Ceylon). Most of the Indian overseas trade at that time with Iran, Arabia and a number of African and European countries was in the hands of Arab and Irani traders. According to Roman historians, Roman and Greek ships sailing to or from Indian ports in those days were manned mostly by Arab sailors. A considerable part of the trade between India and China was also in the hands of Arabs, who thus became fully familiar with the eastern sea-board of India along which too there were Arab settlements at many places.

The Arabs then followed an old-type simple religion of their own. Every Arab clan or tribe had its own separate gods or goddesses whose images were worshipped by members of that clan or tribe. Travellers' records of those days clearly show that the Arabs of that time were a simple, hospitable and generous people. Their relations with Indians were most intimate and friendly and their settlements in India were happy and prosperous.

Then came the time of the birth of the Prophet and of the propagation of Islam. The Arabs and especially the Arab traders continued to visit India as before with only this difference that instead of being idol-worshippers and polytheists, they were now monotheists and had given up idolatry. With them now came to India the new monotheist religion, Islam, with its new social and moral ideals. Thus the entry into India of these Muslim Arabs or with them of Islam had absolutely nothing to do with any type of military invasion of the country.

India in the Eighth Century

Before proceeding, it is necessary to give a brief picture of India at that time. The reign of Emperor Harshvardhan came to an end in the middle of the 7th century, A.D. A number of small states sprang up all over Northern India. The Rajputs moved out of Western history of that period also testifies to the existence of cordial relations between the Arabs and the Indians in those days. It also shows that the Arab traders were treated with love and respect in the country. This was long before any Muslim military invasion of India. In the 7th century A.D., the new religion, Islam, came to India from the south with the Arabs. History reveals that Indians welcomed this new religion with the same cordiality as that with which they had welcomed the Arab traders for hundreds of years. Once it had entered India, Islam too became one of the numberless Indian religious sects. The historian Ronaldson tells us that towards the end of the 7th century A.D., Muslim Arabs had begun to arrive and settle on the Malabar coast. The historian Sturrock writes:

> "From the 7th century onwards, Irani and Arab traders began to settle in large numbers in various ports along the eastern seacoast of India. They married the women of the country. Their settlements, particularly in Malabar, were quite big and important because it appears that from the very earliest time, the policy of the Government in India was to provide all facilities to foreign traders at the seaports." ("S. Kanara", *Madras District Manuals,* p. 180)

Gradually the Muslims began to acquire more and more influence in the country. The Government also provided them with full facilities for preaching their new religion, along with the facilities for trade and commerce and even for acquiring land in the country. By the 9th century A.D., these people had spread over the entire Western coast. We have mentioned that at that time in India, the conflict between the Buddhist and the Jain religions on the one hand and the new sects of Hinduism, on the other, had already started and was in full swing. In contrast with the new Hindu sects mentioned above whose power and influence were increasing at the time, people's attention was naturally and forcefully drawn to the much more simple and easy to understand principles of Islam and its basic tenets of the unity of God and the equality of all men. There was no reason for any hostility or feeling against Islam. Cheraman Perumal, the Raja of Malabar, who had his capital at Kodungloor, himself became a convert to Islam in the beginning of the 9th century and took the name of Abdul Rahman Sanini (*Malabar* by Logan, Vol. I, p. 245).

After his conversion to Islam, he went to Arabia and four years later died there. From Arabia he sent several Muslim scholars and preachers to India. Through them, he also sent instructions to his deputies or successors in Malabar about carrying on the administration and specifically directed that the Arab scholars should be given all help for preaching the new religion. The deputies gladly welcomed the Arab scholars and, at their behest, got constructed eleven new mosques along the Malabar coast for the worship of the One Formless God.

Conversion to Islam of the Raja of Calicut

The Samuri (a form of Samudri), Raja of Calicut, and the Maharaja of Travancore were descended from the same family to which Cheraman Perumal belonged. The coronation ceremonies of the Rajas of Calicut and of the Maharajas of Travancore prescribed for more than a thousand years the memory of Cheraman Perumal's conversion to Islam and his sojourn in Arabia. Up to 1912, it was customary to shave the head of every new Raja or Maharaja at the time of his installation on the *Gadi* in right Muslim style. The coronation robes too were prepared in the Muslim style and the crown was placed on the head by a Mopla, that is, a Mussalman (Quadir Hussain Khan's "South Indian Mussalmans" *Madras College Magazine*, 1912–13, p. 241).

The new Raja or Maharaja, after his coronation, was deemed to have become an out-caste. He could no more dine with the members of his family. A strange legal fiction was kept up to the effect that every Samuri Raja was installed on the *Gadi* merely as a deputy of Cheraman Perumal, pending his return from Arabia. Similarly, every Maharaja of Travancore, when he was handed the sword of office at his installation, had to declare: "I shall wear this sword till the return of my uncle from Arabia" (Logan, *op. cit.*, p. 231).

The Samuri gave every kind of facility to the Muslims in his dominion. No Nayyar could sit by the side of a Namboodiri

Brahmin, but a Mussalman could. Whenever the Samuri went out in a *Palki* (a sedan-chair), Thangal the Muslim divine always sat by his side. The Samuri extended his dominion with the help of the Arabs and other Muslims. This led to great increase in the prosperity of the State. The present city of Calicut was built by a Muslim Quazi of that time. The Rajas of Malabar had considerable naval forces of their own. Most of the naval commanders of the Rajas of Malabar were Muslims and were called "Alirajas". The Samuri also gave great help in the propagation of the Islamic faith. He went to the extent of issuing a general order that at least one child in every Hindu seaman's family should be educated and brought up like a Muslim child. This is the origin of the present-day Mopla Muslim community. The word Mopla means *Maha-pilla,* or the eldest son (Innes: *Malabar and Anjengo District Gazette, p.* 190).

Muslim Preachers, Scholars and Faqeers

It was also during this period that numberless Muslim *Faqeers* and scholars kept coming to India from abroad by land through Afghanistan and by sea through Southern India. They settled down in various parts of the country. They were very well received and were respected everywhere.

Muslim settlements and their importance along the eastern coast of India also went on increasing. It is not necessary here to go into the details of those settlements. In the 11th century A.D., many people, influenced by Najad Vali, a Musalman faqeer, embraced Islam in Madura and Trichinapalli areas. This Najad Vali had been a Turkish prince who had become a *faqeer* and had arrived in Trichinapalli (then called Trisoor) through Arabia, Iran and Northern India. In the 12th century A.D. also, many people in India became converts to Islam under the influence of another *faqeer,* Syed Ibrahim Shaheed. The names of many other Muslim preachers, *e.g.,* Baba Fakhruddin and others, occur in the records of that period. The Hindu Raja of Pennukonda was converted to Islam through the influence of Baba Fakhruddin. It is also recorded that the efforts of these

Arabs and other Muslims brought about great advancement in the trade, commerce and prosperity of India, particularly in the south. The Hindu Rajas of Southern India sent Muslims as their ambassadors to distant countries like China. There were Muslim ministers and prime ministers in several Hindu *Durbars*. Muslims were appointed Governors of Provinces. Hindu Rajas had large Muslim armies.

In the same way, Balhar, the Vallabhi Raja of Gujarat, gladly and courteously welcomed Muslims into his territory. The Hindu Rajas of Kathiawar, of Konkan and of several Hindu States in Central India extended a warm and affectionate welcome to these Muslim *faqeers* and preachers and gave them every help in the propagation of Islam within their respective territories.

About the 11th century A.D., some Hindus in Khambat demolished a Muslim mosque there. At this Raja Sidhraj promptly investigated the incident, punished the guilty and got a new mosque built at his own cost. The Hindu Rajas of those days had Muslim armies with Muslim officers. In the 11th century A.D., the Shia head priest of the Gujarati Bohras, Mullaji, arrived from Yemen (Arabia) in Gujarat and settled there. About that very time, Nuruddin converted to Islam the Kunbi, the Kherwa and the Kadi communities of Gujarat.

From the 8th to the 15th centuries A.D., numberless Muslim saints and *faqeers* settled down in various parts of India, from north to south and from east to west. Because of the purity of their lives and their noble personal character, and because of the simple tenets of Islam, in that era of religious confusion in India, Indians began to embrace Islam in their thousands and hundreds of thousands. The reason and the circumstances of these conversions can be traced even today. In a number of villages in Northern India, the inhabitants contain a large majority of Muslims. If one were to go round such villages and enquire, one would find that the people had accepted Islam because, at one time or another, some selfless and self-sacrificing Muslim *faqeer* of high personal character had lived amongst them. We must remember that all this happened at a time when Muslim political domination had not yet been established in the country or at least had not yet taken root.

Spread of Islam in India

It does not, however, mean that Muslim rule in India did not, in any way, bring about the spread of Islam in the country. There can be no doubt that in every age and in every country religious beliefs of the rulers naturally and inevitably influence those of the ruled. Had there been no Ashok, the spread of Buddhism from one corner of the country to another could not have been so smooth and easy. Similarly, Hinduism could not have so completely and so easily rid India of Buddhism if the Vaishnava sect had not been patronised by emperors like Samudragupta and Chandragupta and if the Shaiva sect had not enjoyed the patronage of Yashodharm Dev (Vikramaditya). We do not even mean that no compulsion of any kind was used at any time or anywhere in converting Indians to Islam. Unfortunately, the history of every country in the world contains instances of the use of a certain amount of compulsion in matters of religion. There are any number of instances of force having been used during the conflict between various Hindu sects on the one side and Buddhism or Jainism on the other in India itself. History, however, shows clearly that:

(i) Islam spread in India long before Muslim invasions.

(ii) Islam spread in India to a considerable extent even before the invasion by Mahmud Ghazni, and that by far the main causes of the spread of Islam throughout India were:

  (a) the piety, the self-sacrifice and the high moral character of the Muslim preachers of the time, and

  (b) the simple and clear-cut principles of Islam which in contrast with those of the numerous Hindu sects then prevailing appeared more beneficial and easier to follow for the common man.

The majority of those who became converts to Islam at that time belonged to the lower castes of Hinduism who had been feeling the injustice meted out to them by the Indian caste-system. The conversion of the rest of Indians in any number to Islam was exactly like the conversion of Indians from the Vedic faith to Buddhism or that from Buddhism to the Vaishnava or the Shaiva religion or that of the Chinese or the Burmese from their former faiths to Buddhism.

The reason why Khalifa Umar issued orders to his Arab army never to launch an attack against India was mainly because the Indian people and their rulers had all through treated the Arab traders like friends and brothers and had accorded complete freedom to preachers of Islam in their territories and because there existed the most cordial relations between the Hindus and the Muslims in the India of that early period. This was also the reason why even for many years after the Arab Empire had reached its full expansion in Asia, in Europe and in Africa, there was no invasion of India by the Arab Muslims.

Gradually, nearly one-fourth of the population of India accepted Islam. As to the question whether force or compulsion played any part in the spread of Islam in the India of those days, we quote below the opinions of only a few historians of the period. Writing about the Indian Muslims, the historian Arnold says:

> "By far the majority of them entered the pale of Islam of their own free will." (*The Preaching of Islam* by T. W. Arnold, 1913, p. 255)

Another historian Townsend says:

> "Its spread as a faith is not due mainly to compulsion." (*Asia and Europe* by M. Townsend, London, 1911, p. 44)

Again, at another place, Townsend writes:

> "Ninety percent of the whole body of the Muslims are Indians by blood, as much children of the soil as Hindoos, retaining many of the old pagan superstitions, and only Musalmans because their ancestors embraced the faith of the Great Arabian." (*ibid,* p. 43)

He says further that even after the establishment of Muslim rule in India, the forcible conversion of the people to Islam was against the inclinations and interests of most of the new Muslim rulers. He writes:

> "The missionary of Islam could not use force and as to the invaders who conquered and remained, they seldom or never wished to use it for the sufficient reason that it was not in their interest. They wanted to found principalities or kingdoms, or an empire, not to wage an internecine war with their own tax-paying subjects or to arouse against themselves the unconquerable hostility of the warrior races of the gigantic peninsula, who were and who remained Hindoos." (*ibid,* p. 45)

From the end of the 13th century to the beginning of the 16th century A.D., during which period the Muslims were continuing their efforts to establish their own Empire in India, the Muslim rulers, according to Sir Alfred Lyall, were:

> "...... generally too busily engaged in fighting to pay much regard to the interests of religion, or else thought more of the exaction of tribute than of the work of conversion." (*Asiatic Studies* by Sir Alfred Lyall, London, 1882, p. 283)

There are doubtless a few instances in which some Muslim rulers who, for political and other reasons or in the supposed interests of Islam in India, did misuse or over-step their powers. As against this the *Farmans,* the orders, and other records of not only Babar and Akbar, but also of most of the other Muslim rulers can be cited to show that they made no distinction between their Hindu and Muslim subjects and did not consider any type of discrimination on the basis of religion in their own interest. History proves very clearly that in the case of 90, nay, 99 per cent Indian Muslims, their conversion to Islam was due only to the high moral character of numberless Muslim *faqeers,* Pirs and Dervashes and also to the social and other specialities inherent in Islam as against the Hinduism of those days.

Arab Seekers after Truth—New Ideas in Religion

The influence of this new faith from Arabia was not limited only to those Indians who had embraced Islam in their hundreds or thousands. The new ideas and ideals preached by Islam made a deep and indelible impression on the rest of the Indian people also, on their ideas, their religious beliefs, literature, their arts, their painting, their science and their architecture—in fact, on the entire culture and civilization of India at the time. Before giving a more detailed picture of this influence, it is necessary that we cast a glance at some aspects of the new Arab civilization after the appearance of Prophet Mohammed.

From the very beginning, Islam believed in One Formless God only. Its tenets were quite simple and its mode of worship easy to follow. Even then, soon after Mohammed's death, Islam began to shoot out fresh branches in various directions. Just as the rulers and statesmen of Arabia began to extend their dominions eastward and westward, in the same way Arab scholars and divines began to enrich their store of knowledge by drawing upon the philosophies, the science, the arts and the literatures of other nations with which they came into contact. In their quest for knowledge, they went to all the four corners of the world.

Translations of Greek, Christian, Buddhist and Other Indian Literary Works into Arabic

The religious scriptures of the Christians were translated into Arabic. So were the philosophical writings of Socrates, Plato and Aristotle and other Greek books on science, medicine, astronomy and other subjects. The Arabs already had contacts with India. To the export of commercial goods from India into Arabia was soon added the export of Indian culture, Indian literature, Indian arts and sciences. In the early days of the *Khaleefas,* Indians occupied several high Government offices in Basra (*Vie d'al Hadjdjadj Ibn Yusuf* by Jean Perier, pp. 249–52). There were a number of Indian settlements in Syria, Kashgar and other places. Before embracing Islam, the people of Khorasan, Afghanistan, Shiestan and Baluchistan followed either the Buddhist or the Hindu religion. In Balkh there was a big Buddha Vihar, whose Buddhist head priests used to be the Vaziers of the Abbasi *Khaleefas* (*A Literary History of the Arabs* by Nicholson, p. 259). All the principal religious books of the Buddhists were translated into Arabic. *Kitabul Bud* and *Bil Bahar Wa Budsip* are still two authoritative works on Buddhism written in Arabic in those days. Similarly numerous Sanskrit writers like Charak and Sushrut, the works of Chanakya and books like the *Panchatantra, the Hitopadesh* and others were translated into Arabic. The life and teachings of Buddha particularly deeply impressed the Muslim Arab scholars of those days. Gradually various types of free thinking, liberal ideas, new schools of philosophy and diverse sects sprang up amongst the Arabs. It was at this stage that Islam gave birth to spiritual monism, *i.e., Adwait vad* and the principles of Sufism.

Spiritual Monism in Islam

At this time, the divines of the Ghulat sect of the Shia Moslems found a place in their tenets for the doctrines of "incarnation of God in human form", *i.e.,* of *Atarvad* and of the transmigration of souls, *i.e., Punarjanma.* They called these doctrines *Halul, Tashbih* and *Tanasukth.* They also held that the human soul could develop and progress right up to the divine status. The followers of the *All Ilahi* sect declared both polygamy and divorce as illegal. They declared also that going to the mosque and performing the enjoined ablutions *i.e., Wuzu,* were unnecessary. Many sects began to question the literal intepretation of the *Quran* and declared the language of many parts of the *Quran* as allegorical (*Heterodoxies of Shiites* by Frielhander, p. J.A.O.S. Nos. 23 and 29). A distinction began to be made between the Unmanifested God *'Nirgun'* (Brahm) and the Manifested God *Sagun* (Ishwar).

Thus many sects came to be established into which people were admitted through particular forms of initiation. Some of these sects declared that the intiated individual could by practice rise to the status of a Prophet or even of God Himself. The Pir or the Guru was considered equal in status to God or sometimes in some respects even higher. The followers of the Motzali sect openly declared that the *Quran* was not an infallible Word of God for all time; but that every human soul received divine revelation from time to time as the human race advanced. Algizali (1057–1152), not satisfied with the *Quran,* the Shariat (Muslim religious law), and the usual Islamic ritualism, isolated himself from all worldly affairs, and sought peace within his own soul through prayers (shaghal), penance (riazat), and meditation (zikr) in solitude. Similar liberal-minded *Sufis* established monasteries wherein spiritual monism wahdat-ul-wajud, *i.e., 'adwait'* was preached, self-denial (*nafskushi*) was emphasised and the way of attaining salvation was said to be devotion (*ishqu, i.e., bhakti*) and Yogic practices (*shagal).* Poets and scientists produced dissenters who disowned even the Prophet and the *Quran,* and ridiculed the ideas of heaven and hell, the *Namaz* (prayer) and the *Roza* (fasts). They proclaimed that the existence of a God who could be defined or described was against reason and illogical. Even Khaleefa Yazeed who died in 744 A.D. was considered and condemned as one of these heretics. The ideas and beliefs of the noted sage Abul Ala Almaari (who died in 1057 A.D.) bore a clear imprint of the Buddha's teachings. He believed in the transmigration of souls, was a strict vegetarian to the extent that he deemed the use of even milk or honey or of leather to be a sin. He preached compassion and kindness towards all living beings and was abstemious in matters like food and clothing. He considered celibacy, *i.e., Brahmacharya,* essential for the progress of the soul. He was a bitter opponent of showy religious practices like going to mosques, performing *Namaz* or keeping the *Roza (Abul Ala the Syrian).* In one of his quatrains, he says:

> "It is true that there is no God but God (*la-Ilah il-Allah*). Yet for one who gropes even in the dark for the heaven which is within you and me, there is no Prophet except his own soul."

The free-thinking of Omar Khayyam is well known. The Sufis learned and adopted the practice of night-long vigils and prayers, of keeping long fasts and other similar austerities from the life of Prophet Mohammad. But the tenets and the teachings of Sufism also bore a clear imprint of Christianity, of Zoroastrianism, of Hinduism and also of Buddhism. The Prophet Mohammad had forbidden retirement from the world, but amongst his followers were many who from the very beginning preached and followed the principle of renouncing the world. They called it "al fararo minaddunia". Orthodox Muslim divines and free-thinking Sufis were constantly at polemic war with each other. Yet for hundreds of years, hundreds of thousands of Muslims came from all direction and still come and gather in Sufi monasteries (Dargahs), and there can be no doubt whatsoever that the Sufis strongly influenced and still influence the life and thinking of the Muslims of all countries in the world.

Mansoor is a household name throughout the Muslim world. His name is well known to the people of other religions also. Mansoor visited India too. His guiding principle of life and constant slogan was *Anal Haque,* which is a liberal translation of Sanskrit *Aham Brahmasmi* and means I am God. For his unorthodox ideas and utterances, Mansoor was imprisoned, tortured and ultimately put to death in 922 A.D. The sayings of Kabir, Dadu, Nanak and other Indian sages of medieval India are full of the thoughts and even the utterances of Mansoor. Mansoor regarded everything as God and declared that all idea of duality was illusion (*maya*). This spiritual monism naturally led to the birth of the idea of the fundamental unity of all religions and of respect for and tolerance of other faiths in the minds of millions of Muslims of that time. In the writings of Sufis are repeatedly mentioned the various stages of Yogic practices—the Samadhi, *i.e.,* spiritual trance, the merits of congregational meetings, *i.e., satsang* and meditation, *i.e., dhyan,* the importance of the spiritual guide, *i.e.,* of the Pir or the Guru, and of *Habs-i-dum, i.e., pranayam.* Devotional music and even dancing in devotional ecstasy have been commended. It is said of Sheikh Badru'ddin, who came to live in India in the 13th century A.D., that even after he had become too old to move, he responded to devotional music, jumped out of his bed and danced like a young man! When questioned as to how the aged and infirm Sheikh could dance, he replied: "It is not the Sheikh who is dancing, it is Love (*Ishqu*) which is dancing" *(Ayeen-i-Akbari* by Blackman and Jarret (Vol. III, p. 368). Undoubtedly, love of God *(Ishqu)* was the Sufis 'religion and their all in all. It was the same thing as the Hindu *bhakti marg.* By salvation or *nijat,* they meant nothing less than losing oneself in and becoming one with the Supreme Being (Fanafi—Allah).

New Religious Movements in Southern India

We have already described the state of religious anarchy in India just before the 8th century A.D. Buddhism had run its course and had been replaced by Shaivism, Vaishnavism and the Shakti sects of Hinduism. The Buddhist principles of high individual morality and of the equality of all men had given place to the worship of a number of gods and goddesses, numerous sects and sub-sects, complicated ritualisms, casteism and untouchability with their discrimination between high and low and innumerable other superstitions which held sway over the people. The Jain king of Madura came under the influence of the teachings of the Shaiva preacher Tirugyan and became a convert to Shaivism. His subjects, however, declined to give up Jainism and at the instance of Tirugyan, he ordered the hanging of a large number of Jains. Such atrocities committed in the name of religion on Buddhists and Jains were reported in those days from many parts of India. It was, therefore, quite natural, under this state of affairs, that the high principles and the moral character of thousands of Mussalman *faqeers* and Sufis who had, in the early centuries of Islam, settled mostly in the South and in the rest of India, should have produced a healthy and beneficial influence on the minds of the people. The minds of many Hindu scholars and sages also turned towards the problem of resolving the confused religious state in various parts of the country. Shankar, Ramanuj, Vallabhacharya, Nimbadittya, Vasav, Madhav and other sages, born in the South one after another, once more gave, in their own respective ways, to their distracted countrymen the message of hope, equality, love and peace.

Influence of Islam in India

Till the 8th century A.D., the movements of social and religious reform in India originated mostly in the North. Thereafter, a change came about and during the 8th century, the South in place of the North began to have the distinction of being the birthplace of such movements. This distinction continued to attach to the South from the 8th to the 15th centuries A.D. Shankar, Ramanuj, Nimbadittya, Vasav, Vallabhacharya and Madhav all came from the South. One important reason for this shift from the North to the South was undoubtedly the fact that most of the Muslim sages, sufis and Dervishes who came to India in that period settled in the South and in the West. There is a clear impress of Islam on the teachings and preachings of the above Hindu reformers and teachers. A learned historian writes:

> "The presence of the followers of Islam stimulated thought on such subjects as caste, spiritual birth and the personality of God." (*Kabir and Kabir Panth* by H. G. Westcott, London, 1907, p. 45)

The historian Barth, in his *Religions of India*, writes:

> "Long before the Afghans, the Turks or their co-religionist Mughal conquerors came to India, the Arabs of the Khilafat had arrived in this country as travellers and had established trade and other friendly relations with the people of the country. Then, from the 9th to the 12th century, followed the powerful religious movements associated with the names of reformers like Shankar, Ramanuj, Anand Teertha and Vasav. Most of the historic religious sects of India originated with these movements and, for a long period thereafter, there was nothing comparable to these sects in Hindustan."

Even a cursory comparison leads one to the conclusion that almost all the Hindu religious teachers of that period drew considerably on contemporary Islamic ideas.

We would now briefly compare the teachings of the principal Hindu religious teachers with the teachings of Islam and Sufism from the 8th to the 15th centuries A.D. This does not, however, mean that the doctrines propounded by the Hindu sages had not existed before that in Hindu religious literature in some form or other. Nor can it be doubted that Hindu sages and teachers like Shankar did quench their thirst for knowledge by drinking at the fount of accumulated ancient Hindu religious lore, and based on it their efforts to guide their own countrymen along the right path. All the same, the comparison which follows will make it clear that they did to a certain extent help themselves to the teachings of Islam in arriving at the doctrines which they formulated and preached. It will also be evident from this comparison that ancient Hindu religious ideas and conceptions after having reached Iran and Arabia came back to their country of birth in a new and rejuvenated form and further enriched the religious treasure-house of this country.

The first to attract our attention is Shankaracharya. He tried to marshal the numerous Hindu religious sects of his time into an organised and united opposition to Buddhism and to provide them with a common philosophical basis. He made many changes or reforms in the then prevalent form of Hinduism. He threw open to all castes the sannyas stage of life. In his work *Manushya Panchak,* he writes:

> "Whoever knows the real essence of existence is my true Guru (teacher) whether he be a twice-born, *i.e.,* a Brahmin or a *Chandala* (untouchable)."

The Vaishnava and Shaiva religious scholars bitterly opposed Shankar at many places. Shankar's spiritual monism (*adwaitvad*) was undoubtedly Indian in origin, but it bore a very strong resemblance to the spiritual monism of the Muslim Sufis of that time. At all events, no one in India before Shankar had given spiritual monism the form which Shankar gave it. There is also at least some sort of resemblance between the strict monotheism of Islam and the spiritual monism of Shankar. In Shankar's time Islam had already come to India. It is recorded that the Hindu Raja of the part of the country wherein Shankar was born had already embraced Islam (Fawcett in the "Anthropology" Bulletin, Vol. III, No. 1). There is in several respects a marked affinity with Islam in the teachings of Ramanuj and other religious teachers, as for example, the emphasis on strict monotheism, the frenzy of devotion, the faith in and devotion to the Guru or Pir, the relaxation of the rigidity of caste distinctions, *etc.* There is at places an amazing similarity of expression between the writings of these Hindu sages and the writings of Muslim Sufis of that period.

The Lingayat sect of Hinduism was founded about the 12th century A.D. Its founders are believed to have been three, named Vasav, Channa Vasav and Ekant Rammayya. The Lingayat sect is a Shaiva sect. The Lingayats believe in one God whom they call Par Shiva, and regard their Guru Allama Prabhu to be His incarnation. As the Muslims have their "Char Pirs" (the four masters), so the Lingayats too have the "Char Aradhya" (the four to be adored). The Lingayat ceremony of initiation is exactly like that of the Sufis. The Lingayats observe no caste distinctions. A Pariah (untouchable) can be admitted into their fold just like a Brahmin. No distinction is made between the two. In a marriage the consent of the bride is considered necessary. Child-marriages are forbidden. Divorce is allowed as also the remarriage of widows. The dead are buried instead of being cremated. There are no after-death ceremonies like the Hindu *shraddha* and periodical oblations to the departed. The Lingayats do not believe in the transmigration of the soul. Inter-dining and inter-marriages are permitted among the Lingayats. Lingayats also call themselves *Jangam* or *Veer Shaiva.* In the first quarter of the 20th century A.D., the Lingayats numbered 5% of the population in Belgaum, Bijapur and Dharwar districts and 10% of the population in Mysore and Kolhapur States. There are undoubtedly many things in the tenets of the Lingayats which are to be found in Islam and which had never before existed in any Hindu sect. *Allam* and *Allah* have manifest similarity.

Similarly, the members of the Siddhar sect believed in one God, rejected the doctrine of the transmigration of souls, disowned the authority of the Vedas and of the *Shastras* as the ultimate proof, and condemned idol-worship and caste-distinctions. They stressed the need of a *Sat Guru* or spiritual teacher. In the sacred books of this sect are to be found, scattered all over, actual words and expressions used in Muslim works or in the writings of the Sufis.

Muslims Making India Their Home

We should now for a short time like to leave aside the question of the influence of Islam on various aspects of Indian life and try to see which other invasions of India by the Muslims took place after the invasion by Muhammad Bin Qasim, how the Muslims established their rule in this country and how the Muslims coming from other countries settled in India and made it their home.

Mahmud Ghazni

Mahmud Ghazni's invasion of India occurred 300 years after the invasion of Sindh by Muhammad Bin Qasim. Mahmud was the ruler of Ghazni. He invaded India, ravaged and plundered some towns, entered into treaties with some Hindu Rajas and took them under his protection, plundered some temples and, it is said, invaded Somnath, broke the idol of Somnath and, laden with immense booty, went back to Ghazni. There is a great difference of opinion among authoritative historians as regards the truth or otherwise of Mahmud Ghazni's invasion of Somnath itself. Writers of history also unreservedly mention and praise many good qualities in the character of Mahmud Ghazni (*Medieval Hindu India* by C. V. Vaidya, Vol. III, p. 104 and *History of Medieval India* by Ishwari Prasad, p. 91). But all this is beside our present subject. It is a historical fact that there were thousands of Hindu soldiers in Mahmud's army. One of his famous commanders was a Hindu named Tilak who had once put down a revolt against Mahmud led by a Muslim commander in Mahmud's army. Anyhow, Mahmud's invasions of India could not have any lasting influence on the life of the country. His invasions can be rated no higher than the plundering expeditions of a greedy highwayman.

Mohammad Ghori

A hundred years later, the Turks began to press the ruling Ghori dynasty of Afghanistan from the west and push them towards the east. The Ghori kings turned further east. This culminated in the invasion of India by Mohammad Ghori. Muslim rule was now established over the Punjab. The political and administrative confusion in India had become worse by the time of Mohmmad Ghori's invasion. By the 13th century A.D., Muslim rule was firmly established over the whole of Northern India. At some places the Rajputs bravely fought the Muslims but they could not unite their forces against the common enemy. Nor had they the requisite statesmanship. Gradually, within the next one hundred years, Muslim rule was established over the greater part of India right up to Mysore.

Non-Indians and Indians

For once, at least India's national life suffered a rude shock. But the Muslims who invaded India settled down in the country and soon became part and parcel of India's population. Their settling down in India and getting completely merged in the Indian people was greatly facilitated by the presence in the country of hundreds of thousands of Indians who had already embraced Islam before the establishment of Muslim rule in the country as well as by the respect for Islam which, as mentioned above, had been generated in the minds of the Indian people generally. Thus in about a single generation these outsiders became Indians to all intents and purposes. Their interests became completely identified with those of the rest of the Indian people. They soon began to find their own prosperity in the prosperity of the Indian people and their own happiness in the happiness of India's vast millions. Besides, in that critical period of India's political and religious life, the country was sorely in need of a strong central administration. This need was fully and successfully met by the Muslims who invaded this country as foreigners and who soon became part and parcel of the Indian people by settling down in India.

No invasion of any people by another can be morally or legally justified. Nor can it be creditable for any country to surrender to outside invader, or suffer a defeat at the hands of an invading army. At the same time, we must admit that no particular community or people has an exclusive right to any particular region, territory or country. The truth is that the division of mankind into nations or nationalities and of the earth into different countries is to a very large extent man-made and artificial. All humanity is but one family and the earth is its abode. The present-day ideas of nation and nationalism, which appear serviceable for the continued, free existence of every people under present-day political conditions are at best a necessary evil. To dilate further on this subject is beyond the scope of this book. However, even under the prevailing conditions, no individual living in a country can or should be considered a foreigner unless he looks upon any other country outside the boundaries of the country in which he lives as his home or as his mother-country, or gathers wealth from the country in which he is living and remits it to his so-called mother-country, thereby enriching the latter at the cost of the former. When any individual once settles down in a country, adopts it as his home and identifies his interests with the interests of all other people living there, he can in no way be considered a foreigner, whatever his religious beliefs or even his personal character may be. For most of the period from the Vedic times to the coming of the British to India, Afghanistan was a part of the country called India. It was regarded as much a province of India as any other. Even then if Afghanistan be considered to be outside India, the invasions of India by Mahmud Ghazni were foreign invasions. The invasion of Sindh by Muhammad Bin Qasim was undoubtedly a foreign invasion. So was the invasion by Mohammad Ghori. But rule over India by Muslims, who had originally come from Iran or Afghanistan, settled down in India and made India their home, could by no means be called foreign rule.

The period of about 250 years of Indian history, *i.e.,* from the end of the 13th to the beginning of the 16th century, was marked by almost constant internecine wars. Thereafter, we have only one more invasion, that by the Mughals. Babar who came from Turkistan and invaded India was a foreigner. Ibrahim Lodi, who was an Indian king, fought Babar the invader on the field of Panipat in 1526 A.D. and was defeated. Babar settled down in India and Mughal rule was established in the country.

The good or the evil accruing to India from Mughal rule is altogether a separate subject. Here we have only to see that just as Islam having once entered India became one of the Indian religious sects like any other sects previously existing, similarly the Muslim invaders, having once settled down in India, became part and parcel of the Indian people and as much citizens of the country as any other section of the people. There are numerous instances in which Muslim rulers of India gallantly fought their co-religionists when the latter invaded India from outside. There are also instances in which Muslim rulers of India sallied forth from the country, invaded other countries outside India, annexed them to their Indian empire and even appointed Hindu Rajas as Governors of the newly conquered territories.

No person can be considered a foreigner in any country simply on account of his or her religious belief. Absolute freedom in matters of religion is a necessary condition of life in every civilized country. During thousands of years of her history, with her broad-minded and cosmopolitan outlook on life and with her spirit of perfect tolerance, India has lived up to this ideal of human civilization much better than any other country in the world. If this view with regard to Indians and non-Indians is not accepted as true in the case of India, then we will have to admit that not only India but also England, Germany, France and practically every civilized country of the world is even today almost wholly inhabited by foreigners. Then could neither the Anglo-Saxons of England be regarded as Englishmen nor could the Aryans of Germany or of India be regarded as Germans or Indians, even though they may proudly acclaim themselves to be the children or even the masters of the soil. The fact of the matter is that the Babar who defeated Ibrahim Lodi was a foreigner but the Babar who broke off all his relationships with Turkistan or with Iran, settled down in India and adopted this country as his home and established his rule in India was as much an Indian as anybody else. Much more so were the other Mughal emperors, who succeeded Babar on the throne of Delhi. The fact that any particular policy followed by any of them was beneficial to India or otherwise makes no difference in this matter. There is no doubt that they were all Indians and their rule was independent Indian rule.

Religion of Humanity

We now come back to the various religious currents that flowed in the India of those days.

We have already spoken of Ramanuj's preachings in the South. Ramanuj was a worshipper of Vishnu. His method was the *bhakti marg,* that is, the way of devotion. His disciple Ramanand carried his spiritual message to the North. The historian Mecauliff writes:

> "There can be no doubt that at Benares Ramanand came into contact with learned Muslims of the time. Rama was believed to be the incarnation of Vishnu. Ramanand at Benares preached the worship of Rama and advocated the way of devotion. He observed no caste distinctions. His followers included persons of all castes and even a large number of Muslims. Out of them, Goswami Tulsidas and Kabir Sahib are the most famous. The former was a high-class North Indian Brahmin and the latter a born Muslim weaver of Benares. The *Ramayan* of Tulsidas is now read all over Northern India. Its language is the Avadhi dialect of Hindi or Hindustani. Tulsidas has written in the language of the people. For his vocabulary he has borrowed freely from Sanskrit as well from Arabic and Persian. He uses

Sanskrit words not in their Sanskrit form, called *tatsam,* but in their popular forms called *tatbhavas* used by the people at large. He may be counted as one of the founders of popular Hindustani of the type later advocated by Mahatma Gandhi. Goswami Tulsidas demonstrated through his immortal work the *Ramayan* that such a popular broad-based language could serve the purposes of highest literature and give expression to the most intricate religious and philosophical thoughts."

Kabir

Kabir was undoubtedly one of the mightiest thinkers and greatest religious and social reformers that India has produced. His philosophy of life was original. He was a mystic and spiritualist to the core. He believed in a religion of the centre, which may well be termed the Religion of Humanity in clear contrast to all other separate religions of the world. He was above all forms, rituals and ceremonies. Born in a Muslim family and brought up in the Hindu city of Benares, he discarded what he regarded as the superstitions of both Islam and Hinduism. In India he was probably the greatest and positively the first propounder of Hindu-Muslim unity. His conception of such a unity was based not upon any political or even social considerations, but upon the deepest truths of existence.

Kabir was born in 1398 A.D. He died in 1518 A.D. There is a story current about Kabir's birth. It is said that he was born of a Brahmin widow, that somebody left the new-born child on the bank of a tank and that the wife of a Muslim weaver, Nuruddeen, saw the child thus lying uncared for, took him to her house and brought him up as her own son. We believe that all this beautiful story is a later concoction and that Kabir, whose full name was Kabiruddeen, was really the son of the Muslim weaver Nuruddeen, who lived in what is now known as Kabir Chawra, Benares. This fact is clearly borne out by the in numerable writings of Kabir and by his entire life itself.

At Benares Kabir got fully acquainted with the teachings of both Hinduism and Islam. Mohsin Fani writes that in his very boyhood Kabir met many Hindu and Muslim divines and learned men and exchanged thoughts with them. For a long period he lived at Jaunpur and also at Jhusi, near Allahabad. At both these places he lived for a time with a number of Muslim Sufis and *Faqeers*, among whom Sheikh Taqui of Jaunpur is the most famous. Kabir has mentioned all this in his well-known work, the *Ramaini*. It was after this that Kabir Sahib started his own congregational meetings in Benares and began to preach his own doctrines.

Kabir's views were so radical and revolutionary that in the beginning he antagonised both the Muslim Maulvis and the Hindu Pandits. Both of them tried to persecute Kabir in various ways and even disturbed his congregational meetings. Ultimately Kabir got thousands of admirers and followers from amongst both Hindus and Muslims. Throughout his life Kabir earned his livelihood from his ancestral profession. Most of his speeches and sermons were delivered while he was simultaneously weaving cloth at his ancestral handloom.

Among the Hindus a belief had been current from very old times to the effect that whoever dies at Kashi immediately gets salvation and on the contrary whoever dies at Maghar (a village 15 miles to the West of Gorakhpur) is reborn as a donkey after death. When Kabir felt his end approaching he insisted upon being taken to Maghar so that he might breathe his last in Maghar and not in Kashi. This he did deliberately to show his disbelief in and contempt for the superstitious belief referred to above. Kabir did breathe his last at Maghar in A.D. 1518 in the presence of tens of thousands of his followers, which included practically an equal number of Hindus and Muslims.

It is said that immediately after Kabir's death, some of his Hindu and Muslim followers began to quarrel amongst themselves. The Hindus insisted that Kabir was a Hindu saint and should be duly cremated. The Muslims, on the other hand, held that Kabir was after all a Musalman by birth and should be buried according to the Muslim custom. Several stories are current about what happened ultimately and how it happened. We may not go into them. The fact, however, remains that up to this day, two places of pilgrimage exist side by side in Maghar just at a small distance from each other. One of these is the *samadhi* of Kabir Sahib, where thousands of Hindus gather every year and pay their respectful homage to the great departed and the other is the *mazar* or tomb of Kabir where thousands of Muslims gather on the same date, year after year and pay their homage to the saint. The occasion is celebrated every year as a great festival in which both Hindus and Muslims join, the Hindus showering flowers on the *samadhi* and the Muslims reciting the *Fateha* at the *mazar* and greeting each other with affection.

Kabir was an uncompromising opponent of the Hindu caste-system and of the theory of untouchability. He held neither the Vedas nor any of the Shastras, nor the *Quran* as infallible guides for all time and under all circumstances. His religion was the religion of love, Prem Dharm of Mazhab Ishq, like that of the Sufis. Through his extremely popular poems (the *Ramaini,* the *Shabds* and the *Sakhis),* Kabir preached the same common religion of love and humanity and of service to both Hindus and Muslims. He ruthlessly denounced ritualism in the religions of both. He preached love for all living beings and the worship of One Formless God.

Kabir accepted the truths which he found common to all religions including Hinduism and Islam, without any discrimination. In his poems, he used current words from all languages, Sanskrit, Persian, Arabic and Hindustani, without any prejudice.

Expressing his anguish at the artificial differences between the two religions and advocating the common essential truths of both and upholding one common universal religion for all, Kabir says:

1. "Oh brother! How can there be two Gods, one of the Hindus and the other of the Muslims? Who has led you astray?"
2. "Allah and Rama, Karim and Keshav, Hari and Hazrat are only separate names of the same One Supreme Being."
3. "These separate names are but separate ornaments made from one and the same pure gold, there is no duality in them."

4. "Only for making oneself understood, they have coined different words, one calls it *Namaz,* the other calls it *Puja.* The thing is the same."
5. "Mahadeo and Mohammad are not two, Brahma and Adam both mean exactly the same thing."
6. "Who is a Hindu and who is Musalman? Both live upon the same earth. One reads the *Vedas,* the other recites the *Quran,* one is called Maulana, the other is called Pandit. These are only separate names. In reality they are all separate objects made out of the same clay. Kabir says, in their delusion of separateness, they have both strayed from the reality. None of the two could realise the God who is the God of all. One slaughters the goat, the other slaughters the cow, both ruin their lives in complete disregard of the unity of all life."

Kabir goes on to say:

> "I am neither a Hindu nor a Muslim. My body is made of the five elements like the body of anyone else and the universal spirit plays and acts within it as in the body of anyone else, Where is the difference?"

The teachings of Kabir bear a clear imprint of the preachings of Muslim *faqeers* and Sufis. No Hindu saint before him had spoken in this strain. He was certainly well acquainted with the *Pindnama* of Fariduddin Attar and with the mystic poems of Jalaluddin Rumi ajid Sheikh Saadi Shirazi. In Kabir's poems we repeatedly get echoes of the utterances of those great saints and seers of the Muslim world.

At one place Kabir says:

> "Jab tu aya Jagat men, Jagat hanse tu roye, Aisee karni kar. chalo, tu hanse jag roye."

That is,

> "When thou wast born in this world, everybody else was laughing with joy, but thou wert weeping and crying.

Now thou shouldst behave in this world in such a way that when thou departest, thou shouldst go smiling and others should be weeping and crying."

The above couplet of Kabir appears to be almost a literal translation of the following famous verse by Sheikh Saadi:

"Yad dari ke Waqt-e zadan-e tu,
Hama Khandan budundoo tu Giryan,
An chunan...zi Ke bad murdan-e tu,
Hama giryan shavand o tu Khandan."

That is,

"Do you remember that when you were born, you were weeping and crying while all others were laughing with joy? Now you should lead your life in such a way that after your death you should go smiling, while all others may be weeping and crying."

Such instances of similarities of thought and expression between the utterances of Kabir and those of Muslim saints and Sufis can be cited almost *ad infinitum*. Kabir's poems are full of Persian and Arabic words and also of similes and metaphors taken from the writings of Muslim Sufis.

Ahmad Shah has compiled a list of over two hundred Arabic and Persian words and expressions used by Kabir in his famous work, *Beejak,* in exactly the same sense in which the Muslim Sufis have used them in their works such as Habib, Mahboob, Ashiq, Mashooq, Musafir, Mukaam, Haal, Jamaal, Jalaal, Saaqi, Sharaab, Qahar, Mehar, Ghaibat, Huzoor, Hairat, Nasoot, Malqoot, Jabroot, Lahoot, Hahoot, Haq and so on. All this shows how far Kabir was indebted to the Muslim Sufis for his teachings and his philosophy of life.

Kabir prefered to preach his religion in Hindi or Hindustani, the language of the people rather than in Sanskrit, the language of the elite. At one place he says: "Sanskrit hai Roop jal, Bhasha Bahta neer." That is, "Sanskrit is like the stagnant water of a well, while *Bhasha,* that is, the language of the people, is like a flowing river."

In Kabir's poems we find at some places an abundance of Sanskrit words and at other places a similar abundance of Persian and Arabic words. At different places Kabir has used different names for the supreme being, such as Ram, Hari, Govind, Brahm, Samrath Saeen, Sat-purush, Rangrezwa, Bechoon (indescribable) Allah and Khuda, but his most favourite name for God is *Sahib.* Kabir confidently claims that he had realised the one supreme spirit, whom he calls *Zaate Paak,* i.e., the Holy Spirit in "you and me", in every living being and in all things. Like the Sufis, Kabir has described God as *Noor,* i.e., Light and propounded the theory of spiritual monism, that is, of *Wehdatul Wajood* or *Adwaitwad.* Kabir's lines in his famous work, the *Ramaini,* very often sound like a literal translation of similar verses of Muslim Sufis like Badruddin Shaheed, Ibna Seena and Gilani. Like the Sufis, Kabir has elevated the Guru (the spiritual teacher) to the status of God. In his *Sakhi,* he says: "If Hari (God) gets angry, there is chance of one being saved but if the Guru, that is, the teacher, gets angry, there is no chance whatsoever." This line of Kabir's sounds like a literal translation of a similar line in Maulana Room's *Masnavi.*

Kabir calls the Guru *siqu ligar,* which means one who cleanses and polishes the soul of the disciple. Kabir was a great believer in the power of love. According to him, Love pervades the entire universe. About the search for God, he says: "Oh man! Where art thou searching for me? I am quite close to thee. I am neither in the Hindu temple nor in the Muslim mosque, neither in Kaba nor in Kailash. If thou art a sincere seeker, thou will find me out in no time. The search will take only the twinkling of an eye. Kabir says, Oh saints, God is in breath of all breaths, present in all beings."

Like the Sufis, Kabir too has invited people to "drink deep" of the wine of Divine Love. He has described almost in the very words of Mansoor, 500 years before him, the journey of the soul to Godhood through spiritual exercises. In his book *Das Muqami Rekhta,* Kabir has described, in his own peculiar way, the incident of Prophet Mohammad's *Meraj,* that is, his well-known accession to Heaven.

The fact is that Kabir drew India's attention towards a universal religion, which is neither Hindu nor Muslim. He has therefore severely and fearlessly criticised the meaningless ritualism and the vain dogmas and superstitious beliefs of both Hindus and Muslims. He was a bitter and unrelenting opponent of the superiority of the Brahmins, and of the caste system and untouchability.

He uses the word "Rama" in the sense of God. In Sanskrit, Rama means He who pervades all. Kabir made it quite plain that his "Rama" was not Rama, the son of Dashrath. He writes: "The Creator did not marry Sita, nor did He build a bridge of stones over the sea."

Kabir has at many places, in the clearest language possible, expressed his disbelief in the Hindu theory of the ten incarnations of God.

About the caste-system and untouchability, Kabir says:

> "Those who have been born and those who are yet to be born are all of the same class. Neither is anyone a Brahmin nor is anyone a Shudra. Let none entertain false pride. The division of men into Hindus and Muslims is a false division. We are one. The lowest of men is he who thinks that he gets polluted by the touch of another human being."

Kabir preached against blind faith in any man or in any written book. He ridiculed all outward forms and rituals. He advised both Hindus and Muslims to rise above all such forms as divided man from man. He preached against the caste-system and against idol-worship. He appealed to both Hindus and Muslims to feel compassion for all living beings, to regard all as children of the same One God and as brothers to each other, to give up all ideas of superiority over others and to serve all to the best of their capacity.

We would like to quote here the following few verses from Kabir:

> "The Hindus say that Hari lives in the East. The Muslims consider the West as the abode of Allah. But Kabir says

> that God lives in every heart and every man should search for him in his own heart. The same one God is Karim as well as Rama."
>
> "All men and women are born in the image of God. Kabir is the child of him, who is both Allah and Rama. Both names are his names. That one God is my 'Guru' as well as my 'pir'."
>
> "Both Hindus and Muslims have to traverse the same path for their salvation. The true teacher, that is the 'Satguru', has shown me that path. Kabir says, hear Oh saints ! Rama and Khuda are both names of the same nameless one."
>
> "The Hindus say that their beloved is Rama. The Muslims say that their beloved is Rahim. Both fight with each other over names and injure themselves. None of them understands the real truth."

Kabir was the first Indian fearlessly to preach one universal religion not only for the Hindus and the Muslims but also for the whole of mankind. His followers included both Hindus and Muslims. Up to this day, both at Kabir Chowra in Benares and at Maghar, near Gorakhpur, thousands upon thousands of Hindus and Muslims gather year after year and pay their homage to the great saint Kabir. Those who call themselves *Kabir-Panthis, i.e.,* followers of Kabir, did not number more than 15 lakhs, in the beginning of the 20th century but Kabir's influence pervades practically every village in India.

During the days of the Mughal Empire, Kabir's ideas and teachings continued to spread all over. The far-sighted Emperor Akbar the Great tried to embody them in his *Deen-i-Elahi,* which means the Religion of one God and to get them accepted by all. In fact, Kabir was the spiritual progenitor of Akbar. Akbar, however, did not fully succeed either because Providence willed otherwise or because of the conditions in and outside the country. Whatever it might be, there cannot be the slightest doubt that the innermost soul of India is hankering after the fulfilment of Kabir's mission. If there is any way for India's salvation, both political and religious, it lies in this direction and if there is any fundamental spiritual truth, it is this.

Kabir's ideas were so original and true, that once more the lead in religious matters was taken up by the North and a whole army of religious preachers, saints, Sufis and faqeers took the message from the North to the South and spread it all over India in the following three centuries.

Muslim Faqeers of the Punjab

In the 15th century, in most of the towns and villages of the Punjab, there lived Muslim Sufis and *faqeers,* just as they had done in the towns and villages of the South in the earlier centuries. Numerous famous Sufi *faqeers* passed their lives in Panipat, Sirhind, Pakpattan, Multan and Ucheh. Amongst them Baba Fareed, Ala-ul-Haque, Jalalu'ddin Bokhari, Makhdoom Jahania, Sheikh Ismaeel Bokhari and Data Ganj Baksh are names well known all over the country for their character, piety and godliness. It was the revolution created by these great spiritual leaders in the minds of the Indian people which ultimately flowered and bore fruit in the shape of the magnificent effort of Guru Nanak who, like Kabir himself and on the same lines, did his very best to unite the Hindus and the Muslims in a common spiritual faith.

Nanak

Guru Nanak was born in A.D. 1469 on the 3rd day of the second fortnight of Vaishakh. In those days, Nanak was a name common amongst both Hindus and Muslims. In his early years, Nanak was taught both Persian and Sanskrit and knew the two languages well. For some time, he was in the service of Nawab Doulat Khan Lodi. At the age of 30, he gave up worldly life and became a *faqeer.* Accompanied by his Muslim disciple, Mardana, Nanak toured throughout India, Ceylon, Iran, Arabia and other countries. It is recorded that over a long period he held religious discourses with Sheikh Sharaf of Panipat, with the Pirs of Multan, with Sheikh Ibrahim, the successor of Baba Fareed and with other Sufi saints of the day. As on the death of Kabir, so on the death of Nanak also, there was a dispute between Nanak's Hindu and Muslim followers about the way of disposing of Nanak's body. Ultimately, the Hindus put up a *samadhi* and the Muslims put up a *mazar* of Guru Nanak. Both were sometime later washed away by the waters of the Ravi.

Nanak's religion also was the religion of unity and love like that of Kabir. His followers likewise included both Hindus and Muslims. Nanak went to Mecca. There like the Prophet Mohammad, he preached the existence of One God and called himself His khaleefa, *i.e*, representative or successor. "There is no God but Allah," he declared, "one of His names is Govind and Nanak is His Khaleefa" (*Guru Nanak's Janmsakhi,* No. 30, Paknama).

In his writings, Nanak has also freely and profusely used Sanskrit, Persian and Arabic words. He declared that Hinduism and Islam were not two separate religions and said:

> "Hindus and Muslims are both children of the same one God. Lacking in true faith they fight with each other, one in the name of Ram and the other in the name of Prophet Mohamad. We are neither Hindus nor Muslims. The Satan of disunity separates the two. We are all one. Our God, the God of all, the one pure being is one. Guru Nanak says: 'Hear' Oh Abdul Rehman, you will be able to realise the true God only when you give up your pride of separateness or superiority."
>
> "The Hindus repeat Rama Rama and the Muslims call Him Khuda, but if we look closely into our hearts, we will find that Rama and Raheem are names of the same one God."

At another place, Nanak says:

> "Neither the Hindus nor the Muslims have found the true way, both have gone astray, driven by the demon of separateness."

> "At His door many a Mohammad, many a Brahma, many a Vishnu, many a Mahesh and many a Rama stands praying and singing of His great and unique qualities in their respective ways."

Like the prophet Mohammad, Nanak also preached unqualified submission to the will of God.

Nanak exposed the futility of going to places of pilgrimage, bathing in particular rivers, senselessly repeating certain names and other forms of ritualism. He declined to accept the final authority either of the *puranas* or of the four Vedas. He preached against idol-worship. Like Kabir, he also expressed his disbelief in the theory of incarnation of God. He condemned the Hindu caste-system as unjust and harmful to society. We quote below a few of his verses in this connection:

> "Let none try to show his superiority over another. There is no high or low. This is my advice to both Hindus and Muslims."
>
> "God's blessings will only be showered on those who fraternise with and regard as their absolute equals in every sense those who are unjustly regarded as low by the cursed caste-system."
>
> "The true God specially favours and honours as His own those who are wrongly condemned as low and lowly."

Addressing the Muslims, Nanak says:

> "Let kindness to all be your mosque, truth your Musalla (the cloth on which prayers are offered), just and honest living your recitation of the *Quran,* purity of character your circumcision, good behaviour towards others your Roza, then alone can you be a true Musalman. Let good deeds be your *Kaaba,* Truth your spiritual teacher, service of others your *Kalama* and *Namaz,* the will of God your rosary, then alone, Oh Nanak! will God bless you."

Exactly similar were Nanak's exhortations to the Hindus.

Nanak laid great emphasis on self-control and purity of character. Like other Sufis, Nanak held the Guru, *i.e.,* the teacher, to be indispensable for the uplift of the soul. The Sufis, Shareeyat, Maarfat, Uqva and Lahoot were given by Nanak the names of Dharam Khand, Gyan Khand, Karm Khand and Sach Khand. There can be no doubt that Nanak was fully acquainted with Sufi literature and freely drew upon it. His preachings to both Hindus and Muslims of one formless God and of one universal religion were exactly on the lines of the teachings of the Muslim Sufis on the subject.

It may be that, in the prevailing conditions towards the end of the Mughal empire and thereafter, the so-called followers of Guru Nanak could not fully live up to the universal ideals preached by him. But this can be said of the followers of almost all great prophets and sages at some time or other.

Other Indian Saints

Besides Kabir and Nanak, a number of other saints and sages such as Dhanna Jat, Peepa, Sena and Raidas the shoe-maker, preached a universal religion to both Hindus and Muslims exactly on the same lines. In the writings of each one of them we come across Sufi ideas and expressions, and the doctrine of the essential unity of both Hindu and Muslim religions, rather of all religions. Raidas has flatly denied the theory that Rama, the son of Dashrath, was an incarnation of God. Some of his poems are also in Persian. He declared God to be the "Sultan of Sultans", that is the King of Kings, and himself as His *Shikesta Banda,* i.e., humble servant. He strongly denounced idol-workship, going to places of pilgrimage, and the caste-system.

Dadoo

Among other prominent successors of Kabir well-known in various parts of the country, one of the most famous names was that of Dadoo. Dadoo, whose real name was Dawood, was born in a poor Muslim family whose occupation was that of ginning cotton. Dadoo was a contemporary of Emperor Akbar the Great. It is said that in the year 1642 Vikrami, Dadoo met Akbar at Fatehpur-Sikri. Akbar asked Dadoo to describe the existence and the personality of God. Dadoo replied in a Hindi couplet which means:

> "Love is the personality of God,
> Love is His body. Love is His existence and love is His dominant colour."

About five thousand couplets of Dadoo are still current in India. Most of them are in easy popular Hindi or Hindustani, but there are a few in Persian also though not in very idiomatic Persian. Though born in a Muslim family, Dadoo was strongly against meat-eating. He preached kindness to all beings. He was a strict vegetarian.

Dadoo says:

> "I see the whole universe as one, all souls are one. They are all pure in their real nature. Evil lies in our seeing duality. All evil arises out of the idea of duality. He who rises above this duality realises God and becomes one with Him."

Describing the various stages of the soul's evolution and comparing the same with Muslim conventional stages, Dadoo says:

> "Oh Dadoo! the presence of God inside my heart is like a tank full of water. Dadoo bathes in that tank. Thus purified, Dadoo performs his *Namaz* before God inside his own heart."
>
> "The body is my mosque. The five senses are my companions in the congregation. Dadoo's own mind is his Mulla or Imam. Thus Dadoo stands before his Allah whom it is impossible to describe. Thus Dadoo performs his *Sijda* and his *Salam.*"
>
> "The whole body of Dadoo is his rosary. On the beads of that rosary Dadoo repeats the name of the All-merciful

> God. Thus Dadoo tries to enter into His mercy. Dadoo's *Roza* or fasting lies in realising the unity of all life by banishing all duality from his heart. Thus Dadoo becomes his own *Kalma."*
>
> "Thus does Dadoo stand before his God all the twenty-four hours in full concentration and reaches that Heaven, where resides the All-merciful God called Rahman."

Like Kabir, again, Dadoo was against all types of religious narrowness or exclusiveness. He strongly advocated Hindu-Muslim unity and preached one common universal religion for all. In his utterances, too, the influence of the Sufis is quite evident. Dadoo says:

> "The same one self resides in all whether he be a Hindu or a Musalman. My delusion that Allah and Rama are two has absolutely disappeared. I see no difference between the Hindu and the Muslim. In both I realise Thy presence and in both I see thee face to face, Oh my God!"
>
> "Oh my Master: what was the path followed by Brahma, Vishnu or Mahesh? What religion did Muhammad follow? What path did Gabriel traverse? They all followed one Allah. Allah alone was their guide and teacher. I wonder whom the people are following ! There is only one Master of the universe, who is indescribable and formless. He is Allah. There is no other God but He."
>
> "Hindus and Muslims are two brothers. They are like the two arms or the two legs of the same body or like the two ears, or the two eyes on the same face. How can they be separated?"
>
> "We are neither Hindu, nor Muslim. We do not bother about the differences of the six schools of Hindu philosophy. We are only the devotees of one God, who is All-merciful."
>
> "The Hindus go to their temple. The Muslims go to their mosque. We go to neither. We worship only the one indescribable God. Our love and devotion to Him are endless. For His worship we require neither the Hindu

temple nor the Muslim mosque, nor any particular form of ceremony. Our sole relationship is with the Invisible One, in whom we live, move and have our being. This body itself is Dadoo's temple and his mosque. The true teacher has shown Dadoo the path of true religion. All worship is to be performed inside the body. There is no need to go out anywhere. Because of empty pride Hindus and Muslims are fighting with each other like two elephants run amock, that is why they are unable to drink deep from the sweet river of life which is flowing within all of us. Dadoo has conquered his own self. That is why he sees the same self and also himself in both the Hindus and the Muslims."

Dadoo condemned idol-worship, the caste-system and going to places of pilgrimage or to the Kaba, just like Kabir. He appears to have believed in the reincarnation of the soul in an allegorical sense. He attached more importance to the teachings of the living Guru or teacher than to the Vedas or to the *Quran.*

Malookdas

Yet another famous saint in the line was Babar Malookdas. He, too, was born during Akbar's reign at Kara in Allahabad district in A.D. 1574 and died during the reign of Aurangzeb in A.D. 1682 at the age one hundred and eight. Malookdas's followers spread as far as Nepal in the east and Afghanistan in the west. They had their regular monasteries in Kabul as well as in Nepal. The mission of Malookdas was exactly similar to that of Kabir and Dadoo. He too preached the one universal religion of love, advocated Hindu-Muslim unity, opposed idol-worship, the caste-system and all types of ritualism and laid stress on kindness to all and service of all.

Malookdas says:

"What is the use of the Hindu *Malu* or of the Muslim *Tasbeeh*?"

"Awake now, Oh Malookdas ! and do not depend upon these separate rosaries."

"No one is a *Kafir* and no one is a *Mlechcha. Sandhya* and *Namaz* are not two separate things, their timings are immaterial. God requires the aid neither of any Yamraj nor of any Gabriel."

"God is Himself quite able to keep the record of the good and bad deeds of every soul and to distribute rewards and punishments accordingly."

"Oh Malookdas ! why do you remain in this delusion of separateness?"

"There is only one God, one religion, Rama and Raheem are names of the same one God."

Twelve Commandments of Sattnamis

Beerbban, the founder of the Sattnami sect, was a contemporary of Dadoo. Sattnamis also call themselves "Sadh". Beerbhan preached monotheism. The name given by him to God was Sattnam, i.e., he whose name is truth. The Sattnamis are against the caste-system and untouchability. They inter-dine and intermarry amongst themselves. Divorce is permitted among them. The Sattnamis are against idol-worship and lay stress on meditation, moral character and the equality of all human beings. Meat and wine are forbidden. During the reign of Aurangzeb, Ishwar Das Nagar complained to the Emperor that the Sattnamis made no distinction whatsoever between the Hindus and the Muslims. In the *Adi Updesh,* the *Bible* of the Sattnamis, are given 12 commandments, which may be summarised as follows:

1. Believe only in one God and do not worship any image made of clay, stone, wood or any other material.
2. Lead a life of humility.
3. Never tell a lie, never talk ill of anybody, never steal or cast a greedy look at another's property.

4. Never listen to anything evil and do not sing anything except hymns in honour of God.
5. Have faith and trust in God.
6. Do not observe the caste-system and do not enter into a controversy with anyone on that subject.
7. Keep your clothes clean, do not put any mark on your forehead nor any rosary round your neck.
8. Avoid tobacco and all intoxicants.
9. Do not kill any living being, nor inflict suffering on anyone.
10. There should be only one wife for one man, and only one husband for one woman.
11. The only place of pilgrimage is the company of good and saintly persons.
12. Do not believe in any superstition nor in astrology nor in any omens.

Undoubtedly these "commandments" were based on a harmonious blending of the best in both Hinduism and Islam.

Babalal, The Teacher of Dara Shikoh

Babalal was the "Guru" or teacher of Dara Shikoh, the brother of Emperor Aurangzeb. His ideas and beliefs were quite similar to those mentioned above. Babalal's discourses with Dara Shikoh are recorded in a Persian book, named *Nadir-un-nikat.* In support of his views, Babalal has freely quoted from the writings of the well-known Persian Sufi poet, Hafiz.

The Narayani Sect

Several other sects of that period made similar efforts for the unification of Hinduism and Islam. Admission to the Narayani sect was open equally to both Hindus and Muslims. People of this sect prayed to God five times a day but with their faces towards the East. Allah was one of the many names used by them for God. They buried their dead.

Pran Nath

During the last days of Aurangzeb, the names of Pran Nath and Dharni Das were also well-known in this connection. Pran Nath has, in his Gujarati work *Qulzum Saroop,* brought out the similarity of the teachings of the Vedas and the *Quran* by giving quotations from both. He was against the caste-system and idol-worship. His followers included both Hindus and Muslims. Everyone initiated into his sect had to sit and dine with both Hindus and Muslims. This formed the main part of the initiation ceremony. *Qayamat Nama* is another important book written by Pran Nath and in it he has very clearly said that both Hindus and Muslims should have one religion and one faith. In the same book he has given the lives of Jewish, Christian, Muslim and Hindu prophets and saints and brought out the fundamental unity of the lives and teachings of all of them. He uses both the words Allah and Khuda among the names of God.

Other Efforts

Essentially the same were the teachings of Jagjeewan Das, Bulla Saheb, Keshav, Charan Das, Sahjo Bai, Daya Bai, Ghareeb Das, Shiv Narayan, Ram Charan and others. Amongst the followers of Jagjeewan Das were to be found people of all castes, Thakurs, Chamars as well as Musalmans. The utterances of Bulla Saheb are full of Persian words and Sufi phraseology. Both Bulla Saheb and Keshav, the former a Muslim and the latter a Hindu, were the disciples of Yari Saheb, a Muslim *faqeer* of Delhi. In those days, Hindu disciples of Muslim *faqeers* and Muslim disciples of Hindu *faqeers* could be counted in hundreds of thousands. Both Sahjo Bai and Daya Bai were women and were the disciples of Charan Das. Charan Das opposed idol-worship and extolled the importance of the Guru. Ghareeb Das was a follower of Kabir. His writings are also full of Persian words and Sufi phraseology.

Ram Charan, the founder of the Ram Sanehi sect, was also a strong opponent of idol-worship. His followers also prayed to

God five times a day, and freely admitted into their sect people of all castes and creeds. Similarly into the Shiva Narayani sect founded by Swami Shiva Narayan were also admitted people of all castes and creeds. Whenever a Shiva Narayani died, his body was buried or cremated or set afloat on a river, according to the last wish of the deceased. The Mughal Emperor, Mohammad Shah, was one of the disciples of Swami Shiva Narayan and the sect flourished greatly for some time under the patronage of the Emperor.

Sadly enough, during the next two or three hundred years, several of these sects underwent a change in their appearance, form and ceremonies beyond recognition. In some cases, the ways and lives of the followers of some of these sects also were newly modelled on lines exactly opposite to the wishes and teachings of the founders. Even so, the original proclamation issued by Emperor Mohammad Shah over his own signature is still (1930) preserved in the principal Shiva Narayani monastery in Ballia district.

The names of Shajanand, Dulandas, Gulal, Bheeka and Paltoo Das, who lived and preached a similar religion of the centre in the eighteenth century are quite well known in history.

Dulandas, a disciple of Jagjeewan, has, in his writings, bestowed high praise on the Muslim Sufis, Mansoor, Shams Tabrez, Nizamuddin, Hafiz, Boo Ali Qualandar, Fareed and others. He calls God "Allah-la makan" that is, Allah beyond space. Some of the verses of Gulal, Bheeka and Paltoo Das are of a very high order from the point of view of poetry, as well as devotion to God. They are all full of Sufi phraseology. They generally address God by the name of "Haque", that is, truth. One of the verses of Paltoo Das can be rendered into English thus:

> "If Ram resides in the East and Allah in the West, Who then resides in the north and in the south?
> Where does the Lord live and where does He not live?
> The Hindus and the Muslims are raising a storm for nothing. The Hindus and the Muslims are quarrelling with each other, And arraying both religions against one another.

Paltoo Das says that the Sahib (The Lord) lives in the heart of everyone.
God is not hidden from anyone. This is the truth."

Worship of Satya Peer

The current of Hindu-Muslim unity on the religious and spiritual planes which flowed in Northern India soon found its counterparts in Bengal and Maharashtra also. In Bengal of the twelfth century, it had become a common thing for Hindus to offer sweets at Muslim Dargahs or mausoleums of Muslim saints, to read the *Quran* and 10 celebrate Muslim festivals. Similarly, the Muslims joined in the celebration of many Hindu festivals and otherwise showed their respect for many Hindu ceremonies Many Hindu customs connected with occasions like marriage had also become common to people of both religions. These currents gave birth to the worship of a new god in Bengal. This new god was then called "Satya peer" which means the God of Truth. Both Hindus and Muslims joined in the worship of Satya peer. It is recorded that Husain Shah, the Muslim king of Gaur in Bengal, was the originator of this sect. It appears that the worship of Satya peer was the precursor of Akbar's *Deen-i-ilahi.*

Chaitanya

Mahaprabhu Chaitanya was born in Bengal towards the end of the 15th century. Dinesh Chandra Sen in his monumental work, *The History of Bengali Language and Literature*, describing the condition of Bengal before the birth of Chaitanya, says:

> "The domination of the society by the Brahmins had become very irksome. As the hereditary distinctions between high and low families became ossified, all caste distinctions became more and more rigid. The Brahmins were supposed to live up to high religious ideals, but because of caste restrictions the discrimination between man and man was continually growing. The people of

> the lower castes were groaning under the tyranny of the higher castes. The people of the higher castes had closed the doors of learning and education for the people of the lower castes. The latter found all chances of entry into higher life closed for them.
>
> The new religion promulgated by the Puranas had become the monopoly of Brahmins, as if it was a marketable commodity."

The simple and easily understood principles of Islam and the equality of all men preached by it created a stir in the life of Bengal at that time. Chaitanya pondered seriously over the situation. He left his home for good and began touring the country. He came into contact with numerous Sadhus and *faqeers* in these tours. Krishna Das, the biographer of Chaitanya, tells us that at Vrindavan Chaitanya met a Musalman Pir who, in accordance with the teachings of his religious book the *Quran,* exhorted Chaitanya to worship only the one Formless God. Yadu Bhatta-Charya writes in his *Hindu Castes and Sects,* p. 464:

> "There are many incidents in the life of Chaitanya which clearly show that he felt great love for the Muslims. There can be no doubt that the teachings of Chaitanya were greatly influenced by the preachings of Muslim Sufis."

Chaitanya preached the service of the Guru and devotion to God. He strongly opposed the caste system and condemned as useless all rituals, rites and ceremonies of the Brahmins. His disciples included Hindus as well as Muslims and people of all classes and castes, high as well as low. Three of his principal disciples, Roop, Sanatan and Haridas were Muslims. Out of all his disciples he loved Haridas the most.

Karta Baba

One of the off-shoots of the sect founded by Chaitanya was called "Kartabhaj". Its founder, Karta Baba, was born through the blessings of a Musalman *faqeer*, who gave him the name of Karta Baba and brought him up himself. Karta Baba's 22 principal disciples came to be known as the "Twenty-two Faqeers". One of them, named Ram Dulal, became Karta Baba's successor. It is said that the soul of the above-mentioned Musalman *faqeer* had entered the body of Ram Dulal. There were several Hindus as well as several Muslims amongst the heads of this sect from time to time. The people of this sect believed in only one God, regarded the Guru as an incarnation of God, recited Guru Mantra, i.e., the secret formula taught by the preceptor five times a day, abstained from meat and wine, observed Friday as a sacred day and spent it in religious discourses, and made no distinction between high caste and low caste or between Hindus, Muslims and Christians. They held community dinners at least once or twice a year, in which all members of the sect participated without distinction.

Muslims in Buddhist Literature

It appears that while atrocities against the Buddhists by Hindus of the Shaiva sect were rampant in Bengal, the Buddhists received considerable sympathy, encouragement and even protection from the Muslims. The Buddhist religious literature extant in Bengal during that period, e.g., *Shoonya Purana, Dharm Pooja Paddhati, Dharm Gajan, Bad Janani,* etc., and the Buddhist songs of those days are full of anger and resentment against the Brahmins and of love and sympathy for the Muslims, Muslim ideals and Muslim religious books. The Buddhist poetic literature of that period reveals some rather strange facts, E.G., that many Muslims going to Bengal in those days refrained from meat-eating.

At one place it is recorded:

> "The Musalmans are praying to God facing towards the West. Some are praying to Allah, others adore Ali, and yet others sing praises of Mohammad Sain."
>
> "The Musalman does not kill any living being and does not eat of any animals."
>
> "He is cooking his vegetarian food on a slow fire."

> "Caste distinctions will now gradually disappear for, look, there is a Musalman member in a Hindu family."
> "Oh God! I know Thou art the greatest of all, I intensely desire to hear the *Quran* from Thy lips."

Saints of Maharashtra

As in Northern India, so in Maharashtra, Hindu saints and sages made strenuous efforts for the unification of Hinduism and Islam. The well-known Maharashtrian scholar, Mahadeo Govind Ranade, writes:

> "The strict monotheism of Islam had entered the hearts of saints like Kabir and Nanak. The worshippers of Dattatraya (the Hindu Trinity) often dressed their god in a way similar to that of a Mussalman Faqueer. The same influence was working on the minds of the people of Maharashtra even more forcefully. Brahmin and non-Brahmin preachers both exhorted the people to believe in the oneness of Rama and Raheem, to give up caste distinctions and Hindu ritualism and follow one common religion of faith in One God and of love for all men." (*Rise of the Maratha Power,* pp. 50–51)

Namdev

Namdev was probably the first saint of Maharashtra who liberated the people from the shackles of the caste system, ritualism and religious narrowness. He preached equality of all men, love of all beings and devotion to one God. Ranade says:

> "The exhortations of Namdev and other saints like him led to the advancement of Marathi literature, the relaxation of caste restrictions, the raising of the status of women, broad-mindedness and kindness to all and to an extent the unification of Hinduism and Islam." The exhortations of these saints, according to Ranade, also led to a decrease in the importance of ritualism, pilgrimages, etc., increase

in the importance of love for all, decrease in the worship of numerous gods and goddesses, and increase in the power of the nation in both thought and action." (*ibid)*

Khechar

The saint Khechar was the teacher of Namdev. It is evident from the teachings of Khechar to his disciple Namdev that Khechar was against idol worship. Khechar says:

> "The stone idol never speaks. How then can it relieve us of our life's ills? People wrongly regard the stone idol as God. But the true God is quite different. If the stone idol could fulfil our wishes, then how could it itself go to pieces when dropped down? Those who worship the stone idol lose everything through their folly. Those who say that the stone idol talks to its devotees and those who believe them are both ignorant."
>
> "The numerous disciples and followers of Namdev included men as well as women, Hindus as well as Muslims, Brahmins as well as non-Brahmins, *Kunbis,* tailors, potters and even the *Mahars* who were regarded as untouchables and also religious-minded prostitutes." (*ibid,* p. 146)

Chokhamela and Bahiram

Chokhamela was a *Mahar* and therefore an untouchable. He was a disciple of Namdev. Once when he tried to enter the famous Hindu temple at Pandharpur and the Brahmin priests would not let him in, he said:

> "What is the merit in being born in a high-caste family? Even if one is born in a low-caste family, if he is true of heart, loves God, treats every living being as equal to himself, does not make any difference between his own children and those of others and always speaks the truth, then he is pure of caste and God is pleased with him. If a man believes in God and loves all men, do not ask him

> his caste. God looks for love and devotion in his children and cares not for their caste." (*ibid,* p. 154)

Bahiram Bhatt, in his search for truth, twice became a convert to Islam and twice reverted to Hinduism. Ultimately he declared:

> "I am neither a Hindu nor a Muslim."

Sheikh Mohammad

In Southern India Sheikh Mohammad has been a famous saint and man of God. His followers still keep a fast in the month of Ramzan like Muslims and also keep a fast on the Ekadashi day (the 11th day of the moon) like the Hindus. They go on pilgrimage to Mecca in Arabia and also to the Pandharpur temple in India.

Tukaram

Tukaram was perhaps the most famous and most universally respected saint of the South. Like Kabir, Tukaram was strongly opposed to the caste-system, idol-worship, sacrifices of animals, lighting of sacrificial fires, *i.e.,* Yajna, Havan and other forms of ritualism. He preached the existence of only One God, whom he generally calls Hari and exhorted the people to worship him alone. He saw and felt the existence of God in the heart of every living being. Yet Tukaram's chief mission for which he worked hard was the unification of Hinduism and Islam. The English rendering of one of his verses is as follows:

> "Oh my dear baba, whatever God wills, that alone happens. God is the creator of us all. He is the king of us all. Our cattle and our friends, our gardens and all our wealth have only a fleeting existence. Oh my friend, my heart is set upon my Master (Sahib). He is my creator, I am riding my mind as one rides a horse. The real rider is the self (Atma). Oh friend (baba)! always talk of God. All

forms are His forms. He has created all in His own image. Tukaram says that he who understands this truth alone deserves to be called a Darvesh."

"Of all the great names the name, 'Allah' ranks first. Repeat it constantly, do not forget it. Verily there is only one Allah. All prophets are his prophets. When we reach that stage all I and thou disappear. There all is one. The distinction between I and thou vanishes. There are no '1' and no 'thou'."

There can be no doubt that through the synthesis of Hinduism, Buddhism and Islam, foundations were being laid at that time in this country, from East to West and from North to South, of a common universal religion of humanity with unity, love and service of all as its creed.

INDIAN ART AND MUSLIMS

Architecture

Just as religious beliefs, so also Indian art, architecture and painting were greatly influenced and this to India's advantage, by the advent of Muslims in the country. Prof. Jadunath Sarkar writes that Indian art and architecture made great progress during the Muslim period. Till the eighth century Indian art and architecture were influenced specially by Buddhist ideals. From the eighth to the thirteenth centuries, Hindu ideals mainly inspired Indian art. Even so, Buddhist influence also was clearly visible. We do not want to enter into the technicalities of the subject. Yet a few things are quite clear. The greatest influence on a country's art-ideals is exercised by that country's geographical conditions. India is a country of impenetrable forests, extreme seasons, mighty rivers, lofty mountains and dense vegetation. That is why in Indian architecture, largeness of size, solidity, complexity and minuteness of detail have always been emphasised. Indian forests are full from end to end of thick intertwined flora and foliage. Wherever and in whichever direction we cast our eyes, we fail to see even a yard of open space. That is why one can hardly find even an inch of bare space on the walls of ancient Hindu temples or palaces. In the Hindu temples of olden times, the foundation is raised on foundation, numerous stories, parapets, and pinnacles rise one above the other and seem to reach the sky, while there is hardly an inch of space or a corner, which is not studded with paintings, engravings and images. Experts in architecture are of the view that the architecture of no other country can compare with that of ancient India in complexity of detail and the immensity of its beauty.

On the other hand Arabia is a vast desert with only a few and far-flung oases here and there. Added to this is the scorching heat of the country, with its limited resources in food and clothing and immense hillocks of burning sand. Naturally, therefore, in early Muslim architecture, huge buildings, plain and bare walls, tall minarets and big domes are conspicuous. The strict monotheism and the iconoclastic spirit of Islam, in contrast with the image worship of India and other countries, gave to the new ideal of Muslim architecture an especial bent and form, which later became consolidated. Anyone whose eyes get satiated with the variety and complexity of Hindu temples naturally gets relief at the sight of a plain Muslim mosque. And similarly, anyone who has been bored by the plainness and simplicity of old Muslim mosques and palaces will find some relief in the complexity and variety of ancient Hindu architecture.

The Mingling of the Two Art Ideals

It is obvious that the meeting and mingling of these two sets of art ideals gave birth to a style of art and architecture grander, more beautiful and more attractive than either. Religious and communal prejudices, however, generally stand in the way of such a unification. But even so, when two separate sets of ideals come into contact with each other, such a synthesis, conscious and voluntary or unconscious and involuntary, is inevitable. Besides, as we have already seen, movements for conquering such prejudices in the field of religion had since the time of arrival of the Muslims in India been continued. As in the religious sphere so in the field of architecture and painting, India began to give birth to new ideals superior to either of the separate Hindu and Muslim ideals. The result and products of these new ideals were also superior to the products of either of them separately. For a comparison of the products of these three sets of ideals, we have to look at the ancient Hindu temples of the South and the temple at Jagannath Puri and at old Muslim mosques at Ajmere and Delhi, as products of the two separate ideals on the one hand, and the imperial palaces of the Mughals at Agra and Delhi and the most beautiful specimen of Indian art and architecture the Taj at Agra as products of the mingling of the two ideals on the other. The Taj at Agra is regarded as one of the most beautiful buildings in the world. It is the crowning achievement of Indian architecture up to the present day. It is positively the most beautiful product of the mingling of the pre-Muslim Indian ideals and the later Muslim ideals in the field of architecture.

Experts on architecture tell us that buildings erected in India before the thirteenth century clearly represent two distinct sets of ideals, while the later Hindu buildings clearly bear the impress of Muslim influence and the Muslim buildings similarly bear the impress of Hindu influence, and in both cases they appear to have increased in beauty and attractiveness. This would explain the vast difference between the Muslim architecture of India on the one hand and the Muslim architectures of Egypt, Syria, Iran and Turkey, on the other.

Besides Delhi and Agra, Rajputana and Kashmir also still have enough specimens of the product of such a synthetic ideal of architecture. Yet other specimens are some of the sixteenth-century Vaishnava temples at Vrindavan, some Jain temples at Sonagarh, several buildings at Vijaynagar and the famous palace of Tirumalai Naik at Madura built in the seventeenth century.

The Hindus, for the first time, began to construct mausoleums over their dead, i.e., Samadhis and Chhatris, about the sixteenth century and this practice undoubtedly came to them from the Muslims. The use of arches in buildings, vaulted roofs and the modern art of gardening are also Muslim in origin. The most beautiful gardens in India today were laid out during the reigns of the Mughal emperors. Amongst them, the Shalimar Bagh of Kashmir, laid out during the reign of Jehangir, is still considered to be the most beautiful garden in the world.

The Art of Painting

Similarly, the meeting of the two sets of art ideals in the field of painting, under the Mughal emperors, also gave birth to a higher and more beautiful art in India. Hundreds of Hindu painters were employed in the palaces of Humayun, Akbar, Jahangir and Shahjehan on very handsome allowances to enable them to improve their art. Reputed painters from Shiraz, Tabrez and even China resided at the Mughal *Durbar.* They all undoubtedly improved and developed their own art with the help of one another. In Persian works and documents of that period occur the names of numerous Hindu and Muslim painters from Jaipur, Gwalior, Gujarat, Kashmir and other places residing at the Delhi *Durbar.* Beautiful paintings and portraits painted by them still continue to amaze experts.

At that period, the newly-advanced Indian art of painting appears to have flourished throughout the country from Delhi and Agra to Jaipur, Jammu, Chamba, Kangra, Lahore, Amritsar and even Tanjore in the South. The ideals originating at Delhi and Agra were followed in the Hindu *Darbars* of Rajputana and the rest of India.

Prof. Jadunath Sarkar writes:

> "... the highest genius was displayed by our artists in this field in the Mughal age ..." (*Mughal Administration,* p. 128)

According to Dr. Beni Prasad numerous English travellers of those days admit that due to the generous patronage and encouragement given by Jehangir, the Indian art of painting at the time was the most advanced in the world (*History of Jehangir,* pp. 92–94).

THE MUGHAL PERIOD

Mughal Invasions

We have now to see what influence the advent of Muslims from outside produced on aspects of Indian life other than those of religion, art, architecture and painting. We have earlier stated that the period of about 300 years after the invasion by Mahmud Ghazni was one of continuous internal warfare and of the setting up of numerous small independent sovereign states throughout India. Then came the Mughal Empire. It was during this period that Muslim sovereignty over India and the influence of the Muslim way of life throughout the country reached its zenith. But before we proceed to narrate the story of Mughal rule over India and its good or bad effects on the country, we would like to review briefly earlier conquests by the Mughals of countries other than India.

The early Mughals were Buddhists. It was the Buddhist Mughal, Changez Khan who, in the beginning of the thirteenth century, sallied forth from his home in Mongolia and conquered Northern China, Tatar and a large part of the rest of Asia. Changez Khan, side by side with his Buddhist faith, also followed some of the more ancient religious customs of his country like horse-worship. He died in 1227. During the next 68 years Changez Khan's successors continued their conquests. They annexed to their Empire almost the whole of Asia except India. They also conquered and ruled over a very great part of Europe. The first Mughal invasion of Europe occurred in 1238. According to European historians, no such great disaster had overtaken Europe since the invasion of Europe by the Arabs in the eighth century. Within a few years, the Mughals brought under their rule the whole of Russia, Poland, the Balkans, Hungary and the entire region up to the Baltic Sea in the north and Germany in the west. This constituted more than half of the then known Europe. Russia was under the rule of the Mughals for full two centuries. It was the same Buddhist Mughals who had conquered the Muslim countries of Iran and Iraq. Much later Hilaku Khan, the grandson of Changez Khan, and the other Mughals who accompanied him, adopted Islam, which was then the religion of the conquered Iranians and Arabs.

The first Mughal invasion of India was by Timur in 1398. Mahmood Tughlaq was then on the throne of Delhi. After plundering and killing both Hindus and Muslims indiscriminately for about 15 days, Timur found that he could not stay in India any longer and left Delhi. His invasion did not have any lasting effect on India or Indian life. The second invasion of India by the Mughals was under Babar in 1526. By that time the Mughals had lived for long years in Iran, a country which was then much more civilized than their native land, Mongolia. These Mughals had thus become much more civilised than the earlier Mughals, who had conquered Iran and the greater part of Asia and Europe. Babar defeated Ibrahim Lodi at Panipat and laid the foundations of the Mughal Empire in India. After his victory at Panipat, Babar made India his home. It was in India that all his later descendants, except Humayun, were born and brought up.

India Needed a Central Paramount Administration

For about 900 years, that is, from the middle of the seventh century after the death of Emperor Harshvardhan, up to the beginning of the sixteenth century there had been no Central paramount administration for the whole of India. During all these centuries, India was a big battle-field between numerous rival states, big and small. This entire period of Indian history was marked by internal dissensions, disunity, political instability and national weakness. India then was sorely in need of a paramount power which could administer the entire country, bring to one focal point the country's scattered energies and thus give it the chance of advancing in various fields of life through countrywide peace and uniform benevolent administration. History bears testimony to the fact that in the sixteenth, seventeenth and eighteenth centuries, the Mughal Empire at Delhi fulfilled this need of the country in full and in an admirable way. From the administrative point of view, as well as from the point of view of internal peace and security, and also industrial progress, art and architecture, prosperity and education of the people, the Mughal period was undoubtedly the most glorious in the history of Indias.

India's Integrity Under the Mughals

Before the Mughal period, the Empires of Priyadarshi Ashoka and of Samudragupta had been the biggest empires in India. But, according to Prof. Jadunath Sarkar, the Mughal Empire at its peak was much bigger than either the empire of Ashoka or that of Samudragupta. Besides, life in the different provinces of India was not so unified during the Ashoka or the Samudragupta period as in the Mughal period. Under those earlier Emperors, each province had its own language, its own system of administration and its own way of life. We quote below from Prof. Jadunath Sarkar:

> "On the other hand, the two hundred years of Mughal rule, from the accession of Akbar to the death of Mohammad Shah (1556–1749), gave to the whole of Northern India, and much of the Deccan also, oneness of the official language, administrative system and coinage and also a popular *lingua franca* for all classes except the Hindoo priests and the stationary village folk. Even outside the territory directly administered by the Mughal emperors, their administrative system, official nomenclature, court etiquette and monetary type were borrowed, more or less, by the neighbouring Hindoo Rajas."
>
> "All the twenty Indian *Subahs* of the Mughal Empire were governed by means of exactly the same administrative machinery, with exactly the same procedure and official titles. Persian was the one language used in all office records, farmans, sanads, landgrants, passes, despatches and receipts. The same monetary standard prevailed throughout the Empire, with coins having the same names, the same purity and the same denominations and

differing only in the name of the mint-town. Officials and soldiers were frequently transferred from one province to another. Thus, the native of one province felt himself almost at home in another province; travellers passed most easily from city to city, *subah* to *subah,* and all realised the imperial oneness of this vast country." (*Mughal Administration*, pp. 129–30)

The Art of Writing History

The historical literature relating to the pre-Muslim period written by Hindus is very scanty, and even the little that we have lacks dates almost completely. In contrast, the books of history, accounts of travels, diaries and biographies written by the Arabs contain exact relevant dates for every incident. Professor Jadunath Sarkar states that the second great benefit derived by Indians from the Muslim rule was that foundations were laid in this country of proper historical literature.

Relations with Outside Countries

After the Buddhist period, India's contacts and relations with outside countries had begun to decline and continued to do so. Foreign trade too was growing less and less. Under Mughal rule, India's relations and contacts with outside countries were revived and re-established. Till about the end of the Mughal Empire, Afghanistan was a part of the Indian Mughal Empire and under the rule of the Delhi Emperor. Thousands of travellers and traders from Bokhara, Samarkand, Balkh, Khorasan, Khwarzim and Iran used to travel to and from India by way of Afghanistan. During the reign of Jehangir, 14,000 camels laden with merchandise came every year to India through the Bolan Pass alone, and went back the same way. Similarly, thousands of ships from and to Arabia, Iran, Turkey, Egypt, Africa, Ceylon, Sumatra, Java, Siam and China arrived at or sailed from the Indian seaports of Thatta,

Bharoch, Surat, Chall, Rajapur, Goa and Karwar in the west and of Machhlipattan, etc., in the east. Professor Jadunath Sarkar calls this the third great benefit which accrued to India from the Mughal rule.

Social and Religious Unity

The fourth great benefit to India from the Mughal rule, in the opinion of Professor Jadunath Sarkar, consisted in the further extension of those currents of religious and social unity which we have already described above in some detail. The fifth benefit was the unprecedented progress and advancement of art, architecture and painting.

In the fields of science, military organisation and discipline and also of fortification, the progress made during the Mughal period was equally unprecedented. The use of firearms, guns and canons was never before so widely current in the whole of India as under the Mughals.

The influence of Muslims on the day-to-day life of the people is clearly visible especially in Northern India. Punjabi, Hindi, Bengali, Gujarati and Marathi languages are even today full of innumerable Persian, Arabic and Turkish words. Most of the high-class sweets in the markets of Northern India have Arabic or Persian names, such as Baloo-shahi, Gulab-jamun, Barfi, Halva, Qala-Qand, Khurma and so on. The preparation of most of these sweets began during the Mughal period. Even in Hindu marriages, Persian articles of dress the 'Sehra and the Jama' are used upto this day.

The Mughals did not, in any way, interfere with the authority or the powers of the ancient village *Panchayats* in India. Professor Jadunath Sarkar says:

> "They (the Mughals) wisely maintained the old system of village administration and the old methods of the collection of revenues intact in the villages of India even to such an extent that mostly Hindus alone were appointed in their Land Revenue Department. The result was that no change of the ruling dynasty at the capital could have

> any harmful effect on the life of the millions of our village people in India." (*Mughal Administration,* p. 139)

The Mughals' Deep Concern for Their Subjects

The *kisans,* i.e., the cultivators of land, and ryots received special consideration and protection from the Mughals. Whenever a new Subedar or Provincial Governor was appointed, the directives given to him invariably included the following:

> "Encourage the ryots to extend cultivation and carry on agriculture with all their heart. Do not screw anything out of them. Remember that the ryots are permanent, that is the only permanent source of income to the State ... See that the strong may not oppress the weak." (*ibid,* pp. 85–6)

Similarly, whenever a new Provincial Subedar was appointed, the Emperor's Especial Minister called the 'Deewan-i-Ala' directed him, *inter alia*:

> "to take very great care that the strong may not oppress the weak, and to suppress all oppressors." (*ibid,* p. 81)

In every Province there was a "Deewan" in addition to the "Subedar" or the "Nazim". The Subedar's duties comprised organising the military, running the Government and supervising the administration of justice. The Deewan's function was the collection of land revenue. Every *Sanad* appointing a Diwan contained the clause that "his most important duty was to extend agriculture and to increase village population". No pressure or compulsion of any kind was permitted on the cultivator in the collection of land revenue. One of the directives given to every Deewan at the time of his appointment was:

> "If the land revenue in the circle of any Amil has been in arrears for some years, then you should realise the arrears

> from the Kisans in very easy instalments, *i.e.,* in instalments of not more than 5 per cent of the arrears at each harvesting." (*ibid,* p. 88)

Similarly, all Foujdars, Thanedars, Karories and Tehsildars, *i.e.,* all military, police, revenue and civil officers, were enjoined strictly to see that those who cultivated the land, the kisans, were not subjected to any hardship whatsoever.

Condition of Kisans

Professor Jadunath Sarkar, after comparing the conditions under which the Indian kisan lived at that time with the conditions under which the kisans of France and Ireland lived at the same time and after showing how the Indian cultivator was much better off at the time than the cultivator either in France or in Ireland, says:

> "But the difference was this that before the advent of the British (that is during the Mughal rule), no kisan in India was ever ejected from the land under his cultivation for default in the payment of land revenue due from him. Nor did any kisan go hungry. According to the Batai system (division of the harvested crops), the land revenue was realised in kind and so the kisan was at a great advantage, because the land revenue payable by him each year depended on the quantity of the crop actually harvested that year. As opposed to this system, the land revenue is now (under British rule) realised in cash, the amount being fixed regardless of the actual crop harvested by the kisan in that year."

Directives and Farmans were repeatedly issued to all officers and feudal chiefs in all the provinces of the Mughal Empire from the Delhi *Durbar* and in the name of every Mughal emperor to the effect that no kisan or cultivator of land should be put to any hardship in the realisation of the land revenue or in any other matter and that absolutely no dues should be realised from any cultivator except those specifically provided for in the law of the land.

The historian, Frederick Augustus, writes:

> "Whenever the Emperor's army passed through villages and its march caused any loss or damage to the property of the cultivators, or the villagers, trustworthy and responsible men were deputed to enquire and arrive at a correct amount of compensation. After that the amount of the loss or the damage was made good to the aggrieved party, either in the form of a remission of the whole or a part of the land revenue payable by the cultivator or, to avoid useless complaints and arguments, the full amount claimed by the cultivator was paid to him then and there on the spot." (*The Emperor Akbar* translated by A. S. Beveridge, pp. 275–76)

Aurangzeb's Proclamation

In 1673, Emperor Aurangzeb issued and published throughout his empire a proclamation forbidding the realization from his subjects of any duty or tax whatsoever on 54 articles listed therein. In the same proclamation, all Government officials and Zamindars were ordered not to accept any present or take any present or take any forced labour from any cultivator. The 54 articles included fish, oil, ghee (clarified butter), milk, dahi (curd), uplay (cow-dung fuel), vegetables, grass fodder, fuel, earthen pots, cotton, village carts, sugarcane, cane juice, cloth printing, camels, use of pastures, the use of roads, of river-ghats, etc. Absolutely no type of duty or tax could be levied on any of these articles in any part of the Empire. It was also laid down in this very proclamation that no duty or tax was to be charged from people going to bathe in the Ganges or to any other place of pilgrimage or from Hindus going to immerse the ashes of their dead in the Ganges or any other river.

Similar Firmans and directives were continually being issued since the time of Akbar. Every Emperor on his accession, and sometimes even during his reign, had to repeat or clarify them, as a precaution against the contingency of any negligence in the matter on the part of any Government official or feudal chief.

Professor Jadunath Sarkar writes:

> "The policy' of the supreme head of the Mughal Government not to commit any exaction on the ryot is manifest from the contemporary histories and letters and can be proved to have been a reality and not merely a pious wish. Several instances are recorded in the reigns of Shahjehan and Aurangzeb in which harsh and exacting revenue collectors and even provincial Viceroys were dismissed on the complaints of their subjects reaching the Emperor's ears." (*Mughal Administration,* p. 108)

The same writer has quoted from a Persian manuscript an instance which "clearly shows how anxious Shahjehan was to treat the kisans with justice and even with generosity".

Shahjehan and the Kisans

One day, Shahjehan, while inspecting the revenue records of the empire found that the revenue realised from a certain village in that year was a few thousand rupees more than that realised from the same village in the preceding year. He forthwith summoned the head of the Department, Deewan-i-Ala Saadullah Khan, and demanded an explanation for the increase in revenue. On investigation, it appeared that the river adjoining that village had somewhat receded in that year and so there was some increase in the area under cultivation in that village. Consequently, the land revenue assessment of the village had also been increased. The Emperor again wanted to know whether the increase in area had been to the ordinary revenue-paying land or to the *Maafi, i.e.,* revenue-free land. On being informed that it was the revenue-free land whose area had increased by the recession of the river, the Emperor became furious and exclaimed:

"The lamentations of the poor, the widows and the orphans of that village had dried up the waters and side-turned the river. The resulting accession was God's gift to them, and you have dared to usurp it for the State. Had my compassion for God's creatures not restrained me, I would have ordered that the Devil of the *Foujdar,* who had exacted revenue for the accession to the *Maafi* land be hanged until dead. As it is, his dismissal will be enough punishment for him and will also serve as a warning to others, not to do such evil acts of injustice. Let an order be issued that the excess revenue thus collected from the people be immediately refunded to them." (India Office Library, Persian Manuscript, No. 370, interleaf facing folio 68)

In 1662, Mohammad Hashim, the Deewan of Orissa, employed a few new Karories (revenue collecters) because they had undertaken to collect more revenue from the same lands than the old Karories had been doing. As soon as the news reached the ears of the Emperor, he at once ordered the dismissal of Mohammad Hashim.

Directives forbidding the realisation of "Abwabs", *i.e.,* of all taxes other the land revenue, from the villagers, were being continually issued from the time of Firozeshah Tughlak (1375) to the time of Akbar (1590) and were thereafter repeated in the reign of almost every Mughal Emperor.

The Mughal Emperors always kept themselves well informed about the happiness or otherwise of the vast numbers of their subjects. Throughout the Mughal period, a huge active and energetic army of 'Vaquey Naveeses' (chroniclers of events), Savaneh Naveeses' (writers of accidents), 'Akhbar Naveeses' (writers of news), Khufia Naveeses' (secret reporters) and others was maintained, through whom news from the remotest corners of the Empire reached the Emperor's ears.

There can be no doubt that throughout the entire period of recorded Indian history, there was never a period in which the interests and the well-being of the tillers of the soil were so well looked after and so well secured as during the time of the Mughal Emperors. That is why a large number of contemporary European and other travellers to India have expressed their unstinted admiration for the prosperity of the Indian villages of those days and have affirmed that it was unequalled by that of any other country in the world (E.g. *Bengal in 1756–57* by S.C. Hill, Vol. I).

The Duties of the Kotwal

In every town throughout the Mughal Empire there was an officer called the Kotwal, in addition to other officials. "The duties of the Kotwal included his seeing to it that there was complete ban on liquor-distillation in the city and he was also responsible for seeing to it that there was no prostitute living anywhere under his jurisdiction " (Manucci, Vol. II, pp. 420–21).

The above statement has been made by a learned European traveller who had seen with his own eyes the conditions actually prevailing in the Mughal Empire during Aurangzeb's reign. The Sanad (letter of appointment) of every Kotwal contained a clause to the effect that "it is your duty and responsibility to see that no theft is committed in your town and that its inhabitants enjoy full protection and are able to pursue their occupations in peace".

Every area had an officer called the "Mohtasib" whose special duty it was to make rounds of every street in the town and to forcibly close any place, if found, where liquor was distilled or sold or which was used for gambling. Out of regard for the feelings of Hindu Sadhus, the use of dry intoxicants, like Ganja and Bhang (hemp) was not so strictly forbidden. The Mohtasib was directed "not to permit the sale of any intoxicants like liquor, etc., in the town and not to permit any public dancing-girl to live inside the town" (*Mughal Administration* by Jadunath Sarkar, P-41).

Prohibition

Moreland the historian writes that Emperor Akbar had ordered the Kotwal of every town throughout the Empire to stop the distillation of liquor within his jurisdiction as far as possible without having recourse to forcible entry into any house. After him Emperor Jehangir forbade, by law, the distillation of liquor throughout the Empire. But it was during the reign of Shahjehan that obedience to this law was strictly enforced throughout the length and breadth of the Empire (*India at the Death of Akbar*, p. 159). The same strictness continued during the reign of Aurangzeb. But during the reigns of subsequent weak Emperors, the royal order could not be so properly enforced everywhere.

The Administration of Justice

We shall now describe briefly the administration of justice under the Mughals. Since ancient times there was a village *Panchayat* in every village of India. The Panchas or members of the *Panchayat* were elected by the villagers from among themselves. The village *Panchayat* was vested with full authority over the municipal affairs of the village. In addition, the *Panchayat* was also entrusted with the protection of the life and property of the people as also with the safety of travellers and traders on the adjacent roads. Every *Panchayat* had Chowkidars under it who received their salaries from the *Panchayat*. The Chowkidars were not in any way under the control or authority of the government. The *Panchayat* was also vested with the authority to hear and decide all civil and criminal cases within its jurisdiction and to punish the guilty or the offenders against law. The *Panchayat* also made arrangements for the education of the boys and girls of the village. We have dealt with this subject in detail at another place in this book. Most of the towns, particularly, the smaller ones, had similar *Panchayats* vested with similar wide powers and authority.

The Mughal Emperors did not, in any way, interfere with the authority or the powers vested since ancient times in the hundreds of thousands of these Indian village *Panchayats*. In fact, they kept these institutions intact. It means that before the advent of the British, the villages of India enjoyed all the right of Sthaniya Swarajya, *i.e.*, local self-government, subject only to the payment of land revenue to the Government.

To help the *Panchayats* in the discharge of their duties as police, a Foujdar was appointed in every district. The Foujdar helped the *Panchayat* only in big dacoities (brigandages) or serious disturbances to peace, etc. To help the *Panchayats* in the performance of their duties as local judiciary a Quazee and a Sadar were appointed in every region covering a large number of villages, for more serious criminal and civil cases, respectively. The Head of all the Quazees in the Empire was called 'Quazee-ul-Quazat' and had his headquarters at the capital. Similarly, the head of all the Sadars in the Empire was called 'Sardar-us-sadoor' and had his headquarters also at the capital. Every Quazee on his appointment was given the following instructions from the Government:

> "Always remain just and honest. Do not favour or be partial to any individual. Always hear and try cases in the presence of both the parties, either in the court-premises or in some Government office. *Never accept any offer or present from anybody, within your jurisdiction, nor attend any function or reception given by anybody in the region wherein you are stationed.*" "Be very careful in writing your judgments or drafting other documents, so that no scholar may put you to shame by pointing out defects in the same."
>
> *"Take pride in your poverty."*
>
> Men of character and learning only were appointed as Quazee or Sadar. The historian, Frederick Augustus, testifies to the fact that under the Mughal Emperors: "... the mass of the employees were both scrupulous and capable." (*Mughal Administration,* p. 37)

In arriving at decisions in law-suits, full consideration was paid to ancient customary laws of the country and also to the Dharm Shastras of the Hindus. The Emperor Akbar appointed a number of able Brahmins as judges and issued directives that law-courts should comply with the provisions contained in the *Manusmriti* and other Hindu Dharm Shastras.

Every Emperor set apart at least one day in the week (often Tuesday or Wednesday) on which he heard appeals and cases of special importance from all over the Empire. The humblest of the subjects had free access to the Emperor and could submit his complaint or petition in person to the Emperor. The Emperor Jehangir, famous for his administration of justice, had hung a golden chain from the outermost wall of his fort at Agra, which reached down to the ground outside. The humblest complainant could tie his petition addressed to the Emperor to the chain and pull it. He was then forthwith brought in and produced before the Emperor.

Liberalism in Religion

Leaving aside the much-debated and at least partly misrepresented time of Aurangzeb's reign, the entire remaining period of the Mughal Emperors in India was undoubtedly an ideal period as regards broad-mindedness and tolerance in religious matters. During the reigns of Babar, Humayun, Akbar, Jehangir, Shahjehan and most of their successors. Hindus and Muslims were treated absolutely alike and on the same footing by the Government in all matters of administration. Both religions were equally respected and neither of them was shown any partiality in any matter whatsoever. The British Ambassador, Sir Thomas Roe, wrote in 1616 concerning what he had witnessed of Jehangir's administration in the following words:

> "Tamerlain's offspring brought in the knowledge of Mohammad, but imposed it on none by the law of conquest, leaving consciences at liberty." (*A General Collection of the Best and Most Interesting Voyages,* edited by John Pinkerton, London, 1811, Vol. VIII, p. 46)

Another Englishman, Capt. Alexander Hamilton, in describing the conditions in Bengal, during the reigns of Aurangzeb and his successors (1688–1723) writes:

> "There are above one hundred different sects ... but they never have any hot disputes about their doctrine or way of worship. Everyone is free to serve and worship God in

his own way, and persecutions for religion's sake are not known among them." (*ibid,* p. 321)

Further,

"The religion of Bengal as established is Mohammadan, yet for one Mohammadan there are above one hundred pagans and the public offices and posts are filled promiscuously with men of both persuasions." (*ibid,* p. 415)

Dr Beni Prasad has in his *History of Jehangir* (p. 100), written that

"the principal festivals of the Hindus as well as those of the Muslims were celebrated with equal enthusiasm and eclat in the *Darbars* of the Mughal Emperors of India. On the Dusshera day, richly-caparisoned horses and elephants of the Emperor were taken out in a procession. On the occasion of Raksha-Bandhan, Brahmins and Hindu feudal chiefs tied the sacred *Rakhi* on the wrist of the Emperor. The Imperial Palaces were illuminated on the occasion of the Diwali festival and even gambling was indulged in in accordance with the Hindu custom. Shivaratri was marked by an unusual festive atmosphere in the Palace. In precisely the same way, the Muslim festivals of Id and Shab-e-Barat were celebrated with the same enthusiasm and eclat."

The birthday of every Emperor was celebrated twice a year, once according to the Muslim lunar calendar and again according to the Hindu mixed calendar.

There can be no doubt that this very broad-mindedness and tolerance in religious matters was the foundation-stone of the Mughal Empire in India. The Emperor Babar laid the foundation of this broad-mindedness in his last Will and Testament to his son Humayun and Humayun, as his successor, conscientiously carried out his father's last wishes. The Emperor Akbar practised and carried this broad-mindedness to a pitch, which will ever remain a landmark in the religious history of the world.

Jehangir and Shahjehan carried out the same policy with wonderful success.

Contemporary Christian Europe

We should remember that it was exactly the period when atrocities and excesses in the name of religion were rampant throughout Europe and were everyday occurrences. In Ireland, no Roman Catholic could inherit the property of his ancestors or be appointed an officer in the army or sit on a judicial bench. In France every member of the Huguenot sect had been deported across the seas. In Sweden no Christian except a member of the Lutheran sect could serve as a jury. In Spain no clergyman was allowed to perform the last rites of a dying Protestant. Not only this, the Government of every country in Europe in those days passed acts of uniformity, according to which no member of any sect of Christianity, other than the sect to which the rulers of that country belonged, was allowed to live in peace in that country. As a result of these atrocious laws, thousands of Catholics, thousands of Anglicans, thousands of Lutherans, thousands of Puritans, thousands of Presbyterians, thousands of Levatois, thousands of Anna Baptists and thousands of Covenanters were burnt alive, put to the sword or tortured to death in the various countries of Europe.

It must be remembered that all these victims of religious persecution were Christians and as orthodox Christians as their countrymen who tyrannized over them. The only difference was that the victims belonged to one sect of Christianity and their persecutors belonged to another sect of the same religion.

Europe and India—A Contrast

Comparing the conditions in Europe with those in India during the same period, the historian Torrens writes:

> "During the reigns of the earlier Emperors of Delhi, to the middle of the seventeenth century, complete tolerance was shown to all religions. Shall they who built

> the tombs of those who, at that very time, were busily employed in making Europe one mighty charnelhouse of persecution, and in colonising America with fugitives for conscience' sake, rise up in judgment against India or load the breath of history with the insolent pretence of having then enjoyed a truer civilization? What if they were taken at their word, and called forth with the covenanters' blood, and the Catholics' blood, and the puritans' blood dripping quick from the orthodox hands that all that time were building scaffolds, rivetting chains and penning penal 'Acts of Uniformity'?." (*Empire in Asia, How We Came by It* by W. M. Torrens, M. P., Panini Office reprint, pp. 96–97)

At a number of places in this book, we have shown that Hindus were appointed to the highest offices during the Muslim and particularly during the Mughal period. Numberless Hindu temples were granted Jagirs and Moafi (revenue-free) lands by every Mughal Emperor. Aurangzeb is supposed to have been rather a narrow-minded Muslim. But even then he had Hindu ministers at his court and Hindu commanders in his Army. More than 250 years have passed since the death of Aurangzeb, yet upto this day (1967) the priests of many Hindu temples in India have in their possession copies of Royal firmans according to which Jagirs or revenue-free lands were bestowed upon those temples under orders of Aurangzeb. The firmans bear the signatures of Emperor Aurangzeb. The Hindu priests of the Temple of Someshwarnath in Arail, near Allahabad, and of the Jangamwari Shiva Temple in Banaras may be cited as instances where the respective priests have still got copies of the said royal firmans in their possession. So far as the peace and prosperity of the people were concerned, the period of the Mughal administration in India was undoubtedly the Golden Age of Indian history. The testimony of numberless European and Asian travellers and of the historical records of the period can be cited in support of this contention. The prosperity, the contentment and the happiness of the people which marked the regime of Shahjehan had probably no parallel in the history of any other country of the world.

The historian Moreland writes that foreign travellers and traders visiting India in those days were amazed to see the efficiency of the administration in protecting lives and property in towns and cities. A number of travellers testify to the fact that, in the first place, very few thefts were committed, and if a theft did occur in any town or city and the stolen property could not be recovered, then the Kotwal of the place had to make good the loss to the victim of the theft out of his own pocket (*India at the Death of Akbar,* pp. 38–39).

Sher Shah ruled at Delhi for some years in between the two reigns of Emperor Humayun. Frederick Augustus writes:

> "Even the few days' rule of Sher Shah did not prove detrimental to the progress of Hindostan. Indeed, arrangements for the use of roads, the facilities for the transport of goods and the security of travellers were even more efficient than ever before." (*The Emperor Akbar,* p. 277)

Among the very first orders issued by Emperor Jehangir on his accession to the throne one was that, throughout the Empire, all roads and government wells along the roads be kept properly repaired and the security and safety of the travellers be well looked after. Another order issued was to the effect that no Government official or Zamindar should evict a cultivator against his will from his holding, for any reason whatsoever (*India at the Death of Akbar,* by Moreland, pp. 46, 129).

A third order was to the effect that no package of merchandise belonging to any trader should be opened at any octroi barrier or on any road for the assessment of the octroi or any other duty chargeable thereon. Jehangir got constructed all over his Empire numerous Serais (travellers' inns), schools, hospitals, tanks, wells and bridges. He appointed Hakeems and Vaidyas (physicians) for the service of the people at State expense in all important towns and banned the sale and consumption of liquor and tobacco throughout his Empire. In no city or town in the world at that time was there any regular government arrangement for public instruction. To make up for this, the Mughal Emperors made grants of Jagirs and stipends to thousands of learned Pandits and Moulvis for the maintenance of Pathshalas and Maktabs, i.e., schools of various languages throughout the Empire. Many English travellers acknowledge the fact that due to the liberal help and encouragement given by the Mughal Emperors to the spread of education, the percentage of literates in India was the highest in the world at that time.

In the field of industry, not only did India fully meet its own requirements, but also in most of the markets of the world, the vast majority of goods displayed and offered for sale were of Indian manufacture. Till the beginning of the 19th century, ships built in India were more beautiful, stronger and more durable than those built at that time in England or in any other European country (*Prosperous British India* by William Digby, pp. 86, 88).

The European traveller, Comte, writes that in the 15th century ships as big as those built in India were not to be seen anywhere in Europe. Englishmen who visited India during the early days of the Mughal Empire have recorded in their diaries that they saw in India ships of far greater size as well as of greater strength and beauty than they had ever come across in Europe. During the days of the Mughal Empire, most of the ships that plied between China and Japan on one side and South Africa on the other had been built in India and particularly in Gujarat. The entire trade from Bengal in the east to Sindh in the west was carried on in Indian ships. Passenger ships built in India were bigger in size than any built elsewhere in the world. From Mexico in the east to England in the west, goods of Indian manufacture loaded on Indian ships were exported to other countries of the world. Indian Muslims went from India on their Haj pilgrimage to Arabia and came back to India exclusively in Indian ships (*India at the Death of Akbar,* pp. 67–77).

Barbosa writes that silk fabrics manufactured in Gujarat were, in the beginning of the 17th century, exported to places as far away as Africa and Pegu. Barthelomew tells us that in those days Gujarat used to supply silk and cotton fabrics manufactured by itself to the whole of Iran, Tatar, Turkey, Syria, Barbary, Arabia, Ethiopia (Africa) and many other countries. Travellers of that period write that the consumption of cloth in India itself at the time was extraordinarily high. Almost all people of the upper and middle classes used to put on silk and wore long and loose overall garments called *Choghas*.

During the reign of Akbar, silk industry developed unprecedentedly. Abul Fazl writes that Akbar himself closely and diligently studied the silk industry. He sent for silk artisans from distant China and other countries and with their help established big silk factories financed by the State at Lahore, Agra, Fatehpur, Ahmedabad and other places.

In the reign of Akbar one rupee could buy wheat in a quantity which, according to the modern metric system, would weigh well over 50 kilogrammes and one could buy a nice pure woollen blanket or rug for a quarter of a rupee.

According to Abul Fazl, there were one thousand shawl-making Government factories in Lahore, besides similar factories in Kashmir and other places. In Agra and in Lahore, there were also Government factories for manufacturing big beautiful carpets of cotton and wool as well as of silk.

Up to the beginning of the 19th century, representatives of the East India Company in India wrote, time and again, to their masters in England that textiles made in England could find no market in India, because they could not compare or compete with those made in India.

The Portuguese traveller Perard writes that in the beginning of the 17th century, Bengal was a very densely-populated province and that practically every home there produced its own cotton textiles and that from the Cape of Good Hope in Africa up to China every man and woman went about clothed from head to foot in material which was the product of Indian handlooms. The Arab traders carried Indian fabrics upto Egypt and Europe and sold the same in the markets of those countries. In those days there was a very great demand for Indian textiles in Ceylon, Burma, Malacca, China, Japan, the Philippines and Mexico and the markets of those countries were full of Indian goods. In a separate chapter in this book, we have described the position of Indian industries during the pre-British period and also how those industries were deliberately ruined by the British.

The history and accounts of European and other travellers pertaining to that period bear testimony to the fact that the India of the Mughal period was more densely populated than not only the European countries of that day but also than the India of the middle of the 20th century at least as far as some provinces were concerned. Calcutta, Bombay and Karachi were then nonexistent, but Agra, Kannauj, Vijayanagar, Golkonda, Bijapur, Multan, Lahore, Delhi, Allahabad, Patna, Ujjain, Ahmedabad, Ajmer and Surat were very densely populated, beautiful and big cities, each one of them being several times bigger than contemporary London or Paris.

No regular and periodical census operations were undertaken anywhere in Europe in those days. In India an estimate of the number of people was arrived at by counting the number of houses in an area. According to Moreland, the population of France in those days was half and the population of England not more than one-eighth of what it was in the second quarter of the present century. About Vijayanagar Abdul Razzaque, Paiz and other travellers state that its population was "unbelievably large at that time". The Hindu Rajas of Vijayanagar maintained a standing army of two million men. Deccan, Gujarat, Punjab and the rest of Northern India were, it is stated, as equally densely populated. It is recorded that at any time a force of armed men could be collected in Agra from the city itself. The number of houses in Gaur, the capital of Bengal, was then 1,200,000, which means that the population of Gaur at that time was not much less than that of London in 1930. From Surat to Lahore, Lahore to Agra, and Agra to Gaur, the number of densely-populated villages and towns through which the European travellers had to pass was so great that it simply amazed them. There can be no doubt that so far as the density of the population and the prosperity of the people are concerned, the India of that day was far ahead of any contemporary country of the world except China.

The Development of Indian Languages

The Mughals and the other Muslims who had migrated to India from outside countries and settled here could not but be influenced by Indian thought, Indian culture and the Indian way of life. They soon became Indian Muslims quite distinct from the Muslims of other countries. The Mughals acquired from Indians the habit of chewing betel-leaves. They adopted as their own language Hindustani, the then prevalent *lingua franca* of India, which they called 'Zaban-i-Hindvi'. In the beginning Babar and his companions spoke the Irani language. Gradually, the Mughals began to use Hindustani in their homes, in their offices as well as in their *Durbars,* and eventually Hindustani became their mother--tongue. For some time, Persian continued to remain the language of their literature and of official correspondence. About the year 1750 they began to use Hindustani for literary purposes too. Naturally many Persian and Turkish words also began to be used in the Hindustani language and became a part and parcel of the language. This Hindustani language soon became the language of the Imperial Court and grew richer and more polished day by day. The beautiful language thus evolved was ultimately called Urdu by which name it is known upto this day. Bahadur Shah, the last Mughal Emperor, was himself a gifted Urdu poet.

Other Indian languages, too, developed to an unprecedented extent during the Mughal period. Jadunath Sarkar writes:

> "It was during the reign of Akbar that, thanks to the splendid contribution of Tulsidas to Hindi and of the Vaishnava writers to Bengali, that a powerful Hindu literature began to develop in the languages of the country. It was the Emperor Akbar who brought into existence a real national Court in India and it was in his reign that India rose to a very great height in the intellectual sphere also." (*Mughal Administration,* p. 146)

Even before the Mughal period, the indigenous literatures of Bengal and of South India had greatly flourished under the Muslim rulers of these parts. Dinesh Chandra Sen, whose *History of Bengali Language and Literature* is considered the most authentic on the subject, states at page 10 of his book:

> "Many influences were at work in developing the Bengali language into a literary language. The most important of these influences was undoubtedly the conquest of Bengal

> by the Muslims. If the Hindu Rajas had continued to be independent, it would have been hardly possible for the Bengali language to get entry into the *Darbars* of the Rajas."

The Muslim rulers of Bengal got the *Ramayan* and the *Mahabharat* translated from Sanskrit into Bengali by employing learned Pandits for the task. Naseer Shah, the Muslim ruler of Bengal, got the Sanskrit *Mahabharat* translated into Bengali in the beginning of the 14th century. The Maithili poet Vidyapati has showered unstinted praise on Naseer Shah and on Sultan Ghayasuddin in this connection. Muslims had very great influence at the court of the Raja Kans, whose successor became a convert to Islam. Kritti Yas, the translator of the *Ramayan,* received great patronage and financial assistance from the Court. The emperor Husain Shah got the *Bhagwat* translated from Sanskrit into Bengali by Naldhar Vasu and as a reward conferred on him the title of "Gunraj Khan". Parangal Khan, the Commander-in-Chief of Husain Shah, had another Bengali translation of the *Mahabharat* done by Kaveendra Parmeshwar. Chhotey Khan, the son of Parangal Khan, who was also the Governor of Chattagram (Chittagong), got the translation of the *Ashwamedha Parva* of the *Mahabharat* done by Shri Krishna Nandi. A Muslim scholar named Ala-ul translated into Bengali the Hindu classic *Padmavat* written by Malik Mohammad Jayaisee. Ala-ul also translated some Persian books into Bengali. Dinesh Chandra Sen writes:

> "There are innumerable instances in which Mughal Emperors and Sardars themselves got Sanskrit and Persian books translated into Bengali. They also gave liberal grants to others for getting such translations prepared. When powerful Muslim Kings of Bengal accorded such a high place to Indian languages in their *Darbars,* naturally the Hindu Rajas also followed their example is ... Thus, the practice of appointing Bengali poets in the *Darbars* of Hindu Rajas had its origin in what the Muslim Kings had done and were doing." (*History of Bengali Language and Literature,* pp. 13,14)

Like the Muslim Kings of Bengal, the Bahamani Kings of the Deccan also very much developed local literatures, industries and the arts. The Adil Shahi Kings used the Marathi language in their offices, and appointed Hindu Marathas to high places in their revenue and military departments. Qutub Shah Dakkhini himself was a gifted Marathi poet and a great lover of Marathi literature. Thus words of both Hindi and Persian languages freely entered the Marathi language.

Besides Hindi, Urdu, Bengali and Marathi and quite like them, the Punjabi and Sindhi languages and literatures also made unprecedented progress during the Muslim period in India. As a matter of fact, it was the period of the rise and development of local living languages and literatures in place of the ancient Sanskrit. The lives of the Hindus and of the Muslims were in this connection so interwoven that the Mishra brothers have, in their book, given a long list of Muslim Hindi poets, and Munshi Shri Ram of Delhi has similarly listed in his book a large number of Hindu Urdu poets. The impress and the influence of Muslim rule and of Persian and Turkish words and idioms on Hindi, Marathi, Bengali and other Indian languages continue upto this day and are indeed indelible.

Development of Literature and Science

In the early days, the Indian sciences of medicine, mathematics and astronomy added considerably to their store of knowledge by drawing freely upon Greek scientific knowledge which became available to them through the Arabic language, Arab ideas and Arab books. Towards the end of the 17th century and towards the beginning of the 18th century, Maharaja Jay Singh, with the object of reforming the Hindu calendar, got constructed new observatories at Jaipur, Mathura, Delhi and Banaras. He also got the Arabic book *Almajasti* translated into Sanskrit. Hindu medical science also enriched itself by borrowing many new things from the Arabs particularly in the field of chemistry.

It was during the time of the Muslim Kings that several new industries, *e.g.,* those of paper-making, of tinning brass and copper utensils, China pottery and various kinds of metal-work were first started in India. Similarly, there were far-reaching and valuable reforms in dress, food, social etiquette, music and other ways of life in India during the time of the Muslim rulers.

In fact, a new synthetic civilization was then developing in all walks of Indian life. That civilization was, strictly speaking, neither Hindu nor Muslim, neither Vaidic nor Buddhist, but a new Indian civilization born of the union of all these civilizations and incorporating the best elements of the ancient Indian as well as the foreign Arab and Iranian civilizations and higher, richer and more beautiful than any of them. The Hindus appeared to be rising above their centuries-old narrow-mindedness, their ancient caste distinctions, their worship of innumerable gods and goddesses, complicated ritualism, priestly domination and diverse ancient superstitions, and advancing towards the all-important goal of the brotherhood of all men, of monotheism and of universal love. Islam in India was undergoing a magnificent transformation and developing into a new Indian Islam, slightly distinct from the original Islam of Arabia. Muslim Sufis were then incorporating in their Islam many philosophical ideas and doctrines of the Hindus and also *Yogic* practices such as *pranayam* and the like which they were adopting as their own. Hundreds of Muslim *faqeers* and Hindu *mahatmas,* like Kabir, Dadoo, Nanak and Baba Fareed were busy demolishing the artificial and harmful barriers separating the various religions and sects in the country and were preaching to all alike one true universal religion of love and service. New and higher ideals were taking shape in science, art, literature and social life. The various languages of India were for the first time giving birth to a new type of high, noble and powerful literature. The entire country was marching ahead towards unity, peace, strength and prosperity. The concepts of one country and one nation, deeply tinged with love for all mankind were leading the whole of India towards a higher and nobler life.

The Emperor Akbar

The greatest, noblest and most magnificent product of this national development that had been growing and blooming for hundreds of years appeared in the middle of the sixteenth century in the person of the illustrious Emperor Akbar the Great. The well-known English philosopher and historian, H. G. Wells, writing about Akbar, says:

> "Free from all those prejudices which disintegrate society and create dissensions, tolerant to men of other beliefs, impartial to men of other races, whether Hindu or Dravidian, he was a man obviously marked out to weld the conflicting elements of his Kingdom into a strong and prosperous whole ..."
>
> "His instinct was the true statesman's instinct for synthesis. His Empire was to be neither a Moslem one nor a Mughal one, nor was it to be Rajput or Aryan or Dravidian. or Hindu or high or low caste; it was to be Indian." (*The Outline of History*, pp. 454–55)

Akbar was the resultant embodiment of those powerful national currents in India which had been active for hundreds of years before his time and which continued to develop even after him. In matters religious, Akbar got his inspiration and encouragement from the illuminating teachings of Kabir.

Centuries before Akbar, the Emperor Harsh used to resort to and worship at the temples of all three—Shiva, Buddha and the Sun in Prayag (modern Allahabad). The worship of Satya peer in Bengal, initiated and propagated by Emperor Husain Shah, in which thousands of Hindus and Muslims joined equally, was an earlier form of Akbar's religious ideology as manifested in his *Deen-i-llahi*. Even so the individuality of Akbar as well as his grand mission was unique in history.

Akbar tried through his *Allah-Upnishad* and his *Deen-i-Ilahi* to lay the foundations of a simple universal religion. In the social field he, in 1573, stopped by law the thousands of years old practice under which a victor in battle forced into his slavery all prisoners of war. He did his best to put an end to forced widowhood, child-marriages, polygamy and animal sacrifice in the name of religion and also the custom of *Sati* (self-immolation by the Hindu widow at the burning pyre of her dead husband). Yet he never attempted to use force or any form of compulsion for imposing any of his reforms. Frederick Augustus tells us that the total amount spent by Akbar in distributing food and clothing every day to the poor and in gifts made during his pilgrimages came to a considerable portion of the Empire's total revenue. Akbar was an earnest advocate of the freedom of women. His Hindu-Muslim marriages also contributed to the fusion of Hindus and Muslims on a more abiding basis. He made great efforts to bring into existence a united Indian nation during his life-time. In fact, Akbar wanted to build up a new India. Akbar's dream did not wholly materialise, but the great movement of synthesis, unity and mutual understanding which he sponsored still goes on. There can be no doubt that the present day efforts to build up a real united Indian nation owe their origin and continuance to Akbar, who was the first to initiate such efforts.

Frederick Augustus writes:

> "Akbar was great as a general, as a statesman creative, and down to the present-day he is unsurpassed as a practical exponent of genuine humanity." (*The Emperor Akbar,* p. 296)

Contemporary Hindu and Muslim Narrowness

Akbar's immediate successors, Jehangir and Shahjehan, during their reigns followed in his footsteps in this matter and kept burning the torch of the said national movement. The movement progressively gained in strength. As we have mentioned above, the period of Shahjehan's reign was the period of greatest peace and prosperity in India, and was in more senses than one by far the Golden Age of Indian history. And yet currents of unity, equality, fraternity, liberalism, broad-mindedness and love of humanity, which were active in India at the time, had not yet been able to cover the entire field of human life in the country. There is no doubt that these national currents were gaining in strength day by day. But, on the other hand, the old narrow mindedness of both Hindus and Muslims had by no means run out their course. We give just one example. If Kabir was one disciple of Ramanand. Tulsidas was another. Both were great. Both were true devotees of God. India is rightly proud of both of them. Both took part in building up the India of the future, each in his own way. Yet while one of them, that is, Kabir, tried to demolish the walls dividing religions from one another and fearlessly preached one universal religion of humanity, the other one, Tulsidas, was distinctly inclined towards the Hinduism of the Middle Ages which hugged the caste system as one of its main doctrines. Religious leaders like Vallabhacharya, and particularly the Shaiva and Vaishnava preachers, were active all over India and were busy in their efforts to keep the nation bound in the narrownesses of the past, instead of leading it towards a brighter and grander future. Among the Muslims, too, while there were, on one side, Sufis and Darweshes who ignored the non-essential rituals prescribed by the Shariat and propagated, like Kabir. one universal religion of love, there was, on the other side, no lack of short-sighted Mullahs who bluntly condemned Akbar, Jehangir and Shahjehan as Kafirs (heretics). It was such narrow-minded people who got Mansoor hanged and had Shams-i-Tabrez skinned alive. In this matter, no others ever did so much harm to the world as those narrow-minded priests and preachers of various religions who failed to see the universality, high morality and love of humanity inherent in their own respective religions, and kept the common people bound in meaningless rituals and ceremonies ordained by custom. They are still doing so. They are keeping intact the time-worn walls which divide the different strands of human society and cut it into pieces. Unfortunately, sometimes, individual interest also leads them in that direction. When the movements initiated by Kabir, Akbar and others like them were about to end this narrowness, once and for all, an event happened which routed for the time these beneficial national currents.

Dara Shikoh and Aurangzeb

Dara Shikoh, the eldest son and rightful successor of Shahjehan, was like his father, grandfather and great-grandfather, a true representative, protagonist and strong advocate of this great national movement for unity. He was a disciple of the well known Hindu saint, Baba Lal Dara's famous work *Nadir unnikat,* in which he has embodied his dialogue with his Guru, Baba Lal, is considered to be one of the best Persian treatises on Vedanta, *i.e.,* on spiritual monism. Dara's favourite epithet for God was *Prabhu* (Master), which was engraved on his seal also. Dara's younger brother, Aurangzeb, aspired to supplant Dara and to ascend the throne himself. All the unifying forces of the country, particularly all Hindus, were naturally on the side of Dara. To defeat Dara, Aurangzeb had to rally round himself all fanatic Mullahs and narrowminded elements in Islam. These elements which had been hindering the unification of the country naturally gained in strength and got a fresh lease of life. The fate of India, for at least the next 300 years, was thus decided on 30th May 1658 on the field of Samugarh, where the short-sighted Aurangzeb won by routing the forces under the liberal-minded and farseeing Dara Shikoh. It is possible that religious narrowness may have been a part of Aurangzeb's own nature. It is much more probable, however, that, as we have hinted above, such narrowness was a political necessity for him. But this makes no difference to our present subject, nor to India's future destiny.

Immediately on ascending the throne, Aurangzeb began to gather round him all narrow-minded Muslim forces in the country. As a ruler, Aurangzeb was not unjust or partial to any community. Highest posts of responsibility in the Empire were bestowed by him upon Hindus and Muslims alike without any discrimination. Unless there was some especial justification for it, he never liked to injure the feelings of his Hindu subjects in any matter whatever. He continued all through the 50 years of his reign strict enforcement of the prohibition against cow-slaughter throughout his Empire, as had been done since the time of Akbar the Great. He always paid special attention to the needs and interests of the kisans, *i.e.,* of cultivators of land. Innumerable stories about Aurangzeb's religious narrowness and partiality are current in the country, and many of them have even found their way into our history text-books. Most of such stones are, however, absolutely without foundation. And yet Aurangzeb was an orthodox Muslim, who believed in and tried to follow all the religious rituals and practices enjoined by Muslim religious law and custom, Maulana Abul Kalam Azad once rightly told the writer of these pages that Aurangzeb cared more for the injunctions issued from time to time by Muslim divines than for the real spirit of Islam.

It could be said of the *Durbars* of Akbar and Shahjehan that they were neither Hindu *Durbars* nor Muslim *Durbars,* but were purely Indian *Durbars.* The same could not be said of Aurangzeb's *Durbar.* Hindus felt proud of Akbar and of Shahjehan as much as the Muslims did. This was not quite possible in the case of Aurangzeb who had stopped the celebration at the Imperial *Durbars* of Hindu festivals like Dusshera, Diwali, Raksha Bandhan and Shivaratri in which the Emperor of India himself used to participate since the days of Akbar the Great. Such joint celebrations at the Imperial *Durbar* became legendary in the reign of Aurangzeb.

Several tar-sighted people in the country, who had been conversant with the previous beneficial currents of national solidarity, resented this trend and tried to resist retrogression. They saw that the policy followed by Aurangzeb was bound to disintegrate the newly knit nation and lead it to ruin. They tried to advise Aurangzeb in the matter. In 1678, when Aurangzeb wanted to revive and re-impose the financially insignificant yet nationally controversial tax called Jazia, which had been abolished by Akbar, Maharaja Sawai Jai Singh said to Aurangzeb:

> "God is not the God of Muslims only. He is the God of all human beings. To Him Hindus and Muslims are all the same. To show any disrespect towards Hindu religious customs or feelings cannot but be contrary to the wishes of the Almighty God." (*Rise of the Maratha Power* by M. G. Ranade, p. 81)

Aurangzeb, however, paid no need to such earnest advice. Naturally, Rajputs, Marathas, Sikhs and other Hindu Rajas and

Maharajas rose up one after another against Aurangzeb. Just as Aurangzeb gathered to his side narrow-minded elements and forces, similarly some Rajputs, Marathas and Sikhs took the help of Hindu narrow-mindedness in support of their opposition. The country was divided into two mutually hostile camps. Within a few years, the fruits of the great and noble efforts made by men like Kabir and Akbar appeared irretrievably lost and the centuries-old national integration movement came to a halt. Aurangzeb was strong, temperate and self-disciplined. It was mainly due to the strength acquired by the Mughal Empire during the period from Babar to Shahjehan that enabled Aurangzeb to quell the rebellions which raised their heads in various directions around him throughout his life. But the Empire which had been founded on the well-being and the goodwill of all its subjects could now be maintained only with the help of the sword. Unfortunately, Aurangzeb's reign lasted a long time. It gave narrowness on either side additional strength and routed the forces and elements working for human equality, liberalism, love and national unity. The Mughal Empire began to disintegrate just about the end of Aurangzeb's rule. The decline of the one and only paramount political power in India sowed the seeds of the ultimate ruin of the country's industries, commerce, literature, peace and prosperity.

After Aurangzeb

It is not improbable that after Aurangzeb's death, the country might have realised its mistake and counteracted the mischief resulting therefrom. If that had happened, the country would have retaken the path which it had followed before Aurangzeb and which had led to increased unity, peace and prosperity. The country did try to do so to a very large extent. The Jazia tax had been abolished only a few days after its reimposition during Aurangzeb's reign itself. Several successors of Aurangzeb also abandoned Aurangzeb's narrow policies and gave proof of their wisdom, liberalism and broad-mindedness. The celebrations of Dusshera and Raksha Bandhan at the Delhi *Durbar* were enthusiastically renewed. The Emperor Shah Alam announced that Shivaji's successor, the Peshwa of Poona was the Vakil (representative) of the Empire in that part of the country. The Emperor also appointed Mahadji Sindhia as the Subedar (Viceroy) for Delhi and Agra and as Chief Administrator of Delhi itself, with the title of "Farzand Jigarband" (dearly beloved son of the Emperor). Akbar Shah, the son of Shah Alam, conferred the title of "Raja" on Ram Mohan Roy, the founder of the Brahmo Samaj and sent him to England as the trusted representative of the Delhi Emperor himself. Innumerable savings and doings of the last Emperor Bahadur Shah can be cited in proof of the fact that Bahadur Shah was a staunch advocate of Hindu-Muslim unity in all fields and was himself a believer in *Sufism* which was the religion of the Centre.

The reaction of this broad and beneficial policy followed at the centre of the Empire soon became distinctly visible in the provinces also. Till after the Battle of Plassey in 1757, the Muslim Subedars of Bengal appointed Hindus as their Deewans in the largest provinces under them. There was not the slightest discrimination between Hindus and Muslims in the treatment meted out to either at the Subedar's *Durbar.* The most trusted follower of Siraj-ud-daula was Raja Mohan Lal, who sacrificed his life in trying to defend Siraj-ud-daula at the Battle of Plassey. Mir Jafar insisted upon appointing Maharaj Nand Kumar as his Deewan in place of the Muslim Deewan Raza Khan. When Mir Jafar died, Nand Kumar brought the holy Ganges water from a Hindu temple and with his own hands gave the last bath to the dead with that water. Exactly similar were the conditions prevailing at the *Darbars* of Ranjit Singh, Holkar, Sindhia, Haider Ali and Tipu Sultan. The famous Maratha statesman, Nana Fadnavis, used to call Haider Ali his "right arm" and the two were as close to each other as real brothers. We have described in this book at the proper place how Haider Ali's policy in these matters was quite as liberal and broadminded and practically the same as that of Akbar the Great. Jagadguru Shankaracharya of Shringeri Math and Tipu Sultan had very affectionate relations with each other. Under the Muslim Nawabs of Oudh, most of the bigger Taluqdars (estate-holders with ruling powers) and important ministers were Hindus and the *Durbar* at Lucknow was always deeply coloured with liberalism, unity and love and regard for each other. A number of other similar instances can be cited from the history of that period. There can be no doubt that India, if she had been given a fair opportunity, would soon have recovered from the evil effects of the mistakes of one man, Aurangzeb, and would have regained her former glory resulting from mutual trust, love and unity.

It was unfortunate for India that, just at the time when the evil effects of Aurangzeb's mistakes were still fresh, and when the Central paramount power at Delhi had become weak on account of those very mistakes, another political power appeared on the Indian stage. This new power saw clearly that its greatest interest lay in this that the mutual mistrust between Hindus and Muslims, resulting from the said mistakes and their other evil consequences, should be kept alive and perpetuated. The interests of the intruder were obviously and in every way quite the opposite of the real interests of India and of the Indian people. This outside power took the fullest advantage of the then confused and disorganized state of the country and of India's consequent prevailing weakness for promoting its own interests and for consolidating itself in the country.

Advent of the British

We have drawn above a comparative picture of the conditions prevailing in India and in England at that time. We have also described the arrival of the British in India. A detailed description of the doings and activities of the British in India for over a hundred years, based upon the statements and writings of authoritative Britishers themselves, will be found later in the pages of this book.

Until the days of Aurangzeb, the position of British traders in India was very nearly the same as that of the vendors of asafoetida from Kabul or of the hawkers of Shilajeet and other similar drugs from Tibet about the beginning of the 20th century. The short-sighted policy of Aurangzeb gave birth to a number of small rival independent states in various parts of India and weakened the Central paramount power of Delhi. Finally it turned back those beneficial currents of mutual goodwill, friendship and love between the Hindus and the Muslims, which, for about 300 years since the time of Kabir, had been continuously working to take the country forward towards abiding national unity, prosperity and happiness. The new enemies of the country got an open field for their intrigues and machinations.

The intrigues of the East India Company in Madras and Bengal started within a few years of Aurangzeb's death and gradually culminated, fifty years later, in the Battle of Plassey. Naturally it was in the interests of the British that the anarchical conditions of the Indian life be strengthened and perpetuated in every possible way. It was also in their interest to see that the beneficial currents of national unity which had received a setback during Aurangzeb's regime did not receive new life.

Reasons for the Success of the Britishers

A serious question which now arises before us is, what were the causes on account of which the more civilized, the more cultured and even the more powerful Indian people again and again fell victim to the intrigues of the less civilized, less cultured and less powerful Britishers of those days? This question will naturally present itself to the mind of every reader of this book. In fact, it is one of the most serious questions of history.

The far-sighted French Commander Dupleix was the first to discover that the sentiments of 'nationalism' and 'patriotism', as understood by the Western people, were practically non-existent in the minds of the Indians of those days. According to Dupleix, it was quite natural and easy for Europeans to make Indians fight amongst themselves and it was thus that India lost her freedom. Dupleix was undoubtedly right to an extent. But we shall have to go deeper into the matter. The English historian, Col. Malleson, says that one of the weaknesses of Indian national character which led them to subjugation was their "... trusting and faithful nature ..." (*The Decisive Battles of India,* Chapter I).

Col. Malleson's statement is nearer the actual truth than that of Dupleix.

In this connection, the first thing we should remember is that for a less civilized people to conquer and subjugate a more civilized people is by no means a new phenomenon in history. The history of the world tells us that many more-civilized nations have become victims of conquest and subjugation by nations less civilized than themselves. In Europe, the Gauls and the vandals who sallied forth from the north and from the east to invade and conquer the vast Roman Empire and shattered it to pieces forever were far less civilized than the Romans. The Tatars and the Mughals who, some fifteen hundred years ago, sallied forth from East and Central Asia and devastated the glorious Empires of Baghdad and Iran were absolutely uncivilized compared with the Arabs and the Iranians of those days. It was the uncivilized peoples of Central Asia who invaded and destroyed the civilized and prosperous Greek Empire of those days. The subjugation of Indians by a nation which was, at that time, less civilized than themselves was only another incident of this kind. This strange phenomenon may be due to three main causes. Firstly, progress in civilization generally breeds habits of living in comfort on account of which the people lose that reckless adventurism which characterises people of lesser civilizations. Secondly, more civilized people cannot utilize their animal powers and animal propensities to the extent to which less civilized people can on account of the development of moral and more human considerations among the former. Thirdly, victory in warfare depends generally on the degree of violence one can commit and it is not necessary that more civilized people may also possess greater means of committing violence than a less civilized people.

Three Main Causes of India's Subjugation by the British

We can clearly discern three main causes of India's disaster at the time, namely:

(1) The feeling of differentiation between persons who belong to one's country and those who belong to another country, which we term as the sentiment of nationalism in these days, was practically foreign to the cosmopolitan Indian mind of those times. Thus the Indian mind was since time immemorial cosmopolitan in the literal sense of that word.

We have stated above that politically there was no strong central power in India at the beginning of the 18th century. A number of big and small "powers" were then desirous of achieving supremacy over others and were busy in efforts to attain it. The Hindus and the Muslims were also in a way falling apart from each other, here, there and everywhere. Under these conditions a third outside power appeared to some people in the country as rather an impartial mediator. Till then Indians had had no bitter experience at the hands of any outsider coming to India, with the exception of a few, like Mahmud of Ghazni or Nadir Shah who left India only after a few days of massacre and plunder. We have shown above that all other invaders till then had invariably made India their home in every sense and had begun to take their full share in the progress and prosperity of the Indian people as a whole. Under these circumstances, the differentiation between people of one's own country and those of any other country could have no special significance for the Indian people. The latter's religious and moral traditions and ideals too could not allow the growth of such a feeling in their minds. Naturally, therefore, they treated the European incomers from across the seas with the same courtesy, love and regard with which they had been treating people in their own country. It thus became quite easy for the British to take advantage of the situation created by the fights for supremacy between Indian rulers, by siding now with one and now with another, and sometimes even by egging on, through their own intrigues, one ruler to fight another for such supremacy.

(2) India's trade at that time both internal and external was several times greater in volume than that of England. But even so, the high position then given to trade and commerce

in the life of European countries, particularly in that of the Britishers, had never been given in India's social life. The English were a nation of traders. They were called by Napoleon "a nation of shopkeepers". The highest in English nobility had their shares in trading companies. As we have already shown, even the Queen of England did not regard it as *infra dig* for herself to own a few shares in a trading venture of a dubious character, like the slave-trade and earn a few thousand guineas every year through it. On the contrary, no Raja or Nawab or landlord in India ever took any part in any trade or commerce, nor did any of those who were connected with any royal *Darbars* have any share in any commercial concern. To earn money through trade or commerce was always considered something low in Indian social life, and since ancient times, had been relegated to a particular class of people. Even agriculture was regarded as a higher and nobler occupation than trade or commerce. Therefore, it was impossible for any Indian ruler to visualise at the time or foresee the political consequences for the country of British trade with India.

At the same time, every Indian ruler always deemed it his bounden duty to provide full security and all facilities to every trader and to help and encourage, as far as possible, all trade and commerce in his kingdom. In the accounts of the reigns of all Indian rulers, big or small, one fact can invariably be noted. It is this that every one of them always took great pains to see that no trader in his realm ever suffered any loss. That was the reason why the Mughal Emperor, Shahjehan, true to the traditions of Asian monarchs, most liberally and generously provided such facilities and gave such concessions to British traders to reside and carry on their trade in the country as no modern ruler of any country in the world would ever dream of providing to traders of any foreign country. The Indian Emperor could never even imagine that his royal generosity would one day prove to have sown the seeds of the ruin of India's trade and industries and would ultimately prove to have been the death-warrant even of the political freedom of India.

The camouflaging of political intrigues and objectives under cover of trade and commerce was something which Indians had never experienced before in thousands of years of their history and which, therefore, could not even be imagined by any Indian ruler at the time. The Emperor Aurangzeb is considered to have been one of the most astute and relentless Emperors of India. Yet, it was Aurangzeb who, when the English Company petitioned to him for the purpose, made a grant of three villages, viz. 'Kali Kata', 'Soota Mati' and 'Govindpur' to the Company as a Jagir, for the construction of a Kothi or business house for purposes of trade with this country. Shortly afterwards, the British traders began to fortify the so-called business house and keep an army there. The local officials complained to Aurangzeb about it. Aurangzeb could had he so desired have stopped the fortification and all the rest with a single order, or he could have easily turned out the British from India on that occasion. But he did not do so. On the contrary, he reprimanded his own officials who had made the complaint and said to them:

> "It is possible that my Indian subjects in the neighbourhood have, out of jealousy, picked up a quarrel with the Firangies. Why should not the poor Firangies make all possible arrangements for their own protection? These outsiders have come from a far-off country and are very hard-working. I shall not interfere in this matter." (*Our Empire in Asia* by Torrens, pp. 14, 15)

Nor had the large Indian commercial community ever before had any bitter experience of any kind at the hands of any foreigners, traders or invaders. The Indian traders had never suffered any loss on account of their contact with traders from any outside country. On the contrary, close contacts between the traders from various countries had always proved beneficial to both sides. It was, therefore, impossible for the Indian commercial community even to think of combining, either in an effort to counteract the political and other intrigues of the East India Company or to have the latter expelled from the country. Let us remember that it was this very Indian commercial community which ultimately suffered the greatest loss on account of the doings of the East India Company. On the other hand, English traders of those days had by that time acquired sufficient experience of ways and means by which they had succeeded in ruining the trade and industries of Ireland and Scotland, both so adjacent to England. So much so that eventually even Scotland had to protect her trade and industries from these destructive onslaughts of the English by enacting the Bill of Security.

(3) Indians had never before any reason for distrusting the pledged word of any foreigner. In India, treaties and royal proclamations had always been deemed sacred and before the arrival of Europeans in Asia, treaties and proclamations made by Asiatic monarchs and rulers were by and large made in perfect good faith. In fact, the character of the English and the Indians of those days differed widely in this respect. The Marathas were then considered to be the cleverest politicians in India. The Marathas invaded Bengal several times. And yet Aliverdi Khan, the Muslim Subedar of Bengal, declared that "the Marathas never committed any breach of any of the treaties entered into by them". During the first hundred years of political relationship between the English and the Indian rulers, perhaps there was not a single occasion on which any Indian ruler had committed a breach of any treaty entered into by him with the English. The fact is that the main cause of the misfortunes of many Indian rulers in those days was that they scrupulously observed the terms of their treaties with the East India Company, even when doing so was obviously detrimental not only to their own interests but also to the best interests of the country itself. Innumerable instances in support of this statement of ours will be found in the pages of this book. On the contrary, concerning the observance or non-observance of the terms of their treaties by the British, Sir John Kaye, the well-known English historian, who had

been Secretary in the Political and Confidential Branch of the India Office in London, writes as follows:

> "It would seem as though the British Government claimed to itself the exclusive right of breaking through engagements. If the violation of existing covenants ever involved, *ipso facto,* a loss of territory, the British Government in the East would not now possess a rood of land between the Brahmaputra and the Indus." (*The Calcutta Review,* Vol. I, p. 219)

Edmund Burke, while impeaching Warren Hastings before the British Parliament, declared: "There is not a single treaty entered into by the British with anyone in India, which they (the British) did not subsequently violate." (*The Impeachment of Warren Hastings* by Edmund Burke).

Difference in the Character of the Two

There are many big and small incidents connected with the relations between Indians and the British in India which bring out the great difference between the character of the two in this matter. It will not be out of place here to give a few such instances. During the battles between Haider Ali and the British, it happened several times that Haider Ali set free vanquished British soldiers and officers on the latter's undertaking not to fight again against him anywhere for at least the next twelve months. But shortly after this, the same British soldiers or officers were seen fighting against Haider Ali in some battle at some place or other in clear violation of their pledged word. On the other hand, Haider Ali invariably kept his word under all circumstances. Once while after having defeated the British at a number of places, Haider Ali was advancing in the territory then in British possession, the British sent an emissary to him to settle terms of peace. Haider Ali promised the envoy that he would talk about the terms of peace on reaching the gates of Madras. Victorious Haider Ali fulfilled the promise he had given to the British envoy. Negotiations were started and victorious Haider Ali agreed to the terms of a peace treaty with the vanquished British. In the battles fought in the territory of Oudh during the War of 1857, we find countless instances of Oudh Taluqdars and Zamindars, who had in their territories openly led the War of Independence, but who had given shelter in their forts and palaces to terror-stricken British, men, women and children, and at the request of those unfortunate people, had even provided them with boats to take them to places of safety in Allahabad and Banaras. But shortly after, those very Englishmen came back to Oudh and fought against their erstwhile protectors and benefactors who had given them shelter only a few months earlier. We may not give here any more instances of this kind. The reader will find any number of them in the pages of this book.

Even among those Indians who now and then gave evidence of treason or treachery to their own country, there were probably one who did not keep their word with the British up to the last.

The truth is that if the history of Europe during the Middle Ages and in the subsequent century is closely studied, it will be found that the sentiments of so-called "patriotism" and narrow "nationalism" in Europe owe their origin to the peculiar social forces then acting on that continent. In the Europe of the Middle Ages the relations between the landlords and the tenants, and between the rich and the poor, continued to be so very strained for a thousand years, that it was quite natural for the discrimination between one group and another or between one class and another to become deeply rooted in the people's mind. Religious fanaticism and prejudices also prevailed in Europe for centuries and helped the growth of the above-mentioned narrow sentiments. Besides, the existence of a large number of small countries, each suffering from acute scarcity of food and clothing and economic rivalries between classes and classes added to the increasing feeling of discrimination between one's own countrymen and outsiders or foreigners.

On the other hand, at no time in the history of India for 2000 years had ever arisen or existed any such causes of social disruption. If now and then there were wars between the rulers of various provinces or States or if there were a few short-lived invasions of the country from outside, none of such incidents produced any lasting effect on the social, industrial, agricultural or economic life of millions of people living in the country or on their mutual relationship, happiness and prosperity.

There can be no doubt that the modern conception of nationalism is the product of struggles born of short-sighted self-interests among SQ-called modern nations. It is true that this feeling of nationalism does, to an extent, raise the individual and lead people to sacrifice their personal interests and even their lives for the good or betterment of the entire nation. But this feeling of nationalism can at best be regarded only as a necessary evil at a particular stage of human evolution. Already, in the second half of the twentieth century, this feeling of nationalism has proved and is proving one of the greatest obstacles in the way of human unity and human brotherhood which are today the most cherished and accepted goal of all our human endeavour on this planet. Whatever it be, there was no ground for the development of this sentiment in the hearts of the Indian people before the coming of the British to this country. That is why Indians of those days made practically no difference between a person of their own country and one from outside, that is, a foreigner.

Therefore, if we look at the whole history of those days rather coolly and impartially, we shall find that the crime of most of those Indians who, during the hundred years of the East India Company's domination over this country, now and then sided with the Britishers against their own country and countrymen, was no greater than the crime of any Indian who, in the struggles for supremacy between Indian rulers, sided now with the one and now with the other. That was the reason why most of these so-called "traitors" scrupulously fulfilled the treaties they made with or the pledges they gave to the representatives of the East India Company.

History clearly shows that, with all their shortcomings, Indians as a rule kept their word, with possibly a few exceptions. On the other hand, unhesitating violation of their treaties by the Company's representatives was the rule to which there were perhaps few exceptions. Yet in spite of their experience of repeated and deliberate violations of their treaties by the British, Indians always trusted the word of the British, all through from 1757 to 1857.

The history of those hundred years also shows that as far as bravery and efficiency in warfare are concerned, Indians were in no way inferior to the British of those days. Colonel Malleson in his book, *The Decisive Battles of India*, has clearly admitted that of the numberless battles fought between the British and the Indians from 1757 to 1857, there was not even one in which the British army was on one side and the Indian army on the other and in which the British had won a victory. There were many battles of this type, but in all such battles the British invariably suffered a defeat. Whenever the British won a battle, it was always a battle in which a section of the Indian army went over to the side of the British and fought against their own countrymen. It is an incontrovertible though shameful fact, that the British did not conquer India with their sword, but that Indians themselves conquered their country with their own sword and handed it over to the British. Enough facts in support of the above statement will be found by the reader in almost every chapter of this book.

Our Decline and Fall

Be that as it may, we have now to understand the sad fact of our country's steady decline during those two fateful centuries, due to our own repeated mistakes and persistent shortcomings. The country which only two hundred years before was considered to be the most prosperous and most powerful country in the world came, after the end of those two centuries, to be regarded as the poorest, the weakest and the most helpless country in the world. In a country in which only one hundred and fifty years ago there was not a single man or woman in any village who did not know how to read and write, the percentage of illiterates reached the figure of ninety-three at the beginning of the twentieth century. The country, which, upto the beginning of the 19th century, was considered to be the most advanced in arts and industries, with possibly the single exception of China, and which supplied cloth and other necessities of life to more than half the then civilized world including England and France, became dependent on other countries for its own necessities of life including cloth to cover its nakedness. All these matters will be dealt with in detail at appropriate places in this book.

But much greater than all these evils which political subjugation can inflict on any country is the loss of character of the people of the subjugated country. The well-known American sociologist, Professor E. A. Ross, writes:

> "Subjugation to a foreign yoke is one of the most potent causes of the decay of national character." (*Principles of Sociology*, pp. 132–33)

Describing the character of the Indians of his time, the Greek historian Arrian says:

> "They are remarkably brave, superior in war to all other Asiatics; they are remarkable for simplicity and integrity; so reasonable as never to have recourse to a law-suit and so honest as neither to require locks to their doors nor writings to bind their agreements. No Indian was ever known to tell an untruth." (*ibid,* pp. 132–33)

It is very distressing to compare the character of the Indians of those bygone days with the character of the Indians of the 20th century, even after two decades of independence. Referring to such a comparison and illustrating his point with similar examples from the history of Egypt and that of Greece under similar circumstances, Professor E. A. Ross says:

"... Alien domination has a blighting effect upon the higher life of the people of India ....." (*ibid,* pp. 132–33)

There can be no doubt that during those two centuries this ancient country moved steadily towards mental, moral and material degradation which the country is finding it difficult to overcome even now.

INDIA REGAINING HER INDEPENDENCE AND OUR FUTURE

India's struggle for regaining her independence began long before Mahatma Gandhi appeared on the scene. Efforts in this direction began as soon as the people felt that they were under a foreign yoke. The first question that arises in this connection is the fixing of the date on which India actually came under British domination and thus of the period for which she remained under foreign domination.

Up to 1757, not a single rood of Indian soil was, in any sense, under the rule of the British or any foreign power. After the defeat of Siraj-ud-daula on the field of Plassey, some administrative rights, like that of collecting Government revenue in certain parts of the country, or rather the task of doing so on behalf and in the name of the Mughal Emperor at Delhi, were entrusted to the British merchants of the East India Company by the Delhi *Durbar* itself. It may further be remembered that up to the year 1842, the British in India acknowledged the Mughal Emperor of Delhi as their Emperor and proclaimed themselves as the "loyal and faithful subjects of the Delhi Emperor". No doubt, the East India Company had begun to mint its own coins in areas partially administered by it. Yet on all coins of the East India Company was engraved the name of the Delhi Emperor as the Emperor of the entire country. A British Governor-General resided in Calcutta as the Chief Administrator of the areas then under the quasi-administration of the East India Company. But in the official seal of every British Governor-General of India were engraved the words: "Fidvi-i-khas Badshah-i-Delhi", i.e., "The special servant of the King of Delhi". Thus legally and constitutionally, the position of the East India Company or of the British Governor-General in India was even lower than that of any Indian ruler then administering any part of the country, under the suzerain authority and in the name of the Emperor at Delhi; e.g., the Nawab Wazir of Oudh or the Nizam of Hyderabad or the Peshwa of Poona or the Maharaja Sindhia of Gwalior.

After the death of Emperor Shah Alam in 1806, on account of the growing weakness of the Delhi *Durbar* and of the apathy, the inexperience and the politically disorganised condition of the people of the country, the British in India began to show indifference and sometimes even lack of courtesy towards the then Emperor Akbar Shah and later towards his successor Bahadur Shah. This was but a natural consequence of the conditions prevailing in the country in the second quarter of the 19th century. Yet such indifference and lack of courtesy on the part of the foreigners gave a rude shock to both the princes and the people of India and opened their eyes to the danger ahead. That is how in 1857 both the princes and the people made a concerted effort under the flag of the Emperor Bahadur Shah to drive out the foreign intruders from the country. We have described in this book at the proper place the causes, the course, and the reasons of the failure of the Indian War of Independence of 1857. The movement did fail in a sense, yet it was the forerunner and laid the foundations of India's final fight for independence under the unique leadership of Mahatma Gandhi which actually freed the country from foreign domination in 1947.

It was on November 1, 1859, after the suppression of the movement of 1857, that the reins of the country's Government formally passed from the hands of the last Mughal Emperor Bahadur Shah to the hands of Victoria, the then Queen of England, who, since that date began to be called the "Empress of India". Thus legally and constitutionally, it was on November 1, 1859, after the forcible arrest and deportation of Bahadur Shah, that India for the first time came under British rule. In constitutional law, it was a successful revolt and a *coup d'etat* by a rebellious group against its acknowledged suzerain.

After full eighty-eight years of foreign domination India regained her independence in 1947. Eighty-eight years or even one hundred and eighty-eight, if we count from the Battle of Plassey, are hardly a very long period, specially in the history of a country of hoary antiquity like India.

We must also remember that efforts for regaining independence never ceased during all those eighty-eight years of foreign rule. Only 13 years after 1859, i.e., in 1872, occurred the great

Kuka rebellion of the Punjab, under the leadership of Guru Ram Singh of the Namdhari Sikhs, in which thousands were arrested from various parts of the Punjab, packed in special railway trains and deported towards Bengal for the crime of trying to free their country from foreign domination. Nobody yet knows the fate of those brave fighters for India's independence. Nobody yet knows whether they were all murdered and buried somewhere in the Sundarbans or drowned in the Bay of Bengal. Their leader Guru Ram Singh was deported to Rangoon and breathed his last in the same house in which the Emperor Bahadur Shah had died a few years earlier, both of them captives of the British.

It must be mentioned that the movement of 1872 under Guru Ram Singh was also a non-violent movement like that under Mahatma Gandhi. Guru Ram Singh advocated the driving out of the British from India exactly as Mahatma Gandhi did later through non-violent non-co-operation. Guru Ram Singh advocated and preached the boycott of British schools and colleges, the boycott of British courts, the boycott of British services and even the boycott of British railways and post offices. His workers and followers utilised other means of transportation and conveyance for spreading their message from city to city and from village to village. The movement was successfully suppressed and yet it was, in many respects, the forerunner and even the inspirer of Mahatma Gandhi's movement, less than 50 years later.

Almost immediately after the failure of the Kuka rebellion came the movement of the Mujahideens in parts of U. P. and Bihar under the leadership of the famous Muslim divines, Shah Waliullah and Shah Azizullah of Delhi. It was an armed movement. Year after year thousands of fighters for India's freedom journeyed from various villages and towns of Northern India to the North-Western Frontier of the country, somehow procured necessary arms and fought a losing battle, trying to turn out the British from the country. Only faith in the righteousness and ultimate victory of their cause sustained them. The last of these Mujahideens or their sympathisers was a Moulvi of Bareilly who was hanged in 1880 for the crime of being a lover of his country's freedom.

Only five years after this, that is, in 1885, was founded the Indian National Congress. The Congress at that time was a body working for the so-called constitutional advancement of India "within the British Empire". But it was a movement in which Indians of all communities, Hindus, Muslims, Christians, Parsees and others joined. Side by side with the Indian National Congress, terrorist revolutionary movements, aiming directly at the turning out of the British from India, continued almost all through that period in various parts of the country. We may not here go into their detailed history.

The British suppressed all these efforts through the use of violence at their command as also through fomenting Hindu-Muslim dissensions, setting the two major communities of India, the Hindus and the Muslims, against each other. It was with this last objective that Bengal was partitioned into two, West Bengal and East Bengal, i.e., Hindu Bengal and Muslim Bengal, in 1905. Simultaneously with the "Partition of Bengal" were started two separate organisations, the Hindu Mahasabha at Lahore and the Muslim League at Calcutta, to counteract the influence of the Indian National Congress for India's national unity.

Then came the great anti-Partition movement of 1905 under the overall leadership of Lokmanya Bai Gangadhar Tilak. It roused the whole country politically as no movement had done since 1857. The sixteenth of October 1905 was the day on which Bengal was partitioned. On every October 16 after that, hundreds of thousands of Hindus and Muslims tied *Rakhis* round each other's wrists with the words "Bhai Bhai Ek Hain, Bhed Nahin Bhed Nahin", which means "We, Hindus and Muslims are brothers, we are one, there is no difference between us." The movement gained strength. The "Partition of Bengal" had to be annulled in 1911. Bengal was again one, only to be partitioned once again, at the time of India's attaining independence in 1947.

Last came the great and unique movement for independence under Mahatma Gandhi's leadership. Mahatma Gandhi appeared on India's political horizon in the year 1915. It was just the time when, partly as a result of six years' incarceration of Lokmanya Tilak and the retirement of Shri Aurobindo Ghosh from political life, political India was passing through a period of comparative frustration. Every movement for freedom till then had some appreciable achievement to its credit. Every such movement also appeared to take the country some steps forward on the road to liberty. Yet none of them, after the great movement of 1857, appeared to lead the country to the cherished goal of freedom from foreign domination. None could develop that mass upsurge, mass organisation and mass preparation for sacrifice which were necessary for driving out the foreign rulers from India.

At the very start of his movement, Gandhiji tried to impress the following two things upon the minds of his followers and also upon the minds of the people at large.

Firstly, that neither on account of impatience nor in undue haste in trying to banish foreign rule from the country should we lose sight of or deviate from those high fundamental principles of morality which from the very foundation of human social life everywhere; secondly, that we should have complete faith in the correctness of our cause and should never allow despair or frustration to obstruct our onward march towards the cherished goal of independence.

The very first India-wide campaign for independence which Mahatma Gandhi led, *i.e.,* the movement of non-violent non-co-operation against the British, started in 1919, produced that unprecedented mass upsurge throughout the country, from the Himalayas to Cape Comorin and from the North-Western Frontier to Assam, which led Lord Reading, the then British Governor-General of India, as early as 1921, publicly to declare at Calcutta: "His (Gandhiji's) programme came within an inch of success ...... I stood puzzled and perplexed."

We have already shown above that India's having come under foreign domination for some time was by no means a unique phenomenon in history. We have said that England herself, for full four hundred years, had been ruled by the Romans, that for long centuries after that the Normans ruled over the British Isles, that the Arabs ruled over practically the whole of Southern and South-western Europe, including Spain, for full seven centuries and that the Mughals had ruled over European Russia for full four centuries. If we carefully read the past history of the present-day western countries, we will also find that much longer time was taken by the English people in trying to throw off the yoke of the Romans or the Normans from their necks, or by the Irish people in freeing themselves from the yoke of the English people, or by the Americans in freeing themselves from the British yoke, or by the people of Italy in liberating themselves from Austrian domination, or by the Russians in freeing themselves from Mughal domination or even from the tyrannical rule of their own Czars than was taken by India in freeing herself from foreign domination.

Soon after the start of Gandhiji's movement, it began to appear that British rule in India was already like a gigantic-looking tree, with a mighty trunk, branches spread far and wide, and even thick foliage here and there, and yet whose roots had already been sapped by internal as well as external weaknesses, whose trunk had become hollow, as if through the action of white ants, and which, therefore, could any time get uprooted through the action of any strong gust of wind.

The above is not only the language of metaphor. The well-known British scientist and philosopher, Edward Carpenter, in his "Ode to England" describes the prevailing condition of his country in the following pithy lines:

> "Oh England, see thee dying before my eyes, Thy veins are choked with yellow dust."

Edward Carpenter, in these lines, evidently refers to the shortsighted greed for gold which then formed the chief characteristic of the ruling classes in England.

Even before the appearance of Mahatma Gandhi, some leaders of thought in India had begun to realise more and more the importance of defining those social and moral principles on which alone the struggle for independence of an ancient and civilised country like India should have been based. They had begun to realise that the narrow unmoral or anti-moral principles on which the newly-risen Western countries had founded their short-lived supremacy were already giving way. Low greed under cover of nationalism—"my country, right or wrong"—was already sapping the foundations of Western civilization. Even science was being prostituted for these low objectives.

The great Urdu poet Iqbal, addressing the people of the West, had prophetically cried out:

"Dayar-i-Maghrib ke rahne walo!
Khuda ki basti dukan nahin hai.
Khara jise turn samajh rahe ho,
Woh kal zar-i-kam-ayar hoga.
Tumhari tahzeeb apne khanjar se
Ap hi, khudkushi karegi.
Jo shakh-i-nazuk pe ashiyana
Bana, woh napaidar hoga."

It means:

"Oh! Ye! Dwellers of the Western realms!
This God's world is not a broker's shop.
The coin which you have taken as a genuine one,
Will tomorrow prove to have been a counterfeit one.
Your civilization will itself commit suicide
With its own dagger.
A nest built on a weak twig.
Will not stand for long."

Another well-known Urdu poet Akbar Illahbadi warned his own countrymen, saying:

"Bhoolta jata hai Europe Asmani Bap ko.
Woh khuda samjhe hue hai barq ko aur bhap ko.
Barq gir jaegi ek din or urh jaegi bhap,
Dekhna Akbar, samhale rakhna apne ap ko."

It means:

"Europe is gradually forgetting its Father in Heaven.
It has taken electricity and steam as its gods.
Electricity will fail one day, and steam will melt away.
Take care, Oh Akbar! that thou too mayest not melt away, along with these false gods of the Western world."

Mahatma Gandhi visualised the danger ahead more than anybody else and decided to give shape to his struggle for India's independence in the light of such timely warnings.

He saw that the entire European civilization of the day, in spite of its wonderful scientific achievements, its topheavy industries and skyscrapers, its organised capitalism, its economic and industrial imperialism over other nations, its colonialism and neo-colonialism, could not continue in real peace and prosperity even for two small centuries. Even towards the end of the 19th century, Europe was already a battle-ground between country and country, between one class and another in the same country and between herself and the rest of the world. Far-seeing and humanitarian thinkers like Rousseau, Mazzini and Marx had already started their search for a more equitable, more human and more abiding way of life. The First World War of 1914–1918 and its consequences gave a further impetus to European thought and movements in this direction. Russia under the Czars was supposed to be the most powerful imperialist country of the West at the time. Even when the First World War was still going on in 1917, the people of Russia began to move towards a juster social order and a more equitable way of life. Yet West European nations, somewhat more intoxicated with their easily-earned gains from less fortunate countries, still stuck to their wrong, unsocial and immoral ways. The danger of a second world war loomed large on the horizon. Mahatma Gandhi saw all this clearly and unmistakably.

Mahatma Gandhi saw that the principles on which ancient countries like India and China bad based their civilizations were of a much higher nature and had enabled the people of these countries to lead a life of comparatively greater peace and prosperity for much longer periods of time. Living on those high social and moral principles, these and other ancient countries had always acted as a blessing and never as a curse to other peoples and countries with whom they came into contact.

Gandhiji went further. He realized that higher religions and spiritual values which man discovered through his thousands of years of sojourn upon this planet could not be ignored. He realised that these values were as important for the future of humanity now as never before. He also saw how religion had, in recent centuries, been misinterpreted, misunderstood and even exploited for baser ends in India itself. He saw how religion, thus misunderstood and misinterpreted, had been one of the factors which brought India under foreign rule and sustained that rule for nearly two centuries. Therefore, one of the first things towards which he bent his efforts was the development of a synthetic outlook on religion, the realization of the basic unity of all religions of the world, of not only tolerance of each other but also right appreciation and equal respect and freedom for all. He realized that the importance which Europe had given to electricity and to low diplomacy leading to ever-increasing exploitation of man by man and of country by country and to principles like those of "divide and rule" should really be given to truth and nonviolence, to human equality and love for all, to the duty that we owe each other more than to the rights we claim from each other. He decided to give form and substance to his struggle for political independence in the light of these high principles.

Mahatma Gandhi saw that one of the principal causes of the decay of our national character, which gradually led to the establishment and continuance of Western domination of this country, in the eighteenth and nineteenth centuries, was our religious differences obstructing the unity of hearts of the people as against the foreign aggressor. He also saw that the remedy lay in our realising two fundamental truths of religious life in this world.

Firstly, that the essential truth of all religions is the same; in one form or another, they try to inculcate in us the same great principles of the unity of God and the brotherhood of man; they all teach us that we should all behave towards one another as members of a common human family. This is the essence of the teachings of all the great religions of the world. In India itself from the early writers of the *Upanishads* to our medieval saints and Sufis like Kabir, Dadoo and Nanak, whom we have already quoted earlier in this chapter, all have been preaching to us this common religion of humanity which is the core of all religions. Therefore, our first task lay gradually and steadily to move towards this one common religion of humanity or the religion of love for all and service of all.

Secondly, we had also to realise that the differences in various religions centred mainly round the language and the forms of worship and that such differences were the natural outcome of the prevailing conditions in which those various creeds were born and sustained. We have, therefore, to develop equal respect for all religions or what Mahatma Gandhi called "Sarva Dharm Samabhava".

In other words, while in every civilized country there must be complete freedom guaranteed to all to follow their own respective religions, their own customs and ceremonies, their own forms of worship, the State should make absolutely no distinction between the followers of one religion and those of another in matters of administration.

Mahatma Gandhi tried to inculcate in the minds of the people of various religions and creeds that spirit not only of tolerance of each other but also of equal respect for each other which produced scenes of national unity all over India, surpassing even the scenes of fraternization during the great national movement for independence in 1857. This was one of the main secrets of the success of Mahatma Gandhi's movement for emancipation from foreign domination. His preaching and practice against the caste system and his insistence upon the removal of untouchability in all forms also formed an essential part of his campaign for national integration and national independence.

Gandhiji also saw clearly that no foreign rule in any country whatsoever could either be established or continued without the co-operation of the ruled.

It was these considerations which gave birth to his movement of non-violent non-co-operation. His movement made a wonderful appeal to the minds of the vast masses of India, including men of all creeds and communities. The movement rapidly gained strength. Gandhiji had to go to jail. He had again to be released very soon. Movement followed movement.

The British had come to India mainly as traders. At the beginning of the century, the drain of wealth from India to England on account of British imports into India had assumed terrible proportions. As a result of Gandhiji's movement, various import associations in Bombay and other places cancelled all their orders for goods from Britain and declined to place further orders so long as the British Government did not settle things with Mahatma Gandhi. It was really a wonderful movement in which the rich capitalists of Bombay and the poor peasants of the villages—all equally participated.

After that there were several big and small Round Table Conferences in England as well as in India. Hundreds of thousands courted imprisonment in various forms of non-violent civil disobedience or satyagraha. More than twelve hundred citizens, including unarmed and peaceful men of all creeds and communities were shot dead in cold blood in Jallianwala Bagh alone. In the famous Qissa Khani Bazar of Peshawar batches of ten each, Pathan men and women, women mostly with babies in arms, crossed against the prohibitory order the line on both sides of which stood British soldiers with loaded rifles, and received bullets on their bare chests. Each batch of ten fell dead on the road. The thing went on till three hundred dead were counted and the soldiers refused to shoot any further. Thus, the movement went on in grim non-violent determination. The whole country was ablaze. No people on earth could possibly continue their domination over another under those circumstances and in 1947 India finally won her independence from foreign domination.

Thus, while every previous effort for India's independence brought the day of emancipation nearer, it was destined for the movement under Mahatma Gandhi, consistent with the highest moral and spiritual ideals of the country, to usher in the dawn of independence in India.

At the time of writing these lines (1967), full twenty years have passed since India got her independence. But it has sadly to be admitted that during this period India has not been able to remove some of the more serious grievances or lessen some of the pressing hardships of the vast masses of the people of the country. Not only this, it is also a painful fact that some of these grievances and hardships have considerably increased since independence. The reason is plain. Most of those upon whom fell the responsibility of administering the country after independence believe more in those Western economic, social and political ideals of life to which we have referred above and against which poets like

Iqbal and Akbar Illahbadi and most of all Mahatma Gandhi had warned us than in those higher moral and social ideals which Mahatma Gandhi tried to place before the nation. We are absolutely clear that our failures during these twenty years, so far as we have failed, are due to our having deviated from the path that Mahatma Gandhi had shown us and that our country's future peace, progress and prosperity depend mainly upon this one thing that, while learning as much as we can from other countries whose social and economic life is mainly based on moral considerations and as such is mass-oriented, we come back to the high moral, social, economic and political ideals placed before us by the Father of our Nation.

1

Europeans Arrive in India

Vasco da Gama and the Portuguese

The twenty-second of May, 1498 was a fateful day for India. It marked the arrival of the Portuguese sailor, Vasco da Gama, off Calicut on the Malabar coast. He was the first European to discover the sea-route to India round the Cape of Good Hope. The present Suez Canal was constructed only 370 years later.

The Hindu king of Calicut, known as the Zamorin (Samuri or sea-lord), gladly welcomed the Christians from across the seas and offered them warm hospitality.

The Portuguese petitioned the Samuri for permission to live and trade in India which was readily granted. Communications with Portugal began to improve and became more frequent. Two years after their arrival, the Portuguese put up a building at Calicut to house their trade activities. In the course of the next three years, the building was fortified with the permission of the unsuspecting Zamorin. A Portuguese army officer, Albuquerque, was appointed its Commander. Albuquerque gradually advanced northwards along the coast and in A.D. 1506 occupied Goa. The simple-minded Indians had no suspicions whatsoever about the real character and intentions of these foreigners. Things went on like this till A.D., 1510 when, it is said, there was some dispute between some officers of the king of Calicut and the Portuguese, who did not hesitate to use force. They set fire to the king's palace and sacked the capital town of Calicut, thus repaying the kind-hearted king who had liberally bestowed favours on them barely 12 years before!

Thus began a chain of events which during the next 300 years demonstrated the insidious efficiency with which a number of European flags followed trade in India and in some other unfortunate countries which happened to be more prosperous, cultured and peace-loving than the Europeans in quest of "fresh fields and pastures new" for their own aggrandisement. It must be remembered that at that time no European country enjoyed either the prosperity or the political power which it does today.

Nor was any non-Christian country outside Europe then ruled by a European Christian power.

We might cast a glance here at the India of that period. India as a whole was, till the middle of the 18th century, a completely independent country. In the spheres of knowledge, sciences, arts, education and public administration, it was one of the most advanced countries in the world. No European country at that time could claim an equal degree of development or progress in any of the different aspects of human culture. For centuries the most eagerly sought-after products of art and industry in European markets were those made in India, which was reputed to be fabulously rich. Arab and Persian traders of the day took Indian manufactures to European markets, and related accounts of the "glory that was Ind". Their listeners had before their eyes the proof of the veracity of these accounts. Naturally, those who valued gold above everything else were irresistibly drawn to the land of gold.

Till then the only trade route from India to Europe was by way of the Arabian Sea, the Persian Gulf, then overland to the Mediterranean ports of Venice and Genoa which were then Europe's biggest distributing and shipping centres. The Italians thus enjoyed the monopoly of handling imports from all over Asia. Their huge profits excited the envy of the North-Western European countries. The obvious way to a share in these profits was for them to discover a less hazardous, quicker and cheaper trade route to and from India. Portugal, Holland, England, France and, to some extent, Spain were the earliest countries to try to reach India by sea all the way. These efforts continued for over a hundred years. But the adventurers were handicapped by the paucity of the knowledge of world geography. Even the elementary knowledge of the four directions in relation to one another was then in its infancy in Europe. Some sailed to the North, others to the North-west or North-east or to the South, all in search of India. Most of the efforts failed and only resulted in the floundering of many ships and the loss of numerous lives. The best-known of these European adventurers was the famous Italian, Columbus, who was supported by the King of Spain. Columbus sailed from Europe towards the west and kept on sailing westwards in his quest for India. He sighted land and dropped anchor off the coast of America, which he believed then and for the rest of his life to be India. That is why the original inhabitants of America have since then been called Indians or "Red Indians". The first European to reach India all the way by sea was, in fact, Vasco da Gama as mentioned above.

The Portuguese in India

Within a hundred years or so of their arrival in India, the Portuguese had become masters of Calicut, Mangalore, Cochin, Ceylon, Div, the Island of Bombay and Negapattam. In addition, they had made such enormous fortunes in India as had astounded the peoples of other European countries.

Some factors in the Indian situation which helped the Portuguese may be mentioned. Politically and administratively India was then split up into numerous administrations, big and small, and there was no Central Government wielding authority over the whole country. The people too did not appear to have any idea of India as *one* country, or of its people as *one* nation. The ancient Hindu Empires had long been extinct and the Moghul Empire was still to be established. Although the Indians of those days knew how to manufacture guns and cannon, they were mostly averse to using them, because of their religious prejudices. This gave the Portuguese, who were experts in the use of firearms, a tremendous advantage. Lastly, the Indians of the day were ignorant of western diplomacy and, when faced with it, were completely at sea.

Two important features of the then Portuguese "trade" in India are also worthy of mention. Portuguese marauders systematically roamed the seas along the eastern and western coasts on a look-out for passing Indian ships which they seized and plundered with impunity. They also occasionally raided inhabited areas along the coast, plundered the inhabitants and, if opportunity offered, abducted men and women whom they turned into slaves. They also brought ship-loads of slaves from the coastal areas of Africa and sold them cheap in India, especially in towns which were under Portuguese control.

The Portuguese of those days were Christian fanatics who believed it to be their religious duty forcibly to convert to Christianity the people under them. A tribunal of the dreaded Inquisition was set up in Goa under whose orders their non-Christian Indian subjects were often burnt alive or otherwise put to death as heretics. That is why most of the Goans today are Christians.

About the beginning of the 17th century, the above-mentioned Portuguese activities began to spread out towards Bengal. But by then the political set-up in India had changed. The Moghul Empire had been firmly established and Shahjehan was on the Imperial throne at Delhi. Bengal was administered by a Subedar (governor) appointed by the Emperor. The Subedar promptly warned the Portuguese against their depredations, but they paid no heed. Shahjehan, thereupon, sent a military expedition against the Portuguese who were completely routed. Their fortified factories and premises were razed to the ground and their seagoing vessels were burnt down. The few survivors were taken prisoner and sent to Agra. This marked the beginning of the end of the Portuguese as a political power in India. Alfonzo de-Souza, the then (1545) Governor of Portuguese India, writes:

> "The Portuguese arrived in India with the cross in one hand and the sword in the other. But when they found abundant gold to be had for the picking, they put aside the cross to free the hand that had held it for filling their pockets with gold. Soon the pockets became too heavy with gold to be held by one hand only. They then threw away the sword too. Thus they became an easy prey to those who followed."

Enter the Dutch

The Dutch came to India towards the end of the 16th century. They had heard in Europe, from the Portuguese, glowing accounts of India's wealth and the fortunes that could be made there. In 1598 their ships began to arrive in India by way of Java. The Portuguese had snatched away the Arab traders' bread. Now the Dutch began to try to supplant the Portuguese. The Moghul Emperor permitted the Dutch not only to establish their trading posts in India but also to fortify them. Policut on the north and Sadras on the south (Madras of the present day) were thus fortified. In 1663 the Dutch had penetrated as far inland as Agra where they had a brewery. They also had business houses at Surat, Ahmedabad and Patna. Their activities then began to expand towards Bengal. In 1675 they established a trading post at Chinsurah. So long as the Dutch were content with amassing wealth, they were successful. Later on, however, they tried to establish their rule in India and so came into conflict with the more astute English, who had in the meanwhile also arrived in the country. The first military scuffle between them occurred in 1759, two years after the Battle of Plassey, when seven Dutch men-of-war suddenly appeared off Chinsurah. The English had by then taken root in Indian soil. Before the Dutch could touch Chinsurah, the English barred their way and with the help of the Nawab of Bengal repulsed them. After that Dutch trade with India declined and in 1805 the last vestige of Dutch rule was wiped off the country by the English who gave them Sumatra in exchange for both Chinsurah and Malacca.

The English Look Towards India

Portuguese trade with India had enhanced Lisbon's importance and prestige in the capitals of Europe. The English felt envious. A Bristol overseas trader first suggested to Henry VIII of England the initiation of a quest for a sea-route to India. For the next 50 years noted English sailors continued their fruitless efforts to reach India by sea, by sailing north-west from England. Ultimately, in 1578, the famous English sailor, Sir Francis Drake, found a clue. He had waylaid a Portuguese ship and whilst plundering it he had come across some navigation charts which were the first pointers the English had ever had about the sea-route to India.

In A.D. 1600, the well-known East India Company was formed under a Charter from Queen Elizabeth I. It is worth noting that in the Royal Charter the Company has been described as a "Society of Adventurers", that is, of people who were out for money and who were not scrupulous about the means they adopted to get it. The Directors of the company had at the very start decided "not to employ any gentleman in any place of charge" (Bruce's *Annals of the Hon'ble East India Company,* Vol. I, p. 128). They had petitioned the Queen that "we must be permitted to carry on our business through men like ourselves because if people even suspect that we would employ gentlemen then possibly many adventurous shareholders of the Company will withdraw their shares" *(Ibid).* This consideration was the guiding principle of the activities and policies of the English East India Company. During the 250 years of its existence, few, if any, of its members or employees could be called "gentlemen" by any stretch of the imagination.

First Englishman Arrives in India

Some 30 years after Sir Francis Drake had found the navigation charts in the plundered Portuguese ship, the first British ship the *Hector* reached Surat in India in 1608. It was captained by Captain Hawkins who was the first Englishman to set foot on Indian soil after having come by sea all the way. Hawkins had brought with him a letter from James I to the Moghul Emperor at Delhi, which he presented to Jehangir at Agra. The Moghul Empire of India at that time was far and away beyond and above comparison with the Kingdom of James I of England in every imaginable respect. Jehangir treated Hawkins with courteous hospitality.

The Portuguese were still in Jehangir's Court and tried very hard to poison his mind against the English but it did them no good. Their influence had begun to wane, yielding place to the English. In 1612, the English seized some Portuguese ships at Surat. The following year (6th February 1613) Jehangir gave permission to the English to construct a house at Surat for their trade. He also agreed to the permanent presence at his Court of an envoy of the English king. Sir Thomas Roe was the first envoy appointed by the King of England. He arrived in India in 1616 and during his tenure of office succeeded by courteous and humble behaviour in extracting from the Emperor many new concessions and facilities for his country's trade with India. The English were permitted to set up new trading houses at Calicut and Masulipattam. The English in India declared themselves to be the subjects of the Emperor of India. Indian Courts exercised jurisdiction over them in all civil and criminal matters including disputes arising between the English *inter se.* Later, however (1624), the Emperor granted the prayer of the English that they may be permitted to try criminal offences committed by any of their employees residing within their business premises. In this connection, we quote an English historian:

> "The Padishah, being a just man and wise, understood their needs, and yielded what they asked, little dreaming that the time would come, when, *from such root of little,* they would claim jurisdiction over his subjects and successors, and, as the penalty of resistance, decimate the one, and imprison the other for life as guilty of rebellion." (Torrens' *Empire in Asia,* pp. 10, 11)

It may be mentioned that Torrens wrote after the closing scenes of the 1857 movement, as a consequence of which the last Moghul Emperor was imprisoned for life.

Shahjehan and the English

Shahjehan expelled the Portuguese from Bengal and in 1634 permitted the English to trade in that Province. Five years later in 1639, the English set up their own trading house in Madras.

Till 1640, the English traders in Bengal, like the Indian traders, had to pay duty on their merchandise. Their ships were not allowed to come up to the Hooghly but had to stop and unload at Pipli, very much downstream. The English had thus to do all their trading at Pipli.

In 1640, a daughter of Shahjehan accidentally got scalded. An English doctor treated her. After the girl had recovered and the time came for rewarding her physician, the English doctor petitioned the Emperor to grant to the English traders in Bengal three new concessions, *viz.*:

(i) exemption of their merchandise from duty;
(ii) permission to bring the English ships right up to the Hooghly; and
(iii) permission to establish their trading houses all over Bengal.

The concessions were granted and in that very year the English established their business house at Calcutta. Shah Shuja was then the Subedar (Provincial Governor) of Bengal appointed by the Emperor. Following the latter's lead, the Subedar provided the English traders with every facility in establishing themselves firmly in Bengal.

In 1661 the King of England received as a dowry from the Portuguese king the island of Bombay, which was then only a small Portuguese settlement. In 1688, the East India Company purchased it from the King of England.

It was a common thing for the English traders in India in those days to seize and plunder any cargo vessel of any other nation on the open seas. They often kidnapped, tortured and even beat to death Indian or other European traders who undersold them and "... they made it a rule to whip to death or starve to death those of whom they wished to get rid .... to murder private traders" (Mill, Wilson's Note. Vol. I, Chap. II). Of their dealings with Indians, an English clergyman writes as follows:

> "As the number of adventurers increased, the reputation of the English was not improved. Too many committed deeds of violence and dishonesty .... the natives themselves were very square and exact to make good all their engagements ..." (*The English in Western India* by Rev. Philip Anderson, pp. 22,32)

As stated above, Surat was the first place in India where the English had landed and later established themselves. They had by now reached Bengal but their ways continued unchanged. According to the English historian, Wilson:

> "The English in Bengal were equally notorious for their quarrels ... The impression of the moral and social tone of the Company's servants in the Bay which has been left on the mind of Sir Henry Yule by his exhaustive study of the records of the time is certainly a dismal one." (C.R. Wilson's *Early Annals of the English in Bengal,* Vol. I, p. 66)

Aurangzeb and the English

It did not take long for the atrocities of the English to reach the ears of Aurangzeb. He immediately ordered their forcible expulsion from India and the confiscation of all their business houses and assets. The English were expelled from Surat, Vishakhapatnam and other places and their business houses and assets were seized. The island of Bombay was besieged. But the English traders there were crafty. They "stooped to the most abject submission" (Mill, Book I, Chap. V), fell at the feet of Aurangzeb and begged for mercy. They made full confession of their misdeeds and solemnly promised future good behaviour if their lives were spared by him. The ruse worked and Aurangzeb was moved to pity. In a fit of magnanimity he not only pardoned them but also ordered the restitution of their confiscated property. Later, in 1699, he even permitted them to construct and fortify some new business houses. During Aurangzeb's reign, his grandson, Azim Shah, was at one time the Subedar of Bengal. As such, Azim Shah gifted three villages on the river Hooghly to the East India Company as a *jagir.* These were Chhootanati, Calcutta and Gobindpur.

After some time news reached the Emperor that the English were constructing Fort William. His reaction is thus described by Torrens:

> "If he (the Moghul) was told of their planting stockade and putting a sort of fortification there, why should he trouble himself regarding it? Likely enough his native subjects around them were jealous and disposed to be quarrelsome. Why should not Firanghees defend themselves as best they might? Poor people! They had come a

> long way, and seemed to work hard—he would not interfere." (*Empire in Asia,* pp. 4–5)

After Aurangzeb, began the decline of the Moghul Empire. The English seized the opportunity. Their atrocities increased and became more frightful. A chain of new trading houses was gradually built up by the East India Company along the eastern and western sea-boards of India. Their trade continued to expand by leaps and bounds. The shareholders and the employees of the East India Company grew richer and richer by plundering the wealth of India. Exactly 50 years after the death of Aurangzeb was laid the foundation of British rule in Bengal, as will be related later.

Enter the French

The French were the last of the European nations to appear on the Indian stage with intentions similar to those of their predecessors. In 1664 a French company was formed on the lines of the English East India Company with the same aims and objects. The French established their trading houses in 1668 at Surat, in 1669 at Machchlipattam and in 1674 at Puducherry (Pondicherry).

The policy of the French in India was to please the local Indian rulers by every means in their power including fulsome flattery. The city of Pondicherry was then in the Carnatic State. The Nawab of the Carnatic, like other rajas and Nawabs in the South, was subordinate to the Subedar of the Deccan appointed by the Emperor at Delhi. Dost Ali Khan was then the Nawab of the Carnatic and Dumas the French representative at Pondicherry succeeded in winning the former's support.

The invasion of the Carnatic by the Marathas provided Dumas with an opportunity. He obtained the Nawab's permission to fortify Pondicherry and garrison it with 1200 European and 5,000 Indian soldiers under a European commandant to help the Nawab against the Maratha invaders. The Marathas were defeated with Dumas's help. The Emperor of Delhi conferred on Dumas, as a token of Imperial pleasure, the title of 'Nawab', with the military rank of 'Commander of two thousand horse'. The whole of the Pondicherry area now came under French administration.

In 1741 Dumas was succeeded by Dupleix. Dupleix was a very capable commander, and called himself 'Nawab Dupleix'. He was the first European in history to be inspired by the ambition of founding a European empire in India. He soon realised that as the various Indian rulers were then fighting one another, it was not difficult for a foreigner to gain political power in the country by helping one of them against the other. He also realised that it was not necessary to bring inforeign troops for the purpose. He saw that Indians made better soldiers than Europeans. They were zealously loyal to their officers and no ideas of nationalism affected that loyalty. They could be very easily trained and officered by Europeans. Dupleix knew how to take full advantage of all these factors. There was, however, one obstacle which he saw clearly, the rivalry of the English.

The English *versus* the French

The English and the French were then fighting in Europe. For about a hundred years Madras had been under the control of the English and was their principal trading centre in India. Dupleix resolved to snatch away Madras from the English. Dost Ali Khan had now been succeeded by Anwaruddin as Nawab of the Carnatic. Dupleix incited Anwaruddin against the English and assured him that he (Dupleix) would hand over Madras to him (Anwaruddin) after the English had been expelled from there. Under that pretext, Dupleix sent a naval expedition under a French commander, La Bourdonnai, for the conquest of Madras. La Bourdonnai took Madras but entered into a pact with the English to give it back to them in return for £40,000. Dupleix took no steps to keep his word with either the Nawab or the English. The disillusioned Nawab marched towards Madras with an army. Dupleix advanced to meet him. The two joined in battle near Madras on 4th November, 1746. Most of Dupleix's army was composed of Indian soldiers. Dupleix won. This was the first victory of a European commander over an Indian ruler. It raised the spirits of the French in India.

The English and the Nawab of the Carnatic now joined hands against the French. In 1748 the English attacked Pondicherry (the French stronghold) but Dupleix's troops repulsed them.

About this time a treaty between France and England was signed in Europe. One of its terms stipulated the return of Madras to the English. Thus ended Dupleix's hopes of expelling the English from the Carnatic. But Dupleix was not a man to be disheartened so easily. The rivalry between the French and the English continued. Each maintained an army in India, consisting mainly of Indian soldiers, and whenever there was a clash between any two Indian rulers, both joined in on opposite sides.

Battles in South India

The political situation in Southern India had deteriorated considerably because of warring factions amongst the Indian rulers there. Nazir Jung was the Subedar of the Deccan appointed by the Moghul Emperor. His nephew Muzaffar Jung had tried to supplant him unsuccessfully and was put into prison by Nazir Jung.

Anwaruddin was the reigning Nawab of the Carnatic, but Chanda Sahib, a nephew of Anwaruddin's predecessor, was trying to supplant Anwaruddin as Nawab.

Sahuji was the Raja of Tanjore. Another claimant, Pratap Singh, wanted to instal himself as the Raja.

The English, the French and the Marathas were, separately, busy trying to exploit these dissensions for their own ends.

The *Durbar* at Delhi was no longer strong enough to settle these disputes in a distant corner of the Empire.

Intrigues followed. The English sided with Nazir Jung (the reigning Subedar of the Deccan) and with Anwaruddin (the reigning Nawab of the Carnatic) and the French helped Muzaffar Jung and Chanda Sahib, who wanted to be the Subedar and the Nawab, respectively.

Chanda Sahib set off the clash in arms by attacking and dethroning Sahuji, the Raja of Tanjore. The Marathas immediately intervened and attacked Tanjore and took Chanda Sahib prisoner. In his place they installed Pratap Singh as Raja of Tanjore. The English now intervened on behalf of Sahuji against Pratap Singh and despatched a military expedition to Tanjore. On arrival at Tanjore, however, the English found Pratap Singh's side to be stronger than their own and so deserted Sahuji and went over to Pratap Singh. For this "favour" Pratap Singh ceded to the English the town and Fort of Devkot. Sahuji was pensioned off and Pratap Singh continued as the Raja of Tanjore.

In the Carnatic, the English had espoused the cause, as already mentioned, of the reigning Nawab Anwaruddin. The French had befriended Chanda Sahib, Anwaruddin's opponent. But, as mentioned above, Chanda Sahib had embarked on the adventure of seizing the throne at Tanjore and had ended as a prisoner in the hands of the Marathas. Dupleix bribed the Marathas to set Chanda Sahib free, and began his efforts to instal Chanda Sahib as the Nawab of the Carnatic in place of Anwaruddin. Dupleix succeeded. In the battle of Ambur (3rd August, 1749), Chanda Sahib defeated Anwaruddin with the help of the French and became the Nawab of the Carnatic.

But Pratap Singh still ruled at Tanjore, technically supported by Nazir Jung, the Subedar of the Deccan. Dupleix, therefore, decided to displace Nazir Jung. Nazir Jung's nephew, Muzaffar Jung, had attempted to supplant Nazir Jung as Subedar and had been imprisoned by Nazir Jung. Dupleix entered into a conspiracy with Muzaffar Jung, who, with French assistance, escaped from his uncle's prison and proclaimed himself Subedar of the Deccan. His first act as the self-proclaimed Subedar was to join Chanda Sahib, now the Nawab of the Carnatic, in attacking Tanjore, where Pratap Singh ruled. The legitimate Subedar, Nazir Jung, who was still in office, sent military aid to Pratap Singh for the defence of Tanjore. A pitched battle was fought between the two factions. Muzaffer Jung was taken prisoner and incarcerated again. Chanda Sahib was replaced by Mohammad Ali, son of Anwaruddin, and proclaimed the Nawab of the Carnatic. Nazir Jung continued as Subedar of the Deccan. Thus Dupleix's machinations again came to nought. But he did not give up. His secret agents assassinated Nazir Jung and Dupleix got Muzaffar Jung proclaimed as Subedar of the Deccan and Chanda Sahib as Nawab of the Carnatic.

Even these tactics, however, did not take Dupleix much farther. The strong Fort of Tiruchirapalli was still in the hands of Mohammad Ali, the English-sponsored Nawab of the Carnatic. The battle for Tiruchirapalli finally decided not only the future of the three ruling families of the Deccan but also that of the English and the French in India. Tiruchirapalli has been said to be the rock on which Dupleix's ambitions and the French hopes in India were dashed to pieces. The battle was fought between Chanda Sahib and the French on one side and Mohammad Ali with the English on the other. Some French troops to help Dupleix were sent from Europe, but the luck of the English prevailed. The French troopship went down with all aboard, somewhere on its way to India. The French side was defeated and in 1754 Dupleix was recalled by the French Government in France. Thereafter the Government of France decided that it would be more in their own interests to keep aloof from India's internal wrangles for political power. The English and the French Companies arrived at an understanding and agreed that neither of them should in future intervene in disputes among the Indian States. The French stuck to that agreement, but the English, time and again, found its breach to be more profitable. The French Company was liquidated in 1769. At the beginning of the 20th century the only French possessions left in India were Pondicherry, Chandranagore and one or two other tiny areas.

Our narrative has now reached the middle of the 18th century. Neither the Portuguese nor the Dutch were able to establish themselves as a political power in India. The story of the English domination of the country now remains to be related.

2

Siraj-ud-Daula—Battle of Plassey

Nawab Alivardi Khan

Aurangzeb died in 1707. The Mughal Empire had passed its zenith. Aurangzeb's death hastened its disintegration. The Subedars of the various provinces became *de facto* independent rulers of their vast territories.

The power of the Marathas was increasing. They started their raids on Bengal. Nawab Alivardi Khan was then the Subedar of the three provinces of Bengal, Bihar and Orissa. He appealed to Delhi for help against the Marathas, but the Delhi *Durbar* had become too weak to help. Alivardi Khan stopped sending the annual tribute to Delhi but still declared himself to be the loyal servant of the Emperor, in whose name he continued to rule the three provinces.

The people of Bengal were and had been happy and prosperous under the rule of Alivardi Khan and his predecessors. The English historian, S. C. Hill, says:

> "I think that every student of social history must admit that the Bengali farmers were much better off in the middle of the 18th century than their counterparts in France or Germany." (*Bengal in 1756–57,* Vol. I, p. 23)

As regards the urban population, Lord Clive has thus described Murshidabad, the then capital of Bengal:

> "The city of Murshidabad is as extensive, populous and rich as the city of London, with this difference that there are individuals in the first possessing infinitely greater property than any of the last city."

There was no discrimination between Hindus and Mussalmans in the Subedar's treatment of his subjects. Most of the smaller States in all the three provinces were ruled by Hindu rajas. Some of the highest officers at the Murshidabad *Durbar* were Hindus. According to S. C. Hill, "almost all the trade and industries of the country were controlled by Hindus".

Plot to Pillage Bengal

It was in Bengal that the foundation of the political supremacy of the English in India was laid, although the English had first landed on the western coast of the country. The shift eastwards to Bengal could have been due to any or all of the following reasons:

(i) Bengal was undefended along its sea-coast. The Moghuls had no navy, whereas along the western coast was stationed the Maratha navy, said to be one of the strongest in the world at that time.

(ii) Bengal was far more fertile and prosperous than the western provinces.

(iii) Probably the English found the Bengalis more docile and easier to be ensnared.

The first plan for the invasion and plunder of Bengal, Bihar and Orissa, with German aid, was formulated in 1746, by an Englishman, Col. Mill, who wrote to Francis of Lorraine as follows:

> "The Mogul Empire is overflowing with gold and silver. She has always been feeble and defenceless. It is a miracle that no European prince with a maritime power has ever attempted the conquest of Bengal. By a single stroke infinite wealth might be acquired, which would counterbalance the mines of Brazil and Peru."
>
> "The policy of the Moguls is bad; their army is worse; they are without a navy. The Empire is exposed to perpetual revolts. Their ports and rivers are open to foreigners. The country might be conquered or laid under contribution as easily as the Spaniards overwhelmed the naked Indians of America."

> "... Ali Vardi Khan ... has treasure to the value of thirty millions sterling. His yearly revenue must be at least two million. The provinces are open to the sea. Three ships with fifteen hundred or two thousand regulars would suffice for the undertaking ... The East India Company should be left alone. No Company can keep a secret." (Quoted from Bolt's *Considerations of the Affairs of Bengal)*

Machinations of East India Company

The objective of the East India Company also was the conquest of Bengal. But Bengal was not conquered by it in Mill's way. The Company followed its own way of machinations. They had quite a lot to do with Hindus in connection with the Company's trading activities. Both were shrewd but not scrupulous business people. In mid-eighteenth-century Bengal, we see the sad spectacle of Hindus conspiring with Christian foreigners for the overthrow of their own rulers. Amin Chand, a rich Punjabi merchant of Calcutta, had been won over by the Company's lavish promises of "a big share of the loot of the Murshidabad Treasury after the Nawab has been finished" and of "such name and fame in England as will surpass any attained in India" by him. The Company's employees were directed to keep Amin Chand happy by "fulsome flattery" (Clive's letters to Watts).

A Col. Scott may be mentioned amongst the English plotters. He had been living in Bengal for a long time, and had assiduously cultivated friendship with some big Hindu rajas and other highly-placed personages, whom he won over with the help of Amin Chand. The latter's purse and the Company's tempting promises had succeeded in undermining the loyalty and integrity of a number of the Nawab's courtiers and of his relatives too.

In the meantime, the putting up of fortifications by the English at Calcutta and by the French at Chandranagore was going on apace.

Nawab Alivardi Khan came to know something about all these activities. He also learned of the intrigues through which the English and the French were then expanding their respective spheres of influence in the South and along the Coromandel coast. He commanded Col. Scott to present himself at his Court. Scott, after promising to attend, slipped away towards Madras. The Nawab ordered both the English and the French to stop forthwith the putting up of any fortifications. He summoned the representatives of the English and the French Companies and said to them: "You are traders. What do you want fortifications for? Whilst you are under my protection, you can have no enemy to fear." Alivardi Khan, however, was by now too old to see that his orders were carried out.

Alivardi Khan's Last Advice to Siraj-ud-Daula

As his end drew near, Alivardi Khan cautioned his successor, young Siraj-ud-daula, in these words:

> "Keep a watchful eye on the power attained by the Europeans in this country. Had it pleased God to spare my life, I would have freed you from this danger. Now my boy, you will have to do it yourself. You must ever be on your guard ... Never think of dealing with all the three (European nations) or of weakening them at one and the same time. The English are the most powerful of the three ... control them first. If you succeed against the English, then the other two will not give you much trouble. Do not ever permit any of them to put up fortifications or to maintain armies. If you make that mistake, you will lose the country." (*Bengal in 1756–1757,* Vol. I, p. 16)

Nawab Alivardi Khan died on 10th April, 1756 and Siraj-ud-daula, then not even 24, succeeded him. By this time, the East India Company had become firmly established in Bengal and had organised a network of underground plots with far-flung ramifications. Emboldened by the growing weakness of the crumbling Moghul Empire which could not help its Subedar in Bengal, they became aggressive and deliberately adopted a discourteous and even a defiant attitude towards the new Subedar.

To start with, no representative of the Company attended the installation *Durbar* of Siraj-ud-daula to present the traditional *nazar* in token of allegiance to the new Subedar. Further, they conspicuously avoided all direct contact with him. If they wanted anything done which needed the Nawab's permission, they bribed the Nawab's officials to get the necessary sanction and would not approach the Nawab. In fact, the English now appeared to be bent on picking a quarrel with Siraj-ud-daula or to provoke him into one. They began flagrantly to contravene the law of the land, and to disregard and disobey not only the Subedar's express orders, but those of the Moghul *Durbar* too. Some instances are given below:

1. Construction of new fortifications in Calcutta and other places including the digging of a wide and deep moat all round their fort at Calcutta.
2. Invitations to such of the Nawab's officials and courtiers as were accused of crimes, including treason, to take refuge in the Company's premises at Calcutta.
3. The Moghul Emperor had been pleased to exempt the Company's merchandise throughout Bengal from all kinds of duty, and the Company's *Dastak* (signed permit) was enough to secure such exemption in respect of all merchandise covered by the *Dastak*. The Company now began to abuse this privilege by selling their *Dastaks* to Indian traders so that their merchandise too became exempt from duty, thus causing a recurring loss to the State Exchequer.
4. The Company without any legal authority whatsoever began to levy and charge heavy duties on the merchandise of Indian traders that entered or passed through the Company's settlements.

Formal complaints about these illegalities and abuses were continuously reaching Siraj-ud-daula, who, however, would not be provoked into taking any drastic action against the Company.

Army Commander Incited to Rebel

An Army Commander of Siraj-ud-daula was approached and the temptation was held out to him that the English would instal him as the Subedar at Murshidabad in place of Siraj-ud-daula. When called to account by Siraj-ud-daula, the Army Commander, in proof of his innocence, produced before him all the letters which the English had written to him (the Army Commander) in this connection, and which incited the Army Commander to rebel against Siraj-ud-daula (*Bengal in 1756–1757,* Vol. III, p. 164).

Raja Durlabh Ram, the Nawab's Dewan posted at Dacca, was won over by the Company and prevailed upon to send his son, Raja Kishen Das, and all his valuable property to Calcutta in order to protect both against any possible action by the Nawab. The Company accommodated Raja Kishen Das in the house of Amin Chand at Calcutta, and when the Nawab ordered them to send Raja Kishen Das back to Dacca, they refused point-blank to obey the order.

Siraj-ud-Daula's Personal Warning and Order to Watts

Watts, the head of the Company's commercial house at Cossimbazar, was summoned by Siraj-ud-daula and told:

> "If the English want to live in this country as peaceful traders, they can do so with pleasure. But it is my order as the Ruler of the Suba, that they must immediately raze to the ground all the fortifications which they have recently put up without my permission." (*Hastings MSS* in the British Museum, Vol. 29, p. 209)

The English, however, ignored the order completely. The work of putting up fortifications was continued, and with greater speed too. Siraj-ud-daula had now no other alternative but to undertake a punitive expedition to put a stop to this persistent defiance of his authority.

Siraj-ud-daula marched on Cossimbazar, and on 24th May 1756, invaded the English fortification there. The besieged, in spite of their guns, could not resist for long, and Watts, their leader, surrendered. Siraj-ud-daula could have ordered the execution of Watts and his English companions as rebels, but he spared their lives, and took them with him on his march to Calcutta (4th June, 1756). He left untouched all the English merchandise stored inside their fortifications and had removed therefrom only arms and munitions.

English Defeat at Tannah

In the meantime English men-of-war had arrived in Calcutta, and the English there had started an open rebellion against Siraj-ud-daula. They had stormed and taken Tannah—a small fortress on the Hooghly, some five miles from Calcutta—which had been garrisoned by a handful of the Nawab's soldiers. So before reaching Calcutta, Siraj-ud-daula re-took Tannah after a short artillery duel between his guns and those on the English ships. The English ships had to retreat after suffering heavy losses.

Anxious to avoid bloodshed, Siraj-ud-daula had during his march to Calcutta made overtures for peace to Watts and offered restoration to the English of all their trading rights and privileges, if the English only paid a token penalty for their past misdeeds and undertook to live peacefully in future. But the English had already made up their minds to destroy Siraj-ud-daula. They were, however, miserably short of men and munitions and so could not hope to succeed in a military action against him. The only effective weapons left to them were bribery and corruption of Siraj-ud-daula's men and supporters. These were extensively resorted to by Watts and his English companions, whose lives had been spared by Siraj-ud-daula at Cossimbazar only a few days before and who were even then accompanying him to Calcutta as his guests. Even Christianity was pressed into service for creating disaffection amongst Indian and European

Christians, of whom there were quite a number (particularly in the Artillery Division) in Siraj-ud-daula's army then marching under him to Calcutta. Three leaflets signed by some clergymen were one after another secretly distributed in the Nawab's army, authoritatively declaring it to be anti-Christian and so sinful for Christians to light on the side of Mussalmans against their own co-religionists.

Treatment by English of Their Indian Helpers

As soon as news of Siraj-ud-daula's march to Calcutta reached the English there, they left their Hindu and Mussalman employees and associates to their fate, and refused to protect them. They now distrusted all Indians, including those who had been assisting them. They even ordered the arrest of Amin Chand without whose help English trade or political power could never have made any progress in Bengal. Others who were arrested included Hazari Mal, a relation of Amin Chand, and Raja Kishen Das (whom the English had previously refused to hand over to Siraj-ud-daula). Amin Chand meekly submitted to the arrest, but the other two courageously resisted but in vain.

Siraj-ud-daula reached Calcutta on 16th June, 1756. On that and the following day there was some desultory lighting, but the main attack against the English was delivered by him on 18th June. In spite of treachery on the part of Christians in Siraj-ud-daula's army, the Company's army could not long withstand the heavy cannonade to which Siraj-ud-daula subjected it, and surrendered to him. This was the second surrender by the English to Siraj-ud-daula, the first one being that at Cossimbazar less than a month earlier. On Sunday, 20th June, 1756, Siraj-ud-daula's victorious army entered the premises of the East India Company and all the Englishmen still there were taken prisoner. Some had succeeded in making good their escape by sea.

The prisoners were later produced before Siraj-ud-daula at a *Durbar* held in the Fort. They humbly prayed for mercy and the "magnanimous Indian Nawab once again granted them full pardon" (Talboy Wheeler's *Early Records of British India,* Vol. I, p. 160). The English historian, James Mill, observes:

> "When Mr. Holwell (the head of the Company's Calcutta House) was produced handcuffed before the Nawab, the latter ordered the handcuffs to be removed immediately and gave Holwell his personal word of honour as a soldier that not a hair of 'your or any of your companions' head, will be permitted to be touched." (*History of India* Vol. III, p. 1179)

Under Siraj-ud-daula's orders, only the arms and munitions were removed from the Company's premises. The merchandise stored therein, or in any other commercial house of the Company was not touched at all.

The English prisoners who had been pardoned sought permission to leave Bengal and join their previously escaped companions in Madras. The permission was readily given.

Many European writers of history testify that most of the Europeans were taken aback, and even alarmed, at this demonstration of Siraj-ud-daula's power.

Siraj-ud-daula changed the name of Calcutta to Alinagar, and appointed one of his Hindu Dewans, Raja Manik Chand, governor of Calcutta and its adjoining territory. He left Calcutta for Murshidabad on 24th June, 1756. On his way, he held a *Durbar* at Hooghly, which was attended by the accredited representatives of the French and the Dutch commercial houses. As a token of loyalty to Siraj-ud-daula, the French and the Dutch representatives presented him with Rs. 3,50,000 and Rs. 4,00,000, respectively. Sirai-ud-daula permitted them to continue their trade activities in Bengal. He still cherished hopes of the English approaching him for a similar amicable settlement.

Siraj-ud-daula reached Murshidabad on 11th July, 1756. Some three months later, he put down a revolt by Shaukat Jung, the Nawab of Purnea. In the battle fought at Raj Mahal, on 16th October, 1756, Shaukat Jung was killed in action and the victorious

Siraj-ud-daula installed a Hindu, Raja Yugal Singh, on the *Gadi* of Purnea. On his return to Murshidabad, Siraj-ud-daula was very warmly felicitated by his subjects.

Siraj-ud-daula had throughout purported to act in the name of the Moghul Emperor and as his loyal servant. The Emperor now signified his approval by issuing a fresh proclamation confirming and continuing Siraj-ud-daula's tenure of office as his Subedar of the three Provinces of Bengal, Bihar and Orissa.

Alleged "Black Hole Tragedy" at Calcutta

Almost all the English writers of history of that period have stated that on the night of 20th June, 1756 (the day on which the English at Calcutta had surrendered to Siraj-ud-daula), 146 Europeans were herded, under orders of Siraj-ud-daula, into a small cell, 18 ft. long and a little less wide, and were kept locked in for the whole night. It was the hottest month of the Indian summer and the cell had only one tiny aperture for air. The prisoners tightly packed against one another suffered agonies and 123 out of the 146 died of suffocation. The remaining 23 that were found alive the next morning were half-dead. The truth of these allegations was taken for granted for a hundred years or more, even though no mention of the so-called "tragedy" or "massacre" was to be found in any of the Company's records of that period. It is further to be noted that in the carefully compiled list of all Europeans who had died in the Company's Fort or premises during that period, only 56 persons have been listed, not one of whom has been recorded as having died of suffocation. All are recorded as having died of wounds or of some disease. Both Clive and Watson mentioned nothing of this incident in their letters to Siraj-ud-daula in December, 1756, letters in which they had enumerated with full details all their grievances against him. Nor was the incident referred to in the long letter which Clive wrote about that time to the Directors of the Company, in which he had detailed all the reasons which, according to him, had justified the Company's harsh treatment of Siraj-ud-daula. Apparently, the story had not been concocted up to that time. The English historian categorically states in his *History of India* (Vol. III, p. 1179) that after their victory over the English at Calcutta, the victorious Indian soldiery "did not ill-treat the defeated English in any way". His testimony, by itself, goes a long way towards exploding the myth of the "Black Hole Tragedy".

The myth has been attributed to Holwell, the head of the Company's establishment at Calcutta. Holwell's exploits in the field of pure fiction are notorious. We quote below from the "letter addressed to the Hon'ble Court of Directors by Clive and others, 1st October, 1765":

> "... In justice to the memory of the late Nawab Mir Jaffir, we think it incumbent on us to acquaint you, that the horrible massacres wherewith he is charged by Mr. Holwell, in his 'address to the proprietors of East India Stock' (p. 46), are cruel aspersions on the character of that prince, which have not the least foundation in truth. The several persons there affirmed and who have been generally thought to have been murdered by his order are all now living, except two ..."

It would, therefore, appear that when it became necessary or expedient to charge either Siraj-ud-daula or Mir Jafar with "horrible massacres" and there were no facts to found the charges on, Holwell provided them out of his own imagination.

English Fugitives at Phalta

Phalta, a sea-port on the Bay of Bengal a little distance from Calcutta, became the rallying point of all the Englishmen who had either made good their escape from Calcutta or had been later permitted by Siraj-ud-daula to leave Calcutta. They all got down at Phalta and stayed there for six months under pretext of waiting for fair weather before resuming their "voyage to Madras". From the Company's business point of view, Madras was a far more important place than Calcutta.

The English fugitives at Phalta soon got busy with two-fold activities. They wrote to Madras and asked for military help and, whilst waiting for it, employed secret agents to bribe and buy over Raja Manik Chand (whom Siraj-ud-daula had recently appointed Governor of Calcutta) and other army chiefs and courtiers of the Nawab, as also other influential people. In the meantime, "in order to deceive the Nawab" (S. C. Hill in *Bengal in 1756–57,* Vol. 1, pp. cxi–cxv), they began to submit very humble petitions to Siraj-ud-daula for permission to resume their trade in Bengal.

It amazed the English at Phalta that Siraj-ud-daula left them in peace there. English writers like Scrafton and Jean Law have also expressed their surprise at this foolhardy forbearance on the part of Siraj-ud-daula.

Military Help from Madras

Army and navy detachments, consisting of 800 Europeans and 1300 Indians, were despatched from Madras about the middle of October, 1756, under the respective commands of the famous Clive (then only a Colonel) and Admiral Watson. The members of the English Council at Madras gave clear and specific instructions in writing to the officers of the expedition, that on arrival in Bengal, they were to overthrow the Nawab by subornation of the Nawab's men, by putting up a claimant for the Nawab's office and by other similar methods (Letter dated 13th October, 1756. *Bengal in 1756–57,* Vol. 1, pp. 239, 240). Under these express orders, the army and navy detachments arrived at Phalta in December, 1756, and began to carry them out. By this time the English intrigues in the Nawab's camp had met with success. Even Raja Manik Chand had succumbed to the temptations held out by the English and had agreed to betray his master and his country.

The strong Fort of Budge-Budge was garrisoned by the Nawab's troops under the personal command of Raja Manik Chand. He had agreed to hand over the fort to the English, but only after a show of resistance. But Clive and Watson had no excuse to attack the fort. So they wrote threatening and insulting letters to Siraj-ud-daula, to which the latter did not send a reply. Nor did the English wait for one. They forthwith invaded the fort. Raja Manik Chand sallied forth with his troops. After about 30 minutes of sham shooting, he retreated taking care to leave wide open the gates of the fort. The "victorious" English entered the fort through the already-opened gates and such of the non-combatant Indian inmates as had been unable to escape were put to death.

The next place after Budge-Budge, at which Manik Chand could have checked the English advance was Calcutta. But there not even a show of resistance was considered necessary by him or by his foreign friends. From Budge-Budge, he went direct to Hooghly and by-passed Calcutta. From Hooghly, he sent a message to Siraj-ud-daula, saying, "1 could not withstand the vast English army" (*Bengal in 1756–57,* Vol. I, p. cxxxviii). Thus, during Manik Chand's absence, the fort at Calcutta also fell to the English quite easily (2nd January, 1757). The English found the fort of Tannah also open and undefended. On 3rd January, 1757, the fort at Calcutta was put under the charge of Drake and his Council.

Pillage of Hooghly and the Massacre

Vast stores of grain had been built up by Siraj-ud-daula near Hooghly and the English knew of it. As a first step, they decided to set fire to it (*Bengal in 1756–57,* Vol. I, p. cxxxviii). The fort at Hooghly was full of costly goods and was undefended. The English occupied it (11th January, 1757) and then for the next seven days systematically plundered the town of Hooghly and the adjoining Indian-inhabited areas and put to death numberless unarmed and unresisting people.

On coming to know of these happenings, particularly of the pillage of Hooghly, Siraj-ud-daula left Murshidabad with an army and advanced towards Hooghly. In *Ive's Voyages* (p. 109) is mentioned the fact that when Siraj-ud-daula approached the English camp, he made a last-minute effort to avoid bloodshed, and wrote a conciliatory letter to Watson, the English commander, offering peace, permission to trade and compensation for the Company's losses in return for future good behaviour and peaceful activities on the part of the Company. He had apparently still to learn how far the foreign traders could be trusted to abide by an amicable settlement.

Finding the Nawab so very keen on peace, the English demanded:

(1) Full compensation for all losses suffered by the Company.
(2) Complete restoration of all the privileges and concessions enjoyed by the Company in Bengal.
(3) The right to fortify any of their settlements.
(4) Permission for the setting up of the Company's mint in Calcutta for minting their own coinage.

Siraj-ud-daula agreed to the first three demands. It was beyond his competence to grant the fourth, as it was the sole prerogative of the Emperor at Delhi to establish a mint or to permit anyone to do so anywhere in the Empire. Lengthy negotiations followed, during which the English came forward every now and then with fresh terms and conditions. Actually, they did not want real peace with Siraj-ud-daula. Their aim was to lull him into a false sense of security for the time being, whilst they themselves continued their intrigues for stirring up a Bengal wide revolt against him. They held out to him hopes of a permanent amicable settlement at Calcutta, if he accompanied them there. Siraj-ud-daula agreed and went. Mir Jafar, his principal Army Commander, accompanied him. On the way to Calcutta, "Siraj-ud-daula discovered some appearance of disaffection ...... particularly in Mir Jaffar" (Scrafton, *Reflections*, p. 66).

Treachery at Calcutta

On his arrival at Calcutta (4th February, 1757), Siraj-ud-daula was ceremoniously received and put up in a sumptuous camp in Amin Chand's garden, and the English planned a treacherous surprise attack on his camp to be made at dawn, the very next morning. Jean Law writes:

> "To deceive him (Siraj) more completely and examine the position of his camp, the English sent deputies the day before the attack they meditated." (*Memoirs*, Vol. III, p. 182)

The deputies (who were really spies) were Walsh and Scrafton. As instructed, they talked with Siraj-ud-daula for some time, on the night between the 4th and the 5th and then retired. They first went to their own tent and, some time later, slipped away in the dark to the English camp. At about 4 or 5 in the morning, under cover of a thick mist, Colonel Clive attacked the Nawab's camp. According to Jean Law, their main target of attack was the tent in which the Nawab had interviewed the English deputies a few hours earlier, and which he was expected to be still occupying. But the Nawab was not there. One of his Dewans had become suspicious about the visit of the English deputies and, after they had left, had persuaded the Nawab to spend the rest of the night in another tent some distance away. The attack thus failed to achieve its main objective. According to Renault:

> "The English had collected, for this surprise attack on the sleeping Mussalmans, their entire army and navy personnel in Calcutta, but they achieved less than nothing. Siraj-ud-daula quickly rallied his men who counterattacked and pressed the English troops hard till they ran helter-skelter to the shelter of their guns on the ramparts of the English fort." (Renault's letter dated 4th September, 1757)

Siraj-ud-daula had with him enough troops to punish this treachery. But, as Renault goes on to say "his ministers, almost all of whom were friendly with the English, pressed him to conclude a peace with the English. He could no longer rely on the loyalty of even his Army Chiefs. He could, therefore, see no alternative to a peace treaty with the English and that too on the hard terms dictated by them." A treaty was signed four days later.

Treaty of Alinagar

This treaty, signed on 9th February, 1757, secured to the English every single concession they had wanted. Its terms may be summarised as follows:

1. The revival of all the concessions till then granted to the English by the Emperor at Delhi was agreed to.
2. All goods in transit to and from any place in Bihar and Orissa, which were covered by the Company's *Dastak* (permit) were to continue to be duty-free.
3. All the trading posts of the Company and all the property of the Company, its employees, clients or customers, seized and confiscated by the Nawab were to be restored and the Nawab was also to pay cash compensation to those whose property had been looted by the Nawab's men.
4. The English were to be free to fortify Calcutta in any way they liked.
5. The English were to have the right to mint their own coinage.
6. The Nawab and his principal officers and ministers were to sign the treaty.
7. Admiral Watson and Col. Clive were to give an assurance, on behalf of the English nation and the English Company, that so long as there was no breach or violation of the treaty by or on behalf of the Nawab, the English would live peacefully is the Nawab's provinces.

The only thing which the English asked for and which the Nawab refused to give was an undertaking by the Nawab to attack and expel the French from his territory.

The English also secured the Nawab's assent to the permanent stay of an English envoy at the Nawab's Court.

It was also agreed that whenever the Nawab requested, the English would help him militarily with men and money.

Fresh Demands

Even before the ink on the Treaty had dried, the English began making fresh demands on the Nawab. Three days after the Treaty had been signed, Clive wrote on 12th February to the Select Committee in England assuring them that:

"additional concessions could be expected from the Nawab", and quite openly suggesting that:

> "the envoy ...... could be used not only for this purpose but also as an agent for carrying on various underground activities and intrigues".

The appointment of a permanent envoy was consequently another calamity for Siraj-ud-daula, because it greatly facilitated the Company's secret intrigues against him.

Watts, head of the Company's Cossimbazar establishment, was the first envoy accredited by the English to the Murshidabad *Durbar.* The arch-traitor, Amin Chand, was sent with Watts as an adviser, and took his money-bags with him. In his *Memoirs of the Revolution,* Watts frankly admits that during his assignment at Murshidabad, he resorted to wholesale bribery of the Nawab's officers, ministers and supporters for the success of the English intrigues.

A week after the Treaty, Watts was instructed, on 16th February 1757, to present to Siraj-ud-daula some new demands which included the following:

(1) The Nawab was not to put up any fortifications anywhere below Calcutta, within a mile of the river Hooghly.

(2) The courts established by the English were to be vested with criminal jurisdiction over Indians with power to pass any sentence including that of death.

(3) The English were to be vested with the authority to try and punish, without any reference to the Nawab or his regular courts, any official of the Nawab who

demanded duty on goods exempted by the *Dastak* (permit) of the Company.

(4) The Nawab was to pay off all debts due to any Indian creditor by the Company or by any Englishman.

The last-mentioned demand was too absurd for words, and the first three amounted to nothing less than a demand for the handing over of some of his own ruling powers and authority to the Company by the Nawab.

The English knew very well that Siraj-ud-daula would not accede to such demands and yet Watts was instructed to make them because their rejection by the Nawab would provide the English with a plausible excuse for a future quarrel with him whenever it suited them to start one. At that time, however, the English had decided that, before any action was taken against Siraj-ud-daula, the French in Bengal must be rendered completely powerless.

After the Treaty of Alinagar, Siraj-ud-daula left Calcutta for his capital, Murshidabad.

English Plan to Attack the French at Chandranagore

Having given top priority to the uprooting of the French in Bengal, the English lost no time in getting ready for their attack on Chandranagore, and their plans were well under way even before the Nawab reached Murshidabad from Calcutta. He came to know of their warlike preparations in violation of the Treaty they had signed barely 10 days earlier. He wrote to Watson on 19th February, 1757, and again the next day, pointing out that 5 or 6 English men-of-war had already arrived in Hooghly and that more were awaited. He further stated that this, with all the other war-like preparations by the English, could only mean that the English were bent upon violating the Treaty so recently signed by them. The Nawab appealed to the English as soldiers, as men of honour and as Christians, to abide by their promise. He also declared that if the English dishonoured their promise and committed a breach of peace by attacking the French, then he (the Nawab) would owe it to his own honour and to his duty to the Emperor to send his troops to help the French against the English.

Watson in his reply dated 25th February, 1757, did not say anything about the English men-of-war at Hooghly, but asserted that obviously some mean person had falsely accused him (Watson) and the English of making preparations to break the peace. Watson concluded his letter by saying:

> "Rest assured that I shall, as in duty bound, preserve the peace."

This was calculated to lull Siraj-ud-daula into a false sense of security till the very last moment.

At this juncture, news was received that the Emperor's army was marching on Bengal as a result of some dispute that had arisen between Siraj-ud-daula and the Emperor's court. Siraj-ud-daula decided to advance towards Patna to oppose the Emperor's army, and wrote to Watson asking for military help in terms of the Treaty. He offered to pay Rs. 100,000 per month as expenses as long as the Company's army was with him. This request provided the English with an excellent excuse for their army to leave Calcutta for the ostensible purpose of helping the Nawab, the real intention being the sack of Chandranagore, to be followed by an attack on Siraj-ud-daula himself.

But the French had not, so far, provided the English with reason or even a plausible excuse for an attack on Chandranagore. On the contrary, they had been suing for peace. As Clive wrote to the Select Committee on 4th March, 1757:

> "The French Governor and his Council at Chandranagore wrote to us that they were agreeable to conclude peace with us. In reply, we said we would gladly welcome an amicable settlement with them and invited their delegation for negotiations. Did not our reply mean that we had agreed to a peace with them? Did we not co-operate with the French delegates in arriving at terms satisfactory to both sides? Have we not agreed that we and the

> French delegates will sign and seal each such term and condition and that both will solemnly promise to observe them faithfully? We have already given our promise to the Nawab to do all that, and he has agreed to take the responsibility of ensuring that neither side violates the Treaty. What will the Nawab think of us now? There is no doubt that he and the entire world will consider us to be nothing but irresponsible and unprincipled triflers."

As a matter of fact, the treaty with the French had actually been drawn up, but at the last minute, Watson had refused to sign it. He was all for going ahead with the attack. But Clive, being more artful, had not agreed. So Clive wrote to the Select Committee as above and thought up the subtle face-saving device of obtaining the Nawab's assent, express or implied, to the English attack on the French. Within a few days, a letter purporting to come from the Nawab was received by Watson. It was dated 10th March, 1757, and was in Persian. Watts, the English envoy at the Nawab's Court, translated it into English. The Nawab was supposed to have concluded his letter with the words:

> "You are sensible and liberal-minded. If your enemy prays for mercy with a pure heart, you may grant it, but you must first be fully convinced about the honesty and purity of his intentions, failing which you can do what you think best."

The letter was a forgery, and Clive had it manipulated through Watts. Scrafton states clearly (*Reflections,* p. 70):

> "The English spent quite a lot of money in heavily bribing the Nawab's ministers and secretaries to have the letter written."

Jean Law also confirms this in his *Memoirs*:

> "...... the secretary must have been bribed to write in a way suitable to the views of Mr. Watts."

Clive's March on Chandranagore

It will be recalled that Siraj-ud-daula had written to Watson asking for military help against the Emperor's army which was then marching into Bengal. Clive wrote to Siraj-ud-daula on 7th March, 1757: "I am coming to your help." The English were now ready and Clive, with his army reinforced by troops from Bombay, started on his march to Chandranagore. The French asked the reason why. Clive wrote to them on 9th March, 1757, deceitfully assuring them: "At present I have no intention at all of fighting your nation." A bare 48 hours later, however, Clive wrote again to the French, accusing them of having sheltered deserters from the English army. He considered it a good enough reason for attacking Chandranagore and on 12th March, 1757, his army was within two miles of its objective. The above-mentioned forged letter conveyed to Clive, as claimed by him (Clive), the Nawab's permission for the siege of Chandranagore by the English. The siege began on 14th March, 1757, and on 23rd Chandranagore surrendered to the English. Later, the French and the English entered into a treaty about other French settlements in Bengal.

It would, however, appear that intrigue and bribery rather than military prowess or valour had helped the English to win. The Select Committee, whilst thanking Amin Chand and Nund Coomar for their help, have recorded in their report dated 10th April, 1757:

> "Had Diwan Nund Coomar's troops not been withdrawn, our victory would have been impossible."
>
> Nund Coomar was a Faujdar (military commander) sent by Siraj-ud-daula with a strong force to Chandranagore to help the French against the impending English invasion, and to protect from the invaders the Nawab's Indian subjects. But, as stated by both Scrafton and Thornton, Nund Coomar was bought or won over by the English "with the help of Amin Chand's money."

As soon as the English arrived, Nund Coomar withdrew his troops from Chandranagore, leaving it and its inhabitants (French and English) to their fate.

Another traitor in the French camp was a French officer, Lieut. de Terrano, who had been heavily bribed to leave open and undefended the door to Chandranagore from the river-side through which the English could get in. Blockman states that de Terrano sent to his father in France some of this illgotten money. The father, although infirm and old, would not touch the money and returned it when he came to know of his son's treacherous act. In utter disgrace, de Terrano is reported to have committed suicide. He had locked himself up in his room. Some days later his dead body was found hanging.

Watson's Threats to Siraj-ud-Daula

The "conquest" of Chandranagore had not only shattered French power in Bengal, but had also cleared the way for the English to have their pre-planned showdown with Siraj-ud-daula. Watson now threw off the mask of friendliness and wrote to Siraj-ud-daula:

> "...... but the time has now come for plain-speaking. If you really want peace in your territory and wish to save your people from disaster, then see to it that I have not the slightest ground for being dissatisfied with you, and perform, within 10 days from today, every single thing which, in the Treaty, you have undertaken to do. Otherwise, remember that the responsibility for the consequences that will follow will be entirely yours .... Within a few days I will send for more men-of-war and troops and will start a conflagration in your territory which all the waters in the Ganga will not suffice to put out."

The undertakings referred to by Watson meant that the Nawab should restore to the English all their business premises and other property, and further pay compensation for their losses. We quote Clive on the Nawab's actions and behaviour during the six or seven weeks after the Treaty:

> "He (Siraj-ud-daula) has fulfilled most of the articles of the Treaty made with us. The 3 lacs of rupees are already paid and goods and money to a considerable amount delivered to us and to our several subordinates, and I have little doubt but that all his engagements will be duly executed." (Letter to the Select Committee dated 30th March, *1757—Bengal Records,* Vol. II, p. 308)

It is thus obvious that Watson's demand was nothing but an excuse for starting hostilities. Even so, Siraj-ud-daula sent a very conciliatory reply explaining the slight delay and assuring Watson that he would very soon meet the rest of his commitments.

Siraj-ud-Daula's Forbearance

Siraj-ud-daula had come to know that the English army had left Calcutta only ostensibly to help him against the Emperor's army (which was then marching towards Bengal) and that the real purpose of the movement of the English troops was an attack on Chandranagore. He immediately wrote to the English: "I no longer need your help." Even when reports reached him that the English army had devastated the countryside along its line of march to Chandranagore and inflicted untold atrocities on his subjects residing there, he only lodged a mild protest. He did the same when a demand was made by the English that the Kalighat area, being a part of the district of Calcutta, should be ceded and handed over to the English representative. Siraj-ud-daula invariably concluded his protests with pathetic appeals to the English to help the growth of mutual friendship "which has already taken roots". It is amazing but true that Siraj-ud-daula had not yet lost all hopes of a lasting peace with the English.

Watts, the English envoy at the Nawab's Court, was kept busy by Clive and Watson, not only in making fresh demands on the Nawab, but also in the sinister secret intrigues against him. As S.C. Hill states:

> "The British agent, having the deeper purse, was able to influence not only the leading men at court, but also the secretaries, and was much assisted by the foresighted cunning of Amin Chand ...."(*Bengal Records,* Vol. I, p. clxxvii)

Mir Jafar was offered Siraj-ud-daula's place, being more influential than the other aspirants and as Watts wrote to Clive, "(Mir Jafar) and his friends were ready to help the English in the dethronement of the Nawab". But apparently, Mir Jafar was not a trusting fool, and so Watts, when recommending Mir Jafar, had to add

> "If you approve of this scheme, which is more feasible than the other I wrote about, he (Mir Jafar) requests you will write your proposals of what money, what land you want or what treaties you will engage in." (Letter to Calcutta dated 26th April, 1757)

Clive again resorted to duplicity. Macaulay states:

> "He (Clive) wrote to Siraj-ud-daula in terms so affectionate, that they for a time lulled that weak prince into perfect security. The same courier who carried this 'soothing letter', as Clive calls it, carried to Mr. Watts a letter in the following terms: 'Tell Mir Jaffar to fear nothing. I will join him with five thousand men who never turned their backs. Assure him, I will march night and day to his assistance, and stand by him as long as I have a man left ...." (Macaulay, *Essay on Clive*)

English Demand on the Nawab

After the English had taken Chandranagore, Siraj-ud-daula had become a little suspicious of them. Consequently, when the

English demanded that the Nawab hand over to them all the French trading centres and all the French nationals in his territory, it proved to be the last straw. The French had been permitted by the Emperor at Delhi (just as the English were) to trade and establish their trading centres in Bengal. The French had never failed or declined to carry out any instructions or orders issued by the Emperor or by the Subedar. Moreover, the English demand amounted to a flagrant breach of the treaty entered into by the English and the French after the fall of Chandranagore. It roused the ire even of Siraj-ud-daula, who wrote to Watson (14th April, 1757) thus:

> "I have said before, and I repeat, that if the English Company wishes to continue its trade then it is not to write to me anything which is not in consonance with the Treaty between us. ... If you do not really wish to fight with me, then before writing to me, study the Treaty signed and sealed by me which you have with you, and write to me accordingly If you want peace with me, then do not write to me anything which goes against the Treaty." (*he's Voyages,* p. 142)

Secret Treaty with Mir Jafar

At midnight, on 4th June, 1757, Mir Jafar signed the secret treaty which Watts brought to him at that hour. Watts had arrived (with the treaty) at Mir Jafar's palace, hidden in a curtained sedan-chair used by ladies. The treaty provided that within 30 days of his installation as Subedar, Mir Jafar was to carry out and fulfil the terms and conditions which may be summarised thus.

Mir Jafar was to pay to the Company ten million rupees on account of war expenses and as compensation for the war-damage to Calcutta. In addition, he was to pay five million, two million, and seven hundred thousand rupees for individual losses suffered, respectively, by the English, the Hindu and the Armenian inhabitants of Calcutta, All French nationals, their trading centres and all their possessions in Bengal were to be handed over to the English, and the French were not to be permitted to live in Bengal any longer. The area enclosed by the Calcutta moat and extended by 600 yards all round it was to be ceded to the English who were also to get the *Zamindari* (landlord's) rights in the vast region to the south of Calcutta, between the Hooghly river and the salt lakes up to Kalpi.

Other terms secured to the English the continuation of all the rights and privileges which Siraj-ud-daula had given them. The parties also agreed to help each other militarily in hostilities breaking out between the English or Mir Jafar and a third party, subject nevertheless to the proviso that Mir Jafar was to bear all expenses whether the help was rendered by him or to him. Mir Jafar also bound himself not to put up any kind of fortifications whatsoever along the river below Hooghly. The Company undertook to help Mir Jafar in suppressing his enemies, so long as he abided by the Treaty. Thus on that night the plot for the overthrow of Siraj-ud-daula was finalised and was ready for execution. But the English had to wait till Watts and other Englishmen in Murshidabad had been evacuated. On 12th June, 1757, Mir Jafar's letter, saying, "Everything ready here", reached Calcutta. The next day, the English army led by Cliveset out from Calcutta on its march to Murshidabad.

Battle of Plassey—Mir Jafar's Treachery

Siraj-ud-daula's army advanced from Murshidabad to give battle to the English. It consisted of 45,000 men under the supreme command of Mir Jafar, with Yar Lutf Khan and Raja Durlabh Ram as his seconds-in-command, and of another 12,000 men commanded by Mir Moinuddin *alias* Mir Madan.

Some 20 miles short of Murshidabad was a dense forest of *palash* trees. Adjoining it was a vast plain called "Palashi" in Bengali or "Plassey" in English.

On 23rd June, 1757, the two armies joined in battle at Plassey. Clive was unable to make any headway. In fact, he was facing defeat, and Siraj-ud-daula's army was in sight of victory when at that critical moment, Mir Jafar, Yar Lutf Khan and Raja Durlabh Ram went over to the English with their 45,000 men. Only the loyal Mir Madan was left to continue the now-desperate fight. He died fighting, and when he fell the Battle of Plassey was over. Siraj-ud-daula was in flight and the English won the day. But, as Col. Malleson says:

> "It was only when treason had done her work, when treason had driven the Nawab from the field, when treason had removed his army from its commanding position, that Clive was able to advance without the certainty of being annihilated." (Col. Malleson in *Decisive Battles of India,* p. 73)

Clive spent the night (23rd of June, 1757) in the nearby village of Dadpur. Next morning he sent for Mir Jafar. By that time, Mir Jafar's guilty conscience had probably made him fear treachery on the part of the English too. He started and his face darkened with suspicion, as the military guard with Clive advanced towards him to "present arms"! His face cleared however, when Clive, hailing him as the "Suba of all the three Provinces", embraced him and assured him that the English would do their "sacred duty" of performing all the promises made to him.

Siraj-ud-daula was in flight and Clive "advised" Mir Jafar to follow in pursuit. Mir Jafar did so and arrived in Murshidabad the next morning (25th June, 1757). Siraj-ud-daula had returned to Murshidabad some 24 hours earlier and spent money lavishly in an attempt to collect a fresh army for trying his luck on the battlefield once again. Some of his courtiers suggested that he might admit defeat and sue for peace—a suggestion which he rejected with contempt. He could not, however, find any supporters. The news of his defeat at Plassey had preceded him and had spread like wildfire, and, "no one worships the setting sun". Then news of Mir Jafar's pursuit reached him. So, at midnight on 24th June, 1757, he stealthily left his palace through a window and disguised as a *Fakeer* (Muslim ascetic) became a fugitive with only three followers, barely 54 weeks after his installation as Subedar of Bengal, Bihar and Orissa.

A few hours later, Mir Jafar entered Murshidabad. Clive had followed him with his troops but, as indicated in one of his (Clive's) letters, he did not venture to enter Murshidabad straightaway, and camped for three days at Syedabad, some six miles away from Murshidabad. On 29th June, 1757, he entered Murshidabad, after having arranged with Mir Jafar the date and time of his entry. He had with him some 200 European and 500 Indian soldiers. In his evidence before the Parliamentary Committee, Clive, sometime later, deposed as follows:

> "...... The inhabitants who were spectators upon that occasion must have numbered some hundred thousands; and if they had an inclination to have destroyed the Europeans, they might have done it with sticks and stones."

But nothing happened and Mir Jafar's installation was fixed for that very afternoon.

Mir Jafar's Installation

In the very hour of his treason's triumph, Mir Jafar's soul appears to have rebelled against what he had done. As he approached the *Gadi* (the throne), his steps faltered and he could not bring himself to sit on the *Gadi* from which, only three days earlier, he had treacherously driven away his young, trusting kinsman and master. Clive had to take him by the hand and make him sit on the throne. Clive was the first to render obeisance to the new Nawab and was followed by the other courtiers in order of precedence (Clive's letter to the Select Committee dated 30th June, 1757).

It was now for the English Company and its English employees and helpers to fill their pockets with the money in the Nawab's treasury. But there was not enough of it, as Clive and his companions discovered on seizing and inspecting it. The English had, therefore, to agree to instalments. It was settled that Mir Jafar was to pay forthwith half of what he had undertaken to pay them, and the other half in three yearly instalments. We quote below from Orme's *History of Indostan* (Vol. II, pp, 187–88):

> "… The Committee by the 6th of July, 1757, received, in coined silver, 72,71,666 rupees … Never before did the English nation at one time obtain such a prize in solid money."

At the division of the booty, the juniormost English officer's share came to 45,000 rupees (over £3,000), but the Indian helpers of the Company were cheated out of their share.

"Payment" to Amin Chand

Amin Chand had very freely advanced the huge amounts of money which the English repeatedly needed for their campaign of intrigues, bribery and corruption. The English did not have to spend a single rupee out of their own pocket. He had been their chief Indian collaborator and supporter throughout the conspiracy which had now achieved complete success. Also, without the unstinted help of Amin Chand, the English could never have developed their trade or increased their influence and power, to the extent of being able to take Chandranagore and ultimately to depose Siraj-ud-daula.

The genuine secret treaty between the English and Mir Jafar contained 13 clauses and was written, as usual, on white paper. But a "Treaty" with fourteen clauses and written on red paper was shown to Amin Chand. The fourteenth clause provided for a payment to Amin Chand of three million rupees in hard cash, plus 5 per cent of the total amount found in Siraj-ud-daula's Treasury. Amin Chand had betrayed not only his soul, his ruler and master, but also his country and his nation. Evidently he had relied upon the proverbial "honour amongst thieves" and had loyally served the English with scrupulous honesty and with all the money that they wanted. He had accepted without question the genuineness of the "red" Treaty shown to him. It was, however, not genuine. Watson's signature on it had been forged at the instance of Clive by one Lushington, because Watson had refused to sign the bogus treaty and so be a party to the fraud on Amin Chand.

Clive admitted, not without some pride, before the Parliamentary Committee, the fact of having got Lushington to forge Watson's signature.

When, after Mir Jafar's installation, the genuine Treaty on white paper was read out to Amin Chand, he shouted:

> "This cannot be the Treaty which 1 had seen, it was on red paper."
>
> "That's right, Amin Chand," suavely replied Clive, "but this Treaty is on white paper." (Clive's evidence before the Parliamentary Committee).

Amin Chand nearly collapsed then and there. His health broke down under the strain of the severe shock. The artful Clive suggested a pilgrimage for its recuperation. Amin Chand undertook one and recovered but died.

Under the English law of that period a convicted forger was hanged. Clive, who had admitted the forgery, got a peerage and a statue in England! In his honour medals were struck in commemoration of the Battle of Plassey!

By such ways and means the foundations of British rule in India were laid on the battlefield of Plassey and most of the credit for it must undoubtedly be given to Clive.

Siraj-ud-Daula's End

Siraj-ud-daula was apprehended and brought to Murshidabad. "The Nawab", according to Clive, "wished to spare his life, but the Nawab's son, Meeran, and some other highly-placed persons considered it essential for the maintenance of peace in the country that Siraj-ud-daula should die." On the night following the day (2nd July, 1757,) on which he had been brought to Murshidabad as a captive, Siraj-ud-daula was murdered by one Mohammad Beg. Siraj-ud-daula was not even 25 then.

Of all the English writers, Col. Malleson is the only one who has been fair enough to do Siraj-ud-daula some justice. He writes:

"Whatever may have been his faults, Siraj-ud-daula had neither betrayed his master nor sold his country. Nay more, no unbiased Englishman sitting in judgement on the events which passed in the interval between the 9th February and the 23rd June can deny that the name of Siraj-ud-daula stands higher in the scale of honour than does the name of Clive. He was the only one of the principal actors in that tragic drama who did not deceive." (*Decisive Battles of India*, p. 71)

3

Mir Jafar

Mir Jafar as "Subedar"

It would appear that the *Durbar* at Delhi, being too weak to do otherwise, subsequently acquiesced in Mir Jafar's occupation of its Subedar's *Gadi,* rendered vacant by the murder of young Siraj-ud-daula. But even so, Mir Jafar was only a puppet Subedar and was completely under the thumb of Clive, who wielded all the authority and power of that office. Mir Jafar was in every way thoroughly incapable of doing anything other than meekly obeying "his master's voice". A wag amongst his courtiers gave Mir Jafar the wickedly apt nickname of "Col. Clive's donkey", and it stuck to him till his death.

Clive now definitely aimed at the establishment of English power and prestige throughout the Subedar's domain, and with that end in view he proceeded to weaken Mir Jafar's authority and prestige by making him unpopular with his subjects, his Hindu high officers and the local governor under him, as these were loyal to the Subedar and they constituted his main source of strength. Ironically enough, Mir Jafar himself was Clive's tool in bringing about his own unpopularity and ultimate ruin. If Clive dictated anything which, in Clive's view, furthered his scheming in the interests of the English domination, then Mir Jafar had to do it, even if it was obviously against his own or his subjects' interests.

The process began with a reversal of the policy of non-discrimination between Hindus and Mussalmans, which had been consistently followed by the Subedars preceding Mir Jafar, who, on assuming office, started dismissing Hindus from all high offices under him and replacing them by his own co-religionists.

Clive's next step was to undermine, through Mir Jafar's own actions (dictated by Clive), the loyalty to the Subedar of his subordinate Hindu local governors and to turn the latter against Mir Jafar by every possible means.

Action Against Raja Ramnarain, Governor of Bihar

Raja Ramnarain, the ablest and strongest of the local governors, was the first to be proceeded against. He had not joined the conspiracy against Siraj-ud-daula, but had formally accepted Mir Jafar as Subedar after Siraj-ud-daula's death. An excuse for action against him was, however, soon trumped up. He was accused, for Mir Jafar's edification, of hatching a conspiracy for the latter's overthrow and also of sheltering some hostile Frenchmen.

On 6th July, 1757, Clive ordered a detachment of some 230 European and 300 Indian soldiers to proceed to Patna (the capital of Bihar) overtly in pursuit of the French fugitives alleged to be sheltering there. The commanding officer, Major Coote, was, however later instructed by Clive that he (Major Coote) should, on reaching Patna, enter into a conspiracy with Mahmood Amin Khan (a brother of Mir Jafar) for Ramnarain's removal from the governorship of Bihar (Clive's letter the Major Coote, 12th August, 1757). Consequently, Major Coote, on his arrival at Patna, did not take any military action, but began to negotiate. He went to Raja Ramnarain's palace and took with him not only Mahmood Amin Khan but also Mir Kassim (Mir Jafar's son-in-law) too. Raja Ramnarain, who had somehow come to know of Major Coote's real mission, met all the three, and conclusively proved that the accusations brought against him were false. He sent for a Brahmin and took the oath of loyalty to Mir Jafar in the Hindu way (as administered by the priest) in the presence of all the three who were completely satisfied. Mahmood Amin Khan and Mir Kassim also swore on the Holy Quran that there were no longer any ill-feelings in their hearts for Raja Ramnarain, whom all the three embraced in token of their continued mutual friendship. Major Coote and his soldiers returned to Murshidabad. But this was not at all what Clive had wanted. So there was further trouble in store for Raja Ramnarain.

Action Against Raja Ramrum Singh, Governor of Orissa

Like Bihar, Orissa was also under the jurisdiction of the Subedar of Bengal. Mir Jafar summoned Raja Ramrum Singh to Murshidabad for rendition of the revenue accounts of Orissa. Clive was then in Murshidabad. Ramrum Singh grew suspicious and, instead of going himself, sent a brother and a nephew of his to Murshidabad with the account books. Both were arrested as soon as they arrived in Murshidabad. Ramrum Singh's suspicions proved to be only too well founded. But he did not lack courage. He also knew that Clive was "the power behind the throne" at Murshidabad. He wrote to Clive: "I have an army of 2,000 cavalry and 5,000 infantry soldiers. If the new Nawab makes the mistake of using force against me or of attempting to take me prisoner, then I am strong enough to resist him successfully. If, however, you will mediate between us and will guarantee my personal safety, then I am willing to meet Mir Jafar personally and shall present a lac (100,000) of rupees as *Nazrana*." Clive considered it impolitic to start hostilities with Ramrum Singh just then and accepted the offer. At his instance Ramrum Singh's relations were set free and he himself was left in peace to rule as Governor of Orissa.

Raja Yugal Singh of Purnea Taken Prisoner

Siraj-ud-daula had installed Yugal Singh as the Raja of Purnea. He was the next victim of Clive's machinations and of Mir Jafar's keenness to instal his own protege, one Khuddam Hussain, as Nawab of Purnea. So Yugal Singh was attacked, taken prisoner and replaced by Khuddam Hussain.

It will be recalled that Durlabh Ram was one of the two seconds-in-command of Siraj-ud-daula's army at the Battle of Plassey, and had deserted with Mir Jafar and gone over to the English. His desertion had materially helped the English to win and Mir Jafar to become the Subedar. He had by now acquired considerable influence and power. Neither the English nor Mir Jafar liked it and so plans were made to bring about his downfall. Durlabh Ram came to know about these plans and forthwith got ready to put up a strong fight. His preparations and strength made the English doubtful about their success against him and so they gave up the attempt to break Durlabh Ram. As a face-saving device, Watts intervened to re-establish peace between Mir Jafar and Raja Durlabh Ram.

Clive Blackmails Mir Jafar

Clive now began to play upon Mir Jafar's suspicions and fears about Raja Ramnarain. He succeeded in convincing Mir Jafar that there was real danger from that quarter, as the Nawab Vazier of Oudh had been approached and had agreed to help Ramnarain against Mir Jafar. The latter was further told that it had thus become essential for him to forestall the imminent attack by Ramnarain and his new ally. Mir Jafar was frightened and apparently consented to a second invasion of Bihar and to the collection by Clive of an army of 50,000 men for that purpose as soon as possible. Clive exploited the situation in the way he had intended to do, and made fresh demands on Mir Jafar for money.

But Mir Jafar was facing bankruptcy. With a depleted treasury, he was owing money all round on account of his commitments. Even his soldiers had not been paid for months and were in a ferment. Clive had collected 50,000 men under his own command, but at the eleventh hour had refused to move a step on the march to Bihar until Mir Jafar paid in full all the debts due by him to the Company and to individual Englishmen. Mir Jafar had never borrowed a copper from either. The so-called "debts" were nothing but the unpaid balances of the price which Mir Jafar had agreed to pay to the Company and to several of the English individually for the Bengal Subedar's *Gadi,* plus many later and fresh demands.

Mir Jafar was helpless and completely at Clive's mercy who could have crushed him with the 50,000 men under him. He had no alternative to submission to the blackmail. So in the words of Malcolm (*Life of Clive*, Vol. I, p. 338):

> "A supply of money was procured for the extraordinary expenses of the army; the *perwannah,* or grant of lands, yielded to the Company, was passed in all its forms; orders were issued for the immediate discharge of all arrears on the first six months of the Nawab's debt, and the revenues of Burdwan, Nuddea and Hooghly assigned over for payment of the rest: "So that", says Clive, (writing on 8th February, 1758, to the Court of Directors), "the discharge of the debt is now become independent of the Nawab ......"

Clive "Invades" Bihar and Wins Over Raja Ramnarain

Clive and Mir Jafar marched on Patna. The overlarge force of 50,000 troops poured into Bihar but its commanders were unable to find an enemy, and the men sat twiddling their thumbs for four months! Actually, Clive had never wanted to makean enemy of a man of the calibre and status of Raja Ramnarain. On the contrary, he was keen on having him as a friend of the English. He had deliberately created the situation with a twofold object. One was to impress Ramnarain with a display of the English Company's military strength so as to convince him that the English were powerful enough either to break him or to ensure the continued exercise by him of all his existing powers and authority if he became their friend and ally. Clive's second objective was to play upon the nerves of both Mir Jafar and Ramnarain long enough till he could manipulate his own choice as an arbitrator or mediator between them. He succeeded. On 28th February, 1758, he presided over a *Durbar* held at Patna, even though Mir Jafar, the Emperor's Subedar of Bengal, was present. By agreement, Mir Jafar's son, Meeran, was appointed the titular Nawab of Bihar, with Raja Ramnarain as his deputy with exactly the same powers and authority as he had till then exercised. For this favour Ramnarain had to part with Rs. 7,00,000 in cash.

Clive did not forget his employers either. He pressed both the Nawab and Ramnarain to grant to the Company the sole monopoly of the production and export of saltpetre in Bihar which produced practically all the saltpetre consumed or sold in Bengal. The value of the monopoly can thus be imagined and to that extent the Company profited at the cost of the indigenous producers of saltpetre in Bihar.

Prince Ali Gauhar's March on Bengal—Clive's Good Luck

One of the titles of the eldest son of the Emperor had long been the "Subedar of Bengal, Bihar and Orissa". It was purely an honorific and carried no administrative authority, duties or responsibilities of the office attached to it. These were exercised by the *de facto* Subedar under the authority of the Emperor, to whom the Subedar was supposed to be responsible. Prince Ali Gauhar, the eldest son of the reigning Emperor, held that title and used it to lead a military expedition to Bengal. Whether or not it had anything to do with the disorder and misrule in Bengal due to Mir Jafar's incapacity as Subedar, the latter's guilty conscience trade him fear the worst. As usual, Mir Jafar ran to Clive for help. Clive left Murshidabad with Mir Jafar's son Meeran, and went to Patna where the prince had arrived. The written records of the period show that at Patna Clive won over the prince by a lavish display of his own unbounded loyalty to the Emperor. The prince led his troops back to Delhi.

In return for this new favour, Clive obtained from his docile "donkey" a Jagir with a clear income of Rs. 3,00,000 per year. It consisted of vast areas of land round about Calcutta, which the Company held from the Nawab's government on an annual rental of Rs. 3,00,000. By the Nawab's grant of the Jagir to Clive, the areas became the private property of Clive and he became entitled to get the said annual rent from the Company.

In addition, Mir Jafar conferred upon Clive the title of "Umra" (nobleman).

Clive's Achievements

Clive had achieved all that he wanted to. He had realised from Mir Jafar, to the last rupee, the full amount which the latter had undertaken to pay to the English in return for the Bengal Subedar's seat. Many new rights and concessions to facilitate the Company's trade in Bengal had been obtained from the Nawab. In addition, the Company had usurped several monopolies. English military strength and English duplicity were treated with respect and were feared throughout the three provinces of Bengal, Bihar and Orissa. Personally, Clive had become immensely rich, besides acquiring the Jagir. "The Nawab's generosity had made" his "fortune easy" (Clive before the Parliamentary Committee in 1777).

On 7th January, 1759, Clive wrote to William Pitt, the Prime Minister of England, as follows:

> "The great revolution that has been effected here by the success of the English arms, and the vast advantages gained to the Company by a treaty concluded in consequence thereof, have, I observe, in some measure engaged the public attention; but more may yet in time be done, if the Company will exert themselves in the manner of the importance of their present possessions and future prospects deserves. I have represented to them in the strongest terms the expediency of sending out and keeping up constantly such a force as will enable them to embrace the first opportunity of further aggrandising themselves; and I dare pronounce, from a thorough knowledge of the Country Government, and of the genius of the peoples acquired from two years' application and experiences, that such an opportunity will soon occur."
>
> "The reigning Soubah ... is advanced in years; and his son is so cruel, worthless a young fellow, and so apparently an

enemy to the English, that it will be almost unsafe trusting him with the succession. So small a body as two thousand Europeans will secure us against any apprehensions from either the one or the other; and in case of their daring to be troublesome, enable the Company to take the sovereignty upon themselves."

"There will be less difficulty in bringing about such an event, as the natives themselves have no attachment whatever to particular princes ...

"But so large a sovereignty may possibly be an object too extensive for a mercantile company; and it is to be feared they are not of themselves able, without the nation's assistance, to maintain so wide a dominion ... It is well worthy of consideration, that this project may be brought about without draining the mother country, as has been too much the case with our possessions in America. A small force from home will be sufficient, as we always make sure of any number we please of black troops ... I shall only further remark, that I have communicated it to no other person but yourself; nor Shall I have troubled you, Sir, but from a conviction that you will give a favourable reception to any proposal intended for the public good." (Malcolm's *Life of Clive,* Vol. II, pp. 119 *et. seq*)

The letter gives a true picture of what the English in India were then planning. Apparently, they were contemplating a revolt against Mir Jafar and/or his son Meeran. Meeran was a young man with plenty of good sense and knew exactly what the real intentions of the English were, and what was at the back of their machinations. Mir Jafar, too, was fed up with their "friendship", and father and son were trying desperately to get out of the clutches of the English. It is probable that Clive suspected this and so had considered it "unsafe" to let Meeran succeed Mir Jafar, and had said so in his letter.

Clive Goes Home

In February, 1760, Clive, who had only a few years ago arrived in India a penniless clerk, left for England, probably the richest Englishman alive.

Appropriately enough, Clive was succeeded by Holwell, the infamous inventor of the "Black Hole Tragedy" myth, who was appointed Governor. Caillaud was appointed the commander-in-Chief of the Company's forces in Bengal. Holwell was Governor for five months only and was replaced by Henry Vansittart. By the time Clive left, the English had already written off Mir Jafar as Subedar. He had outlived his usefulness to the English and "the worm had begun to turn". Nor did the English want Meeran on the scene of their activities, for he had been showing his teeth and was proving a veritable "thorn in the flesh". An opportunity for the elimination of both soon presented itself and the English took fullest advantage of it.

Prince Ali Gauhar started marching on Bengal for the second time, the object being the straightening out of the deplorable state of affairs in Bengal, reports about which had been pouring in for some time. The collection of the cash Imperial tribute, which Bengal had not paid for years, was the other objective. But before he reached Bihar, his father (Emperor Alamgir II) died, and it was as Emperor Shah Alam II that he entered Bihar.

English Tactics

Posing as friends of Mir Jafar and Meeran, the English prevailed upon both to move troops to Patna to check the Emperor's further advance. Col. Caillaud, the new chief of the Company's army, left Calcutta for Murshidabad with his troops and joined Mir Jafar's contingent under the command of Meeran. The two then marched to Patna to oppose the Emperor, which, as Mill says, "was undisguised rebellion" (Vol. III, p. 202).

It is easy to guess that it was the English who had incited and helped Mir Jafar and Meeran to revolt against the Emperor in the hope that father and son would very likely be defeated and they, the English, would thus be rid of both. This is borne out by the fact that the English were simultaneously carrying on secret negotiations directly with the Emperor, who according to Holwell, "had expressed his willingness to accept the terms" proposed by the English *(Ibid).*

Raja Ramnarain, the *de facto* governor of Bihar (as Meeran's deputy), gave proof of his "fast friendship" for the English by rallying forth to oppose the Emperor's army, then on the outskirts of Patna. He was driven back wounded, and the Emperor laid siege to Patna, which, however, was unaccountably lifted after a few days, and his army now marched towards Murshidabad. Caillaud and Meeran, the latter most unwillingly, followed it to Murshidabad where Caillaud pressed Mir Jafar very hard to attack the Emperor's army, which was then within striking distance. This, Mir Jafar and Meeran would not do. Within three days, the Emperor's army turned back to return to Patna. It would appear that no definite plans for the campaign had been decided upon and the Emperor just vacillated between one position and another without achieving anything. Ultimately, he called off the futile expedition and started back for Delhi.

Throughout the operations, Mir Jafar and Meeran were kept under close surveillance lest they went over and submitted to the Emperor, behind the back of the English. Also the latter did not naturally want to leave open any avenue through which Mir Jafar or Meeran could possibly come to know of the English secret negotiations with the Emperor. Caillaud was particularly suspicious, and personally kept an eye on father and son by staying with them in the same tent.

Meeran Found Dead in His Bed

Other ways and means had to be thought of to liquidate Mir Jafar and his son. The English appear to have finally decided upon it, as is indicated by the confidential letters that were now passing between Governor Holwell and Col. Caillaud (May 1760) —letters in which even the murder of Meeran was obliquely referred to. An ingenious scheme was devised.

As has been mentioned, Mir Jafar had, two years previously, appointed Khuddam Hussain as Nawab of Purnea. The English did not like Khuddam Hussain because, being a protege of Mir Jafar, he was a potential enemy of theirs. They consequently engineered a fight between Mir Jafar and Khuddam Hussain, using the technique that had succeeded in pitting Mir Jafar against Raja Ramnarain of Patna. News was brought in to the effect that Khuddam Hussain was plotting against Mir Jafar and using this as a reason, the English prevailed upon Mir Jafar to join them in forestalling Khuddam Hussain's revolt by nipping it in the bud. Caillaud and Meeran led the combined troops against Khuddam Hussain, who naturally opposed force by force. Meeran was unwilling to fight, but the English had intended that the two should, because whatever the result, one of the two, if not both, would be finished. Caillaud forced the issue by starting the fight, but according to Caillaud, he could not succeed against Khuddam Hussain as Meeran refused to co-operate. The Company's troops thus stayed put, facing Khuddam Hussain's force, till 2nd July, 1760.

On the third anniversary of Siraj-ud-daula's murder (2nd July, 1757) and at almost the same hour, Mir Jafar's son and heir was dead. His body was discovered in bed. The news was hushed up and his men did not know about it till they were back in Patna. It was given out that Meeran had been struck by lightning. But, as pointed out by Edmund Burke in his speech to the English Parliament, it was a most peculiar lightning. It had struck without a sound, and had not touched either the tent or the bed in which he had been sleeping. He *alone* was struck!

It is intriguing to find that a month after Meeran's death, ex-Governor Holvell wrote to his successor Vansittart:

> "A party was soon raised at the *Durbar,* headed by the Nawab's son, Miran, and Raja Rajebullabh, who were daily planning schemes to shake off their dependence on the English, and continually urging to the Nawab, that until this was effected his government was in name only." (First Report, 1772, Appendix 9, p. 225)

Was the above statement a justification for, if not a defence of, the means adopted to bring about the dismissal of the English? One wonders.

The Company's Plans for Further Aggrandisement

Clive had, in his letter to William Pitt, asked that the Company should be equipped "to embrace the first opportunity of aggrandising themselves", and, if it became expedient "to take the sovereignty upon themselves". Before he left India, Clive initiated the creation of such an opportunity. Holwell and Caillaud, his successors, carried on his nefarious work, and by the time Vansittart took over as Governor, their plans had taken a definite shape and form. To finalise them the English in Calcutta held several secret meetings under the chairmanship of Vansittart. We quote below from the minutes of the meeting held on 11th September 1760:

> "Our influence has been increasing from time to time since the revolution brought about by Colonel Clive. So we have been obliged to increase our force to support that influence. We have now more than a thousand Europeans, and five thousand sepoys, which, with the contingent expenses of an army, is far more than the revenues allotted for their maintenance. It must, therefore, be proposed to the Nawab to assign to the Company a much larger income, and to assign it in such a full and ample manner, by giving to the Company the sole right of such districts as lie most convenient for management .... It is to be supposed, that such a proposal would meet with all the difficulties that could possibly be thrown in our way ... There seems now to offer such an opportunity of securing to ourselves all we could wish in this respect, as likely may never happen again, an opportunity that will give us both power and right."
>
> (Proceedings at Fort William, First Report, 1772, pp. 228–29)

"Another principal motive" that urged them "to think of changing" their "system" was "the want of money" which they needed for "operations on the coast", the "reduction of Pondicherry", etc.

As has already been mentioned, Mir Jafar had lost his utility as one from whom the English could in future exact all the money that they might need. "With an exhausted treasury ... and vast engagements to discharge" he had been "bled white" already. Nor could he help them any further to help themselves at the expense of an "exhausted country". Consequently, the English had decided to write off Mir Jafar as Subedar of Bengal. The decision was confirmed at the above-quoted meeting.

But, once again, the English were faced by the complete absence of any plausible excuse or ground which could justify their own direct action against their intended victim. Indirect action had failed, as has been narrated above. So the English resorted to their old trick of making such demands as were impossible for Mir Jafar to meet. "He was urged to the severest exactions". (Mill, Vol. III, pp. 213–14). Added to these was the demand for practically sovereign authority over Sylhet and Islamabad areas! Anticipating the certain rejection by Mir Jafar of their demands and their own consequent action against him, the English now cast about for a man to replace him—one who could and would actively further their depredations on a more extensive scale. As fate would have it, it was Mir Jafar himself who unwittingly provided the English with just the man they were looking for. When the demands had been formally made, Mir Jafar sent to Calcutta his trusted and clever son-in-law, young Mir Kasim, to discuss them.

Secret Treaty with Mir Kasim

In the meantime the English had, on 15th September, decided to try and get Mir Kasim and Raja Durlabh Ram to join them in their plot for the removal of Mir Jafar. Governor Vansittart was deputed to contact Mir Kasim and Holwell was to approach

Durlabh Ram with the idea of using him as a contact man between the English and the Emperor in an effort to win the latter over to the English side. Next morning Vansittart and Holwell reported complete success of their respective missions.

The next 10 days or so were spent in discussing and drafting the secret treaty between Mir Kasim and the English. According to Malleson the treaty was signed on 27th September, 1760, and it was therein recorded that the parties thereto had agreed:

(i) That Mir Kasim was to be appointed the Grand Vazier and vested with all the powers and authority of the Subedar and that Mir Jafar was to be allowed to continue as the nominal holder of that office on an annual pension for life,

(ii) That in return for the military help which the English agreed to give in future to Mir Kasim at his request, the districts of Burdwan, Midnapore and Chittagong were to be immediately ceded to them in perpetuity,

(iii) That Mir Kasim must redeem, by payment in cash, the jewellery which Mir Jafar had pledged with the Company,

(iv) That all efforts to re-establish on a firm footing the Emperor's rule in Bengal, Bihar and Orissa would be jointly thwarted by both the parties,

(v) That neither of the parties should arrive at any understanding or settlement with the Emperor without the consent of the other,

(vi) That the English should be granted special privileges for the acquisition of lime in Sylhet and,

(vii) That immediately on assuming office as Grand Vazier, Mir Kasim should pay Rs. 20,00,000 as under:

To Vansittart—5,00,000

To Holwell—2,70,000

The balance to be distributed amongst the other members of the Council and in addition Mir Kasim should advance a "loan" of Rs. 5,00,000 to the Company.

We can hardly do better than quote the comments of W. M. Torrens, M.P., on this "transaction". He writes:

> "The iniquity of this transaction finds few apologists even among those who have taken upon themselves to dress and to enamel Oriental deeds for European view. The treaty with Mir Jafar still subsisted ... He was the sworn and blood-knit ally of the Company; and if ever men were bound by decency to maintain at least the forms of good faith, the Governor and Council of Calcutta were so bound. Yet, being so, for the sum of £ 200,000 to them privately paid, and for the cession of three rich and populous provinces they sold their too confiding friend and ally" (*Empire in Asia*, p. 42).

After closing the deal, Mir Kasim left Calcutta for Murshidabad. Two days later, Vansittart followed him with some companions to bring pressure to bear on Mir Jafar. On arrival, they stayed at the Company's Cossimbazar House, which faced Murshidabad across the river.

Mir Jafar's Dethronement and Deportation

Vansittart and Mir Jafar met and discussed matters on the 15th, 16th and 18th October, 1760. On the 18th Mir Jafar was given written memoranda containing the English complaints against him, their new demands and their proposition about Mir Kasim. Mir Jafar declined to hand over the reins of his government to Mir Kasim. The English and Mir Kasim had now gone too far to retract and decided to use force.

At about 3 A.M. on 20th October, Caillaud crossed the river, with two companies of European and six companies of Indian soldiers, and surrounded the sleeping Nawab's palace. His mental reactions, when he woke up, are thus pictured by Malleson:

> "Well indeed, on that eventful morning, might the thoughts of the old man have carried him back to a

period little more than three years distant, when on the field of Plassey, he too in secret compact with the same English had betrayed his kinsman and master to obtain the seat which another kinsman was now by similar means wresting from him. What to him had been the power thus basely and dishonourably obtained? All the agonies of the preceding fifty-eight years of his life paled before those which he had suffered during the three years he had ruled as the Nawab in the usurped place of Siraj-ud-daula. He could not but contrast his position, threatened by the men to whom he had sold his country, with that which he would have occupied if at Plassey, he had been loyal to the boy-relative who had, in the most touching terms, implored him to defend his turban. With the prestige of having been the main factor in the destruction of the insolent foreigners who had since dictated to him, and who now threatened to dethrone him, he would have wielded real power; his name would have been honoured, his country would have been secure. But now—a glance from the window showed him the red-coated English soldiers rallying round the standard of his kinsman in revolt against him. Would Mir Kasim show him more mercy than he had shown to Siraj-ud-daula? The reflection of the fate to which he had abandoned his kinsman and master must have passed through his mind." (*Decisive Battles of India,* pp. 131–32)

A letter from Vansittart was sent which maddened Mir Jafar to the extent of threatening a desperate resistance. But he soon realised his utter helplessness and surrendered to *force majeure.* According to the English interpreter, Lushington, Mir Jafar's last message to Caillaud before surrender was:

> "You had installed me on the *Gadi* and, if you so desire, you have the might to remove me. You have deemed it proper to break your promises. I have not. If I too had a tricksome mind, I could have collected an army of 20,000 and fought you to a finish. My dead son had warned me — in vain."

The pathetic appeal cut no ice with the English, who dethroned Mir Jafar and deported him to Calcutta, where he was kept under detention and allowed a pittance of Rs. 2,000 per month for his personal expenses. Later, when the old man sought permission to go on a pilgrimage to Karbala, it was refused.

W. M. Torrens, M. P., was not the only Englishman who had condemned the Company for having "sold their too confiding friend and ally". The Company felt compelled to give some sort of justification for their sordid action to the proprietors of the East India Stock. Holwell's fertile imagination and facile pen were once again commissioned and, on 10th November, 1760, a letter written by Holwell to the Company's Directors was read out at a meeting of the English officers of the Company at Calcutta. It had been affirmed in that letter that:

> "That Nawab Jaffir Ali Khan was of a temper extremely tyrannical and avaricious, at the same time very indolent, and the people about him being either abject slaves and flatterers, or else base instruments of his vices; ... numberless are the instances of men, of all degrees, whose blood he has spilt without the least assigned reason."

Attached to this letter was a list of men and women alleged to have been murdered by Mir Jafar's orders. It was only after Mir Jafar's death that Clive's lie was detected. In his letter dated 1st October, 1765, he stated: "The several persons there affirmed to have been murdered are all now living, except two!"

Company's Gains

The English saw to it that:

(i) The three districts of Burdwan, Midnapore and Chittagong, whose combined revenues represented a third of the total revenues of Bengal, were forthwith ceded to the Company in perpetuity by the grant of formal *sanads,* and,

(ii) The promised Rs. 20,00,000 was immediately paid in cash to them.

The next day, 21st October, 1760, Vansittart and Caillaud wrote to the Select Committee at Fort William:

> "The advantages to the Company are great indeed ... A supply of money will be sent with the Colonel for the payment of the troops at Patna, and we have even some hopes of obtaining three or four lacks besides to send down to Calcutta to help out the Company in their present occasions and at Madras."

Yet another gain was the increase in the Company's income from its mint. The Company's first rupee had been minted, after the Battle of Plassey, on 19th August, 1757. Since then the Company's rupees (called the "Calcutta rupees") had been in circulation, but only at a discount, because compared to the Murshidabad rupee, the Calcutta rupee contained less silver and weighed less. So the Company was not making much by minting the coins. The English now took steps to remedy this. The very next day after he had usurped the Murshidabad *Gadi,* Mir Kasim granted the *Purwanah* (licence) to the Company to mint their own silver and gold coins, subject to the condition that the Company's coins were exactly of the same weight and composition as the Murshidabad Government coins. At the same time he issued strict orders that no discount was to be charged on the Company's coins and that no one should refuse to accept them. These orders naturally helped the Company to increase its income and resources.

4

Mir Kasim—Subedar-"Rebel"-Fugitive

Mir Kasim's "Inheritance"

When Mir Kasim took over, the state of affairs in the administration and the condition of the people in Bengal were deplorable and tending to become worse still. He saw that the *Durbar's* finances were in a terrible disorder. Revenue was coming in most irregularly. The army had not been paid for many months, and the cash balance in the treasury was next to nil. Expenses were growing and were already ahead of the income which was shrinking continuously. Like Mir Jafar, he too realised that it was not going to be easy for him to fulfil the lavish promises he had made to the English, who pressed him for payment. To pay the English he borrowed as much as he could, then took recourse to extortion from the landed and monied classes, with the help of the soldiers in the Company's employ. Finally, to meet the still-unsatisfied and growing demands of the English he had to sell the *Durbar* jewellery and even had to melt the gold and silver plate in the palace for minting coins with which to pay the English.

Mir Kasim's licence to the Company to mint their currency was subject to the condition that the Company's coins had exactly the same weight and composition as the Murshidabad Government coins. The English ignored the condition completely and minted coins of heavily alloyed gold and silver. The people too ignored Mir Kasim's strict orders and would not accept the Company's coins except at a discount. The Company then made the infamous request that Mir Kasim should permit them to mint their coins with exactly the same design, inscription, shape and form as the Murshidabad coins. Mir Kasim declined to be a party to this wholesale fraud on his subjects. To keep the English satisfied he, however, issued an ordinance making it an offence for anyone to refuse to accept the Company's coins without a discount. He further began to penalise the people, including landlords and businessmen, who either refused to accept the Calcutta coins or wanted a discount on them. This led to widespread disaffection amongst these classes and as they naturally wielded a certain amount of influence, plots for a revolt against the new Nawab began to be hatched.

Burdwan Countryside Devastated

The *sanad* granting Burdwan to the Company (October, 1760) provided that the landlords and tenants of lands throughout the district were to continue as before. The only change effected by the *sanad* was that the Company's employees, instead of the *Durbar's* officials, would thereafter collect the revenue. It was further provided that the Company would use the money to maintain a force of 2,500 Europeans and 8,000 Indians for the security of the Empire and for providing help to the Subedar (Mir Kasim).

It will be recalled that more than two years previously, Mir Jafar had assigned to the Company the revenue from Burdwan district for only so long as the unpaid balance of the "debt" claimed by the Company remained outstanding. Since then the district had been under the virtual control of the Company, who collected the revenues through *telangas* or their soldiers imported from Madras. The *telangas* had been maltreating the villagers and extorting from them, besides the revenue, their own private levies and perquisites. Every kind of violence to person or property was resorted to. The people in the countryside bore it all for over two years and then began to desert their homes and fields. Raja Tilak Chand, the Zamindar (landlord), repeatedly complained to the English at Calcutta and asked for relief which was never vouchsafed. Many *purgunnas* (sub-districts) of Burdwan were completely deserted by the cultivators and Tilak Chand's losses in revenue were mounting up to hundreds of thousands of rupees. Neither the Subedar nor the English seemed to care. Then Mir Kasim granted Burdwan (in perpetuity) to the Company, which made the suffering Raja and his people subject to the tender mercies of the English and their *telangas* for all time. The cup of their misery was full. However, Raja Tilak Chand made a last effort to get some sort of succour. He wrote to Vansittart about the widespread misery in Burdwan and at the same time brought up-to-date the account of payments due by him as revenue. His appeal for protection fell on deaf ears and the *telangas'* atrocities continued.

In utter despair, Tilak Chand prepared to fight Mir Kasim as well as the English. He entered into an alliance with the Raja of Birbhoom and raised a force. The Council in Calcutta sent a force under Capt. White to suppress the revolt. There was a clash between the two forces on 28th December, 1760, in which the Raja's force was defeated. The Raja of Birbhoom fled to the hills and his capital, Nagore, too was occupied along with Burdwan by the Company's troops.

Gross Abuse of Concession

Duty on merchandise had long been one of the most productive sources of Government revenues in India. During the Moghul regime Indian trade with Iran, Arabia, Egypt, Italy, Spain, Portugal, England, Burma, China, Japan and other countries kept thousands of Indian cargo-vessels busy with the transport of merchandise, on which duty had been paid to the Indian Government. In addition, every trader in India had to pay to the Government transit duty on whatever merchandise he conveyed from one place to another. So the magnitude of the revenue from this source can well be imagined. In 1640, the then reigning Emperor had, as a mark of his pleasure, exempted from duty such merchandise as the East India Company exported or imported into the country. The exemption was strictly limited to the exports and imports by the Company itself and did not cover those by any individual Englishman whether or not in the Company's employ. Nor did the exemption apply to goods in transit from one place to another within the country.

All that was needed to secure the exemption was the Company's *Dastak* (permit) covering the goods in transit. When Siraj-ud-daula was the Subedar, the Company began to abuse the concession not only by using their *Dastak* to cover goods in transit inside the country, but also by selling their *Dastak* to private individuals to enable them to evade the duty on their merchandise. The evil grew during Mir Jafar's regime, and as soon as Mir Kasim occupied the *Gadi,* it became a common practice of the Company's employees and other Englishmen to get the Company's *Dastak* for their own private use. The English historian, Mill, writes:

> "The Company's servants, whose goods were thus conveyed entirely free from duty, while those of all other merchants were heavily taxed were rapidly getting into their own hands the whole trade of the country, and thus drying up one of the sources of the public revenue. When the collectors of these tolls, or transit duties, questioned the power of the *Dustuck,* and stopped the goods, it was customary to send a party of sepoys to seize the offender and carry him prisoner to the nearest factory". (*History of India,* Vol. III, pp. 229–30)

Another Englishman, Verelst, discloses another device adopted for the evasion of the duty. He writes:

> "At this time many black merchants found it expedient to purchase the name of any young writer in the Company's service ... and under this sanction trade was carried on without payment of duties ... So plentiful a supply was derived from this source that many young writers were enabled to spend £1,500 and £2,000 per annum, were clothed in fine linen and fared sumptuously every day." (*View of Bengal,* pp. 8, 46)

The Directors of the Company too admitted (in their letter of 8th February, 1764) that this private trade of the Company's servants, writers, agents and others was unlawful and a shameful misuse of the *Dastak* unauthorised in every way and was a two-fold wrong perpetrated on the Nawab and his natural subjects. Nevertheless, the "wrong" continued as before.

The Emperor, as a measure of protection to the indigenous traders in salt, betelnuts, tobacco, timber, dried fish, etc., had promulgated an order forbidding all Europeans from trading in the listed articles. During the Mir Jafar regime the English set these orders at nought and forcibly began to trade in these articles too. Mir Jafar had protested but it was of no use. At first the English paid duty on these goods but as soon as Mir Kasim took over, they stopped paying all duties. Later, they unlawfully seized the monopoly of buying or selling, at their own price, any kind of goods that they wanted and used force to prevent any Indian trader from dealing in them. The trade was carried on "in the prosecution of which", according to Verelst, "infinite oppressions were committed". And these oppressions were committed under the ostentatious protection of the Company's sepoys and the English flag, which every Englishman, engaged in these activities, hoisted on his place of business. We quote Warren Hastings:

> "I have been surprised to meet with several English flags flying in places which I have passed ... By whatever title they have been assumed, I am sure their frequency can bode no good to the Nawab's revenues, the quiet of the country, or the honour of our nation ... Many complaints against them (sepoys) were made to me on the road; and most of the petty towns and serais were deserted at our approach and the shops shut up from the apprehensions of the same treatment from us. (In a letter to the President dated Bhagalpur, 25th April, 1762)

In the second half of the eighteenth century tyranny and oppression of the people were rampant to an extent unapproached by any in the world's history. We cannot do better than let Edmund Burke sum up the terrible conditions of which helpless Bengal was the victim. In his address to the English Parliament, Burke said:

> "Commerce, which enriches every other country in the world, was bringing Bengal to total ruin. The Company, in former times, when it had no sovereignty or power in the country, had large privileges under their *Dustuck* or permit; their goods passed without paying duties through the country. The servants of the Company made use of this *Dustuck* for their own private trade, which, while it was used with moderation, the native

Government winked at to some degree; but when it got wholly into private hands, it was more like robbery than trade. These traders appeared everywhere; they sold at their own prices, and forced the people to sell to them at their own prices also. It appeared more like an army going to pillage the people, under pretence of commerce, than anything else. This English army of traders, in their march, ravaged worse than a Tartarian conqueror ... Thus this miserable country was torn to pieces ... In vain the people claimed the protection of their own country courts." (Impeachment of Warren Hastings)

Frustration of Traitor-Turned-"Patriot"

The plight of the people of Bengal apparently moved an erstwhile traitor to penitence. At the back of the French settlement of Chandranagore, Nund Coomar had been sent by Siraj-ud-daula to help the French and to protect his own Indian subjects against the English invaders. Nund Coomar flagrantly abused his master's confidence and treacherously left the battle-field with his troops, thus betraying the French and his own countrymen. As the Select Committee said in its report, the English "victory" over the French "would have been impossible" had "Diwan Nund Coomar's troops not been withdrawn". Whether or not Nund Coomar had been paid for his treason, he now turned a new leaf, and cast himself in the role of a "patriot" struggling to rid his country of the hated English. He threw himself, heart and soul, into plans for an armed attack on Bengal, that is, on Mir Kasim and the English, carried out under the Emperor's flag and under the leadership of the Marathas, who had by no means given up their keen rivalry with the English for the domination of the country. The Emperor was in Patna. Nund Coomar contacted both. The Marathas agreed. The Rajas and Zamindars of Burdwan, Birbhoom and other places began to muster under the Emperor's flag to join the attack. The preparations were still going on when the Third Battle of Panipat was fought and lost, dashing to pieces Nund Coomar's hopes of staging a come-back.

The battle was fought on 6th January, 1761, between the Afghan invader, Ahmed Shah Abdali, and the combined Indian forces of the Marathas, Mussalmans, Hindus, Rajputs, Jats and others led by the Maratha Confederacy. On the eve of the battle, however, the leaders fell out amongst themselves. Their followers fought fiercely and inflicted heavy losses on the Afghan forces, before the latter won the day. Ahmed Shah did not dare to venture any further with his decimated force and so returned to. Afghanistan. But the battle had thrown out of gear the Maratha Confederacy which had formed the backbone of Nund Coomar's plans. The Marathas, the last of the competitors with the English for the domination of Northern India, were thus put out of the way, leaving a clear field for the English.

> "With the battle of Panipat, the native period of Indian History may be said to end. Henceforth the interest gathers round the progress of the merchant princes from the far west." (*India on the Eve of the British Conquest* by Professor Sydney Owen)

Tripartite Understanding Between the Emperor, Mir Kasim and the English

Early in 1760, the English representative, Major Carnac, who had replaced Col. Caillaud as commander-in-chief of the Company's forces, arrived in Patna where the Emperor was then staying. Mir Kasim was also there.

Mir Kasim presented to the Emperor a very large amount of money in lieu of the arrears into which the Subedar's annual tribute to the Emperor had fallen, and undertook to send in future, Rs. 24 lacs every year, as tribute to the Emperor from the revenue of Bengal, Bihar and Orissa. He also promised that the Murshidabad coins would in future bear the inscription "Shah

Alam II". The English made a similar promise with regard to their coins minted at Calcutta.

The Emperor, in March, 1761, gave his *ex post facto* sanction to Mir Kasim's Subedarship of the three provinces and issued a *Purwanah* (official notification) to that effect.

The English made two requests, both of which were turned down by the Emperor. One was that the Emperor be pleased to grant the Company similar *Purwanahs* with regard to the regions then under the *de facto* possession and control of the English. The other was that the *Diwanee* of the three provinces of Bengal, Bihar and Orissa may be taken away from the Subedar and granted to the Company. That meant that the Company and not the Subedar would, thereafter, have the authority to collect the government revenue in the three provinces and would be accountable for it to the Subedar and the Emperor.

At that time the Emperor too was having his own troubles. There were rumours, not altogether groundless, of another claimant to the Imperial throne. Shah Alam was, therefore, anxious to hurry back to his capital. He expressed the wish that the English accompany him back to Delhi with their army and also expressed his willingness to grant them the coveted *Diwanee* in return.

The English, however, were quite unable to take advantage of this offer as they did not have enough troops to send to Delhi without leaving almost undefended their possessions in Bengal, practically at the mercy of the host of enemies they had made due to their depredations.

In June, 1761, the Emperor left Patna for Delhi.

Raja Ramnarain under Duress

Ramnarain, according to the English themselves, had long and consistently, been their "firm friend" and "well-wisher". Unfortunately for himself, he also had the reputation of being very rich and both the English and Mir Kasim wanted money very badly. The English technique for getting it was by kidnapping important people and handing them over to Mir Kasim to extort sufficient money for both parties. Governor Vansittart had Ramnarain treacherously arrested and handed over to Mir Kasim's custody, under the pretext that Ramnarain owed money to the Subedar on account of arrears of revenue. The charge was "groundless" as stated, 12 years later, by Carnac in his testimony before the English Parliament's Select Committee. It is intriguing to find that on 17th July, 1761, Col. Coote wrote to the Governor and his Council that Mir Kasim was willing to pay the English Rs. 7,50,000 for doing what they did to Ramnarain. Thus it was that innocent Ramnarain was incarcerated and subjected to extortion for as much money as could be got out of him. Mill criticises the incident, but from another angle. He writes:

> "This was the fatal error of Mr. Vansittart's administration; because it extinguished among the natives of rank all confidence in the English protection; and because the enormity to which, in this instance, he had lent his support, created an opinion of a weak or corrupt partiality." (Vol. III, p. 224)

By 1762, Mir Kasim had geared up the administrative machinery so well that the annual income now exceeded the expenditure. In addition, all the arrears of pay due to the army had been paid up-to-date. Further, all the financial liabilities to the English had been discharged to the last rupee. What was better still, his subjects were satisfied with his administration. To provide effective protection for his administration against the ever-growing, baneful and corrupting English influence, Mir Kasim decided to shift his capital from Murshidabad to Monghyr and spent most of his time there.

He put up very strong fortifications around Monghyr and recruited an army of 40,000. He had drilled and trained in the European way and in the use of European arms by efficient European instructors. He also put up a huge workshop for casting cannons. The cannons produced were admitted to be superior in every way to those made in Europe.

This did not, of course, suit the English at all, who discovered that in replacing Mir Jafar by Mir Kasim, they had "caught a Tartar" of whom they must rid themselves, by fair means or foul.

Case of Kettle Calling the Pot Black

The ball was set rolling by some half-a-dozen members of the Select Committee in Calcutta who on 11th March, 1762, wrote to the Directors of the Company to the following effect:

> "We could cite innumerable instances of Mir Kasim's atrocities and extortions ever since he became the Subedar. But it would make the letter too long. We would give only one instance of Ramnarain whom he had removed from the Deputy Governorship of Patna. We have been considering it to be in our best interests to support Ramnarain in his office as he has always been, admittedly, a man of his word. Ramnarain has been put in irons by Mir Kasim who will keep him like that till money to the extreme limit has been extorted from him. After that, Ramnarain would doubtless be put to death. Mir Kasim has extorted huge amounts of money from most, if not all, of those who have helped the English. Several have died of tortures resorted to for extorting money. Many have been basely murdered, or to escape dishonor have committed suicide, as many Indians do ... Mir Kasim is increasing the strength of his army and is training them in the European way and in the use of the European arms. He is also putting up new fortifications ... All the accusations levelled against Mir Jafar by Governor Vansittart were false and were made with the sole object of turning people's minds against him. All the people are extremely dissatisfied by the replacement of Mir Jafar by Kasim."

Our readers would no doubt note that, as stated before, it was the English Governor Vansittart who had taken Ramnarain into custody and handed him over to Mir Kasim! Mir Kasim extorted money from Ramnarain and from the other victims provided by the English through their sepoys. Whether or not the English and Mir Kasim divided the booty, the fact is incontestable that both were equally guilty.

English Atrocities

A network of the Company's trading posts covered the whole of Bengal and Bihar. All trade in consumer goods, from salt to timber was monopolised by them. The Company's employees bought and sold at their own prices under a show of force. Even standing crops were not spared. If any dealer or cultivator or consumer dared to protest or resist, he was forthwith made an example of by the Company's sepoys, who were always available at the posts on which the English flag was hoisted as confirmed by Warren Hastings himself. Not a copper was collected as octroi or duty by any of the Nawab's outposts.

> "The annals of no nation contain records of conduct more unworthy, more mean, and more disgraceful than that which characterised the English Government of Calcutta during the ... years which followed the removal of Mir Jafar ... The results of this shameful and oppressive system were that the respectable class of native merchants were ruined, whole districts became impoverished, the entire native trade became disorganised and the Nawab's revenue from that source suffered a steady and increasing declension. In vain did Mir Kasim represent, again and again, these evils to the Calcutta Council." (Malleson's *Decisive Battles of India,* pp. 133, 137)

The English were not yet ready or strong enough to go on ignoring completely the Nawab's repeated representations about these "evils" and so decided to dispose them of in their own way. Governor Vansittart and Warren Hastings visited Mir Kasim at Monghyr on 30th November, 1762. Mir Kasim presented his grievances which can be summed up as follows:

> "...... Every village and district ...... was ruined through the oppression of the English, the subjects of the Sarkar (Nawab's Government) were deprived of their daily bread, and the collection of the revenues was entirely stopped, so that it lost nearly a crore of rupees." (*Calendar of Persian Correspondence, p.* 194, No. 1695)

After a couple of weeks' talks, the Treaty of Monghyr was executed between Vansittart and Mir Kasim on 15th December, 1762).Vansittart and Warren Hastings both signed it and the same day both wrote to the Council at Calcutta, profusely praising the fairness and liberality of its provisions as also Mir Kasim's sincerity and truthfulness. Vansittart left Monghyr assuring Mir Kasim that on arriving at Calcutta he would see to it that all differences were satisfactorily settled.

One of the clauses of the treaty provided that the English would in future pay duty on certain articles (salt, tobacco, betel-nuts, etc.) at the rate of 9 per cent, but the Indian dealers would have to pay 25 per cent duty on the same articles. This rank injustice towards his own people was agreed to by Mir Kasim who was, according to Malleson, "anxious for peace at any price short of sacrificing his own independence". (*Ibid,* p. 140).

Vansittart, contrary to the assurance he had given Mir Kasim, began, on his return to Calcutta, sending fresh troops to the Company's trading posts for the continuation of the atrocities already being committed. At about the same time the Council at Calcutta convened a meeting and formally decided to send official instructions to all the trading posts and the agents of the Company, forbidding them in so many words, to act in accordance with any of the terms of the Monghyr Treaty. They were further directed to deal appropriately with such of the Nawab's officials as attempted to have the treaty terms carried out. It is reported that it was stated at this very meeting of the Council that Vansittart had accepted a bribe of Rs. 7,00,000 from the Nawab for signing the treaty. Anyway, the treaty was broken before the ink on it had dried.

After awaiting some sort of action in compliance with Vansittart's three-month-old assurance, Mir Kasim wrote to him on 5th March, 1763:

> "For three years the Government has not received a single thing or a single copper from the English. On the contrary, the English have been and are continuously subjecting government officials to penalties and fines and realising the same by force."

The complaint met the same fate as the previous ones had done and the evasion of duties, as well as the exaction of duties from the Indian merchants by the English, continued unabated.

Whilst the Indian merchants were being eliminated in this way, the income from duties levied by the Nawab's Government was reduced to nil. At this stage Mir Kasim made an ingenious move to meet the situation effectively. On 22nd March, 1763, he ordered the abolition of duties on all kinds of merchandise throughout his territory and the removal of all outposts which were supposed to collect the same. The abolition could not affect his income from duties because he was unable to collect any. The English would not pay, and the Indian merchants either bought the Company's *Dastaks* to secure the exemption of their merchandise or stopped dealing in merchandise subject to duty.

The abolition hit the English hard. Not only did they lose their customers who purchased their *Dastaks,* but the abolition put the Indian merchants on a footing of equality with them, so far as the cost of the merchandise of either was concerned. The Indians lived economically and so could make a profit even if they sold cheaper than the English could. There was a boom in the business of the Indians, resulting in renewed prosperity all round, including agriculture. People had more to spend and paid less for what they got. The English had lost their monopoly through the inevitable economic reactions of the abolition.

English Reactions

It was impossible for the English to forego quietly the huge profits hitherto earned for them by their monopoly of practically all the paying trades. Their Council at Calcutta hastily passed a resolution that the Nawab should be made to withdraw his order which abolished the duties as it was illegal (!) and that he should be forced to re-impose the abolished duties on his subjects (!!).

They re-doubled their efforts to acquire the coveted *Diwanee* of Bengal, Bihar and Orissa for which they were in secret correspondence with the Emperor. At the same time, they hastened their plans for Mir Kasim's overthrow. He came to know about the latter and wrote to Vansittart:

> "I understand that many Englishmen are plotting to instal a new Subedar."

As the plot had not yet been perfected, Vansittart cleverly replied:

> "The story that the English wish to put up another Nazim has been concocted by tricksters."

Another step which the English took was to depute Hay and another Englishman to negotiate a new treaty with Mir Kasim. The latter was informed by Vansittart that the two deputies would be reaching Monghyr for the purpose. Mir Kasim wrote back:

> "Treaties between men are rightly supposed to have some reasonable span of life, so to make a new treaty every year is improper ... You are sending deputies to negotiate a new treaty with me at the same time you are sending your troops all around and these are the troops for whom I have paid you in advance by granting you Zamindaris to the tune of Rs. 50,00,000."

The English went a step further still, and vehemently protested when Mir Kasim ordered the detention of two of his own subjects. One of them was the same Jain Jagat Seth who had joined and helped the English in their plot to overthrow Siraj-ud-daula six years earlier, and the other was his brother Swaroop Chand. Mir Kasim had learnt that both were the moving spirits of one of the most active cells of conspiracy against him which was located in his own capital and so had ordered their detention at Monghyr. The English did not have the slightest right to object but Vansittart did, obviously because "any stick is good enough to beat a dog with".

"Negotiations" with English Deputies

The English deputies arrived in Monghyr and on 25th May, 1763, faced Kasim with eleven new demands in writing on behalf of the Company. It is significant that some six weeks earlier (on 14th April) the English had alerted their army and the "negotiations" were a patent pretence. The demands were so preposterous that their rejection by Mir Kasim was a foregone conclusion and that was exactly what the English wanted as an excuse for starting armed hostilities.

Some of the demands were:

(i) The Nawab must agree to accept *in toto* and in writing whatever the English Council decided about duties or taxes on merchandise, trade or business or business agents,

(ii) The Nawab must re-impose the abolished duties on the merchandise of his subjects and English merchandise should continue to be duty-free,

(iii) The Nawab must make good the financial losses suffered by the English and their employees individually due to the recent abolition of duties,

(iv) The Nawab must agree to punish any of his own subjects if and when so desired by the English.

In making these demands the English were following the same old technique that they had adopted in the past with a slight difference. This time the negotiators impudently refused to listen to what Mir Kasim had to say about his own grievances.

Attack on Patna at Night

The English were now quite ready and were evidently spoiling for a fight. They had agent at Patna named Ellis. Like other agents of the Company, he too had been provided with troops. Ellis started giving no end of trouble to the Nawab's Deputy-Governor at Patna, whose routine orders he openly flouted. Mir Kasim complained to Vansittart but, as usual, nothing happened.

Ellis now received instructions from Calcutta to be ready to attack the fort at Patna the moment he received the order to do so.

Whilst Mir Kasim was holding "peace" talks with the two English deputies, he was shocked to see English boats loaded with arms and ammunitions passing Monghyr on their way to Patna. He stopped the boats and did not allow them to proceed. On 2nd June, 1763, he wrote to Vansittart:

> "The Company's demands are most improper and have been made in violation of the existing treaties ... the Company should recall its troops from Patna."

In reply, he was bluntly told that far from being recalled, the troops in Patna were being strongly reinforced.

As soon as Mir Kasim stopped the boats, the Company recalled the two deputies and ordered Ellis to go ahead with the attack on Patna. Ellis did, and at midnight on 24th June, 1763, occupied the fort at Patna.

Mir Kasim had at last reached the limit of his forbearance and dispatched his army to dislodge the English. His army counterattacked, re-took the fort and the town, and inflicted on the English the loss of 300 European and some 2,500 Indian soldiers. Ellis and his colleagues were taken prisoner and sent to Monghyr.

Mir Kasim ordered the detention of the two negotiators at Monghyr, but one of them got away in an English gun-boat and headed for Calcutta. Mir Kasim ordered his apprehension and return to Monghyr. The boat was stopped near Cossimbazar and the deputy was asked to go ashore. He declined and started firing on the Nawab's men, who boarded the boat and in the melee he was killed.

Mir Kasim's Last Protest and First Demands

On 28th June, 1763, Mir Kasim wrote to Vansittart and his Council:

> "... Mr. Ellis attacked the Patna fort at night like a robber, and plundered the market-place, the traders and inhabitants of the town quite a number of whom were killed. Pillage and killings continued till the next afternoon ... Since your men have wantonly and cruelly ravaged the town, plundered property worth many lacs of rupees and ruined and killed people, justice demands that the Company should make good the losses and pay compensation to the people in the same way as the Company itself exacted compensation for similar "losses" in Calcutta. You Christians have proved to be curious "friends". You entered into a treaty and swore in the name of Jesus Christ to abide by it. On the express condition that the army to be recruited and maintained by you will always be by my side and help me in my need, you got me to grant you a part of my territory to meet the expenses. As all the atrocities have been committed by you through that very army, it is clear that your real intention has all along been to use it for destroying me. I demand in the name of justice and fairness that the Company should give adequate compensation for all the atrocities committed and on all the money extorted from my people by the Company's agents in my territory. I would also trouble you to please return

> to me Burdwan and the other regions granted by me as peaceably as you got them from me."

At long last, Mir Kasim was at bay, but it was too late. He had been patient and forbearing far too long.

"Declaration of War" Against Mir Kasim—Mir Jafar Proclaimed Subedar

Mir Kasim's letter was received in Calcutta on 7th July, 1763. The same day the English Council of the Company published its "Declaration of War" on Mir Kasim. It also announced to the people that Mir Jafar had again been installed as Subedar in place of Mir Kasim, and mustered its troops from all over Bengal in Mir Jafar's name and under his flag. Further, people were asked in Mir Jafar's name to co-operate with and help his troops. It need hardly be mentioned that the Council of the English traders had never been given by anyone the authority to depose a Subedar of the Emperor or to replace him by their own nominee.

It must, moreover, be noted that Patna had been attacked, pillaged and occupied by the Company's regular troops some two days *before* the so-called declaration of war.

On 5th July, 1763, two days before "war" was declared, the Company's army started from Calcutta on its march to Murshidabad. It was commanded by Major Adams. To defend Murshidabad, Mir Kasim's army left Monghyr. It was commanded by Mohammad Taqi Khan.

Syed Mohammad Khan, the Deputy-Nazim of Murshidabad, had already been won over by the English, and he created difficulties and obstructed Taqi Khan's efforts. Even in Taqi Khan's army, seeds of disaffection had been extensively sown by secret agents, prominently mentioned amongst whom is one Mirza Eeraj Khan, who betrayed Mir Kasim and Taqi Khan. There were two or three skirmishes between the Company's and Mir Kasim's troops, in one of which Taqi Khan met his death. In another some 200 Europeans and Christians in Mir Kasim's artillery deserted at the crucial moment and went over to the English.

Udvanalah

Nature and Mir Kasim's foresight had combined to turn Udvanalah into an almost impregnable stronghold. On two sides it was bound by the Ganga and the deep river Udvaualah, which formed a confluence with the Ganga. On the third it was flanked by the unscalable Rajmahal hills with a lake at their foot. On the fourth side it was bordered by deep wide moats overlooked by battlements of the fortifications constructed by Mir Kasim. On the battlements were mounted over a hundred heavy guns. Beyond the moats was an extensive treacherous swamp. Access to Udvanalah was possible only by a narrow lane of solid earth which wound its tortuous way through the swamp, and its course was a well-kept secret which the Company's commanders did not and could not know.

It was here that Mir Kasim's army made its last stand.

Siege of Udvanalah and Its Fall

The Company's army laid siege to Udvanalah. Old Mir Jafar too was there.

For a whole month the besiegers subjected Udvanalah to a very heavy cannonade but it had no visible effects. There were frequent sorties too on the besiegers after midnight. An abstemious Mussalman Commander, Mirza Najaf Khan, led them. He sallied forth by the secret route and, after inflicting losses on the besiegers in lives and property, would return the same way. The besiegers could not pursue him. It was a stalemate and the English were in despair. However:

> "It was the act of a single individual which converted the despair of the English into confidence; it was the consequence of that act which changed the confidence of Mir

Kasim's army into despair. The individual on this occasion performed the divine function for the English army." (Malleson's *Decisive Battles of India*, p. 157)

This individual was an anonymous English soldier. Some time earlier, he had left the English army and entered the Nawab's. The recruitment of this Englishman by Mir Kasim in his army proved to be the most potent factor leading to his downfall. This English soldier very carefully studied the secret passage through the marsh which Mirza Najaf Khan used in his sorties on the besiegers. After memorising it, he slipped away one night to the English camp and within an hour led the English army into the besieged stronghold. The defenders were caught napping. They had relied too much on the impregnability of their stronghold and on the utter inability of the English to take it. They had become complacent and careless. They were taken completely by surprise and lost 15,000 men in battle. "Adams" (the English Commander) "not only conquered Mir Kasim's army, he massacred it too." (*Ibid*, p. 160).

One of the reasons contributing to the fall of Udvanalah is stated to be the absence of Mir Kasim himself that night. Had he been there in person to alert and guide his officers and encourage his men .... "it is more than probable that the English Company would have been left, from that day, without a single foot of ground in these Provinces." (*Consideration of Indian Affairs* by Bolts, p. 43).

There were also quite a number of traitors in Mir Kasim's army. Some of the high-ranking officers were Europeans, Christians and Armenians and their instinctive loyalty was not to the Mussalmans who were fighting their co-religionists. From the 11th century onwards the followers of the cross and the crescent had been at war with each other. The latter had more than once conquered and ruled the former, the repeated defeats rankled in their hearts and the hostile feelings have persisted throughout the centuries. The inability to visualise and evaluate the potentialities of this hostility has, time and again, proved to be fatal for many Indian and other Asiatic rulers. Amongst Mir Kasim's officers was one Khoja

Gregory *alias* Gurdhin Khan. He had a brother, Khoja Petroos, who was a rich merchant in Calcutta. Major Adams contacted Gregory and the other Armenians in Mir Kasim's army through Petroos and succeeded in winning them over to the English side.

With the fall of Udvanalah on 4th September, 1763, the last hope or chance of the success of the Indian Subedar's struggle for power against the foreign traders was lost forever. Mir Kasim met with a disaster from which he could not recover. But even so, he did not lose heart and would not surrender to the foreigners. From Udvanalah he went to the Fort at Monghyr. It was a strong fort too and Mir Kasim after arranging for its proper defence left for the Azimabad Fort. In his absence the commandant of the Monghyr Fort, Arab Ali Khan, was bribed and so surrendered it to the English without firing a shot. The English now pursued Mir Kasim. It has been stated that Mir Mohammad Ali Khan the commandant of the Azimabad Fort also handed it over to the English in return for a pension of Rs. 500 per month. Mir Kasim was thus surrounded on all sides by traitors.

The English, though "victorious" so far, still had two more things to accomplish. One was to take Mir Kasim into custody and the other was to rescue Ellis and his other English companions who were still held under detention by Mir Kasim.

Mir Kasim had a Frenchman, Gentil, in his personal employment. On 19th September, 1763, Adams and Carnac wrote to Gentil:

> "... If you can contrive means for the delivery of our gentlemen from the power of Cossim Ally Khan and will convey them to us, you may place a firm reliance on the gratitude of the English; and we promise you fifty thousand rupees immediately." (Long's Records, pp. 332–33).

Plot for Taking Mir Kasim Prisoner—His Escape

Vansittart and Warren Hastings got Khoja Petroos (the aforementioned Christian merchant of Calcutta) to write to his brother

Khoja Gregory *alias* Gurdhin Khan, who, as mentioned before, was an officer in the Nawab's army, for help in this connection. Gurdhin Khan appears to have agreed. One night Mir Kasim was awakened from sleep by one of his trusted secret agents and told, "Your commander Gurdhin Khan is selling you to the *Firangis*. The plot is ready. Some outsiders and your prisoners have joined Gurdhin Khan."

For three months, Mir Kasim had been treating Ellis and his companions with great consideration and generous hospitality. When, however, he discovered that these people had abused his trust and hospitality and were plotting against him and that they had collected arms for the execution of their plot, he ordered their execution as rebels. So Ellis, all his English companions (except Dr. Fullerton), Jagat Seth and his brother Swaroop Chand, and other conspirators including their leader Gurdhin Khan were executed at Patna.

Thereafter, when the English advanced towards Patna, Mir Kasim crossed the river Karmnasa with some troops and artillery and on 4th December, 1763, he left his territory and entered the territory of Shuja-ud-daula, the Nawab of Oudh.

Thus ended Mir Kasim's three years of rule as Subedar. His subsequent struggles and death will be related later. In the opinion of many, Mir Kasim was, to a certain extent, the last Indian who went all out to safeguard and preserve the independence of Bengal and perished in the attempt.

5

Mir Jafar Again

As mentioned before, the English in Calcutta, on 7th July, 1763, proclaimed throughout Bengal, Bihar and Orissa, that Mir Mohammad Kasimali Khan had been deposed on account of his "tyrannies" and "Mir Mohammad Jaffir Ali Khan Bahadur" had again been installed on the *Gadi.* The proclamation also appealed to all the Government officials and the people "to muster under the flag of Mir Mohammad Jaffir Ali Khan Bahadur to help him to firmly establish his Subedarship and to defeat all the efforts of Kasimali Khan" to re-occupy the *Gadi.*

Price Paid by Mir Jafar

The English had earlier got Mir Jafar to execute an agreement about which the historian Elphinstone says (*Rise of British Power in India*, p. 397):

> "Most of the English affirmed that the re-installation of Mir Jaffir was nothing else but the restoration of his just right to him; but even so they did not hesitate to impose on him new and harder terms."

By the agreement, all the concessions, including the three districts granted by Mir Kasim, were confirmed. The other terms may be summarised as follows:

(i) The Nawab's army was to consist of no more than 12,000 infantry and 6,000 cavalry.

(ii) The duty of 25 p.c. on all the merchandise of the Indian traders, which had been abolished by Mir Kasim was to be re-imposed.

(iii) With the exception of salt on which a duty of 2½p.c. was made payable by the English traders, all other merchandise of the latter would be duty-free throughout the territory, and they would have the right to trade in any other commodity anywhere without paying any duty.

(iv) Mir Jafar was to pay to the English:

(a) Rs. 30,00,000 for war expenses,
(b) Rs. 25,00,000 for the English army,
(c) Rs. 12,50,000 for the English navy, and
(d) An estimated Rs. 5,00,000 as compensation for the financial losses suffered by the English on account of the abolition by Mir Kasim of duties on the merchandise of the Indian traders. The amount actually realised on this account was Rs. 53 lacs as against the 'estimated' Rs. 5 lacs which Mir Jafar had agreed to pay!

But, as Scrafton writes, the Nawab was now no better than a mere bank with whom the English had unlimited credit against which the Company's employees could draw any amount and as often as they liked.

Bengal in 1764

A picture of the condition to which the Administration and the people of Bengal were reduced during less than 15 months of Mir Jafar's second "rule" is provided by the long list of grievances which he detailed to the Council at Calcutta (September, 1764) in a vain attempt to get them redressed. It may be summarised thus:

(a) Illegal, forcible and continued occupation of:

(i) the forts at Patna, Monghyr and other places,
(ii) as many as 40 travellers' rest-houses at Patna and
(iii) numerous villages without paying any government revenue.

(b) Abuse of the concession to mint coins by minting base coins which were lighter in weight too.

(c) The loss of poor people's livelihood caused by the Europeans who forcibly monopolised the poor people's trade in salt, betel-nuts, tobacco, etc., and unlawfully prevented them from dealing in these commodities.

(d) Forcible acquisition and sale of all foodgrains by the Company's men at their own prices, so that enough foodgrains even for the Nawab's Army, were not available.

(e) Cruel ill-treatment of the countryside people by the sepoys who passed that way on the Company's business.

(f) Offenders, even against the Government, were given refuge in the Company's factories and business premises, and traders in Patna and Murshidabad who refused to pay Government duties were protected by the English.

(g) Two new markets were set up by the English and the traders and customers of the old government markets were compelled to have dealings only with the English markets. The Government markets were ruined, causing heavy losses in revenue.

As usual, nothing happened.

Mir Kasim's Last Efforts

The Emperor Shah Alam was staying at Phaphamau (Allahabad). Shuja-ud-daula, the Nawab of Oudh, was the Prime Minister of the Mughal Empire, and the Emperor's principal supporter. Mir Kasim approached both and related to them all that had happened in Bengal. Shuja-ud-daula took an oath on the Holy Quran that Mir Kasim would be re-installed on the Murshidabad *Gadi*. Mir Kasim did something more. He still had with him his artillery and a body of troops. He sought and obtained permission to subdue the rebellious Raja of Bundelkhand, against whom Shuja-ud-daula was preparing to lead a military expedition. Mir Kasim invaded Bundelkhand with his own artillery and troops and subjugated the Raja, who undertook to pay up all arrears of the Imperial tribute. Victorious Mir Kasim returned to Allahabad. The Emperor and his Nawab Vazier were so pleased with Mir Kasim that they immediately started preparations for invading Bengal and attacking the English with the object of restoring the *Gadi* to Mir Kasim.

In the meantime, Shuja-ud-daula, as the Emperor's Prime Minister, addressed to the English Governor and his Council a communication giving them:

(a) An opportunity to answer and explain the serious charges detailed against them, and

(b) An ultimatum in case they persisted in their extra-commercial and unlawful political and other objectionable activities.

Pointed attention was drawn to the numerous favours, concessions, privileges, grants of settlements and business houses, *jagirs* and titles which the Emperors of Hindustan had, from time to time, conferred upon the English Company and individuals, on a scale which, perhaps, "exceeded proper limits", and which certainly exceeded the help given to any other European nation.

> "In spite of all these favours," the communication proceeded, "you have interfered with the Emperor's rule and administration, occupied Burdwan, Chittagong and other areas in the Imperial territories, and, without the Emperor's permission or consent, have, at your own will, removed and replaced one Subedar by another. You have imprisoned the *Durbar's* officials and men, and have affronted and committed grave contempt of the Emperor's authority in other ways too. You have sheltered the rebels against the Emperor. You have not only ruined the country's trade and commerce, but have also caused very heavy losses to the Imperial revenue. The inhabitants of the country have been subjected by your men to untold atrocities. Even now you are continuing to occupy by force of arms fresh Imperial regions, the recent ones being several *Purgunnahs* (sub-districts) and villages in the Allahabad Province, which have been attacked and pillaged."

"There can be no understandable reason for all these unlawful activities on your part, other than that you have intended to set at nought the *Durbar's* authority, and are resorting to these actions with the deliberate intention of establishing your own political rule over the country."

"Please let me have full particulars. Have you done all this under instructions from your King or the Company in England, or of your own bat? 1 want to know, so that I can take proper steps to remedy all these evils. If you have been doing it all on your own to achieve your own unlawful ambitions, then 1 call upon you to desist immediately from all interference in the country's administration, and to limit your activities exclusively to trade and commerce, as you did in the beginning. If you do that, then the *Durbar* will help you, more than ever, in expanding your trade."

"Please send one of your senior high officers as your representative, who can give me a true picture of all the circumstances and all necessary explanations. I shall then take appropriate action."

"Should you, God forbid, persist in your present attitude and continue to disregard any authority except your own, then the sword of justice will inevitably come down on the heads of the rebels, who would then feel the weight of the Emperor's wrath—which would be like God's anger. Then it will be too late for you to admit the error of your ways, and to submit humble petitions for merciful consideration. As it is, the Emperor has already shown you more than enough consideration. I have written to you as 1 wanted to give you a last chance. Do what you think proper but send me a reply soon."

English Reaction

Along with the above letter from Shuja-ud-daula, the English also received information about Mir Kasim's imminent return to Bihar with the Emperor and Shuja-ud-daula. They correctly assessed the strength of the latter's army and had no illusions about their own ability to cope with it in a battle fought in the open. When Mir Kasim had left Bihar, the English had advanced from Azimabad (Patna), crossed the river Sone and camped at Buxar. Now they hurriedly left Buxar, re-crossed the Sone and went beyond the walls of Azimabad.

Getting no satisfactory reply from the English, Shuja-ud-daula, taking the Emperor and Mir Kasim with him, advanced with his army and besieged Patna.

The English had a very anxious time, but their traditional ability in intrigues helped them at this juncture too. They knew that the Emperor was himself in grave difficulties because of the growing strength of his opponents in Delhi, and was looking for help in all directions. The English exploited the situation, and started by insidiously creating distrust between Shuja-ud-daula and the Emperor. They approached the latter behind the back of the former, and assured him of their own sincere "loyalty and faithfulness" to him. They even offered to undertake the subjugation of Shuja-ud-daula, and to hand over the latter's entire territory of Oudh to the Emperor. All this did not win over the Emperor to the English side, but it certainly succeeded in making him quite indifferent to the result of the siege of Patna.

Then the rainy season started. Shuja-ud-daula, partly because of the rains and partly because of the Emperor's attitude and the initial success of English machinations, lifted the siege of Patna and retired to Buxar, where he decided to stay till the rains were over.

Mir Jafar Summoned

When Mir Jafar became the Subedar for the second time, he appointed Nund Coomar as his Dewan or minister. It will be recalled that Nund Coomar was the 'repentent' traitor who had deserted at Chandernagore and gone over to the English. Later, he had plotted to overthrow the English with the help of the Marathas, but the plot was scotched by the Third Battle of Panipat.

Now Nund Coomar advised Mir Jafar to propitiate Shuja-ud-daula and the Emperor and get the latter formally to confirm his second tenure of office as Subedar. The English came to know about it, and, as any amicable direct settlement between Mir Jafar and the Emperor could not but be against their own interests, they dismissed Nund Coomar from his post of Dewan to Mir Jafar, and peremptorily summoned the latter from Patna to Calcutta. Mir Jafar had to obey. The incident appears to have created some unrest amongst the Company's Indian soldiers at Patna, but it was quickly put down and the agitators were shot.

The English feared that if the siege of Patna was allowed to drag on, Shuja-ud-daula would quite possibly get the Marathas to help him, and so they decided to end the 'war' as soon as possible. Major Munro was sent from Calcutta to take over as commander-in-chief of the Company's forces at Patna. He was specifically instructed to attack Shuja-ud-daula and to end the hostilities immediately. Munro took prompt action. He marched to the Rohtas Fort and it was surrendered to him, as arranged, by its commandant, Raja Sahumal. Munro had approached Sahumal through Dr. Fullerton and Syed Ghulam Hussain, (the author of 'Seourul Mutakhreen', who admits the fact) and had promised Sahumal everything that he had wanted. Needless to say, not one of these promises was ever kept and the go-between, Ghulam Hussain, could not help Sahumal when the latter appealed to him.

The Battle of Buxar was fought on 15th September, 1764, between Munro's troops, who had sallied forth from Azimabad, and Shuja-ud-daula's besieging army. It raged the whole day and ended in the complete rout of Shuja-ud-daula's army which left many thousands dead on the battle-field. Shuja-ud-daula had to retreat and many more of his men got bogged in the quagmire of the Ganga and perished.

Some of the reasons responsible for the disaster have been stated to be the deterioration of relations between the Emperor and Shuja-ud-daula, and between the latter and Mir Kasim. The Emperor had become definitely, though covertly, hostile to Shuja-ud-daula, and was only marking time. He had been toying with the idea of joining the English, who had sent him some very attractive offers which had finally decided the issue in favour of the English. So the Emperor had been, for some time, perfecting his plans to go over to the English. When the Emperor himself was behaving like that, it is not difficult to imagine the numbers in Shuja-ud-daula's army who followed the Emperor's lead and passively or actively sided with the enemy, whom they were supposed to fight.

Emperor Changes Sides

As soon as the battle was over, Shah Alam openly left Shuja-ud-daula, went over and camped with the English army. The English forthwith hailed him as "our Emperor" and offered him their obeisance as his humble subjects. Accompanied by the Emperor, the English crossed the Ganga and from there sent an invitation to Shuja-ud-daula's Dewan, Beni Bahadur, to come and start negotiations for a treaty. The English tried to assure Beni Bahadur that the Company had strictly forbidden its employees to "conquer" any further territory in Hindustan, but even so, no treaty materialised. Then, it appears, the Emperor went towards Allahabad.

Shuja-ud daula retreated to re-form his army with the intention of putting up a fight once again, and the English followed suit.

Mir Kasim's End

Mir Kasim knew that if he were caught, the fate that awaited him at the hands of the English would not be any better than that meted out to Siraj-ud-daula. He, therefore, escaped from Buxar and went to Allahabad. From there he proceeded to Bareilly where he stayed for some time. For the next 12 years he was a homeless wanderer till death mercifully overtook him at Delhi in 1777.

Chunargarh Fort was on the way of the returning English army. The English commander had with him a *Purwanah* (order or authorization) in favour of the Company, signed by the Emperor, which he presented to the commandant of the fort, Mohammad Bashir Khan, who wavered. The garrison, however, decided to ignore the *Purwanah* and resist the English. Finding their commandant to be still hesitant, they got hold of him, threw him on the road outside the fort, and courageously put up a spirited defence. The English brought up their guns and shelled the fort, but it took them several days to effect a small breach in one of its walls, through which they tried to enter one dark night. But the defenders repulsed them, inflicting heavy losses on them. The English, thoroughly beaten, gave up and resumed their journey to Allahabad. Their army had never yet succeeded in getting the better of the Indian army in any fair fight.

Fall of the Fort at Allahabad

The garrison of the fort at Allahabad too put up a very stiff resistance, but the English were lucky enough to find a friend who knew all the secret ways and passages to get in and out of the fort. This was no other than Najaf Khan who, a little over a year before, had, by his nocturnal raids, harassed and battered the English besiegers at Udvanalah. For some reason, he had now joined the English and helped them to effect an entry into the Allahabad Fort. The English were helped, too, by a very superior heavy gun made in India, which they had seized at Buxar in the loot of Shuja-ud-daula's camp.

Shuja-ud-daula had by no means given up the fight. He again attacked the English army at Kara, with the help of some Maratha troops of Malharrao Holkar. There were one or two minor skirmishes, till Maharaja Shitab Rai intervened, and, as a mediator, got a treaty executed between the Company and Shuja-ud-daula. It contained the following terms:

1. Shuja-ud-daula was to pay to the Company as reparation, Rs. 25 lacs down, plus another Rs. 25 lacs in yearly instalments.
2. The territory comprising Allahabad, which was then part of the Oudh Province, was to be separated

and set apart for the Emperor's benefit. The town and the Fort of Allahabad were to be used for the Emperor's residence exclusively, and a detachment of the Company's army was to be quartered in the fort for the Emperor's security.

3. Ghazipur and its adjoining region were to be ceded to the Company.
4. A representative of the English was to be stationed permanently in Shuja-ud-daula's Court, but was not to interfere in any way in the Nawab's administration.
5. In future, an enemy or friend of one party was to be treated as an enemy or friend by the other.

There can hardly be any doubt that, had not the Emperor himself played into English hands, Shuja-ud-daula would have, at Buxar, succeeded in putting an end to the growing English political power. As it was, he was very heavily handicapped by the hopeless incapacity of Emperor Shah Alam.

Company's Last Extortion from Mir Jafar

Mir Jafar had been used as a ladder by the English for climbing up to the top of their ambitions, a ladder which was heartlessly kicked away as soon as the objective was reached. In October, 1764, the Company made him agree to pay Rs. 5 lacs per month. He was exceedingly hard up during his last days which were made most miserable for him by the Company. In the words of Sir William Hunter, his death "is said to have been hastened by the unseemly importunity with which the English at Calcutta pressed upon him their private claims to restitution". Mir Jafar died in February, 1765, at the age of 65, in his palace at Murshidabad.

6

After Mir Jafar

Mir Jafar's eldest son, Meeran, having, as related, predeceased him, the second son, Najmuddaula, succeeded his father as Subedar. But Spencer who had succeeded Vansittart refused to recognise Najmuddaula as Subedar unless he executed a fresh agreement. It had become impossible for Najmuddaula to function as Subedar without the consent of the "Governor-in-Council" and resistance was equally out of the question, as the latter's armed forces far exceeded those of the Murshidabad administration. The principal terms of the proposed agreement were:

1. The new Nawab was to create a new post of Deputy-Subedar, to which a nominee of the English, Mohammad Raza Khan, was to be appointed, who as Deputy, would carry on the entire administration in the Nawab's name.
2. No one in the administration's Finance Department was to be dismissed or appointed in future without the previous consent of the English Council.
3. The Murshidabad Treasury was to pay regularly Rs. 5 lacs per month for the expenses of the Company's army.
4. The strength of the Nawab's army was never to be in excess of what was absolutely necessary for the collection of revenue and maintenance of the Nawab's prestige.
5. The English would in future have the right to carry on any trade, anywhere in the territory, without being liable to pay any duty, octroi, levy or tax whatsoever.

Najmuddaula had to accept all the terms, though they reduced his administrative authority to a mere shadow. In addition, he was made to "present" Rs. 20 lacs to Spencer and his colleagues.

The new Nawab wanted to appoint Nund Coomar as his Dewan. But the English over-ruled the appointment and arrested Nund Coomar and brought him to Calcutta.

Clive's Return to India

The trade and commerce of the English had increased by leaps and bounds, and so had their ambitions. For the attainment of their ambitions, the Directors of the Company in England considered it essential to send Clive back to India, and so Lord Clive was appointed Governor of Fort William. On his way out, he touched Madras and received news of Mir Jafar's death. He, according to Wheeler (*Early Records of British India,* pp. 329–30),

> "... was delighted at the news. He was anxious to introduce the new system for the Government of the Bengal provinces, which he had unfolded to Pitt more than several years before. He would set up a new Nawab, who should only be a cypher. He would leave the administration in the hands of native officials. The English were to be the real masters; they were to take over the revenues, defend the three provinces from invasion and insurrection, make war and conclude peace. But the sovereignty of the English was to be hidden from the public eye. They were to rule only in the name of the Nawab and under the authority of the Emperor."

Clive reached Calcutta in May, 1765, and learned that Spencer and his colleagues had recognised Najmuddaula as the Nawab Subedar and had in the bargain filled their own private pockets with Rs. 20 lacs. He was very angry because he had intended to instal on the Murshidabad *Gadi,* a six-year-old grandson of Mir Jafar. Anyway, Clive got busy with steps for the implementation of the plan chalked out by him.

Clive Extorts Rs. 5 Lacs for Himself

The Emperor was still in Allahabad, and Clive decided to go to meet him. On the way, however, he stopped at Murshidabad, and succeeded, with the help of Mohammad Raza Khan, in collecting from the helpless Subedar Najmuddaula Rs. 5 lacs as his "present". Before leaving, he so arranged matters that almost all the power was in actual practice wielded by the English and the Subedar was reduced to a mere figurehead.

From Murshidabad Clive went to Benares, where both General Carnac and Shuja-ud-daula resided at the time. Clive met the latter on 2nd August, 1765, and coerced him with threats of fresh hostilities into modifying and adding to the terms of the agreement which had been executed between him and the Company less than a year before. The new terms were:

(i) The ceding of Allahabad and Kara to the Company to hold the same "for the Emperor", and

(ii) The increment in the amount payable to the Company as reparation from Rs. 50 lacs to £600,000.

Emperor Signs Death Warrant of Mughal Empire

Clive then proceeded to Allahabad. He met the Emperor on 9th August, 1765. It was a fateful meeting because, at it Shah Alam granted the Dewanee of Bengal, Bihar and Orissa to the English Company, thereby digging the grave of the Mughal Empire itself. The grant of the Dewanee meant:

1. That the Company was vested with sole and exclusive authority to collect all government revenue and other dues in Bengal, Bihar and Orissa, and out of the collections

    (i) To send to Delhi as Imperial revenue Rs. 26 lacs, and

(ii) To meet the expenses of the Murshidabad *Durbar.*

2. That the Company was to retain the balance as its property.
3. That the Subedar was to discharge only the remaining administrative duties.

Thus were created two governments in the territory—one for show, to be carried on by the Indian Subedar, and the other, the real *de facto* government, to be carried on by the English Company at Calcutta. Having achieved his purpose, Clive left for Calcutta.

Death of Najmuddaula

On the day Clive left Murshidabad for Benares, Najmuddaula died under suspicious circumstances. Both he and Mohammad Raza Khan had accompanied Clive to see him off, as far as a garden outside the city. On the way back, young Najmuddaula was seized with a terrible pain in the stomach, and he died as he reached his palace. Rumours of foul play persisted. Colour was lent to some of these rumours by these two facts. One was that after accepting a present of Rs. 5 lacs from Najmuddaula, Clive wrote to the Court of Directors: "It is impossible therefore to trust him with power, and be 'safe'." The other fact was that in his letter to William Pitt, Clive had written about Meeran, Mir Jafar's heir: "... It will be almost unsafe trusting him with the succession." By a strange coincidence, Meeran too met with a mysterious death, not long afterwards. In any case, the Company benefited by Najmuddaula's death to the tune of over Rs. 13 lacs a year. The Company had, at the time of the grant of the Dewanee, agreed to pay Rs. 55 lacs a year to the Murshidabad *Durbar* for its expenses. The Company reduced it to Rs. 41,80,000 when Najmuddaula's younger brother became the nominal Subedar.

Thereafter, the real government in the three provinces was carried on separately by each of the three Deputy-Subedars appointed by the English. The Subedar was a mere cypher in every sense. Henceforward, the history of Bengal will be exclusively a narrative of what the English governors did there.

Company's Employees as Freebooters

In their overpowering greed for personal wealth, the English employees of the Company, high and low, had now thrown overboard not only the distinction between right and wrong but the Company's interests too. They openly resorted to free-booting which they carried on

> "... with impunity in Bengal and elsewhere ... The counting-house was deserted continually for marauding expeditions ... During this period the business of a servant of the Company was simply to wring out of the natives a hundred or two hundred thousand pounds as speedily as possible, that he might return home" ... (Torrens' *Empire in Asia,* pp. 82–83)
>
> "... we think the vast fortunes acquired in the inland trade have been obtained by a scene of the most tyrannic and oppressive conduct that ever was known in any age or country." (Letter from the Court of Directors to Lord Clive dated May, 1766)

One cannot easily imagine a stronger or more authoritative condemnation of the nefarious activities of the Company's English employees—not excluding Clive himself.

Clive's Taxation and Commercial Policies

The Company had the authority to tax any merchandise at its own discretion. Clive's obvious policy was to tax the necessities heavily and the non-essential commodities somewhat less. An essential commodity like salt was subjected to the heavy duty of 35 p.c. and in addition the employees of the Company were given the monopoly of the salt trade. Thus even the poorest had to suffer. The Company collected all the taxes.

The monopoly in salt was followed by the forcible acquisition of the monopolies of other commodities too, so that before long, all worthwhile trade in Bengal, Bihar and Orissa came under the absolute control of the English or their men, agents and sub-agents.

Bolts, an Englishman, was expelled from the country, because he had detailed in his book the ways and devices through which the Company's agents had destroyed the flourishing industries and handicrafts of Bengal. Verelst, who succeeded Clive as Governor, testifies in one of his letters that before the advent of the English political authority, products of arts, crafts and industries in Bengal not only reached every corner of India but crossed the seas on its East and West to reach even far-off countries. Thus "money flowed into Bengal in a thousand ways". But all those ways were closed now. The European traders exported to Europe shiploads of merchandise produced in India, but the country never received a penny in return, as the full price of the exported goods was paid out of the amounts realised and collected in Bengal. But that was not all. The English also realised from Bengal, in one form or another, all the money they needed to meet their expenditure in other Indian Provinces and even in their Chinese Settlements. "During three years the exports of bullion from Bengal exceeded five million sterling, whilst the imports of bullion were little more than half a million." (*Early Records of British India* by Wheeler, p. 375).

Wholesale downright inhumanity was resorted to for getting all that money. We quote from the official records of the Company to describe what was happening when, due to total failure of rains, Bengal found itself in the grip of a terrible famine. Whilst thousands were dying of hunger all round, "some of the agents saw themselves well situated for collecting the rice into stores; they did so. They knew the gentoos (Hindoos) would rather die than violate the principles of their religion by eating flesh. The alternative would, therefore, be between giving what they had or dying. The inhabitants sank; they had cultivated the land, and saw the harvest at the disposal of others. In some districts the languid left the bodies of their dead unburied." (*Short History of the English Transactions in the East Indies,* p. 145).

Even the Directors of the Company were moved to write in their letter dated 18th December, 1771, that the employees of the Company should absolutely and exclusively control the supply of rice and other grains which led directly to an acute scarcity of foodgrains all round.

Clive's Departure and Warren Hastings' Appointment

Clive left India for good in 1767, and was succeeded by Verelst as Governor of Fort William in Bengal.

Each of the three provinces comprising the Suba of Bengal was ruled, independently of one another, by Shitab Rai, Mohammad Raza Khan and Jasarat Khan, as Deputies of the Company. It is interesting to note that during this period was started the training of Englishmen in the procedure, practice and know-how of revenue work. They were systematically assigned to work under the guidance of all the Indian revenue officials. The English trainees later controlled and often supplanted their erstwhile teachers.

It would appear from one of Verelst's letters that the English had a lot to do with the postponement of the Emperor's return to Delhi and the prolongation of his stay in Allahabad. Evidently, Verelst wanted the Emperor to come to Bengal but, in the interest of the Company, he dared not make the suggestion. He hoped for some way of getting the Emperor himself to express a wish to visit Bengal.

In August, 1769, Cartier took over from Verelst as Governor of Fort William in Bengal. Nothing of any political importance happened in Northern India during the Cartier regime, except that Emperor Shah Alam left Allahabad in 1771 and went back to Delhi. An outline of the Governor's normal and routine functions at this time is to be found in A. F. Scholfield's Preface to the third volume of *Calendar of Persian Correspondence.* He writes:

> "Fom the tangle of plot and counterplot, of intrigue and suspicion, the personality of the Governor of Fort William in Bengal, to whom most of the letters in this volume are addressed or in whose name they were issued, does not emerge with any great distinction."

Warren Hastings took over from Cartier in 1772.

7

Warren Hastings

Warren Hastings had poor education and had come out to India as a clerk of the Company on a salary of Rs. 40 per month. He worked for a long time with the Company's Agent at the Murshidabad *Durbar.* He served his apprenticeship in diplomacy, intrigues and machinations under Clive and proved to be an apt pupil. In addition he took the opportunity to familiarise himself with the traditions, customs, beliefs and the mental make-up generally of the country's people. The finished product turned out to be much craftier and far more unscrupulous than Clive himself.

So far as increase in or accession to the territory under the Company's rule is concerned, Warren Hastings did not achieve much. Yet his tenure of office as Governor (1772–75) and then as the first Governor-General (1775–85) is rightly considered as of utmost importance in the history of the establishment of British rule in India. It was Clive who laid its foundations, but it was Warren Hastings who persistently and successfully undermined the political authority of the Indian rulers of the time and thus consolidated and built up the foundations on which the superstructure of the British Empire was ultimately raised. Apart from his activities in the north of India as Governor, his regime as Governor General covers the First Maratha War and the wars in the south with Haider Ali and Tipu Sultan. These wars will be dealt with in later chapters. We shall confine ourselves in this chapter to what Hastings did in the north.

London Pressure on Warren Hastings

Throughout the 13 years of Warren Hastings' assignment in India, the Directors of the Company continuously pressed him to collect and remit more and more money from the country. Their thirst for money grew with the satisfaction of each demand and became insatiable. It can hardly be wondered at if, as Lord Macaulay put it,

> "The object of Mr. Hastings' diplomacy was at this time simply to get money ... by some means, fair or foul". (*Critical and Historical Essays,* Vol. III, p. 244)

Warren Hastings did not fail to exploit the opportunities that came his way for lining his own pockets, but he always did so without any detriment to his employers' interests.

1. When in 1765, the Emperor granted the Diwanee to the Company, Clive agreed, as provided in the grant, that the Company would pay the Emperor Rs. 26 lacs every year as Imperial revenue. The Company did so till 1771 when the Emperor left Allahabad. Next year, Warren Hastings, on taking over, stopped further payments.
2. Clive had compelled Shuja-ud-daula in 1765 to cede the region comprising Allahabad and Kara to the Company which it undertook to hold in trust for the Emperor. Warren Hastings sold the territory back to Shuja-ud-daula for Rs. 50 lacs, which went, not to the Emperor, but into the Company's coffers.
3. Clive had reduced by over Rs. 13 lacs the Company's previously agreed annual payments to the Murshidabad *Durbar.* Warren Hastings unilaterally reduced it still further.

Other 'Reforms'

Simultaneously, Warren Hastings effected many changes calculated to replace the Indian personnel by the English in all the higher grades of the Company's administration of the Provinces including the Company's Indian Deputies at the head of the Administration in each of the Provinces.

The Englishmen who had undergone training by working under the Company's Deputies and other revenue officials had by now learnt all about administrative and revenue work and were now competent to carry on independently.

Warren Hastings started with Mohammad Raza Khan, the Deputy of Bengal at Murshidabad, and Shitab Rai, the Deputy of Bihar at Patna. Both were charged with embezzlement and breach of trust, arrested and brought to Calcutta for trial.

Nund Coomar, who had been changing sides every now and then and had been deported by the Company from Murshidabad to Calcutta, was now bought over by Warren Hastings to help him in proving Mohammad Raza Khan's guilt. The price paid was Warren Hastings' promise to make him the Deputy of Bengal. Nund Coomar did his best but Warren Hastings did not keep his promise.

Strangely enough, both the accused were found "not guilty" and were discharged by Warren Hastings. The reason was later stated by the frustrated Nund Coomar to be the heavy bribes running into lacs of rupees which had been paid to Warren Hastings. Anyway, the Deputies were not reinstated and the three Provinces were brought under the direct rule of the Company which appointed its own officers, collectors and judges throughout the Suba of Bengal.

The Civil and Criminal Courts were shifted from Murshidabad to Calcutta and within a year in 1773 a Supreme Court was established at Calcutta, with Sir Elijah Impey, a boyhood friend of Warren Hastings, as its first Chief Justice. It had jurisdiction over Bengal, Bihar and Orissa. A beginning was thus made for the ultimate removal of the seat of the government of the Suba of Bengal from Murshidabad to Calcutta, the headquarters of the Company. It was calculated to demonstrate that the ruling powers over the entire Suba were now in fact exercised by the Company exclusively.

Extermination of Rohillas

Rohillas were Pathans whose homeland, Rohilkhand, bordered the Oudh territory of the Nawab Vazier Shuja-ud-duala. Mill, in his *History of India* (Book V, Chap. 1), describes the Rohillas thus:

> "Their territory was one of the best governed in Asia; the people were protected, their industry encouraged, and the country flourished steadily. By these cares, and

> by cultivating diligently the arts of neutrality, and not by conquering from their neighbours, they provided for their independence."

The English "had not the slightest pretence of quarrel with the Rohillas" (Torrens' *Empire in Asia,* p. 111). The Rohillas had entered into a treaty with Shuja-ud-daula and had been observing it scrupulously.

These were the people against whom Warren Hastings entered into an alliance with Shuja-ud-daula in 1773. The allies agreed to invde Rohilkhand jointly, but that Shuja-ud-daula would meet the entire cost of the expedition. It was further agreed that Rohilkhand was to be handed over to Shuja-ud-daula against Rs. 40 lacs to be paid by him to the Company.

> "On the 17th April 1774 the allies in iniquity entered Rohilkhand. In vain the brave but out-numbered people sued for mercy ...... Seldom, if ever, have what are calculated the rights of victory been more inhumanly abused. Every man who bore the name of Rohilla was either put to death or forced to seek safety in exile." (*Ibid,* p 110)

Shuja-ud-daula got Rohilkhand and paid the promised price of Rs. 40 lacs to the Company. Warren Hastings, too, according to some accounts, received Rs. 2 lacs for himself.

It was all done within a week. The once-prosperous Rohilkhand was plundered and devastated mercilessly. "The Rohillas should be exterminated", Warren Hastings had written in one of his letters.

First Governor-General of India

Next year 1775, Warren Hastings was promoted to be the first Governor-General of India. Till then, there had been separate Governors and their respective Councils at the head of each of the Company's administrations in Madras and Bombay, in addition to the Governor of Fort William and his Council in Bengal. All the three administrations were independent of one another. With the appointment of Warren Hastings as Governor-General of India, the Governors of Madras and Bombay were brought under the administrative control of the Governor-General of India.

A few months later, Warren Hastings wrote "finis" to the career and life of Nund Coomar. Frustrated and furious, Nund Coomar presented a long petition to the Council at Calcutta, accusing Warren Hastings of numerous extortions of bribes and many atrocities. He supported these accusations with full particulars, *e.g.,* names, addresses and amounts, etc. In the opinion of the Council, a *prima facie* case had been made out against Warren Hastings, but Warren Hastings, who was still a Governor, refused to appear before the Council and defend himself on the ground that the Council had no authority to hear complaints against the Governor.

As a counterblast Warren Hastings charged Nund Coomar with having committed forgery some five years earlier in 1770. Nund Coomar was tried by the Supreme Court at Calcutta. Whether or not the witnesses and the evidence produced for prosecution or defence were sufficient or reliable to prove his guilt has never been settled. The fact remains that Nund Coomar was convicted and sentenced to death, even though no law of the country, Indian or English, had prescribed the death penalty for forgery. The fact that the presiding judge was Sir Elijah Impey, an old friend of Warren Hastings, and that the latter himself was the prosecutor as also the Governor-General of India at that time, may or may not have had something to do with the sentence which was not provided for by law. Nund Coomar was hanged on 5th August, 1776, in the presence of thousands of Indians and according to Mill, he faced death with unprecedented calm and courage.

Depredation of Benares

Benares State was a tributary of the Nawab Vazier of Oudh, who concerned himself only with the collection of the annual tribute due to him, and not with the State's administration which was carried on by its ruler, Maharaja Balwant Singh. "His people were happy, and the country prosperous .... the peasantry fearless of unjust exaction or personal wrong, cultivated their fields like gardens, and throve on the fruits of their industry." (Torrens' *Empire in Asia,* p. 124). But, unfortunately, as it turned out, the Maharaja had the reputation of being the richest of the Rajas in that part of India, and so became the natural victim of the Englishmen's lust for money.

In 1776, Warren Hastings somehow succeeded in getting the Company the grant of Benares State from the Nawab Vazier of Oudh. The Company forthwith issued a *sanad* whereby,

(i) All the ruling powers of the reigning Maharaja Balwant Singh were vested in his son Chet Singh, and

(ii) An English "Resident" was posted in the Benares *Durbar.*

Warren Hastings was now faced with the necessity of increasing the armed forces of the Company. So he ordered Chet Singh to maintain three battalions of infantry under English officers which were to be at the disposal of the Company. It cost Rs. 5 lacs a year. Chet Singh protested, but had ultimately to carry out the order.

Two years later, Chet Singh was ordered to maintain a similar cavalry regiment. He refused and so provided Hastings with an excuse for military action. He immediately marched on Benares, ordered the arrest of Chet Singh and surrounded his palace. Chet Singh escaped with his life, but with little else. The palace was ransacked and the town was thoroughly looted.

Warren Hastings installed a youth of 19 from the ruling family, as the titular Maharaja of Benares. Almost all the ruling powers of the Maharaja were vested in the English Resident. The annual tribute payable by the State to the Company was raised to Rs. 20 lacs. The condition of the people under the new administration is thus described by Torrens (*Empire in Asia,* p. 125):

> "Misery and distraction took the place which had recently been occupied by comfort and content .... two years later, when Hastings revisited the ...... he found *it* one of desolation."

Torture of Oudh Princesses

On the death of Shuja-ud-daula, his son Asaf-ud-daula succeeded him as the Nawab Vazier of Oudh with its capital at Lucknow. The dying Nawab Vazier had placed his mother and his wife under the "special protection" of the English Government headed by Warren Hastings, who had "accepted the trust". The two old princesses dwelt in the palace of Fyzabad which Shuja-ud-daula had bequeathed to them, and "were supposed to have derived under his will vast treasures". (Quotations from Torrens).

In course of time Asaf-ud-daula was bled white, not only by the never-ceasing English demands for more and more money, but also by the heavy annual contribution he was obliged to pay to the Company for the maintenance of the subsidiary force. At last he reached the end of his tether and could pay no more. He personally approached Warren Hastings and pleaded poverty.

The two met at Chunar and agreed upon a sordid "device for replenishing the exchequer of Calcutta without exhausting that at Lucknow." (Quotation from Torrens). "It was", says Lord Macaulay, "simply this, that the Governor-General and the Nawab Vazier should join to rob a third party, and the third party whom they determined to rob was the parent (mother) of one of the robbers."

But apparently, even Warren Hastings could not bring himself to have the gates of the Fyzabad palace forced open by the English troops and the aged women robbed—women whom he had taken under his "special protection". To justify this cowardly breach of trust, an adequate reason had to be found. So, a conspiracy with Chet Singh for resisting the English was imputed to the intended victims, but still the imputation had to be proved and "proved in a respectable way". Sir Elijah Impey's services were requisitioned.

So, the Chief Justice of the Supreme Court at Calcutta and Chief Magistrate of England in the East, left Calcutta and arrived at Lucknow.

> "He took a number of affidavits which accused the Begums of complicity with Chet Singh in his supposed conspiracy against his lawful masters, the Company. Sir Elijah did not

read the affidavits, or hear them read. They were in a dialect he did not understand, and he had no time to wait for an interpreter ...... This scandalous prostitution of his high authority being completed ...... he returned to Calcutta ...... The farce concluded, tragic scenes began. The palace of Fyzabad was surrounded by English troops. The Princesses were told that they were captives, and required to deliver up their gold and jewels. On their refusal, these ladies were subjected to semi-starvation and their servants to torture. Unable to bear their groans and tears, the Begums gave up casket after casket, and store after store until the sum of spoil was reckoned at £ 12,00,000. Then, and not till then, their wretched menials were allowed to go. Such are the bare outlines of the dreadful tale." (Torrens' *Empire in Asia,* pp. 126–128).

It might be noted here that in 1787, Sir Elijah Impey was impeached for "crass corruption, positive injustice .... intentional violation of the Acts under which he held his powers". But the then rulers of England did not punish him, holding it sufficient that the man had been exposed. Thus the man who had sent Nund Coomar to the gallows for forgery even though there was no provision in law prescribing the death penalty for it, and who had deliberately provided a false excuse for the robbery of the aged and defenceless princesses of Oudh got off very lightly.

Devastation of Gorakhpore

In 1778, Warren Hastings, according to James Mill, transferred one of his officers, Col. Hennaway, from the Company's service to that of the Nawab Vazier who was pressed to vest Col. Hennaway with full civil, revenue and criminal jurisdiction and authority in the districts of Gorakhpore and Bahraich. Within three years,

"...... the country, from a very flourishing state .... had been reduced to misery and desolation; that taxes were levied not according to any fixed rule, but according to

> the pleasure of the Collector; that imprisonments and scroungings for enforcing payment were common in every part of the country; that emigrations of the people were frequent; and that many of them were so distressed as to be under the necessity of selling their children." (Mill, Book V, Chapter 8).

When the Nawab came to know of the atrocities, he dismissed Col. Hennaway immediately. Mill has stated that Col. Hennaway was in debt when he entered the Nawab's service, but when he was dismissed three years later, he had not only paid off all his debts, but had a large sum in hard cash. Another Englishman, Colebrooke, in a letter to his father in England, wrote:

> "...... the plundering of the Begums and the extermination of Rohillas may be forgotten, but the cruelties enacted in Gorakhpore will for ever be quoted to the dishonour of the British name."

It would be an utterly wrong assumption to imagine that only the princes, the rich and the highly-placed suffered as the result of Hastings' "crooked politics and shameless breaches of faith". It must be remembered that the Company was legally vested with the right and the authority to levy and realise taxes, land-rents and all revenues throughout Bengal, Bihar and Orissa. We quote again from Colebrooke's above-mentioned letter:

> "I may confine myself to stretching the land rents to the utmost sum .... A proprietor of an estate under the Mogul Government seldom paid half of the produce of his estate, and in small properties much less; he was further allowed to take credit for a certain sum by way of pension or held rent-free lands in lieu thereof. Under the Company, a landholder is allowed ten per cent of net produce as his share ...... It was Mr. Hastings who filled the country with collectors and judges who adopted one goal, easy fortune. These harpies were no sooner let loose upon the country than they plundered the inhabitants

with or without pretences .... Justice was dealt out to the highest bidders by the judges, and thieves paid a regular revenue to rob with impunity .... The treatment of the people has been such as will make them remember the yoke as the heaviest that any conqueror put upon the necks of conquered nations."

Impeachment of Warren Hastings

It has been stated in the minutes of the Company's Council at Calcutta dated 11th April, 1775, that during the three years that had then passed since his appointment as Governor, Warren Hastings had amassed a private fortune of "over forty lacs". Further, "Hastings acknowledged to having taken a hundred thousand pounds from Asaf-ud-daula in 1782" (Talboys Wheeler in *Short History of India*).

One can easily visualise the size of Warren Hastings' total fortune from the two items authenticated above, plus those that have not been recorded.

Burke's famous impeachment of Warren Hastings in the British Parliament gives all the details of Warren Hastings misdeeds and atrocities during the thirteen years of his administration of the country. It is a "must" for all students of the history of India of that fateful period. The Parliament heard the case for seven years whilst Burke proved all his charges by documentary evidence. In the end, the British Parliament acquitted Warren Hastings of all charges, apparently because, whatever Warren Hastings was stated to have done, the Parliament believed he had done very largely in the interests of the English nation and for the consolidation of English rule in India. The impeachment is stated to have cost Warren Hastings Rs. 10 lacs. The Company, however, compensated him by granting him a pension of Rs. 40,000 a year for 28 years, and by paying him most of it in advance.

8

The First Maratha War

By the middle of the 18th century, Maratha power, under the able leadership of Peshwa Balaji Bajirao, had reached its zenith. A weak descendant of Shivaji still occupied the *gadi* of his illustrious ancestor at Satara, but he did so under the Peshwa's wing. All power and authority, however, rested in the strong and capable hands of the Peshwa, who had established his capital at Poona. The Poona *Durbar,* as the Peshwa's Government was called, ruled the vast Maratha Empire extending from Attock in the North to Karnatic in the South, and from the western boundary of Bengal in the East to the Khandala Bay in the West.

The main pillars of the Maratha Confederacy, as it has been called, were four Maratha rulers of big and practically independent States, viz., Sindhia of Gwalior, Holkar of Indore, Gaikwad of Gujarat and Bhonsle of Berar. All four of them acknowledged the paramountcy of the Peshwa, paid him tribute and held their respective armies at the disposal of the Poona *Durbar.*

Origin, Growth and Decline of the Peshwas

Balaji Vishwanath, the first Peshwa, had obtained from the Mughal Emperor, Farrukhsiyar, the Charter of Self-Government for the Maratha Dominion, and had undertaken to maintain an army for the defence of the Emperor's territory in the South. The Emperor had also passed an order that for the maintenance of this army, *chowth* or one-fourth of the revenue of the remaining territory, under the Emperor's *Suba* in the South, was to be paid to the Marathas.

Thereafter, the successive Peshwas continued to acknowledge the Delhi Emperor as the Emperor of India and their suzerain, albeit only in name. It was in the Emperor's name that Peshwa Balaji Bajirao sent an army to the North beyond Delhi to reconquer the Punjab and wrest it back from the Afghans who had invaded and occupied it. Balaji Bajirao's brother, Raghunathrao—better known as Raghoba—was put in command of this army. He drove the Afghans out of the Punjab province and back across the river Attock. Although the conquered province was made a part of the Maratha Dominion and placed under a Maratha governor, it was all done in the Emperor's name and the governor was styled the Emperor's Subedar.

Within a few years, however, the Maratha domination of the Indian political scene began to wane. It was caused very largely by internal dissensions among the leading members of the Confederacy and the separatist tendencies of some of the Maratha rulers who had constituted the Confederacy's main strength. These dissensions had simmered for some time before they raised their ugly head in 1761 at the Third Battle of Panipat, which, as mentioned before, the Marathas lost.

The defeat cost the Marathas their prestige and political influence not only at the Emperor's Court but also throughout Upper India up to and beyond the Ganga. Rot had set in and the only person who could have stopped it was Peshwa Balaji Bajirao. But he died within a few weeks of the defeat at Panipat. He was succeeded by his minor son, Madhavrao, under the guardianship of his uncle Raghoba (Raghunathrao), who acted as Regent during the Peshwa's minority. Raghoba was a man of strong will, courageous and had proved himself to be a capable military leader in his conquest of the Punjab. But he was ambitious too, and it made him short-sighted and so thoroughly unscrupulous that in the pursuit of his ambitions, he did not hesitate to commit even cold-blooded murder. Later, he proved to be quite incapable of preventing the defection of the Maratha rulers from the Maratha Confederacy.

English Reactions and Plans

As stated by Grant Duff *(History of the Mahrattas)* "the Court of Directors were desirous of seeing the Mahrattas checked in their progress". Consequently, the Panipat shock to the solidarity of the Maratha Confederacy gave the English abundant satisfaction. The growing power of the Marathas in Northern India had threatened to develop into a serious obstacle in the maintenance of English domination in political, economic and military spheres in that region, and of its extension to other parts of the country. The English now considered themselves to be free, at least for the time being, of the Maratha menace in the northeastern regions of India. But they too had equally important possessions and vested interests in central, western and southern India, which had still to be safeguarded against a resuscitation of the Peshwa's power which was by no means dead yet.

To consolidate the Company's position on the Western coast, the Directors impressed upon the Governor of Bombay and his Council, "in the strongest manner", the urgency of their acquiring some additional "valuable" regions along the coast, to wit, "Salsette and Bassein," with their dependencies, and the "Marhattas' portion of the Surat Provinces. "These are the objects," wrote the Directors in their letter dated 31st March, 1769, "which you are to have in view in all treaties, negotiations and military operations, and that you must be ever watchful to obtain."

The English had also realised that the threat to their existence in Southern India could and would become extremely serious if the Peshwa succeeded in enlisting the support of Hyder Ali and the Nizam for driving out the English from the south. They, therefore, planned to use every possible artful device for creating and promoting friction, bickerings and clashes among all the three, so that the chances of their combining against the English were reduced to a minimum.

Further, to prevent any possible resurgence of the Peshwa's power, and to guard against the resulting Maratha interference with the expansion of the English domination in Bengal and North-eastern India, the English also planned somehow to get the Marathas deeply involved in their internal dissensions.

"In more earnest prosecution of these plans," the Directors sent a special agent, Mr. Mostyn, to India, "with instructions from the Court of Directors, that he should be sent immediately to negotiate with Madhorao, the Peshwa ...... for the cession of the island and peninsula of Salsette and Bassein". (Mill, Vol. III, pp. 423–24). The "cession" of these two places was only one of Mr. Mostyn's mission. "Mr. Mostyn was sent to Poona by the Bombay Government for the purpose of ...... using every endeavour, by fomenting domestic dissensions or otherwise, to prevent the Marhattas from joining Hyder Ally or Nizam." (Grant Duff's *History of the Marhattas*, p. 340)

The English had not had much difficulty in winning over Raghoba, who, as Regent of the minor Peshwa Madhav Rao had acquired a good deal of power and influence at the Poona *Durbar*. Raghoba was easily, perhaps willingly, convinced by the English that Nizam-ul-Mulk, the Emperor's Subedar in the South, was about to attack the Marathas. The allegation was baseless. But the English, with the help of Raghoba, persuaded Madhav Rao who had now attained majority, to enter into an alliance with the Governor of Bombay as a precaution against the Nizam's attack, should it materialise. An agreement was eventually executed by Madhav Rao and the Governor of Bombay. It was to the effect that if the Nizam attacked the Marathas, the English would help the Marathas with their army and war materials and that, in return for such help, the Peshwa would cede to the Company the island of Salsette and the Bassein Fort.

The Nizam never attacked the Marathas, so the coveted Salsette and Bassein were not ceded to the Company. But the agreement did serve to put the English and the Peshwa *Durbar* on a friendly footing. Probably, that was what the English had wanted. The English now had an approach to the Poona *Durbar* and soon established some sort of a status there. This in turn provided them with ample opportunities for carrying on their intrigues in the very stronghold of the Maratha hegemony.

The stage was thus set for the start of Mostyn's machinations, when he arrived on the scene ostensibly as the Bombay Council's representative at the Poona *Durbar*.

Mostyn at Work

Mostyn began very cautiously with Raghoba co-operating whole-heartedly. But at the Poona *Durbar*, they were pitted against the famous Nana Fadnavis, a far-sighted statesman and politician of rare acumen and calibre. He knew full well what the English and Raghoba were up to. According to historian Torrens, "Nana Fadnavis respected and admired the English, but only at a distance. He studiously avoided any close political contacts or collaborations with the English, and howsoever great or imminent the crisis that faced him, he consistently refused to accept any military help from the English on a long-term basis or understanding."

That was why Nana entirely disapproved of the above-mentioned agreement between Madhav Rao and the Governor of Bombay. The Peshwa, too, was now under Nana's influence and had been free of Raghoba's tutelage since he had attained majority. So, after some exploratory conversations, Mostyn realised that it was not going to be an easy task to get Salsette and Bassein from the Peshwa, but he continued his efforts. He now tried to sow dissensions between Nana and Raghoba and then prevailed upon the latter to try somehow to bring the Peshwa back again under his (Raghoba's) influence. Raghoba appears to have bungled, for he only succeeded in making Madhav Rao so angry that the latter ordered his detention, but released him shortly afterwards. Utter failure faced Mostyn and Raghoba, when the young Peshwa, aged only 28, suddenly died, in circumstances not entirely free from suspicion, on 18th November, 1772. He had no son and had nominated his younger brother, Narayanrao, as his successor. Within a few months, Narayanrao was murdered on 30th August, 1773. We quote from Sir Henry Lawrence's statement in the "Calcutta Review", Vol. II, p. 430:

> "Raghoba afterwards murdered Narain Rao ...... and was supported by the British Government, a very evil chapter in Anglo-Indian history."

Within less than three weeks of the murder, the Council at Bombay wrote to their agent Mostyn, who was at Poona:

> "...... to improve diligently every circumstance favourable to the accomplishment of that event (the possession

of Salsette and Bassein), and on no account whatsoever to leave the Marattha Capital." (Mill, Vol.III, p. 425).

Raghoba lost no time in proclaiming himself the Peshwa in succession to the murdered Narayanrao.

Mostyn now turned his attention to another item of his mission, namely, the engineering of a clash between the Marathas and the Nizam as well as Hyder Ali. Raghoba was now as much a puppet in English hands as Mir Jafar had been in Bengal. Mostyn prevailed upon Raghoba to declare war against the Nizam and Hyder Ali and sent him south with an army. This proved to be a wrong step, taken as it was before Raghoba was firmly in the saddle at Poona. The Poona *Durbar* and the people were violently opposed to Raghoba's usurpation of the Peshwa's *Gadi* with the help of the English. During Raghoba's absence from Poona on his expedition to the south, the opposition gained considerable strength under the able leadership of Nana Fadnavis and his colleagues in the government, so that Raghoba, after meeting with nothing but disaster and disgrace in the south, could not venture to return to Poona and went away to Gujarat.

In the meantime, the murdered Narayanrao's widow gave birth to a posthumous son on 18th April, 1774. The Poona *Durbar* unanimously proclaimed the infant to be the Peshwa in succession to Narayanrao, and the people hailed the event with unfeigned delight. Mostyn was in Poona, but what could he do?

It was, however, imperative in the English interest that no one else but their puppet, Raghoba, should occupy the *Gadi*. They got Raghoba to come to Surat to sign a treaty and on 6th March, 1775, Raghoba (purporting to be the Peshwa) signed the treaty whereby he assigned to the English, with immediate effect, Salsette, Bassein and a part of the Surat Province. In return, the English promised to send Raghoba with the Company's army to Poona and to instal him on the Peshwa's *Gadi*. The "treaty" had no legal sanction and it led to what has been called the First Maratha War.

The Battle at Arras

Accordingly the Bombay Council sent an army to Gujarat, under the command of Col. Keatinge to join forces there with Raghoba's troops and then to march on to Poona and instal Raghoba on the *Gadi.* The Poona *Durbar* sent their army under the command of Senapati Khadke to intercept the Company's army. The two armies joined in battle at Arras (in Gujarat) on 18th May, 1775. Raghoba and his helpers were defeated suffering heavy losses. As the rainy season was due to start any moment, Senapati Khadke did not follow up his advantage and instead returned to Poona, thus leaving in Gujarat a clear field for Raghoba and the English to carry on their intrigues.

As it happened, Gujarat then offered a most favourable opportunity for the success of the English design of weaning away the Gaikwad, the ruler of Gujarat, from his allegiance to the Peshwa and from the Maratha Confederacy.

Some years earlier, the reigning Gaikwad, Maharaja Damnajirao, had died, leaving behind him four sons born of his three wives. Two of them, Sayaji and Govindrao had been fighting among themselves for years, each claiming the *Gadi.* Fatehsinh, the cleverest of the four brothers, had been siding with Sayaji. The Bombay Council sent their veteran agent, Mostyn, from Poona to Gujarat. Mostyn approached Fatehsinh and, after some time, succeeded in getting Fatehsinh to agree to a treaty between the English and the Gaikwad.

In pursuance of this treaty, Sayaji (whom Fatehsinh had favoured) was installed on the *Gadi* with the help of the English, who, in return, got from the new Maharaja Gaikwad territory with an annual income of several lacs of rupees. The Gaikwad family had up till now owed allegiance to the Peshwa, but the new Maharaja, Sayaji Gaikwad, disowned it and broke away from the Maratha Confederacy. His was the first open defection.

It was about this time that Warren Hastings, who had been the Governor of Fort William in Bengal for three years, was appointed the first Governor-General of all the Company's possessions in India, with authority over the Governors of Bombay and Madras and their Councils.

Hastings' Direct Negotiations with Poona

The Bombay army's defeat and the resulting failure to instal Raghoba as Peshwa, placed the Governor of Bombay and his Council in a difficult position so far as the Peshwa Government was concerned.

The Bombay Government had occupied Salsette and Bassein under the "Treaty" signed at Surat by Raghoba as the (self-proclaimed) Peshwa. They had done so in anticipation of the success of their attempt to put Raghoba on the *Gadi.* The attempt had failed, and there was hardly any chance of Raghoba becoming the Peshwa in the near future. On the other hand, the English attempt had irretrievably antagonised the Poona *Durbar* against them.

The Poona *Durbar* had rejected the Surat "Treaty" as invalid, and the Bombay Government, after having gone to war with the *Durbar,* could hardly approach it with the request that they may be allowed to retain possession of Salsette, Bassein, *etc.,* to which the Bombay Government had no right, legal or moral.

It was in these circumstances that Warran Hastings thought of a plan of starting direct negotiations with the Poona *Durbar* in his capacity as Governor-General. He sent a special representative, Col. Upton, to Sakharam Bapu, the Prime Minister at Poona, to express the Governor-General's deep regrets for the Bombay Government's unauthorised military action against the Peshwa Government in support of Raghoba. Col. Upton was to explain that the military action had been taken without the permission of the Governor-General, and that the latter's consent to the Surat "Treaty" had never been obtained by the Bombay Government. Upton was further to convey an assurance by the Governor-General that the English did not at all want either to help Raghoba or to fight the Peshwa Government. He carried with him a letter to this effect signed by Warren Hastings and addressed to Sakharam Bapu. Hastings had concluded the letter with fervent protestations of the English friendship for the Poona *Durbar,* and with the request that the English might be permitted to retain possession of what they had taken under the Surat "Treaty". Thus the most important part of Upton's mission was to negotiate for and obtain the acceptance of Warren Hastings' request for the continued English occupation of Salsette and Bassein.

Upton in Action

Col. Upton went to Purandar, where the Poona Ministers were then in residence. On arrival he found that he had been given an extremely difficult assignment. He was pitted against shrewd politicians like Sakharam Bapu and Nana Fadnavis, who could correctly evaluate the Governor-General's professions and who saw clearly not only what was behind them but also the full implications of the proposals.

Col. Upton was called upon to explain the obvious inconsistency in the English position. Whilst the Governor-General disapproved of and disowned the Surat "Treaty", he yet wanted to retain the territory occupied under it. Upton was repeatedly asked if the Governor-General's professions and his denunciation of the "Treaty" were sincere. He obviously could not give the real reason as that would have exposed the hollowness of the Governor-General's profuse assurances of English friendship for the Peshwa; nor could he think of any other reason which could be plausible enough for such astute diplomats. After a few weeks, on 7th February, 1776, Upton wrote to Warren Hastings that his proposition was not at all acceptable to the Poona *Durbar*. But he stayed on at Purandar trying to wear away the Poona Ministers' opposition. After some months of futile efforts, he decided to go back to Calcutta. He was on the point of leaving Purandar, when the Poona Ministers, so it is stated, asked him to put off his departure. He agreed to it.

As subsequent events proved, there had been a change, as sudden as it was inexplicable, in the Poona Ministers' previous adamant attitude, and they were now willing to enter into negotiations with Upton for a fresh treaty, which was eventually signed on 6th June, 1776. Upton then returned to Calcutta.

Treaty of Purandar and Its Reaction

The treaty was executed between the Peshwa *Durbar* and the Company whose seal was affixed to it. Its main clauses may be summarised as follows:

(i) The Surat "Treaty" was declared invalid and cancelled.

(ii) The English undertook to withdraw their support from Raghoba and never again to render him any help.

(iii) The English undertook to vacate and restore possession of the Bassein Fort to the Poona *Durbar.*

(iv) The Poona *Durbar* undertook to make provision for a maintenance allowance to be given to Raghoba.

(v) The Poona *Durbar* agreed to the retention of the island of Salsette by the Company, and "as a token of friendship" granted to the Company as a Jagir, the city of Broach and its adjoining areas which had an annual income of three lacs of rupees.

(vi) It was agreed that a representative of the Company was to be permanently stationed at the Poona *Durbar.*

As soon as the Directors of the Company in London came to know of the above terms, they wrote to Warren Hastings, and insisted on the Company's keeping "under every circumstance of all the territories and possessions ceded to the Company by the treaty concluded with Raghoba" and directing him forthwith to "adopt such measures as may be necessary for their preservation and defence" (Mill, p. 436).

In subsequent letters, the Directors stated very clearly that it would be foolish to give up an important region and fort like Bassein. They directed their English employees in India not to withdraw their support from Raghoba, and to find or create some excuse or other for a breach of the Treaty of Purandar or to provoke the Marathas into committing one. They further directed their Madras Governor to be ready for war and for rendering military help to Warren Hastings should an occasion arise.

Thus the Company evaded compliance with the terms of the treaty it had signed, sealed and delivered. They did not give up and deliver possession of the Bassein Fort, nor did they cease to help and support Raghoba. They further insisted upon planting Mostyn at the Poona *Durbar* as their representative, in spite of strong protests of the Ministers, who had had bitter experience of the trouble and mischief which Mostyn was capable of creating, and which, they feared, he would be directed by his employers to create again.

Mostyn in Action

The fears of the Ministers turned out to be only too well founded, as Mostyn, soon after his arrival, got busy with his intrigues and succeeded in winning or buying over Moroba, one of the Ministers, and in creating serious trouble between Moroba and Nana Fadnavis, as also between Nana Fadnavis and Sakharam Bapu, the Prime Minister. The internal quarrels developed to such an extent that Nana Fadnavis was relieved of his post, which was given to Moroba. Nana Fadnavis left Poona in disgust and went away to Purandar. Mostyn now had a clear field to use Moroba for the success of his scheme. He got Moroba to send a secret message to the Bombay Council asking them to bring Raghoba immediately to Poona for being installed on the Peshwa's *Gadi.* The Bombay Council immediately prepared to send Raghoba with an army to Poona. Warren Hastings, too, as soon as he got the news, ordered a large military force to proceed from Bengal to Poona. But, before either of the armies could start, Moroba's treachery was discovered at Poona and he was imprisoned. The Poona *Durbar* recalled Nana Fadnavis and, as Sakharam Bapu the Prime Minister wanted to retire on account of old age, Nana Fadnavis was made the Prime Minister. Mostyn was not by any means dismayed by the unexpected change in the Poona Ministry, and continued his efforts to convince Nana Fadnavis and his colleagues that the Company did intend to abide by the Treaty of Purandar and would shortly implement it. He did not succeed.

Hastings Clears Way for Bengal Army

The Bengal army's route to Poona lay through the territories of several Indian rulers, and opposition to its passage was expected, particularly from Bhonsle, Holkar and Sindhia (who were still Members of the Maratha Confederacy and loyal to the Poona *Durbar)* if the real objective of the army's march was known. So Warren Hastings gave out that the Bengal army was proceeding to the western coast to defend it against an impending French attack, and not to fight against any Indian ruler, including the Poona *Durbar.* Holkar and Sindhia were then at Poona and apparently believed the story, for they raised no objection. With Bhonsle, the Raja of Berar, Warren Hastings went a step further and "overtures were made to the Raja of Berar through Mr. Elliot, who was deputed, with the view to detaching him from the Confederacy, and who was empowered to offer him the full support of the Governor-General in his claim to the possessions of the Raja of Sattara, and to the situation of Peshwa" *(Origin of the Pindaris).* Warren Hastings' "overtures" failed to detach Bhonsle from the Confederacy, but secured to the English Bhonsle's friendly neutrality and a peaceful passage for the Bengal army. There were some minor oppositions still, some of them armed too, but the opponents were either defeated or won over by offers of English friendship, or, as in the case of Bhopal, were even bought over.

Nana Fadnavis was not hoodwinked by the fantastic story about the imminence of a French attack, and had no illusions about the real motive of the Bengal army's march. He protested vigorously and when protests were of no avail, began to prepare for an appeal to arms. The army marched on.

Bombay Army Meets with Disaster

The Bombay Council did not wait for the Bengal army to reach Poona, but on 22nd November, 1778 dispatched its own army with Raghoba to instal him on the Peshwa's *Gadi*. For the cost of the expedition Raghoba was supposed to have borrowed money from the Company and had been nude to execute a bond for the repayment of the loan. The army distributed appeals to the people along its line of march for help to Raghoba. It met with no opposition till it reached Khandala.

Nana Fadnavis had kept himself well posted about these developments and at the right moment dispatched his army to stop the Bombay army from advancing any further. Sindhia and Holkar were then at Poona and were entrusted with the command of the Maratha army.

The Company's army, commanded by Col. Egerton, was out-manoeuvered by the Marathas, who proved to be better tacticians. They retired before the advancing English army, and kept retiring till both reached the plains of Talegaon, some 18 miles from Poona. Then Egerton discovered that he had been lured into a trap set by the Marathas. He was encircled on three sides by a vast Maratha army, which was rapidly closing in. In desperation he tried to save his army. He blew up his ammunition, dumped his heavy artillery into a nearby lake, and on the midnight of 11th January, 1779, attempted to cut his way through. The Marathas foiled that attempt and after a bitter and bloody struggle, the Company's army surrendered and was disarmed by the Marathas. On the 13th January an armistice was signed and negotiations for a peace treaty were started. The Bombay Council's army had sustained its second defeat at the hands of the Marathas since the First Maratha War began.

A treaty was duly signed and sealed, whereby the English agreed to surrender to the Peshwa *Durbar*, Raghoba and the Maratha territories (Broach, Surat, etc.) in their occupation. They also agreed to hand over to the Peshwa *Durbar* written instructions addressed to Col. Goddard commanding the Bengal army which was marching on Poona, directing him to go back. Finally, two English officers were handed over to the Maratha Commander, Mahadji Sindhia, as hostages for due compliance by the English with the undertakings.

Warren Hastings declined to accept the treaty, and ordered Goddard to ignore it completely and to continue his march on

Poona. So, when the Poona *Durbar's* representative presented to Goddard the written instructions directing him to go back, he did not comply with them, and trotted out the old excuse that he was not marching to attack the Peshwa *Durbar's* territory, but only to defend the Company's western sea-coast against an impending French attack. Incidentally, the Bombay Council, too, had written to Goddard, cancelling the instructions to withdraw, which the *Durbar's* representative would bring him. Accordingly, Goddard continued to advance and reached Surat on 26th February, 1779. It may be mentioned here, that the English had correctly gauged the strength which Mahadji Sindhia's loyal membership had lent to the Maratha Confederacy. He was a very able army commander and was a fully trusted colleague of Nana Fadnavis. They rightly concluded that the best way to cripple Nana Fadnavis and the Maratha Confederacy was to win over Mahadji Sindhia. With that end in view they started making overtures at Talegaon itself, and held out temptations which Mahadji could not resist. The immediate English objective was to secure the release of Raghoba and the two English officers, whose custody as hostages had been entrusted to Mahadji. The latter was agreeable to set the hostages free for a consideration which the English readily promised.

Secret Pact between Company, Mahadji and Raghoba

A secret pact was made between the English and Mahadji to which Raghoba was also a party. Under the pact the English promised to give to Mahadji, the Broach territory and Rs. 41,000 in cash for his men. Mahadji was also to be vested with full powers of administration over the Peshwa territory which he was to exercise in the name of the titular. *Diwan* of the Peshwa, to which office Raghoba's minor son, Bajirao, was to be appointed. Raghoba himself was to receive an annual pension of Rs. 12 lacs from the Peshwa *Durbar* and was to live in far-off Jhansi. For the price which the English promised to him, Mahadji freed the hostages and also allowed Raghoba to join the English again. Defeated on the battle, field, the English had, by intrigue, secured the future co-operation of the commander who had defeated them, but who lost to them the battle of diplomacy.

Counter-steps by Nana Fadnavis

Faced by the arrival and stationing of the Bengal army in Gujarat, Nana Fadnavis was convinced that the English were determined to flout the treaty signed by them at Talegaon. So he prepared to fight. Unaware of the secret pact which Mahadji Sindhia had made with the English, Nana Fadnavis sent him at the head of a strong army to drive the English out of Gujarat. At the same time he sent Bhonsle with a force of 30,000 men on a march to Bengal, the English stronghold. Nana Fadnavis did not know that Bhonsle's loyalty too had been undermined by the English who, as mentioned before, had established friendly relations with Bhonsle. The latter dallied on the way to Bengal. Before starting he had written to Warren Hastings assuring him that his (Bhonsle's) march to Bengal would be only a show for the benefit of Nana Fadnavis and his colleagues. "I propose", he wrote, "not to reach Bengal before the monsoon and then the rains would provide me with a plausible excuse for returning." He carried out his plan. Mahadji reached Gujarat in compliance with Nana Fadnavis's instructions, but the hopes generated by the English promises had neutralised him already.

Goddard in Action

Col. Goddard, whilst carrying on his preparations for a full-scale attack on Poona, had also written to Nana Fadnavis more than once proposing negotiations for a peace treaty. The latter had insisted that as a condition precedent to the starting of negotiations, the English deliver forthwith to the Poona *Durbar*, in accordance with the terms of the last treaty, the island of Salsette and the rebel Raghoba. The English would not part with either.

Goddard then sent marauding expeditions to plunder the Peshwa's subjects in their Gujarat territory. Mahadji did not, lift even his little finger to oppose them. When Nana Fadnavis came to know of these raids, he sent troops under Holkar to protect the Peshwa's subjects and territory against the marauders. But Mahadji did not co-operate with Holkar and the latter, unaided, was unable to cope with Goddard's army.

On 16th March, 1780, Mahadji sent a representative to Goddard asking that in compliance with the secret pact, Raghoba may be sent to Jhansi so that he (Mahadji) himself could go to Poona with Raghoba's son to seize authority and assume control of the Peshwa Government, with the promised help of the English. Goddard refused point-blank and denounced the secret pact. Mahadji was terribly disappointed and Goddard considered it no longer advisable to let Mahadji stay on in Gujarat with an army under his command. Within a few days Goddard unexpectedly attacked Mahadji and his army. The latter were completely caught napping, and before they could recover, Goddard pressed home the advantage, and drove Mahadji and his army out of Gujarat.

The English perfidy turned Mahadji into a dangerous foe, like a scotched snake, and Warren Hastings hastened to crush him effectively. Mahadji's principal stronghold was his fort at his capital, Gwalior. A tributary of the Sindhias, the Rana of Gohad, was won over to the English side with the promise that, when conquered, the Gwalior Fort would be given to him. A force under Capt. Popham was sent to reduce the Fort. The Rana of Gohad helped, the Fort fell to the invaders on 4th August, 1780, and was handed over to the Rana. Thereafter, Col. Carnac was sent to Gwalior by Warren Hastings, whose troops pillaged and devastated several regions in the Sindhia territory. In order to finish Mahadji once for all, Warren Hastings next tried to incite some rulers of nearby Rajasthan to attack him, but fortunately for Mahadji, these attempts failed.

Nana Fadnavis's Efforts to Unite India

Goddard's continued attacks on the Peshwa's territory and Mahadji's evident defection spurred Nana Fadnavis to make an all-out effort to unite the Indian princes and rulers in a concerted action against the foreigners, who had come to trade and now seemed determined to stay on to rule. He concentrated on the princes and rulers in the south and addressed appeals to the Nizam of Hyderabad, the Nawab of Arcot, Sultan Haider Ali of Mysore and several others, both Muslims and Hindus. He succeeded in making a pact with the Nizam and Haider Ali whereby the parties agreed to launch attacks on the English possessions adjoining the territory of each of them. Nana had already done his part by sending, as stated before, an army of 30,000 men to invade Bengal.

He wrote to his representative at the Mughal *Durbar* to approach the Emperor and explain to him very clearly the political strategy of the English whose aim now was nothing less than the sovereignty of the whole of India. The representative was further instructed to inform the Emperor that in the south, the Nizam, Haider Ali, the Nawab of Arcot and the Peshwa had joined hands to fight and put down the English. Finally, the representative was to appeal to the Mughal Emperor, to lead as the Emperor of India, the united front of the Indian rulers against the English peril. The appeal to the Emperor fell on deaf ears as the astute Warren Hastings had already established cordial contacts with the Emperor and the Delhi *Durbar*, with the object of getting both to tide with the English. However, Nana Fadnavis's efforts were not entirely fruitless elsewhere, even though he failed to unite the whole country.

Nizam Won Over by Warren Hastings

Warren Hastings came to know that Nana had made the pact with the Nizam and Haider Ali. He at once set to work to break up the alliance against the English. He made overtures to Haider Ali but cut no ice with him. He approached the Nizam with the concocted story that the Emperor was going to dismiss the Nizam as his Subedar in the south, and to replace him by Hyder Ali. Further as a proof of the English friendship for the Nizam, Warren Hastings restored to him the Guntur region, which the English had, some years previously, seized from the Nizam and given to Mohammad Ali, the Nawab of Karnatic. The Nizam succumbed to the English blandishments and deserted Nana and Haider Ali for the English.

Goddard and His Bengal Army Defeated by the Marathas

Whilst Warren Hastings was busy with his intrigues in the South, Goddard marched on Poona, his original objective. He did not get anywhere near Poona, as he was intercepted by a Maratha force commanded by Holkar, Phadke (who had routed the Company's army at Arras) and Parashuram. There was a fierce battle at Bhorghat which Goddard lost. He was forced to retreat in disorder and disgrace with his Bengal army, just as the Bombay army had done from Talegaon a little over a year ago. This was the third and most crushing defeat of the First Maratha War which the English army had sustained at the hands of the Marathas.

Haider Ali in Action in the South

As soon as he received word from Nana, Haider Ali, true to his promise, started a series of attacks on the adjoining English possessions. The Madras Council's resistance proved futile, as their forces were defeated time and again by Haider Ali. They were brought down to their knees, and approached Nana with prayer for peace, swearing by everything they held sacred to abide faithfully by the new treaty to be entered into by them.

The Treaty of Salbai

The disaster of Goddard's defeat in the attempted invasion of Poona and the repeated reverses in the south inflicted by Haider Ali on the Madras Council's army thoroughly demoralised Hastings. He now sought safety in peace at any cost. But he met with an initial difficulty as he could not get a suitable mediator. Bhonsle, when approached, did not have the hardihood to face Nana as a mediator after his (Bhonsle's) treachery in respect of the march to Bengal. Ironically enough, it was Mahadji Sindhia, whom Warren Hastings, was forced to approach and to request him to mediate, which Mahadji did.

Negotiations lasted many months and ended at Salbai in a meeting of the representatives of the Company and the Poona *Durbar* for settling the terms of the proposed treaty. It was agreed:

(i) that the possession of all those portions of the Peshwa's territories which the English had obtained up to date by force or by guile was to be restored to the Peshwa *Durbar,*

(ii) that the *status quo* of 1775 in respect of the Gaikwad's territory and the whole of Gujarat would be re-established and maintained,

(iii) that Raghoba was to be given a life pension of Rs. 25,000 per month and permitted to live in any one place,

(iv) that the agreement between the English and the Rana of Gohad, whereby the latter had been given the Gwalior Fort, was to be cancelled, and the Fort restored to Mahadji Sindhia.

The treaty was inscribed on 17th May, 1782, but Nana Fadnavis could not bring himself to sign it, because that would have meant the betrayal of the true friend and faithful ally of the Peshwa, Haider Ali, who was then fighting the English. Haider Ali's death on 6th December, 1782 was a severe blow to Nana's plans and hopes of ridding the country of the English. In despair he signed the Treaty of Salbai.

Thus ended the First Maratha War, in which the English lost to the Marathas every single battle. Looking back, one cannot help concluding that it was the Maratha Confederacy which lost the War. It marked the beginning of the end of its solidarity. Of its four main pillars of strength, Gaikwad had openly deserted, Bhonsle had been won over by Hastings and had in a way become more dangerous as an ally than he would have been as a renegade; Sindhia had been siding alternately with the English and the Peshwa *Durbar* according to his own interests. He was the most powerful and most capable military leader of them all. Only the fourth, Holkar, had been able to resist the English overtures and remained loyally steadfast in his allegiance to the Maratha Confederacy. It may be that the traditional rivalry and the resulting hostility between the Sindhias and the Holkars had contributed to the latter's continued loyalty to the Confederacy.

Warren Hastings had thus succeeded once again in his intrigues which some years later he admitted, not without some pride, before the British Parliament in these words:

> "I won one member (the Nizam) of the Great Indian Confederacy from it by an act of seasonable restitution; with another (Moodaji Bhonsle) I maintained a secret intercourse, and converted him into a friend; a third (Madhoji Sindhia) I drew off by diversion and negotiation and employed him as the instrument of peace."

9

Battles in the South—Haider Ali-Tipu

The growing English domination of the Indian political scene had no more irreconcilable an opponent than Haider Ali. He was gifted with courage as well as brains and throughout his life struggled unremittingly to rid the country of the English peril.

Haider Ali was brought up in the best of schools—adversity. His father, Fateh Mohammad, was the first in a long line of pious Muslim divines to take up service to earn a livelihood and enlist as a soldier. After some brief spells of service in the armies of the Nawab of Arcot and the Maharaja of Mysore, Fateh Mohammad joined the army of the Nawab of Seera as the commandant of the Balapur Kalan fortress. When Haider Ali was only three the fortress was attacked by a neighbouring ruler and Fateh Mohammad was killed in action. Haider Ali and his elder brother were taken prisoner with their widowed mother and subjected to torture for ransom. A first cousin of Haider Ali who was a subaltern in the Mysore army was stationed at Shrirangapattam, the capital of Mysore. Haider Ali's widowed mother appealed to him for help and he hastened to the rescue of the children and their mother. He paid the ransom and took all the three with him back to Shrirangapattam, where he saw to it that when the boys grew up they received adequate military training. As they came of age, the two brothers joined the Mysore army.

The political status and the set-up of the Mysore *Durbar* at this period may now be briefly described. At the behest of the Emperor at Delhi, the Mysore *Durbar* was paying the *chowth* (monetary tribute) to the Marathas, but otherwise the state was completely independent in all respects. The Emperor or his subedar in the South, the Nizam of Hyderabad, exercised no authority or control over the state or its Hindu Maharaja. The Maharaja too did not rule, he merely reigned. Traditionally, he occupied the position of titular head of State and not that of its administrator or ruler. For generations, his duties had been exclusively religious which he performed in the privacy of his palace. His people saw him only twice a year. The entire administration was carried on by the Prime Minister, called the *Daiva* or Dalvai. The office of the *Daiva* was hereditary.

The war between the rival claimants to the *Gadi* of the Nizam of Hyderabad gave Haider Ali his chance. The Mysore *Durbar* and the French were allies of Muzaffar Jung whom the late Nizam had nominated as his successor. The war ended in a victory for Muzaffar Jung. Haider Ali was only a trooper at the outbreak of the war, but he covered himself with distinction in all the battles to such an extent that his bravery and capability as a future military leader attracted the attention of Nandi Raj who was then the *Daiva.* Nandi Raj took Haider under his wing and by 1775 Haider Ali had risen to the high military position of *Foujdar* (army commander) of Dindigul. It did not take him long after that to become the commander-in-chief of the Mysore army. He had acquired extensive knowledge and experience of the latest methods of warfare through fighting for years by the side of the French against the English. He now used them to improve the army under his command. He employed a number of French instructors and artillerymen to train his soldiers, and so brought up the Mysore army to the highest standard of efficiency attained by any army in the country.

But internal dissensions between the Ministers of the state marred the smooth running of its civil administration. The trouble owed its origin to Khanderao, a Maratha Brahmin who had at the instance of Haider Ali himself been appointed a Minister. Khanderao turned out to be an ambitious and scheming person, loyal only to himself. By his intrigues, he somehow succeeded in getting the *Daiva* Nandi Raj removed and getting himself appointed as the *Daiva* or Prime Minister. He them betrayed the Mysore *Durbar* and his patron Haider Ali to the Marathas secretly inviting them to attack the capital city of Mysore. Haider Ali had thus to fight not only the Marathas but Khanderao too. The people and the ruling family of Mysore gave unstinted support to Haider Ali who succeeded in foiling the attempts of both. With unanimous public approval, the Maharaja of Mysore dismissed Khanderao and appointed Haider Ali to the highest office in the state. Haider Ali now became the *de facto* ruler of Mysore. After some time the Emperor at Delhi honoured Haider Ali by appointing him Subedar of the Seera Province near Mysore.

The English at War with Haider Ali

The English did not at all like that a man of Haider Ali's calibre should be the ruler of a powerful state almost next door to their possessions. They hastened with their intrigues to undermine the loyalty of Haider Ali's friendly rulers as a first step towards bringing about his downfall. They started with Mohammad Ali, the Nawab of Karnatic, who was very friendly with Haider Ali, and won him over with the promise of giving him the Baramahal region in Mysore territory, and then without any reason attacked Baramahal in 1767. About the same time an English army about 50,000 strong commanded by General Smith advanced from Madras against Haider Ali.

To resist the English, Haider Ali made a pact with the Nizam of Hyderabad. It was agreed that the armies of both were jointly to invade Karnatic and its nearby English territory. The Nizam sent his Vazier, Rukn-ud-daula, with an army of 50,000 to help Haider Ali. In the meantime, General Smith had attacked and taken several frontier fortresses of Mysore, including the important ones of Vaniyamwadi and Kaveripattam. He advanced to reconquer them. The Nizam's Vazier, Rukn-ud-daula, accompanied him. What Haider Ali did not know, however, was that the English had already contacted the Nizam and his vazier and had arrived at some understanding with both. Haider Ali was thus severely handicapped in his resistance to the advancing Madras army under Gen. Smith, although he did not realise it till much later.

The Madras and the Mysore armies under Gen. Smith and Haider Ali, respectively, faced each other at Trinmalli. The Nizam's army too was with Haider Ali, but under the pretence of leading the attack on the English, it advanced and stationed itself between the Madras and the Mysore armies. Then suddenly the Nizam's army started retreating in a mad rush right into the

Mysore army behind it. Pandemonium reigned and Haider Ali had to retreat with his army in disorder. The incident was hailed as a "victory" for the English and was celebrated at the Madras Fort by a salvo of a hundred guns. But the English commander did not follow it up, nor was a single soldier of Haider's army killed, wounded or taken prisoner.

Of the battles fought elsewhere, Haider's army won only a few. The back of his resistance was broken and a considerable area of Mysore territory passed into English hands Haider now found himself practically isolated. The Nawab of Karnatic had openly gone over to the English and the behaviour of the Nizam's army at Trinmalli left hardly any doubt as regards the Nizam's attitude. Haider Ali was under other pressures too. The Maratha invasion was still a real threat to Mysore's integrity. Again his own administration of the State was of recent origin and it would have been unwise for him to be away from his capital for very long.

In these circumstances, Haider Ali sent an emissary to the English to seek peace. It turned out to be a false move on his part. It gave the English the impression that Haider Ali had been forced down on his knees and that it was now easy enough for them to conquer his entire territory. Consequently they treated Haider's emissary with contempt and turned him out. The affront put Haider Ali on his mettle and spurred him, single-handed as he now was, to an all-out and determined effort for the expulsion of the English from his territory.

Two Interesting Incidents

We digress here to relate two incidents stemming from Haider Ali's set-back at Trinmalli.

As soon as Haider's mother who was in her seventies heard of her son's reported "defeat", she got together a thousand horsemen and camel-riders and a cavalry corps of 200 armed but veiled women and set out in a palanquin to give her moral support to Haider Ali. In spite of the rainy season and the difficult terrain, she travelled over 200 miles within a few days, and when asked by her son why she had undertaken that arduous journey at that age, her reply was characteristic. She said that she wanted to see for herself how courageously a son of hers was enduring his defeat. "I am completely satisfied, thank God," added the proud mother, "and as my presence in your camp might distract your attention from the work before you, I am returning immediately." This she did and on her way back, she had the additional satisfaction of hearing that the day after she left, Haider Ali had attacked and taken back from the English the strong fortress of Vaniyamwadi.

Some time before Trinmalli, Haider Ali had dispatched his son Tipu by a circuitous route to Madras with a force of 5,000 horsemen. He himself remained behind to check Smith's advancing army. Tipu was only 18 then. He marched with lightning speed and one morning suddenly appeared in Madras. The Governor was strolling in a garden some distance outside the Fort. The Members of his Council and Mohammad Ali were also with him. Catching sight of Tipu's fast-moving cavalry on the outskirts of the city, they ran like rabbits to the shelter of a small ship in the harbour. They did not even wait to collect their helmets and swords. Mohammad Ali rode away on a horse. Tipu took possession of the nearby St. Thomas Hillock and the adjoining English territory and encamped there. Smith later succeeded in dislodging Tipu by a clever trick. After Haider Ali's retreat at Trinmalli, Smith sent a camel-rider to Madras who posed as a messenger from Haider Ali with a personal message for Tipu from his father. The pseudo-messenger told Tipu that Haider Ali had been defeated at Trinmalli and that he commanded Tipu to return forthwith. Inexperienced Tipu was taken in by the ruse. He took counsel of the commanders under him and all of them advised him to return as in the circumstances it was no longer feasible to invade the Madras Fort. The news of the English "victory" at Trinmalli was conveyed to the Fort by the same messenger and, as mentioned before, a hundred guns were fired in celebration. Tipu left St. Thomas Hillock and rejoined his father.

Haider Ali Re-Conquers Lost Territory

Having decided to carry on the fight alone, Haider Ali had launched a three-pronged campaign against the English. He had himself undertaken the task of re-conquering all the fortresses on the eastern frontier of Mysore. He had also dispatched a part of his army, commanded by Faizullah Khan, to drive away the English from other parts of the State. The expedition to Madras under Tipu was the third prong of this campaign calculated to divide the English forces and thus lessen their pressure against him.

The most important of the fortresses which the English had occupied on the eastern frontier was Kaveripattam. It was surrendered to Haider Ali by the English commandant after three hours of intensive shelling. Haider Ali then re-captured Vaniyamwadi. The next fortress he attacked was that of Amboor. The English garrison at Amboor dumped the stock of ammunition into a tank and set fire to the armoury. Even so, Haider Ali got 18 brass cannons, 3,000 guns and a considerable quantity of ammunition and provisions. Amboor too surrendered to Haider Ali after only a few hours of bombardment by his artillery. Haider Ali invariably permitted the English officers and soldiers to depart with their private and personal property. To the Indian soldiers, he offered the choice of either going home or enlisting in his army. Most of them chose the latter. This contrasts with the behaviour of the English commander who attacked the small fortress of Dharampuri which was flying the white flag of surrender. The officer commanding the garrison, his family and all the soldiers were put to the sword, even though they had surrendered to the English!

Smith lost all the battles against Haider Ali and had to retreat in disorder. To help Smith, fresh troops under Col. Wood were sent from Bengal, but it was no use. Haider seemed unconquerable and by the end of 1768 he had recovered every inch of Mysore territory which had passed into English hands only a short time before.

English Strategy, Success and Failure

Whilst Haider with his main army was busy on Mysore's eastern frontier in recapturing the State's territory from the English, the latter sent an expedition from Bombay to attack Mangalore, the most important western fort and town of Mysore. Mangalore fell to the English when it was attacked.

Haider had to fight on two fronts now. On the eastern border he was fighting and repelling the Company's troops commanded by Smith and Wood. On the western border, Mangalore had fallen and had to be re-taken. Undismayed, Haider rose to the occasion. He immediately sent Tipu with 3,000 horsemen to Mangalore and himself followed shortly after with re-inforcements leaving the rest of his army, under the command of his relation Makhdoom to continue the fight in the east against Smith and Wood. The two English officers took advantage of Haider's absence from the eastern front and marched on Bangalore with their combined forces. Next to Srirangapattam, Bangalore was an important eastern town of Mysore. But they never got even within sight of it.

Tipu proved himself to be a worthy son of a worthy father. Even before the latter could overtake him with re-inforcements, Tipu had fought a bloody battle lasting three days with the Bombay army and inflicted a crushing defeat on it. The English commander of the Bombay army, 46 English officers, 380 English and over 6,000 Indian soldiers of the Company were taken prisoner by Tipu. Before Haider joined his son, he had already captured Mangalore, which had been occupied by the Bombay army for less than a month.

After arranging for the proper defence of Mangalore, Haider and Tipu returned eastwards for the defence of Bangalore which, as mentioned before, was now threatened by the combined forces of Smith and Wood. He divided his forces into three detachments which converged on the advancing English force from three sides and inflicted defeat after defeat on Smith and Wood, whose troops were routed, and retreated in complete disorder beyond the limits of Mysore State.

Haider Ali Marches on Madras

After expelling the English from the entire Mysore territory, Haider carried the war into the enemy's camp. He advanced into the territories of the English and of their friend and ally, the Nawab of Karnatic. The Company's army could not check his onward march. Nawab Mohammad Ali of Karnatic was frightened out of his wits, and as Haider's army was daily getting nearer to and nearer to Madras, the English Governor and his Council lost their nerve completely and sent their emissary, Capt. Brooke, to Haider Ali to sue for peace. The latter's reply was: "I shall soon be at the gates of Madras and will then listen to whatever the Governor and his Council have to say."

> "I shall soon be at the gates of Madras and will then listen to whatever the Governor and his Council have to say."

Capt. Brooke returned empty-handed to Madras.

Haider was there some 130 miles from Madras. He sent back to Mysore his heavy equipment and executed a lightning march on Madras. It took him no more than three days to travel over 120 miles and on the fourth morning he was barely ten miles from the Madras Fort, with only the St. Thomas Hillock between him and the Fort. The English quickly sent a large force to the hillock to stop Haider's further advance. But Haider out-manoeuvred them. He made a detour and approached the Fort from the side which was undefended, whilst the Company's force was awaiting him at St. Thomas Hillock on the other side, some two or three miles beyond the Fort. He could have easily sacked the Fort and town of Madras, but had given his word to Brooke that he would give a hearing to the English at the gates of Madras, and in accordance with the tradition of the Orient, he kept his word. He informed the Governor of his arrival and the latter immediately sent Dupriex, the Governor-designate of Madras, and Beauchier to negotiate the truce. As Col. Malleson writes:

> "Hyder, in fact, was master of the situation. The native town and the private houses of Madras were at his mercy.

In the panic which his arrival had caused the fort itself might have fallen. He was in a position to dictate his own terms, and virtually, he did dictate them" (*The Decisive Battles of India*, p. 230).

First-ever Treaty between George III and Indian Potentate

Until this all the treaties between the English and the Indian rulers were executed by the East India Company on behalf of the former. Haider, however, insisted that the treaty under negotiation must purport to be between King George III of England and Haider Ali Khan, the Mughal Emperor's Subedar of Seera. The English had to agree.

The treaty was signed and sealed on 15th April, 1769. Its main provisions may be thus summarised:

1. Permanent peace and amity in future between the parties and their respective subjects.
2. Restoration of *status quo* as regards the territory of either party, which had been conquered or occupied by the other during the hostilities.
3. The province of Karoor was taken away from the Nawab of Karnatic and ceded to Haider Ali.
4. Payment of a considerable amount of money by the English to Haider Ali as war expenditure and reparations.
5. Both the parties undertook to help each other in case a third party attacked either of them.
6. Replacement by the English of a ship of Haider Ali's which they had seized at Bombay by a ruse, by an armoured man-of-war equipped with 50 guns.
7. The English guaranteed the due observance of all the terms not only of their own treaty but also of the treaty between Haider Ali and the Nawab of Karnatic, which was separately executed at the same time.

Under the latter treaty, Mohammad Ali was allowed to continue as the Nawab of Karnatic but only as a tributary of the Mysore *Durbar* to whom he was to pay an annual cash tribute of Rs. 6 lacs.

As a consequence of the military reverses repeatedly inflicted by Haider Ali on the Company, the value of its shares in the London market had fallen to about 40 p. c. of their face-value. The Directors had been frantically pressing the Madras Governor and his Council to conclude peace with Haider Ali as soon as possible. However, when the peace treaty had been executed, the Directors wrote to the Governor that by entering into such a treaty he had "given to the Indians good grounds for believing that they could treat the Company with contempt at their will with impunity". Accordingly, soon after the treaty had been signed and sealed by them, the English began to look out for an opportunity or an excuse to repudiate it.

English Violate Treaty

The opportunity sought by the English presented itself when the Marathas suddenly invaded Mysore territory for the fourth time. Under the treaty, the English had bound themselves to help Haider Ali if his territory was invaded, but when the latter asked them to fulfil their promise, they simply refused to do so. Haider was, in these circumstances, forced to make peace with the Marathas by paying some money and ceding some territory.

Incidentally, it did not take Haider long to recover the territory which, because of the English perfidy at the critical moment, he had had to cede to the Marathas. He had been keeping himself fully posted about the internal dissensions and the resulting events at the Poona *Durbar.* When he came to know of Narayanrao's assassination by the latter's uncle, Raghoba, and of Raghoba's intrigues with the English, he dispatched an expedition under his son, Tipu, who wrested back from the Marathas all that territory. Afterwards, the Marathas made peace with Haider Ali.

The English refusal to help him against the Marathas naturally created some doubts in Haider's mind about their good faith. The English had gained nothing by their breach of faith with Haider Ali. They had failed to weaken Haider or to neutralise Maratha hostility. But the failure seems to have spurred the English to sustained efforts throughout the decade that followed the treaty to bring about Haider's downfall. As already mentioned they had, as guarantors, signed Haider's treaty with their friend, the Nawab of Karnatic and had undertaken the responsibility of making the Nawab observe it. They disliked doing it because under the treatly the Nawab was to pass out of their control into that of Haider Ali. So after the treaty they encouraged the Nawab to ignore it entirely. Further, they incited a number of other tributaries of Mysore to rebel against Haider. But the latter quelled all the rebellions and brought the rebel tributary rulers to their knees. The Raja of Chittaldrug had also rebelled. At the battle of Chittaldrug, which he won, Haider Ali was completely disillusioned and was convinced of the utter unscrupulousness of the English.

English Sue for Fresh Peace

With the disappearance of the last vestige of his faith in the English professions of friendship and in their peaceful intentions, Haider resorted to the best form of defence—attack. He openly declared his intention of attacking the English possessions and forthwith started getting ready for it.

At this juncture fortune favoured him with a powerful ally in Nana Fadnavis. For some years Haider had been at peace with the Marathas. Nana Fadnavis, like Haider, had become quite convinced that the intentions of the English were no longer confined to trade, and that the acquisition of political control over the country by the elimination of the existing rulers was their main objective. Nana Fadnavis realised that the only effective way of checking the English was a combination of the two most powerful indigenous rulers—the Mysore *Durbar* and the Peshwa *Durbar.*

In 1780 Nana Fadnavis sent a special envoy to Haider Ali, the *de facto* ruler of Mysore. The envoy, Ganeshrao, was empowered to propose an alliance of the Marathas and Mysore against the English. Haider welcomed the proposal. The matters in dispute, which had kept alive for years the hostility between the Marathas and Mysore, were forthwith settled amicably. Haider and Nana entered into a close alliance with the object of driving the English out of India with unstinted mutual help and co-operation.

News of Haider's open preparations for an attack on the English possessions and of his alliance with Nana Fadnavis with the avowed objective of driving them away upset the English. The Madras Council repeatedly sent emissaries to Haider Ali to sue for another peace treaty. But Haider had had enough of treaties with the English and rejected contemptuously their overtures for peace. He confronted Grey, one of the English emissaries, with the undeniable past breaches of faith by the English and treated him more like a secret agent than an accredited envoy.

Haider's Campaign Against the English

Haider Ali began with the invasion of Karnatic in July 1780. He split his army into several divisions leading one under his own command. His sons, Tipu and Karim Saheb, led a division each. Senior Hindu and Muslim army commanders were deputed to lead other divisions. Karnatic thus faced a multi-pronged attack and fort after fort, region after region, fell to Haider's rapidly-moving army. The Company's forces commanded by Col. Caseby were posted at different strategic points for the defence of the Karnatic territory. The Nawab's troops too had joined Caseby. Even so, they were unable to stem Haider's victorious march and had to fall back after every engagement. When Porto Novo, an important foreign trade centre, handling merchandise worth millions of rupees, was conquered by Haider's second son Karim, and Haider himself was nearing Arcot, the capital of Karnatic, the Nawab sought safety in flight to Madras.

Early in August 1780 a part of Haider's cavalry, advancing towards Madras, reoccupied St. Thomas Hillock opposite Madras and the fort and town were once again in danger of being sacked. The Company's troops under Gen. Monroe advanced from Madras and a second body of troops under Col. Bailey left Guntur for the defence of Arcot which was threatened by Haider. Haider sent a division under Tipu towards Guntur to intercept Bailey's force. On 20th September 1780, Tipu's and Bailey's forces joined in battle at Poorimpak. In spite of the reinforcements which Monroe had sent to Bailey, the English army was routed by Tipu. Its artillery was blown up, thousands of Indian soldiers and 700 Englishmen were killed in action and some 2,000, including Bailey and Sir David Baird, were taken prisoner.

General Monroe was then at Ganji and Haider himself was marching against him. After Bailey's crushing defeat, Monroe decided that discretion was the better part of valour, dumped his artillery and heavy equipment into a big lake near Ganji and retreated to Madras. Haider occupied Ganji and conquered the adjoining fortresses and the entire region. Then he returned to Arcot and invaded its fort. The siege lasted three months and the town of Arcot fell to Haider, but not before both sides had sustained heavy losses. As an instance of Haider's magnanimity towards the English, it may be mentioned that he sent the surviving Englishmen to Madras under an escort (Col. W. Miles' *History of Hyder,* p. 395).

Haider's Death—Peace with Tipu

The disastrous defeat of Bailey and the cowardly retreat of Monroe without firing a shot dismayed Warren Hastings, who sent a large force from Bengal to Madras under Sir Eyre Moote. Haider was then conquering the Company's strongholds and ports along the coast below Madras. Sir Eyre Moote reached Madras on 5th November, 1781, collected some two lacs of pagodas from the fugitive Nawab Mohammad Ali of Karnatic for army expenses and spent the next three months at Madras in preparation to check Haider's victorious advance. Two battles were then fought and lost by Moote, who retreated to Madras each time. Fresh troops to aid him were then sent from Bengal. The third and last battle was fought in September 1782 at Arni, and Sir Eyre Moote sustained such a crushing defeat that he gave up all hope and returned to Bengal with the remnants of his army.

We digress here to give an example of the courage and determination with which Haider's soldiers and even their women fought the Company's troops—an example provided by the defence of the fortress at Manniarguddi. One night, when most of its small garrison was away getting supplies, a detachment of the Company's army advanced to take the fortress by surprise. It was then held by only 20 men under a *Naik* (Corporal). They were hopelessly out-numbered by the attacking force but the *Naik* and his men decided to fight on. The womenfolk enthusiastically joined them. The men were stationed on the walls and the women speedily collected heaps of big stones on the battlement and boiled huge cauldrons of water. The gates of the fortress were closed against the advancing enemy, who tried to climb the walls. They were met by showers of stones and the scalding water. The men shot the attackers down in numbers. The attack was thus repulsed and the enemy forces were scattered and ran for their lives.

To resume our narrative, Sir Eyre Moote's defeat at Arni made it quite plain that Haider could not be checked by the English and that he would succeed in driving them out of Southern India. Nana Fadnavis was confident of Haider Ali's success and evaded signing the Treaty of Salabai. At this stage, Fate intervened to help the English. Shortly after his victory at Arni, Haider Ali got a carbuncle on his back and had to return to Arcot. He knew that he would not recover, but so devoted was he to the task of driving out the English that even from his sickbed, he issued orders for the march of an expeditionary force of 5,000 horsemen to Madras. Tipu was fighting elsewhere. Haider sent for him. Meanwhile, he personally gave his last detailed instructions to his Ministers, chief amongst whom were two Hindus, Poorniya and Krishnarao. Before Tipu could return to his bedside, he died on 6th December, 1782 and Tipu succeeded him. Like his father, Tipu continued the fight against the English with such undiminished vigour and success that the English were reduced to a condition of "debility, dejection and despair" (Mill, Vol. IV, p. 222). In 1783, they abjectly sued for peace with profuse assurances of keeping faith in future. Tipu lacked the experience of his father and was taken in by the English guile. On 11th March, 1784, the Treaty of Mangalore was executed between Tipu Sultan and the English, whereby the latter undertook to (i) abstain from any interference in matters relating to Mysore, (ii) maintain friendly relations with Tipu and his heirs and (iii) render all help to Tipu and his heirs against their enemies.

In return, Tipu generously restored to the English all their territory and possessions which he and his father had conquered.

Haider Ali—Soldier-Statesman

Haider Ali was a little over 60 when he died. He had begun his career in the Mysore Army as a *Naik* (Corporal). At the time of his death, he was Sultan Haider Ali Shah of Mysore, a State with an area of more than 80,000 sq. miles and a net annual revenue of over Rs. 3 crores. He had under his direct command 1,15,000 men in his infantry, 19,000 in his cavalry and 10,000 in his artillery. In addition, he had at his disposal an auxiliary force of 1,80,000 armed men. His armoury had six lacs of shotguns, two lacs of swords and 22,000 cannon. He was the only Indian ruler of the period to maintain a strong and fully armed navy for the defence of the State's sea-coast. Its commander, Ali Raza, used it too for annexing to the State numerous islands in the Malayan Archipelago.

It is an interesting coincidence that, like the famous "little corporal" who rose to be the Emperor of France, Haider Ali too has often been described as "Hyder Naik" by some historians.

Haider was quite illiterate. For his signature he inscribed only the first letter of his name and that too scrawling it upside down. But what he lacked in education, he made good by his keen intellect. It was of a very high order and this has been testified by Indian and foreign historians alike. His memory was prodigious and like Napoleon, he had the amazing gift of applying his mind to a number of things at the same time. He dictated simultaneously several letters, dispatches and orders, whilst he discussed affairs of state with his Ministers and solved complicated problems relating to them.

Haider was neither partial to his co-religionists nor prejudiced against non-Muslims. A number of high officers in the State were Hindus. So were his principal ministers and advisers. He treated Jagadguru Shankaracharya of Shringeri Math in Mysore with great reverence and, when occasion arose, he never hesitated to seek his advice. He banned cow slaughter and participated in the Hindu festivals. The *eclat* with which he celebrated *Dussehra* has not been surpassed to this day (1929), although Mysore has been ruled by Hindu Maharajas for 130 years. He was unusually broad-minded and hated religious shibboleths. He would not sport a beard or tolerate any quarrels on the grounds of religion.

Once a violent dispute broke out between the Shia and Sunni sects of Muslims and he sternly warned the leaders of both parties that they would be mercilessly crushed if they did not stop it immediately.

As dauntless military leader and war tactician, he was unrivalled and was invincible throughout his life. He was an adept not only in the arts of war but also in those of peace, and in both he was an outstanding figure. He was a sagacious and far-sighted statesman, an unusually efficient administrator and a just ruler. His army worshipped him and his subjects adored him. He was ever accessible even to the humblest seeking justice and severely punished those who went against his strict standing orders or prevented any victim of injustice from approaching him personally. Once, a favourite *Jemadar* of his, Hyder Shah, suppressed an old woman's petition. Haider Ali learned of it and ordered that the *Jemadar* be flogged in his presence. Some of his courtiers prayed that the *Jemadar* may be pardoned. Haider's reply was characteristic:

> "I cannot accede to your request. There can be no greater sin than prevention of a direct contact between a king

> and his subjects. The strong must protect the weak. God has made kings only for the protection of the weak. A king who tolerates the victimisation of his subjects and does not punish the wrong-doers richly deserves to lose the trust and affection of his people and the latter have a right to rebel."

Haider Ali practised what he preached and harshly punished any official who victimised any of his subjects.

The people of Mysore State were happy and prosperous under Haider's rule. Agriculture, industries and trade flourished with unstinted State help and encouragement. Haider lavishly patronised traders, craftsmen and artisans.

Like all brave men, Haider admired bravery in his enemies. He invariably treated with large-hearted consideration those whom he defeated in battle.

He despised pomp and lived like an ordinary soldier, often on a soldier's rations. At his public *Durbars* he treated his soldiers as his equals and never sat on the throne except on Id Day and that too on the insistence of his people. Like Napoleon, his stamina was limitless. He passed several nights in succession on horse-back in pouring winter rains.

Such was Haider, the inveterate enemy of the English marauders who struggled all his life to drive the English out. As we have said before, on him alone were centred all hopes for the preservation of India's independence which was then very seriously threatened by the English. He was a terror to the English and had he lived longer, the course of Indian history would have run differently.

10

Sir John Macpherson—Acting Governor-General

John Macpherson first came to India in 1767 as paymaster of an English ship. He was an educated man and knew how to look after himself and his own interests. Scruples did not bother him. The situation in Karnatic offered a promisingfield for his scheming activities. He went there in 1768.

As has been narrated, Mohammad Ali had become the Nawab of Karnatic solely because the English had helped him. In return Mohammad Ali had ceded to the English considerable territory with an annual income of about Rs. 1,600,000. For some time they treated him with a certain amount of respect and consideration. He was even accorded the privilege of exchanging personal presents with King George III of England. Later the English began to deal with him in exactly the same way as they had been dealing with the Nawabs of Oudh. Mohammad Ali was fleeced on one excuse or another not only by the Company but privately by its employees too. When he had been bled white and he was bankrupt, he was prevailed upon to borrow money from English merchants and moneylenders to meet their ever-recurring and increasing demands. He was now very heavily in debt. The demands were continuing all the same, and he did not know how to extricate himself from this impossible situation. At this time Macpherson approached him with the suggestion that all his troubles would end if Mohammad Ali sent him (Macpherson) as his accredited agent to England to plead his cause with the Ministers of the English Government. Mohammad like a simpleton agreed to this and thus opened an easy way for Macpherson to get more and yet more money from the Nawab for feathering his own nest.

He arrived in England and unsuccessfully tried to bribe the Prime Minister by offering him a "loan" of over Rs. 7,000,000. But he did succeed in establishing close personal relations with other Ministers and the Directors of the Company and these led to his employment by the Company for service in India. He returned to India and eventually rose to the position of an important member of the Governor-General's Council at Calcutta. When in 1784

Warren Hasting returned to England, Sir John Macpherson was appointed the Acting Governor-General. He refused to pay to the Delhi Emperor Shah Alam the arrears of the agreed cash tribute due from the Company amounting to Rs. 40,000,000. He also continued Warren Hastings' practice of fleecing the Nawab of Oudh. His successor, Lord Cornwallis, in his confidential letter of 8th August, 1789 addressed to the Secretary of State for India in England (the Rt. Hon'ble Henry Dundas), has repeatedly referred to Sir John Macpherson's "ill-earned money, his flimsy cunning and shameless falsehoods .... his duplicity and low intrigue". It might be added that on his return to England Sir John Macpherson got himself elected to the British Parliament through bribery, corruption and malpractices which were later proved. He was then unseated. The fact that persons of the calibre of Warren Hastings and Sir John Macpherson were appointed the first two Governors-General of India has of course its own significance which will be apparent to our readers.

11

Lord Cornwallis (1786–93)

Under the Regulating Act of 1773, the Board of Directors of the Company in England appointed the Governor-General who was bound by the decisions of his Council. This had severely handicapped Warren Hastings on several important occasions, who thus had responsibility without the backing of power. Moreover, the English territory in India had considerably increased and was likely to increase further. It was consequently considered necessary by the rulers of England that control of the political affairs of the Company should vest in a body responsible to the British Parliament. Pitt's India Act, passed by Parliament, therefore provided for a Board of Control appointed by the Crown. The Board had the authority to appoint the Governor-General, who was empowered to act at his discretion with or without the concurrence of his Council or even against its decisions. The authority of the Company was thus limited to the management of its trade and commerce and the control of its political affairs gradually passed out of its hands into that of the English Crown. Lord Cornwallis was appointed permanent Governor-General by the Board of Control in consultation with the Board of Directors and in 1786 took over from Sir John Macpherson, the *pro tempore* Governor-General.

Instructions to Cornwallis

In the meantime, England had been defeated in the American War of Independence and lost not only her possessions but also her prestige which was at its lowest ebb. To rehabilitate her prestige somehow, her rulers decided to redouble their efforts towards the expansion of their territory in India leading to the acquisition of supreme political power over the country. As was borne out by the English official dispatches of the period, Lord Cornwallis was plainly told that what had been lost in India must be made good and that he give top priority to the achievement of that objective. Lord Cornwallis was a man of peace, but orders were orders and they had to be carried out at any cost even at the risk of war. He rightly expected the strongest opposition from Tipu and decided to bring about his downfall. He entered into a new agreement with the Nizam, under which the Company's subsidiary force maintained by the Nizam in his territory could be used for the contemplated attack on Tipu. The Nizam undertook to co-operate. Lord Cornwallis then took steps to enlist the support of the Marathas, as only with the Nizam's help he could not hope to succeed against Tipu.

The Marathas were then carrying on negotiations with Tipu for an alliance. Cornwallis instructed George Forster to proceed at once to Nagpur and see to it that the negotiations fell through by persuading the Maratha ruler Mudaji Bhonsle and his colleagues to join the English. As mentioned earlier, Mudaji Bhonsle had done a friendly turn to Warren Hastings and was still friendly with the English. Lord Cornwallis in his letter to Forster dated 23rd October 1787 wrote:

> "If the Marhatas have engaged or resolved to keep peace with Tipu, it is not probable that our solicitations would induce them to depart immediately from that plan."

Forster was therefore instructed to spare no pains to incite the Marathas "to form a close connexion and alliance against Tipu as a common enemy". Lord Cornwallis wrote similarly to the English Resident at Poona instructing him to win over the Peshwa *Durbar* too. He supplemented these efforts by promising to the Marathas and the Nizam a third share each in the territory conquered from Tipu if both of them helped the English to defeat him. The promise tipped the scales in favour of the English. All the three entered into a "triple alliance" which has been designated as "a plundering confederacy for the purpose of extirpating a lawful prince" by the famous English politician Fox. The English Government, when informed of this alliance against Tipu, sent out to India a contingent of soldiers and as a further help advanced as a loan five million pounds to Lord Cornwallis.

Third Mysore War

Everything was now ready for the war against Tipu but a plausible excuse for starting it was still lacking. Tipu had scrupulously observed the Treaty of Mangalore which he had made with the English in 1784 and, as Governor Holland of Madras wrote, "Tipu did not at all intend to fight the English, and if the latter had any *bona fide* grievance, he was willing to settle the matter amicably by correspondence." It was alleged, however, that Tipu was preparing to attack the Raja of Travancore, then an ally of the English. Tipu assured the English that he had no such intention and did not want to break the peace. But the English would not be convinced, for as Lord Cornwallis wrote to the Madras Governor, "Tipu's unpreparedness provided the very best opportunity for the Company." Thus it was that in June 1790, the English trampled under foot the treaty with Tipu, and sent an expeditionary force from Madras under Gen. Meadows to attack Tipu. To help Meadows, re-inforcements from Bengal were sent by Col. Maxwell. Meadows also succeeded in suborning some of Tipu's commanders.

Meadows Repulsed

Tipu advanced from Mysore to oppose the invading force. In spite of all the advantages on his side, Gen. Meadows could not get even within sight of Mysore territory. In all the battles he fought with Tipu—and there were several—Tipu's army steadily pushed him back and drove him beyond Karnatic, large parts of which were re-occupied by Tipu. After some six months of struggle in which his forces suffered heavy losses, Meadows was forced to return to Madras.

Cornwallis Takes a Hand

On 12th December 1790 a huge army under the personal command of Lord Cornwallis himself left Calcutta for Madras. He was joined by the Maratha and the Nizam's armies. It may be mentioned parenthetically that the Peshwa *Durbar's* playing the English game was an ominous portent not only for Tipu but also for the future of the indigenous political powers and the independence of the country. Then Tipu received another blow. The European officers and men serving in Mysore since the time of Haider Ali were won over by bribery and corruption to the Company's side. As Thornton says in his *History of British India,* "Tipu's European servants were now quite as ready to exercise their skill and knowledge for his destruction as they had been previously assiduous in using them for his defence." Thus Tipu had to fight not only three powerful enemies converging on him from all sides, but also treachery in his own camp. Tipu was at bay and fought doggedly with the courage of desperation. But the odds were against him. Bangalore was taken and sacked by the invaders. Under Lord Cornwallis's order, the inhabitants of the town were subjected to, what Mill calls, a "deplorable carnage". Lord Cornwallis then advanced on Seringapattam (Srirangapattam), the capital of Mysore. As he neared the capital, Tipu now in despair sent him a messenger with several camel-loads of fruits in token of his desire for peace. Lord Cornwallis returned the fruits untouched and sent back the messenger without giving him a hearing. "The fact is that the English in India, at that time, had been worked up into a mixture of fury and rage against Tipu more resembling the passion of savages against their enemy than the feelings with which a civilized nation regards the worst of its foes." When Seringapattam was besieged, Tipu tried once again for peace with the English and the Marathas and sent an envoy, but Lord Cornwallis did not permit the envoy even to come near him. At about the same time he ordered Meadows to attack and take the Tower of Somerpeet, then considered to be the key-stone of the Seringapattam fortifications. The Tower was successfully defended by its commander, Syed Ghaffar. Meadows was repulsed with a loss, it is said, of some 200 English soldiers killed. He could not bear the disgrace of this defeat and shot himself in his tent. The bullet however did not kill him, and before he could fire a second time, the pistol was snatched from him by Col. Malcolm who had rushed into the tent on hearing the first shot. Lord Cornwallis's army was now in occupation of Lal Bagh on the eastern outskirts of Seringapattam. Haidar Ali's grave was in Lal Bagh and, needless to say, it did not escape desecration.

Treaty of Seringapattam

Lord Cornwallis's success against Tipu was very largely, if not entirely, due to the help given to him by the Nizam and the Marathas, particularly by the latter. Apparently, the Marathas saw no advantage in prolonging the war and reacted favourably to Tipu's overtures for peace. It is stated that the Marathas, particularly Nana Fadnavis, pressed the English to conclude peace with Tipu and Lord Cornwallis could not afford to offend the Marathas by opposing their wishes. Thus, the Treaty of Seringapattam was signed on 23rd February 1792. Under its provisions, helpless Tipu had to cede half of his dominion to the English and their allies and pay them a war penalty of Rs. 330 lacs in three yearly instalments. He had, moreover, to hand over to the English, his two sons aged 8 and 10 as hostages for the due payment of the penalty. The ceded territory was equally divided amongst themselves by the Company, the Nizam and the Marathas.

Thus ended the war which had been started by the English under the pretence that since Tipu had committed an act of war against the Company by attacking Travancore, the English had to help the Raja of Travancore who was in alliance with them and under their protection. It is remarkable, however, that no further mention of Travancore is to be found in the official records of the war or in the provisions of the treaty.

Further Expansion of Company's Territory

With Tipu's elimination as an opponent of the English, a very serious obstacle in the way of the expansion of their territory in India was removed, and the alliance with the Marathas further facilitated the process. Next year Lord Cornwallis annexed practically all the French possessions in India and then proceeded to carry out his employers' instructions for the acquisition of Guntur province. These instructions had been given to him when he left England, but he had postponed action as it would have led to the Nizam joining Tipu against the English. After the war with Tipu, Lord Cornwallis considered it safe to act and sent Capt. Kenna way to the Nizam for acquiring Guntur from the latter. According to Mill (Vol. V, p. 225) it was settled that "no intimation was to be given to the Nizam of the proposed demand, till after the arrival of Capt. Kennaway at his court. The Government of Madras, under specious pretences, conveyed a body of troops to the neighbourhood which held themselves in readiness to seize the territory before any other power could interpose either with arms or remonstrance." The Nizam was never noted for his courage and could not refuse the demand when it was made. No force was needed and Guntur was added to the Company's territory without even a fight. The payment of the annual tribute to the Delhi Emperor in return for the grant to the Company of the *Dewanee* of Bengal, Bihar and Orissa was finally stopped by Lord Cornwallis, and the last vestige of even the semblance of the Emperor's sovereignty over these provinces was wiped off. It is amusing to note that the Company still declared themselves to be the subjects of the Delhi Emperor! The latter was, of course, too weak to enforce high rights or to check English rapacity.

The Nawab of Oudh, too, was treated by Lord Cornwallis in a similar way. Warren Hastings had quartered in Oudh a very small force of the Company, officered exclusively by Englishmen and had saddled the Nawab with the entire cost of maintaining it. The Nawab had been assured that it was only a temporary measure taken for the defence of his territory. As Mill says, "Oudh was never faced by any particular threat of invasion." The Nawab requested Lord Cornwallis to fulfil Warren Hastings' promise and remove the army from Oudh. Lord Cornwallis insisted that the army must stay on in Oudh and that too at the Nawab's expense! Thus the Nawab, a friend and ally of the English, was for a number of years blackmailed into spending some Rs. 50 lacs per year for maintaining the Company's army so that the English could use it for satisfying their inordinate hunger for the domination of India aimed at by the rulers of England.

Cornwallis's "Reforms"

In order to establish English rule firmly over the Company's Indian territory, Lord Cornwallis entirely excluded Indians from important administrative and executive posts. But he met with difficulties in replacing Indians by Englishmen or other Europeans in the higher and well-paid posts. He was pestered by highly-placed persons in England who wanted him to appoint mostly the English n'ver-do-wells. It is recorded that the Prince of Wales very often pressed his good-for-nothing favourites and boon-companions on Lord Cornwallis for appointment and the latter yielded for some time. But when the Prince of Wales wrote to him to appoint one Treves as the Chief Judge at Banaras, the limit was exceeded and, be it said to Lord Cornwallis's credit that he refused to do it on the ground that it would be ridiculous to appoint a raw, inexperienced and untrained youth like Treves as a Chief Judge. It may be mentioned that Treves was the son of a notorious moneylender from whom the Prince of Wales had borrowed money!

Village Panchayats

From very ancient times almost the entire population of India had lived in villages and the "village community was…the unit of social, industrial and political existence" (Torrens' *Empire in Asia*). "Time out of mind", continues Torrens, "the village and its common interests and affairs have been ruled over by a council of elders, anciently five in number, now frequently more numerous, but always representative in character, who, when any dispute arises, declare what is the customary law, and who, when any new or unprecedented case occurs, occasionally legislate" (pp. 100, 101). According to Torrens, every criminal case or civil dispute was tried by the *Panchas* or jurors, elected by the people for each case and their decision was final and binding on the parties. The *Panchas* were elected from all castes and walks of life in the village without distinction. Either of the parties to the case was entitled to object to and prevent the election of any *Panch.*

Another English writer, Sir John Malcolm, has this to say about the village *Panchayats:*

> "The village institutions of India were competent, from the power given them by the common assent of all ranks, to maintain order and peace within their respective circles. In Central India, their rights and privileges never were contested even by tyrants, while all just princes founded their chief reputation and claim to popularity on attention to them."

The village headman or the *Mukhiya* was also chosen by the villagers and was usually a self-sacrificing man of high moral character and courage. The *Mukhiyas* invariably supported a just ruler and stoutly opposed an unjust or tyrannical one. Generally, they were a bulwark of defence for the people and life of their villages against injustice or tyranny. According to Sir John, if a villager was forced by some calamity to migrate and leave his field and house in his native village, he or his descendants could always return and resume possession of the field and the house. "Every wall of a house, every field, was taken possession of by the owner without dispute or litigation."

Yet another Englishman, Sir Thomas Munro, who was well-acquainted with other parts of India, writes:

> "In all Indian villages there was a regularly-constituted municipality, by which its affairs, both of revenue and police, were administered, and which exercised to a very great extent magisterial and judicial authority."

Sir Thomas has given details of the several functionaries of the village municipalities or *panchayats* and of their respective duties in their several spheres. The collection of revenue was entrusted to one, whilst the preservation of peace, law and order was the duty of a different official, the two being independent of each other. A constabulary was also maintained for the security of the village and its people. Every cultivator was the full owner of the fields cultivated by him. "The people", writes Sir Thomas, were "simple, harmless, honest and having as much truth in them as any people in the world."

To sum up, the village *Panchayats* had been the backbone of India's social, economic and political structure for thousands of years.

Extinction of Panchayats

The extinction of *panchayats* began in Bengal, when Mir Jafar and Mir Kasim ruled it as puppets of the East India Company. The process coincided with the era of organised trade and commercial loot and of naked brigandage by the Company. But the deathblow to the village *panchayat* revenue and judicial system was given with the passing of the Regulation Act by the English Parliament in 1773. To quote Torrens again:

> "These municipal institutions, which confessedly had been scrupulously respected in all former changes of dynasty, whether Mohammadan or Maratha, were henceforth to be disregarded, and many of them to be rudely uprooted by the new system of foreign administration. Instead of the native *panchayat* was established an arbitrary judge ... No wise or just historian will note these things without expression of wonder and condemnation."

Effects of Judicial "Reform"

The replacement of the village *Panchayats* by copies of the English law-courts has been lauded as a "reform" but it had a very deleterious effect on the character of the Indian people as recorded by Mill. "The new courts" procedure involved long delays and was so complicated that only professional lawyers could follow it. A class of legal practitioners called pleaders sprang up Seeking justice became too expensive for the poor. The rulers and the ruled were treated alike under the laws which were designed to help the former in collecting revenues cheaply and easily. Incidentally, the reforms provided jobs for thousands of incapable English youths and a fertile field for widespread chicanery, litigation, fraud, forgery, perjury, bribery and general corruption of the people. The corruption was intentional for Lord Cornwallis knew that the main source of strength of foreign rule lay in the weak character of the subjugated "natives" and so deliberately set about corrupting it by every means in his power.

The famous English positivist, S. Lobb, called the new legal "system" "miserable" and asked:

> "Can anything be conceived more thoroughly immoral than the system of Western advocacy which we are doing our best to introduce into the country? Are not our law-courts hotbeds of corruption, and is not the love of litigation contaminating and thoroughly perverting the national mind? Why not let the people settle their own disputes as far as possible?"

Permanent Settlement

The Permanent Settlement has been rightly described as the most important measure of Lord Cornwallis's tenure of office. It was adopted to save the Company from bankruptcy. After acquiring the *Dewanee* of the three Provinces of Bengal, Bihar and Orissa, the Company had been increasing the rate of the land revenue year after year and to such an extent that the cultivators were no longer able to earn even a bare living. They gave up their vocation and miles and miles of fields lay fallow. Another consequence was the terrible famine of 1770. The Company's income from land revenue was dwindling fast. When Lord Cornwallis took office, the Company's coffers were almost empty. To save the situation, the Directors had instructed him to fix the land-revenue once for all. Accordingly, the Permanent Settlement was made by him. Under it, the *Zamindar* (landlord) was assessed to a permanently fixed revenue and was made responsible for its payment as also for the payment of the revenue then in arrears. It was simultaneously enacted that the lands of the defaulting *Zamindars* would be immediately confiscated and auctioned by the Company. The actual cultivators, the farmers or the *ryots* were reduced to the status of mere tenants and as such were completely at the mercy of their *Zamindars*. The auctioned lands were usually knocked down to people subservient to the Company and a new type of weak *Zamindars* came into existence.

A Contrast

In the parts of the country which were under the Company's administration, widespread misery, poverty, ruined peasantry and de-populated regions met the eye. The countryside was, in the words of Edmund Burke, "turned into a desert". On the other hand, in the vast territories ruled by the Marathas, Tipu, the Nizam or the Nawab of Oudh, there were flourishing countrysides, fields growing bumper crops, and villages populated by a prosperous and contented peasantry. For the people of India, even the recurring internecine wars had not been half as disastrous as the Company's misrule, with its attendant evils of wrongful exactions, unlawful extortions and systematic loot had been for the hapless people of "British India". The latter were never, even during the worst of times preceding the Company's advent, reduced to such straits as they were during the 30 years of the Company's administration. This is proved by what a number of foreign and Indian writers have put on record and is further vouched by the Company's official records, notably by its "Fifth Report of 1812"

Cornwallis Leaves India

After ruling as Governor-General for seven years, Lord Cornwallis returned to England. His was a very special and important contribution towards the establishment of British rule in India on a firm and permanent basis. He was succeeded by Sir John Shore.

12

Sir John Shore (1793–98)

During Warren Hastings' regime, Sir John, then a plain Mr. Shore, was an ordinary employee of the Company in Bengal. He proved himself to be an apt pupil of Warren Hastings in intrigues and machinations and soon became a valuable aide of his. In the words of Edmund Burke, "Mr. Shore" was "materially concerned as a principal actor and party in certain of the offences charged upon Mr. Hastings." When the Ministers and the Directors of the Company in England proposed to send him as the next Governor-General, Burke wrote to the Chairman of the Court of Directors: "... it is for the prudence of the court to consider the consequences which possibly may follow from sending out, in office of the highest rank and of the highest possible power, a person whose conduct, appearing in his own records, is at the first view very reprehensible." Burke also strongly protested against Mr. Shore's appointment by a letter addressed to Henry Dundas, the Secretary of State for India. But these protests were of no avail. Those in authority simply ignored them and appointed Sir John Shore as Governor-General. Sir John arrived in Calcutta and took over on 28th October 1793.

In the same year the life of the Company was extended for another 20 years by a fresh Royal Charter.

Mahadji Sindhia's Mysterious End

Within four months of Sir John's assumption of office, Mahadji Sindhia suddenly died at Vanowri, near Poona. He had arrived at Poona sometime earlier for consultations with the Peshwa and Nana Fadnavis. Grant Duff has attributed Mahadji's death to high fever. Another historian, Keene, alleges on the authority of *Tareekh i-Muzaffari* that "Mahadji had been waylaid the evening before by an armed gang deputed by Nana" who, in Keene's opinion, "had without doubt sufficient reasons for desiring Mahadji's death". Mahadji may have been murdered and not have died a natural death as stated by Grant Duff, but it is iniquitous to accuse Nana of complicity in the murder, because there is complete absence of any motive on Nana's part as he had no reason whatsoever to wish for Mahadji's death. There are, however, pointers to the existence of motives and reasons elsewhere which could have inspired the murder.

According to Grant Duff, Mahadji's "power and ambition, his march to Poona, and above all, the general opinion of the country, led the English to suspect him; and we accordingly find in their records various proofs of watchful jealousy". Grant Duff also records the fact that soon after Mahadji's arrival in Poona, a Delhi newspaper published a report to the effect that the Delhi Emperor had written to Mahadji and the Peshwa requesting their help in the realisation of the money tribute due to him from the Company which Lord Cornwallis had finally declined to pay. The English knew about it and knew also that Mahadji would soon be going to Poona for consultations with Nana Fadnavis as regards the measures to be jointly taken for the realisation of the tribute from the Company. The English believed that a formidable alliance against themselves, between the Emperor, Nana Fadnavis and Mahadji with the last-mentioned as its leading spirit was on the way. The alliance, according to English thinking, was likely to lead to an attack on Calcutta by the forces of all the three commanded by Mahadji. This was an impending disaster which had to be averted at all costs. The English considered Mahadji to be the root-cause of the trouble and the Company's official correspondence amply bears out the facts that (*i*) the English started intrigues and plots against Mahadji and (*ii*) instigated Holkar to attack Mahadji's State immediately after the latter had left for Poona. At the same time the English broke off relations with the Sindhia *Durbar* and recalled the English Resident posted there. Lord Cornwallis then in England wrote to Sir John Shore on 7th September 1794: "The death of Sindhia ...... will nearly remove every political difficulty of your Government."

It will be recollected that some 15 years earlier, Warren Hastings had won over Mahadji who had become a willing tool in his hands in his "designs against the few remaining territories of the Moghul Emperor" (Burke). One of the temptations to which Mahadji succumbed is stated to be Warren Hastings' promise to pay him in future the annual tribute which the Company had been paying to the Moghul Emperor. In furtherance of his designs, Warren Hastings had advised and helped Mahadji in collecting a strong army officered mostly by Europeans and with de Boigne, recommended by Warren Hastings, as the Commander-in-Chief. With this army, Mahadji had, at the instigation of Warren Hastings, attacked and occupied some of the Emperor's territory not far from Delhi and had virtually held the Emperor himself in duress. But as described earlier (Chapter VIII), Mahadji was soon disillusioned by the perfidy of the English and became their bitter and unrelenting enemy. There can, therefore, be little doubt that Mahadji had been for years a painful thorn in the English side. His death not only removed it but also completed the disruption of the Maratha Confederacy headed by the Peshwa, as Mahadji was its last, most powerful and most capable supporter amongst the Indian rulers. No wonder, Lord Cornwallis felicitated the Governor-General of India on Mahadji's death.

Elimination of Nana Fadnavis

With Haider and Mahadji gone, Nana was isolated as the last redoubtable fighter for India against its domination by the English. But even so he was continuing the struggle and was still a formidable barrier in the way of the English ambitions. The English Resident at Poona wrote in one of his letters: "As long as Nana remained supreme at the Poona Court, they (the British) should never dream of obtaining a firm footing in the Marhatta kingdom."

The English had engineered plots against Nana time and again, but they did not stand a chance because Nana had the unstinted support of Madhorao II (Madhorao Narayan), the reigning Peshwa, who invariably followed Nana's advice. So the removal of Madhorao Narayan from the Peshwa's *Gadi* had become essential to the success of the English plot to bring about Nana's downfall. Fortune again favoured the English with another death—that of Madhorao Narayan. "On the morning of 25th October, the

Peshwa jumped down from a balcony of his palace ... He was seriously hurt and lived for only two days thereafter" (Grant Duff). Some English writers have stated that the 21-year-old Peshwa had committed suicide because of a quarrel with the powerful Nana Fadnavis. Reports to that effect may have been circulated at the time for rousing public indignation against Nana. The Peshwa may have fallen down accidentally or may have been pushed off the balcony by some secret enemy or traitor. But his death did provide the English with the one chance they had been waiting for. It will be recalled that when in 1773, the English were keen on replacing the reigning Peshwa Narayanrao by Raghoba, the latter with the support of the British Government had Narayanrao murdered. The English were even keener on Nana's downfall which could not be accomplished so long as Madhorao Narayan occupied the *Gadi.* Thus it may be that the latter had to go the way his murdered father (Narayanrao) had gone 15 years previously. How the English brought about Nana's elimination may now be narrated.

The late Peshwa (Madhorao II) left no son, only a widow, Yashodabai. The English wanted a puppet of theirs, the deceased Raghoba's son Bajirao, to succeed as Peshwa. Nana had been holding Bajirao in detention at Poona for some time. They persuaded Holkar who was now under their influence to go to Poona and support Bajirao. Holkar, after discussions with Nani and other Ministers, agreed that someone approved by all should be adopted by the widow, as she was entitled to do under the Hindu customary law and that the adopted son should succeed Madhorao II. In January 1796, Nana informed Mallet the English Resident accordingly, as he had promised to do. Nana also informed Mallet that only the selection of a suitable boy for adoption was pending.

The English acted swiftly. Mallet had not completely failed in stirring up discontent against Nana amongst people who mattered. Some of them had believed in the reports about Nana's complicity in Mahadji Sindhia's murder. Then there were the disgruntled followers and supporters of Raghoba. Apparently Mallet had succeeded in combining all such people and these were ready to support Raghoba's son. With the help and active support of Mallet and his co-conspirators, Bajirao escaped from detention and before Nana and the Ministers could select a boy for adoption, Bajirao was proclaimed Peshwa by his partisans and occupied the *Gadi.* Once in full power, he forthwith used it to "feed fat the ancient grudge" he bore against Nana Fadnavis. The latter tried to escape the fate Bajirao had in store for him but failed, and had to spend the next few years in prison.

Breach of Faith with Nizam

There was a dispute over money between the Nizam and the Marathas, which the former, relying on the English support, disdainfully declined to settle peacefully. The Marathas were left with no alternative but to use force and they invaded the Nizam's territory. Tipu also was then hostile to the Nizam. Sir John Shore was the Nizam's only hope, but he refused to help. For years, the Nizam had the Company's Subsidiary Army stationed in his territory for the specific purpose of protecting him against attack. This force, too, declined to come to his rescue. The Nizam was defeated by the Marathas at the battle of Kurdala on 15th March, 1795, and had to make peace with them on their terms.

The Nizam then asked Sir John to take away the Subsidiary Army from his territory and began to organise his own army. As a measure of defence he posted his troops along the borders of his territory. Sir John strongly objected to this and threatened the Nizam with military action if he did not forthwith withdraw his troops from the borders. The Nizam ignored the threat and the English feared that he might join the Marathas or Tipu against themselves. They took recourse to intrigue, won over the Nizam's son Alijah and incited him to rebel against his father. To quell the rebellion, the Nizam had to call in his troops from the border. The revolt was put down and Alijah taken prisoner but it unnerved the Nizam so much that he submitted to the terms dictated by Sir John Shore. He and his descendants thereafter continued to be the humble servants of the English and rendered every help in firmly establishing the Company's rule.

Attempt to Grab Karnatic

We have narrated before how Nawab Mohammad Ali of Karnatic was fleeced and when he had been sucked bone dry, how he was compelled to borrow from English traders to meet the ceaseless demands of the Company and its employees. The scandal attracted the attention of some Members of Parliament who asked questions embarrassing to the Ministry which had been helped in the Parliamentary election by funds provided by some of the creditors of Nawab Mohammad Ali, amongst whom may be mentioned Paul Benfield. The matter was hushed up (Thornton).

"The system of torture by which the possessions of the Indian princes have been wrung from them", as stated by William Howitt, was "the skilful application of the process by which cunning men create debtors, and then force them at once to submit to their most exorbitant demands". Lord Cornwallis had manoeuvred a treaty with Nawab Mohammad Ali whereby the English had acquired full control over the Karnatic army and several districts of the Nawab's territory had been "mortgaged" to the Company in lieu of the "debts" allegedly due from him. He died on 13th October 1795, and was succeeded by his son Umdal-ul-Umra, who "inherited" all these fictitious debts of his father. Two weeks later, on 28th October, Sir John wrote to the Governor of Madras, "you must press the new Nawab to cede to the Company the entire State." The Nawab did not agree. So at least for the time being the English attempt to grab his State did not succeed, although it did expose their real intentions with regard to Karnatic.

Annexation of Rohilkhand

There was trouble in Rohilkhand. On the death of its ruler Nawab Faizullah Khan, his younger son, Ghulam Mohammad, murdered his elder brother, Ali Khan, the rightful heir, and seized the *Gadi.* Sir John Shore decided, according to Mill, to take away the State from Faizullah's family. Sir Robert Abercrombie advanced with the Oudh army to accomplish it. In the clash of arms at Bitovra, the Rohillas initially gained some advantage but they were ultimately defeated. The English confiscated the State of Rohilkhand and its treasury was given away by them to the Nawab Wazir of Oudh.

Sale of Oudh "Gadi"

Asafuddaula, the Nawab Wazir of Oudh, was the next victim of English rapacity. Lord Cornwallis had, in the Treaty of 1788, given the Nawab a solemn undertaking that the amount of Rs. 50 lacs which the Nawab had to pay every year to the Company for the maintenance of the latter's Subsidiary Army, would never be increased. Sir John, however, wanted a stronger army to be at his disposal, but at another's expense, so that it could be used for the expansion of the English possessions in Northern India, not excluding Oudh itself. In pursuit of this aim he wrote in a letter that "we must not in the least consider our treaties with Oudh" (Mill). He pressed the Nawab to agree to spend another Rs. 5 lacs year and maintain an additional force of one regiment each of English and Indian cavalry. The Nawab courageously refused. Sir John forcibly took into custody the Nawab's Vazir, Maharaja Jhaoo Lal and himself went to Lucknow in March 1797, and coerced the Nawab into accepting the additional burden, and thus committed breach of the promise given by Lord Cornwallis. The Nawab could not bear the shock of this perfidy, fell ill and died shortly afterwards. He was succeeded by his son Wazir Ali. The succession was at first formally recognised by Sir John, who did not hesitate to rescind the recognition later. It happened this way. The deceased Nawab, Wazir Asafuddaula, had a brother, Saadat Ali, who lived in Banaras and was supposed to have a better claim to succeed Asafuddaula. "Seeing that a better bargain could be made with the brother of the deceased Wazir, Sir John Shore repaired to Banares, and proposed to the latter ... to dethrone Wazir Ali, offering the support of the Company on the intelligible condition that the subsidy should be largely increased and their support should be paid for otherwise in money and kind. To this stipulation, the bold and barefaced aspirant to the princedom "gleerfully consented" and, after a preliminary process at Lucknow, termed in the Parliamentary Return of Treaties "a full investigation", and "purporting to be an enquiry into the spuriousness of Wazir Ali's birth, that prince was deposed and Saadat Ali was proclaimed Nawab Wazir of Oudh in his stead at Lucknow, on 21st January, 1798." (*Dacoities in Excelsis* by Major Bird, Assistant Resident at Lucknow).

On 21st February, 1798, a treaty was executed between Sir John Shore and Saadat Ali whereby the latter undertook:

(i) to pay in full the debts claimed by the Company,
(ii) to cede to the Company the Allahabad Fort and pay Rs. 8 lacs for its repairs,
(iii) to pay Rs. 3 lacs for repairs to the Fatehgarh Fort,
(iv) to pay some lacs of rupees to be specified later for expenses incurred on the movement of the Company's armies,
(v) to pay Rs. 12 lacs to compensate the Company for its expenditure in getting Saadat Ali installed as Nawab Wazir,
(vi) to pay an annual pension of Rs. 11/2 lacs to the deposed Wazir Ali and,
(vii) to increase the annual payment to the Company on account of the Subsidiary Army from Rs. 56 lacs (which Asafuddaula had been forced to agree to pay less than a year before) to Rs. 76 lacs.

It was also provided in the treaty that no European other than an employee of the Company would be permitted to reside anywhere in Oudh.

Major Bird had estimated that the Company thus got within a year a million pounds in cash besides the Allahabad Fort. Sir Henry Lawrence has thus commented on the treaty ("Calcutta Review" for January, 1845):

> "What will perhaps most strike the English reader of Sir John Shore's treaty is the entire omission of the slightest provision for the good government of Oudh. The people seemed as it were sold to the highest bidder ... Saadat Ali was ... a more promising sponge to squeeze than his

> nephew ... He (Sir John Shore) made the *Musnud* of Oudh a mere transferable property in the hands of the British Governor ... We are obliged entirely to condemn the whole tenor of Oudh negotiations."

English Possessions Outside India

In 1795, Sir John Shore had driven the Dutch out of India and annexed to the Company all their possessions in the country. Thereafter by degrees, he drove out the Dutch from Ceylon, Malacca, Bandar, Ambiyana and other Asiatic countries. The French possession of Mauritius and the Spanish possession of fertile Manila were also annexed to the British Empire. All this was done mostly with money wrung out of India.

England Honours Sir John Shore

For valuable services rendered, Sir John Shore was raised to the peerage and in March 1798, he returned to England. He had followed closely in the footsteps of his ideal in politics, Warren Hastings, and his services to England were no doubt at par with those of Clive and Warren Hastings. He was reputed to be a "staunch Christian" too!

13

Marquess of Wellesley

Some years before his selection as the next Governor-General, Wellesley was appointed a Member of the Board of Control constituted by the British Crown in 1793 under Pitt's India Act, which was invested with the management of all political affairs of the Company, the sole authority to make war or peace and the power to appoint Governors-General. From then onwards, he had continued to be in close touch with Prime Minister Pitt and the ex-Governor-General Lord Cornwallis, and under their guidance had carefully studied the Indian political situation. Pitt was a staunch imperialist and Wellesley was his apt pupil. Before he left for India, Wellesley was invited by Pitt to stay with the latter for a whole week during which the two discussed full and elaborate plans for the establishment of the British Indian Empire. Thus coached, Wellesley left for India and on his way out stayed for two months at the Cape of Good Hope, arriving in Calcutta in May 1798.

At the Cape, Wellesley had the advantage of discussing his plans with two Englishmen, Major Kirkpatrick and Sir David Baird, both of whom had first-hand experience and up-to-date knowledge of the state of affairs in the territories of the Indian rulers. Major Kirkpatrick was a veteran and astute politician who had served under Warren Hastings and Cornwallis as the Company's Agent and Representative at Mahadji Sindhia's Court, at Hyderabad and in Nepal. He had had a lot to do with the secret collection of information about the routes to Nepal and its military strength. Kirkpatrick had also had a hand in the replacement of Frenchmen by Englishmen in the Hyderabad Army. Sir David Baird had once been imprisoned by Tipu. With their collaboration, Wellesley was able to develop his plans further and evolve a scheme for the destruction of the political power and authority of the Indian rulers. His letters from the Cape to Pitt and to Dundas, the Minister dealing with Indian affairs, give a clear indication not only of the instructions which he had been given by the two but also of his plans. He wrote to Dundas on 23rd February, 1798: "Bear in mind the state of the native powers in India at this moment;

and recollect that the greatest advantage which we now possess is the present deranged condition of those interests." Consequently, Wellesley decided to exploit this advantage and planned to make the "native powers" enter into a "subsidiary alliance" with the English, one by one. A "subsidiary alliance" meant in effect that in return for some financial help, the Company would render military help to the Indian State by taking over the control of its army and its defence and would guarantee its security as also that of its ruler. "The subsidiary system was nothing more than a delusion ... these countries were not ostensibly conquered; the sovereign was allowed to remain on his throne, with all the trappings of royalty, but substantial power was transferred from him to the person of a political agent" ("Asiatic Quarterly Review," January 1887).

Wellesley's mission is best stated in his own words:

"I will", he wrote to Lady Anne Barnard, "heap kingdoms upon kingdoms, victory upon victory, revenue upon revenue; I will accumulate glory and wealth and power, until the ambition and avarice even of my masters shall cry mercy."

To further his plans, Wellesley also took steps to propagate Christianity in India. Under his orders, Sunday began to be observed as a holiday throughout the Company's possessions, and the publication of newspapers on Sundays was banned by law. For providing the Company with low-paid English-knowing Indian minor officials and clerks, a college was established in Fort William at Calcutta. Instruction in the Christian religion was made an essential part of the curriculum. The Bible was translated into seven different languages by the college and copies were widely distributed free of cost.

14

Nizam Forced into "Subsidiary Alliance"

Wellesley had written to Dundas from the Cape of Good Hope (28th February, 1798): "Peshwa's power and influence are declining so rapidly that, it is neither necessary nor feasible to attack the Marathas." He had decided to attack and destroy Tipu but, as he wrote to Dundas in the same letter, "we will need the help of other Indian rulers, and the Nizam's own army cannot be depended upon to side with us against Tipu". As a matter of fact, that army had once before sided with Tipu against the English. It became essential, therefore, that the Nizam's own army be somehow disbanded and replaced by a new subsidiary army of the Company, thus leaving the Nizam without any armed forces under his control. This could be accomplished only if the Nizam was trapped into seeking a subsidiary alliance with the English.

The Plot

It was a common practice of the English officers of the Company to win over by bribery the Ministers of Indian rulers. In Hyderabad, too, this was done. The Nizam's Wazir Azimul Omra, and some of his courtiers were bribed and won over through Capt. Kirkpatrick, the English Resident at the Nizam's Court. Capt. Kirkpatrick was the brother of Major Kirkpatrick who had coached Wellesley at the Cape of Good Hope, and was an expert in hatching plots with the courtiers of Indian rulers. He had taken to Indian dress and the Indian way of living. He had married the daughter of a Muslim courtier in Hyderabad and was popularly known there as Hashmat Jung.

The plot hatched by the bribed Azimul Omra and Capt. Kirkpatrick was that the former would quietly start disbanding the Nizam's army bit by bit, without the knowledge of the Nizam. When the entire army had been disbanded, the Company's army which was to be kept ready at hand was to take the place of the Nizam's disbanded army. The Nizam was to be kept entirely in the dark till the change-over was complete, and the Nizam faced with a *fait accompli.* It was rightly expected that the Nizam, very considerably weakened as he was by his defeat at the hands of the Marathas at Kurdala (*vide* Chap. XII), would be incapable of doing anything about it. We quote below from the secret instructions which Wellesley sent to Capt. Kirkpatrick on 8th July, 1798:

> "... you will urge to Azimul Omra in the strongest terms the necessity of his taking every precaution to prevent the propositions ... from transpiring; and you will suggest to him the propriety of dispersing the corps in small parties for the purpose of facilitating its final reduction ... Should Azimul Omra consent, in the name of the Nizam, to the proposed conditions, you will then require the march of the troops from Fort St. George."

A week later, Wellesley wrote to General Harris, the Governor of Madras, to keep the Company's troops ready to march to Hyderabad. He wrote further:

> "The measure forms part of a much more extensive plan for the establishment of our alliances"

and impressed upon General Harris the absolute necessity of:

> "... the most strict attention to secrecy in the whole of this proceeding ... you will communicate the whole proceeding to the Residents at Poona and Hyderabad for *their* information *only,* and not to be imparted to their respective Courts".

A month later Wellesley again wrote to General Harris saying "my letter of the 16th July must have made it plain to you how vital my plan was for the continued existence of the English rule in India."

Plot Succeeds

It appears, however, that Azimul Omra although won over was hesitating and delayed doing his part. In the meantime the Company's troops had started for Hyderabad from Madras without waiting for the disbanding of the Nizam's army. Any delay in the execution of the plot obviously imperilled its success. But, "fortunately for us," writes Sir John Kaye, "the Nizam's army revolted at the right moment ... and arrested its French officers and commander." Just then, the army from Madras arrived on the scene, surrounded Hyderabad, demanded the instant dismissal of the Nizam's army and its replacement by the Company's troops. The Nizam was helpless. Till a few hours earlier, he had no inkling of what had been brewing. He now found himself hemmed in by the Company's army with his own army in revolt and his *Durbar* honey-combed with treacherous cells. The only way out was submission to the English Resident's demands and the Nizam submitted. He signed the Treaty of Subsidiary Alliance on 1st November 1798.

What Sir John Kaye has omitted to explain is, how it happened that the Nizam's army revolted "at the right moment" just when the Madras army was at the gates of Hyderabad. Had the English agents been busy stirring up disaffection in the Nizam's army and inciting it to revolt "at the right moment"? We wonder whether it is just English luck, pure and simple, or the English foresight in providing a second string to their bow, that deserves the credit for the opportune revolt. Perhaps it was a combination of both that led to the success of the plot.

Effects of Treaty

The Treaty tolled the knell of the Nizam as an independent Indian ruler. It stationed in his dominion and at his expense a force 6,000 strong, equipped with artillery and officered by Englishmen. The Nizam was also bound not to employ any European without the prior sanction of the Company. Actually, he was not free even to employ Indians of his choice as his Ministers. After the death of Azimul Omra the English forced him to appoint their own nominee, Mir Alam, as his Prime Minister. Thus the first independent Indian ruler to be hounded by Wellesley into a Subsidiary Alliance was virtually held in duress by the English and, ironically enough, had to pay for the army which kept him there.

Camouflage

An attempt was made to camouflage the ugliness of the real happenings by the wording of the Treaty's Preamble which read:

> "Whereas Nawab Nizam-ul-Mulk Asaf Jah Bahadur in view of the importance of the existing friendship has expressed the wish that the strength of the Honourable Company's army in his employment be increased, etc."

The attempt, founded on an utter falsehood, did not, however, succeed in throwing dust into the eyes of the British public and so another lie was tried. It was declared that as attacks on English possessions by the French and by Tipu were feared it had become absolutely necessary that such of the Indian rulers as were likely to join the French or Tipu be paralysed.

Wellesley Rewarded

The Ministry in England sent Wellesley a special dispatch expressing their intense satisfaction with the Hyderabad Treaty. The Company's Directors granted him an annual pension of £ 5000 for 20 years, beginning with the date of the Treaty. Capt. Kirkpatrick and his assistants were also rewarded by promotions, etc.

On 8th July, 1798, the day on which he wrote to Capt. Kirkpatrick, Wellesley had also written to the English Resident at Poona on identical lines. But efforts to bribe and win over any of the Ministers or courtiers of the Poona *Durbar* did not make any headway. The *Durbar* had not yet become utterly characterless or lacking in political wisdom like the Hyderabad Court. Although Nana Fadnavis was in prison, the men at the helm of affairs were too alert and far-sighted to be taken in by the English guile and the English did not find it easy to suborn any of them or lead them "up the garden path".

15

Tipu Sultan

By the 1792 Treaty of Seringapattam (Chap. XI) Tipu had to cede to the English, the Marathas and the Nizam half of his dominion and to pay them as war-penalty Rs. 330 lacs. One-third of this amount was realised from Tipu at once, and for the balance, he was given two years' time to pay.

Cornwallis was then Governor-General and as his letters written at the time indicate, he fully expected that Tipu would be quite unable to pay within that time such a huge amount, because even the territory that had been left to Tipu was devastated and could not bring in any appreciable revenue. Cornwallis had, therefore, counted on Tipu's failure to pay, as an excuse for gobbling up the remaining half of his territory. But Cornwallis's expectations failed to materialize. Tipu was a very capable administrator who always performed what he promised. We quote the English historian Malcolm:

> "... I shall take a short retrospect of the leading features of his (Tipu's) conduct since 1792 ... With that unremitting activity and zealous warmth which we could look for in a prince, who had come to a serious determination by every reasonable means in his power to regain what he had lost, Tipu worked hard. This was first marked by an honourable and unusually punctual discharge of the large sum which remained due at the conclusion of the peace to the allies. Instead of sinking under his misfortunes, he exerted all his activity to repair the ravages of war. He began to add to the fortifications of his capital—to remount his cavalry, to recruit and discipline his infantry, to punish his refractory tributaries, and to encourage the cultivation of his country, which was soon restored to its former prosperity." (*Wellesley's Dispatches,* Vol. I)

All this was gall and wormwood to the English.

Wellesley's Decision to Destroy Tipu

During his stay at the Cape of Good Hope, Wellesley had come to know about Tipu's recovery from the crippling blow of 1792, and about the restoration of his State's "former prosperity". Earlier in England he had been infected by Cornwallis's view that Tipu's very existence constituted a grave menace to the English interests in India. He had, therefore, decided even before he landed at Calcutta to crush Tipu by every available means. Wellesley's efforts to paralyse the Nizam and the Peshwa were only stepping-stones to the ultimate accomplishment of Tipu's destruction.

False Accusations

But Tipu had not violated any of the terms of the 1792 treaty. An excuse had, therefore, to be found for attacking him. So, it was stated, on the strength of a "notification" alleged to have been published by the French in Mauritius, that Tipu had sent special emissaries to Mauritius in a bid to get the French to join him against the English.

On 9th June, 1798, Wellesley sent a "copy" of the alleged "notification" to General Harris, the Governor of Madras, and directed him to alert his army for operations against Tipu. On 20th of the same month he informed General Harris of his "final determination ... to assemble the army upon the coast ... with the object of striking a sudden blow against Tipu" and added "you will, of course, feel the absolute necessity of keeping the contents of this letter secret." On 23rd June, 1798, General Harris wrote back to Wellesley that the latter's suspicions and fears were groundless, and that it would be impolitic to go to war with Tipu at that time. On 6th July, 1798, Josiah Webb, Secretary to the Madras Government, wrote to Wellesley:

> "Whatever French troops there were in Mauritius have been recalled to France, and even the French ships have left, thus any conspiracy between Tipu and the French is manifestly impossible."

Tipu Hoodwinked

Wellesley's first letter to General Harris about assembling "the army on the coast" was sent on 9th June, 1798. Five days later, on the 14th Wellesley wrote a very cordial letter to Tipu, and as a further gesture of goodwill agreed to withdraw his earlier claim to the Waynad region which the Company had been claiming for some years. Tipu was taken in, and reacted just as cordially. He wrote back to Wellesley: "You are my sincere well-wisher and I am convinced that you will always maintain our cordial relations" (Tipu's letter to the Governor-General received in Calcutta, 10th July 1798). On 4th November, 1798, Wellesley again wrote very cordially to Tipu to lull his suspicions which had been somehow aroused. Wellesley was not yet ready to strike.

Wellesley Throws off Mask

Only five days after the second friendly letter, Wellesley, on 9th November, 1798, wrote a strongly-worded letter to Tipu in which he said "Do not imagine that I could be unaffected by the negotiations carried on by you with the enemies of my country." He further informed Tipu by this letter, that Major Doveton would soon be reaching him (Tipu) with the demand for the cession of such of his districts as were needed by the Company. Evidently, Wellesley's preparations had now been completed and his campaign against the Nizam of Hyderabad had also been successfully concluded. He wrote to the Commander of his Navy, Rennier (14th November, 1798): "Hyderabad has been settled and our preparations for war have been fully completed on either side of the sea-coast ... This is a good opportunity and I have decided to take advantage of it for the purpose of rendering Tipu absolutely powerless either by threats only or by war."

Preparations for War

The Nizam and his new Wazir, Mir Alam—appointed on the insistence of the English—rendered very substantial help by providing a force 18,000 strong, consisting of 14,000 cavalry, and the entire Subsidiary Army. The Madras contingent numbered 4,000 and Bengal contributed 2,000 men. In addition, a sizable force from Bombay, under General Stuart, also joined in. Altogether Wellesley had an army of over 25,000 at his disposal. Even so, Wellesley was not confident of success against Tipu, and had recourse to the standard technique of the English in India, *viz.,* bribing and corrupting such men in the opposite camp as could deliver the goods. Wellesley appointed a "commission" of five, consisting of his brother Col. Wellesley, Col. Close, Col. Agnew, Capt. Malcolm and Capt. Macaulay, with the object of winning Tipu's men over to the English side. He considered it "both just and expedient to do so" (*Wellesley's Dispatches,* p. 442). The Commission's efforts effectively undermined Tipu's resistance and contributed very largely to his defeat and downfall.

Ultimatum to Tipu

Wellesley wanted to be personably near the scene of operations and so arrived in Madras on 31st December, 1798. Here he got Tipu's reply to his letters. Tipu in his reply vehemently protested his innocence and fervently expressed the hope that the terms of the 1792 treaty would be adhered to by all the four governments that had signed it.

On 9th January, 1799, Wellesley wrote once again to Tipu and demanded the immediate cession of all his towns and ports along the sea-coast to the English. A reply was demanded within 24 hours. The letter was virtually an ultimatum.

Declaration of War

The Company's army led by General Harris began its march on Tipu's dominion on 3rd February, 1799. Tipu wrote to Wellesley on the 13th, urging an amicable settlement and proposing that Major Doveton may be sent to him to start negotiations for peace. Wellesley took no notice. Tipu repeated his request. Wellesley ignored it, and formally declared war on Tipu on 22nd February, 1799. The Company's forces invaded Tipu's dominion by land and sea simultaneously.

Traitors in Tipu's Camp

Tipu did not have a chance. To start with, he was told by his own men that the Company's force was only four or five thousand strong and was thus milled into sending out a comparatively small body of horsemen to check the enemy's advance. It was commanded by Tipu's trusted Brahmin Minister, Poornea, who instead of engaging the invaders in battle kept going round them in circles, and even severely reprimanded a detachment of his cavalry which had courageously attacked the enemy!

On hearing that the Company's army was continuing to advance unchecked, Tipu himself set out with a force but was again misled about the route which the invaders had taken, and so went the wrong way. As soon as he discovered his mistake, he retrieved it by marching rapidly to where General Harris's force then was, and engaged it at Gulshanabad. In the battle that ensued, he inflicted very heavy losses on the enemy. At this juncture, Tipu learned that another force from Bombay, under General Stuart, was marching on his capital, Seringapattam. He, therefore, instructed his army-commander, Kamruddin Khan, to press home the initial advantage gained against General Harris, and himself rushed to the rescue of his capital. But Kamruddin Khan had already sold himself to the English and instead of attacking the Company's army, he deliberately manoeuvred his own force into utter confusion and the English won the day. By marching continuously for two days and nights, Tipu caught up with General Stuart's force and attacked it immediately. The Bombay force was routed and sought refuge in a nearby forest. Tipu was again deceived by someone and led to believe that the English army had given up the fight and was on its way back to Bombay. In reality it had taken the forest route to join General Harris.

Battle for Seringapattam

Almost immediately after Tipu's return to Seringapattam, General Harris's army too arrived there. Immediately facing it was the Fort and beyond it was the city. The English army heavily bombarded both. Some of Tipu's advisers suggested his flight from Seringapattam, others advised him to surrender and to sue for peace. Tipu did neither and made up his mind to fight to the last and if necessary, to go down fighting. It appears that he was not even aware that he had already been betrayed by Poornea and Kamruddin Khan, for he sent out from the Fort a force, commanded by both of them, to fight the besiegers. Both betrayed Tipu for the second time, and would not attack the English. Brave and loyal cavalrymen in their command repeatedly sought permission to charge the enemy but it was refused every time. The English army advanced unscathed and reached Mahtab Bagh, the key bastion of the Fort. The bastion was for a long time successfully defended by its intrepid and loyal commandant, Syed Ghaffar, who had, in 1791, defeated and repulsed General Meadows at the siege of Somerpeet tower, another bastion of the Seringapattam Fort. The English tried to bribe Syed Ghaffar but failed. They then look recourse to secret intrigues with some of Tipu's closest associates and these advised Tipu to entrust the defence of the main Fort to Syed Ghaffar, and to replace the latter at the Mahtab Bagh bastion by a new commandant. The new commandant was a creature of the English and surrendered the bastion to them without fighting, thus clearing their way to storm the main Fort.

Syed Ghaffar Murdered—Tipu Trapped

Amongst those who had sold themselves to the English was one Dewan Mir Sadiq, Tipu's principal informant and adviser at that time. Ghazi Khan was one of Tipu's loyal and trusted officers and was manning the ramparts of the Fort. Mir Sadiq had Ghazi Khan murdered, and when the wall of the Fort was breached with the connivance of his co-conspirators, he did not inform Tipu about it.

The next victim was the loyal Syed Ghaffar, the brave defender of the Fort, who was murdered by the traitorous conspirators. The latter signalled to the English besiegers who started pouring into the Fort immediately through the breach in the wall they had made.

Tipu was then in the city, behind the Fort. He had just sat down to his meal when news of Syed Ghaffar's murder and of the English soldiers' entry into the Fort was brought to him. He left the food untouched, mounted a horse rushed to the Fort with the few officers and men who were at hand and entered the Fort through a back door.

Mir Sadiq following close on Tipu's heels had all the doors leading out of the Fort locked and barred, so that Tipu was trapped inside the Fort and could not evade falling into English hands. He (Mir Sadiq) was giving strict orders to the sentries at the door, through which he himself was going out, not to open it on any account or for anybody, when an alert and loyal soldier saw what he was up to and shouting, "Take thy punishment, thou cursed devil, who wants to run away after delivering his God-fearing Sultan into the hands of the enemies," cut Mir Sadiq down then and there. It could not, however, help Tipu in any way, who had by now realised the hopelessness of the position into which treason had landed him.

Tipu's Last Fight

Tipu's position was desperate. He had only a handful of men with him and the Fort was packed with the soldiers of the English army. The odds against him were heavy. But with the courage which desperate situations invariably evoke in the brave, Tipu rallied his men declaring, "We must fight and defend the Fort to our last breath death can come only once, why care when?" He put himself in the forefront of his men and started shooting at the European officers of the enemy. Several of them fell to his gun. A bullet hit his chest, but he continued firing. Then a second bullet hit him. His horse received several shots and crumbled under him. In jumping off, he dropped his turban. He threw away the gun and drew his sword. Bare-headed and on foot he continued to hack with his sword, whilst blood ran down his chest, till he fell down. As he lay prostrate, a European soldier tried to snatch away Tipu's jewelled belt. Tipu's sword flashed for the last time and cut off the soldier's leg at the knee. A faithful follower pressed him to surrender and throw himself at the mercy of the English. Tipu indignantly spurned the suggestion. Next moment, a third bullet entered his right temple, killing him instantly. He died a gallant soldier's death, fighting to the last. When his body was recovered from under a heap of dead men, the sword was still firmly clasped in his hand!

Tipu's Son Inveigled into Surrender

Fateh Hyder, Tipu's eldest son, was fighting the English near Karighat Hill, some distance away from the Fort, when he heard of his father's death. He hurried back and assembled some ministers and noblemen in a council-of-war. They were, however, divided about the course to be taken. Jahan Khan, of whom more will be narrated later, led the group which advocated a continuation of the armed struggle. Others, headed by Poornea (who had already been won over by the English) pressed for immediate cessation of hostilities and suing for peace. At this juncture, General Harris personally called on Fateh Hyder and very courteously made an offer of peace. He publicly pledged his solemn word that the English would instal Fateh Hyder on his father's throne, if he surrendered to them. Poornea's group prevailed upon Fateh Hyder to accept the offer and lay down arms. Fateh Hyder surrendered and this removed all chances of the English occupation of the Fort being disturbed by armed action.

General Harris's promise to Fateh Hyder later turned out to be no better than a ruse resorted to for inducing him to surrender. It was flagrantly broken within the next 48 hours or so, when all the 12 sons of Tipu, his brother Karim Sahib, and the ladies of his household were taken into custody and deported to the distant fortress of Rai Vellore.

The Pillage

Tipu was killed on 4th May, 1799. That very day the invaders took possession of the city. By a proclamation issued in Wellesley's name, it was announced that his army would protect the life and property of the citizens and would not permit any atrocities. Nevertheless, unchecked loot, wholesale atrocities like murder and even rape by the soldiers, both English and Indian, were rampant throughout the city for a number of days. This has been admitted by several English officers in the letters they wrote about that time.

Tipu's palace was later thoroughly pillaged. His treasury was full of gold and jewellery. The English soldiers of the Company plundered it. The throne made of solid gold was broken up. Caskets containing diamond and pearl necklaces and other articles of jewellery were impounded. The value of the loot has been estimated to exceed £11,000,000 or about Rs. 12 crores. Tipu's large collection of rare books, manuscripts and other valuables were shipped to England.

The English Celebrate Tipu's Death!

Sir John Anstruther, the then Chief Justice of Bengal, wrote to the Governor-General on 17th May, 1799, that "his (Tipu's) was the only power strong enough to repel our armies" and that "our Empire in India" had by reason of Tipu's death "become firmly established, safe and secure'. The event was, therefore, celebrated with eclat by the English at Calcutta. Victory processions were taken out and a thanksgiving service was held in the new cathedral, which was attended by the Governor-General and all the English officers.

Honours and Rewards Distributed

Wellesley, who till then was "Earl Mornington", became "Marquess Wellesley". General Harris received a peerage with the title of "General Lord Harris of Seringapattam". All the Englishmen who had taken part in the fighting were rewarded. Nor were the traitors who had betrayed Tipu forgotten. Many of them received pensions and *Jagirs.*

Dismemberment of Tipu's Kingdom

The Company reserved for themselves the "lion's share". The Nizam too received a slice, and the rest of the territory was left to be "ruled" by a scion of the last Hindu ruler of Mysore, a boy of five, whom the English installed as the "Maharaja" and appointed the arch-traitor Poornea the boy's Wazir and guardian.

"Treaty" with Infant Maharaja

On 8th July, 1799, the Company entered into a fresh treaty with the new "Maharaja". Its main provisions may be summarised thus:

(1). The Company's Subsidiary Army was to be permanently stationed in Mysore and the State was to pay to the Company 7 lacs of pagodas (about Rs. 25 lacs) every year for its maintenance.

(2). The English were vested with the sole and complete control of all the forts and the army of Mysore.

(3). The Governor-General was vested with the authority to intervene, at his discretion, in the administration in all the departments of the State, and his decisions and directions were binding on the Maharaja who would have to carry them out.

(4). The only right the Maharaja was left with was to receive an annual personal allowance of not less than one lac of pagodas.

Lone Lover of Freedom

Malik Jahan Khan was one of the top personalities at the council-of-war held by Fateh Hyder after his father, Tipu, had been killed, and, as previously stated, he had advocated the continuation of the fight against the English. He had been overruled but could not reconcile himself to Fateh Hyder's surrender. When the English occupied Seringapattam, he rode out alone from the city as he would not submit to the foreigner's rule. Within a short time he collected an army of about 30,000 infantry and cavalry. For the next two years he harassed the English and their friends by surprise attacks in the region between the rivers Krishna and Tungabhadra. His fame spread far and wide. He was called *Dhoondiya Bagh* (Tiger) by the people. His last battle was with the troops commanded by Col. Arthur Wellesley, in which he was delivered treacherously into Col. Wellesley's hands by the Afghans of Karappa and Kurnool. Several English writers have called this lover of freedom a "robber", as they have called Chhatrapati Shivaji a brigand.

Thus ended the rule of Haider's descendants over Mysore. Even the high office of the "*Daiva*" of Mysore, which was held by Haider, was abolished.

Efforts to Calumniate Tipu

Sir John Kaye, who after 1857, was for some time the secretary-in-charge of the "Political and Confidential Section" of the office of the Secretary of State for India, has recorded: "It is a custom among us .... to take a native ruler's kingdom and then revile the deposed ruler" (*History of the Sepoy War* Vol. III, pp. 361–62). When Sir John wrote, the "custom" had been followed for over a hundred years.

All the English writers of Indian history, with the solitary exception of James Mill, as also some hired Indian writers, have done their best to paint Tipu black. Perhaps no historical figures in the world have been calumniated more than the Indian leaders who resisted the growth of the English political domination of their country.

One of the principal and oft-repeated accusations is that Tipu was a bigoted Muslim who oppressed non-Muslims. We would point out that accusations of bigotry against the Mussalman rulers in India have ever been pressed into service for promoting hatred and hostility between the Hindus and the Muslims. That Tipu was a devout Muslim is true, but there is a world of difference between bigotry and devotion to one's own faith. We quote from James Mill's *History of India*:

> "Another feature in the character of Tipu was his religion, with a sense of which his mind was most deeply impressed. He spent a considerable part of every day in prayer. He gave to his kingdom or state a particular religious title, *Khudadad* or God-given; and he lived under a peculiarly strong and operative conviction of the superintendence of a Divine Providence. His confidence in the protection of God was, indeed, one of his snares; for he relied upon it to the neglect of other means of safety."

We have considered it necessary to undertake a little research of our own in order to make up our mind about Tipu's "bigotry" and his treatment of non-Muslims. We have been helped in our quest, amongst others in Mysore, by Dr. Shamshastri, the scholarly Director of the Archaeological Department of the Government of Mysore, and by Shri Shrikantia, Vice-Chancellor of Mysore University, to all of whom we are deeply grateful.

Two Proclamations of Tipu

We came across only two documents which could possibly lend colour to the alleged charge of religious bigotry of Tipu. We now deal with them briefly.

One is a proclamation issued by Tipu when he was battling with the combined forces of the English and the Nawab of Karnatic. It is an appeal addressed to the Muslims living in his enemy's territory calling upon them, in the name of Islam, to refuse all help to the foreigners, and to migrate to Mysore. Reinforced by quotations from the *Quran,* and from the Persian poems of the famous Hafiz, it declared that for Mussalmans to help the foreigner against their own country was heresy. It also announced that all the Mysore State officials had been ordered by Tipu to offer not only asylum to the would-be emigrants, but also security of life and property, as also a means of earning a livelihood.

The other document relates to Indian Christians in Mysore State and must be interpreted in the light of its background. Haider had treated the European Christian missionaries who bad come to his dominion with broad-mindedness and had not only allowed them complete freedom to preach and propagate Christianity, but had also liberally provided them with all the facilities that they wanted. But in the wars which Haider and Tipu had to fight against the English, the missionaries and the Indian converts to Christianity had abused that magnanimity. "The true value of missionary labour in India ... for the consolidation and strengthening of British rule ... can hardly be over-estimated" (Editorial in *The Statesman* of 23rd February 1887). They became willing tools in the hands of the English for suborning and sowing disaffection amongst European officers and soldiers in the Mysore army. Handbills with the signatures of European missionaries were widely distributed amongst the Europeans telling them that they "as Christians were not bound by the oath of loyalty to Haider or Tipu, even though it had been taken by them on the Bible and the Cross"! The second document is a proclamation or general order issued by Tipu to his Indian Christian subjects living along the sea-coast, on "hearing about their persistent disloyalties". He, like Haider, had the bitter experience of his Indian Christian subjects' disloyalty and even treachery. The order offered the Indian Christians the alternative of their conversion to Islam or externment from Mysore State.

We leave it to our readers to decide for themselves whether it was religious zeal ("Muslim bigotry" as it has been called by Tipu's traducers) or political exigency which led Tipu to issue such an order. Excepting Christians, no other non-Muslim community is covered by this order.

Tipu's Treatment of Hindus

We have not come across any authentic document or statement about any ill-treatment of Hindus, who outnumbered his subjects belonging to all other communities. On the contrary, there is an overwhelming evidence in the historical records of his fair and friendly treatment of the Hindus.

His two chief advisers, Poornea and Krishnarao, were both Brahmins, the former being his Prime Minister. The Hindus occupied the highest posts in the Mysore *Durbar* and State. He treated the Jagadguru Shri Shankaracharya of Shringeri Math (in Mysore State) with great veneration as is borne out by some 30 letters written by him to the Jagadguru, which are still extant. In one of them, written in 1791, he requested the Jagadguru to arrange for the ceremonial holy recitation (Path) of *Shat Chandi* at State expense. He endowed Hindu temples in Nanjangooda, Shrirangpattam, Melkote and other places with *Jagirs* and often made presents to them in cash and kind. Two temples in Bangalore, one right in front of and the other adjoining his two palaces, as also one very near his palace at Shringapattam still bear mute testimony to his broad-minded toleration of other religious faiths.

His non-Muslim subjects' trust and confidence in Tipu as regards religious matters is indicated by an incident which is on record. Some Hindu Nairs of Malabar coast sought his advice about their conversion *en masse* to Christianity. Tipu said to them:

"The Raja is the father of his people, and as such my advice is that you stick to your ancestors' religion."

Tipu's Concern for His Subjects

Tipu's "unremitting activity and zealous warmth" as a ruler have been testified to by writers like Malcolm. That he was a very capable and benevolent administrator who gave topmost priority to his subjects' welfare is amply borne out by the historical records of that period. His people were, by far, more prosperous and contented than people in the adjacent Company-ruled regions. They were self-reliant and not subject to any arms-restrictions as people under the Company's rule were. He was particularly friendly to the rural population. Forced labour in villages was totally abolished and oppressive methods of collecting rents or revenue were strictly banned. If any official, howsoever highly placed, was discovered to have been guilty of such practices, Tipu punished him severely. State officials were forbidden to interfere in any way or adjudicate in the internal affairs or disputes of the village communities. These were invariably managed and settled by the village *Panchayat* exclusively. For further development of agriculture, he had, in 1793, started the construction of a dam on the Kaveri river to store water for irrigation. He himself laid its foundation-stone which bore an inscription in Persian. We give below the translation of an extract from it:

> "... This dam is being constructed by the Khudadad Government, at the cost of lacs of rupees, as an act of charity in the name of Allah. Anyone who brings under cultivation any uncultivated land and grows crops, vegetables or fruits by irrigating it with water from this Bund, will be charged by the Khudadadad Government only 75 p.c. of the present government-share of the land-produce ... the newly cultivated land shall belong to the cultivator and his descendants for as long as the earth and sky last, and no one shall dispossess him on any account."

Our readers will no doubt note that Tipu encouraged agriculturists by reducing the government cess even though he provided them with additional irrigation facilities.

Tipu was killed within two years of his laying the foundations of the dam, remnants of which and the stone with the above inscription, came to light when digging for the foundations of the present Kaveri dam. The stone is still preserved in the gateway of the group of the present buildings of the dam.

The development and progress achieved in trade and industry during Tipu's rule of Mysore, particularly in cotton, woollen and silk textiles, was unprecedented and has not been equalled up till now (1929).

His iron and steel workshops manufactured commodities for civilian consumer use, as also superior cannon and guns with two or three barrels.

Tipu, Man and Soldier

Unlike his father, Tipu was a learned man, and was fond of scholars. His *Durbar* was graced by many learned Hindu pandits and Muslim divines. His extensive library was filled with valuable and rare books.

As mentioned Wore, Tipu was deeply religious. He lived a simple, clean and disciplined life. His daily meals consisted mostly of almonds, milk and fruit. He never touched liquor or any other intoxicant.

Tipu had great respect for women and did everything to safeguard their honour and virtue. In his battles he took every possible precaution against molestation by his soldiers of the women of the vanquished foe and came down with a very heavy hand on anyone found misbehaving in this respect. Twice in his battles with the Marathas, a number of Maratha women, some of them wives of Maratha Sardars, fell into his army's hands. On both the occasions, he treated them with respectful consideration, put them up in separate tents, and although the war was still on, sent them to the Maratha camps in palanquins escorted by his soldiers. (*Tipu Sultan* by Col. Miles).

A brave and able military commander, Tipu was the worthy son of a worthy father. He won his first battle when he was only seventeen. He could never get over his defeat in 1792 by the combined forces of the English, the Marathas and the Nizam. The odds against him were heavy but he felt the defeat and the humiliating treaty which followed it so much that as a sort of penance, he gave up sleeping on a bed and used to lie down on the bare floor with an odd piece or two of rough canvas under him! He had "come to a serious determination by every reasonable means in his power to regain what he had lost" (Malcolm). He lived up to what he often said: "It is better to live like a lion, if only for two days, than to live like a sheep for two hundred years." Of the many epitaphs on Tipu's tomb, one of the aptest is "Shamshere Gum Shud" (the sword is lost). According to the numerical value assigned to the Persian alphabet, the phrase "Shamshere Gum Shud" gives the year of Tipu's death. "Lost" indeed was the sword wielded by a selfless patriot and ardent lover of freedom who, like his father, refused to have any truck with the enemies of his country's freedom. To our shame, it must be admitted that during the 150 years following Aurangzeb's death, Haider and Tipu were the only two and two of all the Indian rulers and princes, who would not and did not at any time join the empire-hungry English against their own country. Had he so wished, Tipu, too, could have bartered his countrymen's freedom for a mess of pottage. But even his enemies admit that he fought to the last drop of his blood against foreign domination and preferred to die fighting in the attempt rather than be dishonoured by a charge of treason against his country or his people.

16

States of Oudh and Farrukhabad

Oudh

The prosperous region of Oudh, then called "The Garden of India", had long been coveted by the Company. After the Battle of Buxar, the Company had entered into a treaty with the Nawab Wazir of Oudh (1765), whereby the latter had agreed to the permanent posting of an English Resident at his *Durbar.*

The principal duty assigned in those days to the English Residents at the *Durbars* of the Indian rulers and princes was to sow and nurture the seeds of dissension at their respective *Durbars* as also to start and carry on intrigues against the ruler or the prince. To facilitate the performance of this duty, the Residents took to Indian dress and the Indian way of living. They employed teachers (*Munshis*) for learning the language of the region and familiarising themselves with the manners and customs of the people amongst whom they lived.

We have narrated (*vide* Chapter XII) how Sir John Shore had in 1798 sold the Oudh *gadi* to Saadat Ali and entered into a "Treaty of Perpetual Friendship" with him.

Wellesley's Move Against Oudh

After finishing Tipu and virtually annexing Mysore State, Wellesley turned his attention to Oudh. An opportunity to put the screw on Saadat Ali soon presented itself. Wazir Ali, whom the Company had at first recognised as the legitimate Nawab of Oudh and then deposed to make room for their stooge Saadat Ali, engineered a revolt against the latter. Saadat Ali was able to put it down only with the help of the Company's Subsidiary Army stationed in Oudh. After the revolt had been quelled, Wellesley wrote to Nawab Saadat Ali on 5th November, 1799, "advising" him that certain "reforms" in the Nawab's own army should be carried out. These "reforms" were to the effect that, barring the minimum number of men required for the collection of revenue and for ceremonial occasions, the rest of the Nawab's army should be disbanded and replaced by the Company's cavalry and infantry, and the Nawab should pay for the replacements an additional amount of money over and above the Rs 76 lacs which he was already paying for the maintenance of the Company's Subsidiary Army in his State.

Wellesley did not allow the Nawab any time for his reply nor did he wait for it. On the contrary, close on the heels of his letter he dispatched a regiment of the Company to be stationed in Oudh and declared the Nawab responsible for its maintenance. He also ordered a second regiment to be in readiness to march to Oudh immediately after the first had arrived there.

Nawab Saadat Ali's Reaction

On 11th January, 1800, the Nawab sent a letter of protest to Wellesley through Scott, the English Resident at Lucknow, his capital. His "remonstrance" was, in the words of Major Bird, the Assistant Resident at Lucknow, "as reasonably stated as it was justly founded". The Nawab referred to clause 17 of the above-mentioned 1798 "Treaty of Perpetual Friendship", whereby it was agreed that "the Nawab will continue to have exclusive authority and full control over his hereditary kingdom and its domestic affairs, as also over his army and his subjects."

"If", protested the Nawab, "the administrative control of my army is taken out of my hands, then it is an obvious negation of the rights and authority secured to me by the Treaty ... I am confident that the Company does not intend to commit an infringement of the Treaty from which I have not moved a hair's breadth, and never shall ... What I fear most is that by the Company's action, if persisted in, not only will the Company's good name and the people's faith in its promises suffer, but my prestige in and outside my country will be lost too ... it would mean the end of my rule ...." He also pointed out that by the unnecessary disbandment of his army, thousands of his faithful servants would be deprived of their livelihood which would be very detrimental to the welfare of his subjects. He concluded his letter with the expression of the hope that "in view of the Company's large-heartedness and your kindness, full control of my army will be allowed to remain in my bands as provided in the Treaty".

According to Major Bird, "a haughty reply was made by the Governor-General", who declined to take delivery of the Nawab's letter because it was "so impertinently worded" and directed that it be returned to the Nawab with the warning that if he again dared to express any doubts about the good faith and honesty of the English Government, he would be suitably punished.

Historian James Mill's Comments

> "A party to a treaty fulfils all its conditions with a punctuality, which, in his place, was altogether unexampled; a gross infringement of that treaty, or at least what appears to him a gross infringement, is about to be committed on the other side; he points out clearly, but in most humble language, savouring of abjectness much more than disrespect, the inconsistency which appears to him to exist between the treaty and the conduct; this is represented by the other party as an impeachment of their honour and justice; and if no guilt existed before to form a ground for punishing the party who declines compliance with their will, a guilt is now contracted which hardly any punishment can expiate. This, it is evident, is a course by which no infringement of a treaty can ever be destitute of a justification. If the party injured submits without a word, his consent is alleged. If he complains, he is treated as impeaching the honour and justice of his superior; a crime of so prodigious a magnitude as to set the superior above all obligations to such a worthless connection." (*History of India,* Vol. VI, p. 191)

Bare-faced Blackmail

On 2nd January, 1801, Wellesley sent an ultimatum to Nawab Saadat Ali demanding that "he should either abdicate and retire on an annual pension or cede to the Company half of his dominion in return for the two English Regiments already stationed in Oudh."

Wellesley also sent to the English Resident a draft of the Treaty which the Nawab had to sign if he accepted the second alternative. The Nawab repeatedly protested against this high-handedness but it was of no use. On 28th April, 1801, Wellesley instructed the English Resident "to use the Company's army and forcibly occupy half of the Nawab's territory, should he decline to cede it amicably."

"My objective", Wellesley categorically stated to the Resident, "is to destroy completely the military strength of the Nawab, and to acquire for the Company full and unfettered civil and military administration of the entire dominion of the Nawab."

The Nawab was helplessly at the mercy of the English, his erstwhile "friends", who had long been under numberless obligations to the Nawabs of Oudh. He was hemmed in by the English troops and subjected to ceaseless pressure by the English Resident and by Henry Wellesley, brother of and Private Secretary to the Governor-General. On 14th November, 1801, he signed the Treaty dictated by Wellesley, whereby half of his dominion was ceded to the Company. The ceded half consisted of the most fertile portions of Oudh yielding an annual revenue of Rs 135 lacs. The Marquess of Wellesley appointed his brother Henry Wellesley, the first Lieutenant-Governor of the new "British Province" constituted of the territory forcibly annexed.

A Vote of Thanks to Accused

On 9th March 1808, Lord Folkstone speaking in the English Parliament, frankly admitted that Nawab Saadat Ali had been throughout honest and patient but helpless, and proved to the hilt the dishonesty and rank injustice with which he (Lord Folkstone) charged Wellesley. Another Member of Parliament, Mr. R. Thornton, referred to the "Treaty" in these words: "... one might as well call a robbery committed by a footpad on a traveller on Hanslow Heath a treaty." Like Warren Hastings, Marquess Wellesley too was put on trial before Parliament. He was charged with this gross injustice which was fully exposed in speeches delivered by some broadminded members. The "trial" lasted three years, and ended with the Parliament's vote of thanks to the Marquess for this real service of his to the "British Empire"!

Farrukhabad

Farrukhabad was a small tributary of Oudh. It was ruled by a Nawab who paid Rs 4 lacs every year as tribute to the Nawabs of Oudh. An English Resident had also been posted at the Farrukhabad *Durbar*. During Cornwallis's regime, the Resident began to interfere in the internal administration of the State to such an extent that the Nawabs of Oudh and Farrukhabad lodged strong protests. Lord Cornwallis had to recall the Resident. He also gave an undertaking that in future no English Resident would be posted at Farrukhabad nor would there be any interference in the internal affairs of the State.

Wellesley in Action

Within six months of the annexation of the half of Oudh, Wellesley ignored the promises given by Lord Cornwallis and in November, 1801, sent his brother Henry to Farrukhabad with instructions somehow to get the reigning Nawab, Imdad Hussain, to agree to the cession of his territory to the Company in return for a yearly pension of a lac of rupees. Imdad Hussain had only recently attained majority. The Governor-General had given specific instructions to Henry Wellesley to the effect that the latter was to win over, by tempting promises of lavish rewards, such of Imdad Hussain's relations, friends and advisers as were willing to be bought and to intimidate by threats such as were not amenable to bribery. Henry carried out these instructions but even so it did not prove an easy task to get Imdad Hussain to sign away his State. Consequently, he was summoned to Lucknow under the orders of the Governor-General.

Underhand Tactics Succeed

On his arrival at Lucknow, Imdad Hussain was amazed to discover that the seal of his signatures had somehow found its way into the hands of the English Resident. Be that as it may, it has been officially stated that on June 4th, 1802, Nawab Imdad Hussain Khan signed at Bareilly the document or deed whereby he ceded his entire territory to the Company in return for an annual pension of Rs. 1,80,000 payable by the Company to the Nawab and his descendants.

Henry Wellesley was appointed the first administrator of the erstwhile Farrukhabad State.

17

Annexation of Tanjore

We have briefly related in Chapter 1 how the Company sent a force to Tanjore in support of Sahuji who claimed the *Gadi,* and how the English deserted him at the crucial moment and went over to the reigning Raja of Tanjore, Pratap Singh, who in return for this favour, ceded to the Company the town and Fort of Devkot. According to Torrens, "This was the beginning of the conquest of Hindostan."

Some years later, in 1762, the English helped Nawab Mohammad Ali of Karnatic to attack Tanjore. We might mention here that for generations the Nawabs of Oudh and Karnatic had been the milch-cows of the English, who instigated and helped the Nawabs to re-imburse themselves by plundering their neighbours. It was in pursuance of this policy that the invasion of Tanjore by Karnatic was helped by the English.

After the invasion the English adopted the role of mediators and an agreement was patched up between the combatants, whereby Tanjore became a tributary of Karnatic and agreed to pay to Karnatic an annual tribute of Rs. 4 lacs. The English also guaranteed that never again would Tanjore be attacked by the Nawab of Karnatic. But the latter did attack Tanjore in 1771 and the Company's Governor of Madras ignored the guarantee and the undertaking given by the Company in 1762, and helped the invader with the Company's troops. Meanwhile Raja Pratap Singh had died and his son, Tuljaji, had succeeded him as Raja of Tanjore. Tuljaji saved his skin by paying a very large amount of money to the Company and the Nawab of Karnatic. Two years later, in 1773, the Nawab invaded Tanjore for the third time with the collaboration of the English. The Nawab, who had no money of his own, had no alternative but to get money in this way for meeting the constant unlawful demands made on him by his so-called English "creditors" and the Company's officers. At every invasion of Tanjore, the amount of the tribute payable by its Raja to Karnatic was increased, but the former regularly paid it.

This state of affairs continued till 1787, when a formal "Treaty of Perpetual Friendship" was executed by the Raja of Tanjore with the English Company. Some six years later, Tuljaji died. He had no son of his own but had adopted Sarboji. The English exploited the opportunity for getting a stooge of theirs, Amar Singh, installed on the Tanjore *Gadi.* They got some *Pandits* to declare that Sarboji's adoption was invalid according to the Hindu *Shastras,* and so he could not succeed the deceased Tuljaji as Raja. The English then forcibly installed Amar Singh on the *Gadi* with the help of the Company's troops.

By then, the English had also discovered some "defects" in the 1787 Treaty to remove which they got the new Raja Amar Singh to execute a fresh treaty in 1793. Under its provisions the Company took over, for all time, the defence of the Tanjore principality and the Raja, in return, undertook to pay a very large amount of money to the Company every year. An English writer describes Amar Singh thus: "The Raja of Tanjore (Amar Singh) was a man of extremely great character and high principle and exceedingly well disposed towards the British Government." (*Life of General, the Right Honourable, Sir David Baird, Bart.* Vol. I. p. 119). But the English had not yet reached their goal of ending, once for all, the Indian rule over Tanjore. The 1793 Treaty was only one of the means to that end. Their next step was to post McLeod as English Resident at Tanjore and to get a Christian missionary, the well-known Rev. Poomartz, appointed as tutor to young Sarboji. Both were commissioned to start intrigues and plot against Raja Amar Singh and his *raj* generally. We would quote again the English writer about McLeod's activities:

> "...... circumstances graudally transpired which convinced ... the Raja ... that this civil servant of the Honourable East India Company had been placed at the Court of Tanjore for no other purpose than that of inducing, or even (if necessary) compelling the unfortunate Raja to give up his territory and become a pensioner of the said Honourable East India Company for the remaining term of the natural life ...... The Honourable East India Company was not exceedingly scrupulous as to the means by which territory was to be acquired"[1] (*Ibid*).

McLeod's behaviour towards Raja Amar Singh became so impudent that the latter complained about it but it was all in vain. To intimidate Amar Singh, McLeod would sometimes ostentatiously parade the Company's army before his palace—an army paid for by Amar Singh and supposed to be at Tanjore for his protection!

On 23rd January, 1796, McLeod ordered Col. Baird, the Commandant of this army, to see to it that neither Amar Singh's *Sirkeel,* Shivrao, nor any of his two brothers, Trimbaji and Shankarrao, was allowed to go out of the Tanjore Fort. On the 24th, he suddenly surrounded Amar Singh himself with the Company's soldiers and coerced him into signing a paper ceding all his territory to the Company. The very next day, Amar Singh wrote to the Governor-General, Sir John Shore, and said: "The Resident held me in duress, told me all kinds of lies and forced me to sign that paper. Consequently, my State must continue to be mine." The English plan to tell the world that Amar Singh had, of his own free will, ceded his territory to the Company was thus upset by proofs of coercion produced by Amar Singh. Moreover, the English conspiracy inside Tanjore had not yet matured fully. Under the circumstances, Sir John had to order the maintenance of the *status quo.* For the next two years, Amar Singh was allowed to continue his rule over Tanjore, and in the meantime, underground activities to further the English conspiracy against him were continued.

It was at this stage that Wellesley took over.

Wellesley Annexes Tanjore

Wellesley had been directed, before he left England, to obtain possession of Tanjore anyhow. He had also undertaken, as mentioned before, "to heap kingdoms upon kingdoms". Raja Amar Singh, on the other hand, had scrupulously observed the treaty with the English and had not in any way provided the English with even a plausible excuse for action against him. But as the above-mentioned English writer has put it "... whenever policy of aggrandisement seemed to warrant the measure, a pretext was never wanting to the Honourable East India Company to remove a native prince". (*Ibid,* p. 138).

Sarboji was now made the central figure in the English intrigues and pitted against Amar Singh. McLeod and the missionary Rev. Poowartz, were the moving spirits behind these intrigues. Amar Singh was accused of grossly ill-treating Tuljaji's widows and Sarboji and Rev. Poowartz supported the accusation by his own testimony. The widows and Sarboji were then brought to Madras to save them from further ill-treatment. Then the English suddenly "discovered" that Amar Singh, whom they themselves had manoeuvred to instal and whom they had been acknowledging as the rightful Raja for some ten years, was not entitled to the *Gadi,* but that Sarboji was the rightful heir! The earlier declaration about the invalidity of Sarboji's adoption, which the English had obtained from some *Pandits* was now at the instance of the English reversed by some other *Pandits,* who declared that Sarboji's adoption by Tuljaji was quite valid and in accordance with the Hindu-*Shastras.* Without the slightest reference having been made to him, Amar Singh was suddenly deposed one fine morning by the very army of the Company for the maintenance of which he had been paying the Company all the past ten years!

The same army installed Sarboji on the *Gadi,* who immediately ceded the principality of Tanjore to the English by a formal treaty and voluntarily became a pensioner of the Company. To quote once again the English writer, "interest declared for the possession of Tanjore—justice upheld the claims of the Raja, the undoubted heir, the legally acknowledged prince, the actual possessor of the territories" (*Ibid,* pp. 161, 162). We have only to add that the historian Mill, too, acknowledges the selfishness and the injustice of the English action.

18

End of Karnatic Nawab's Sovereignty

We shall now take up the thread of the story of Karnatic from the point at which we left it in Chapter XII.

In a certain "treaty" executed after the Mysore War of 1792 between the Company and Nawab Mohammad Ali, a clause had been inserted of which Wellesley now took advantage. It provided that, if in future war broke out in or near Karnatic, the Company would have the right to occupy such parts of the Karnatic dominion, and for such period as the Company might deem necessary for its success in the war.

Wellesley declared war against Tipu on 22nd February, 1799. Two months later, on 24th April, 1799, he wrote to Nawab Umdat-ul-Umra, the son and successor of the late Nawab Mohammad Ali, and, on the strength of the above clause, "advised" the Nawab to hand over to the Company at least for the duration of the war, administration and the revenue collection of his State. The "advice" was not unaccompanied by threats. Before the Nawab's reply was ready, Tipu was killed in action (4th May, 1799) and Seringapattam was occupied by the English. The army which "conquered" Seringapattam consisted also of the Subsidiary Army for the maintenance of which Umdat-ul-Umra had been paying to the Company nine lacs of pagodas every year.

On 13th May, 1799, Nawab Umdat-ul-Umra replied to Wellesley's letter, politely but firmly rejecting the preferred "advice". Congratulating Wellesley on the English victory against Tipu, the Nawab also claimed a share in the conquered territory proportionate to the cost met by him of maintaining the Subsidiary Army which had taken part in the fighting and contributed to the victory. Recalling that part of the Karnatic territory had been taken away and given to Haider Ali by the English in the past, when the latter had entered into a treaty with Haider Ali, the Nawab also asked for its return now that the English had conquered Haider Ali's entire dominion.

Wellesley realised that Umdat-ul-Umra was a hard nut to crack and, as it would have militated against the Company's interests either to accept or to reject outright any of the Nawab's just and legitimate demands, Wellesley did not even acknowledge the Nawab's letter.

Instructions from England

On 5th August, 1799, Wellesley received a letter from the Secretary of State for India in the British Parliament, saying "we are at present tied up by our treaties with the Nawab of Karnatic, but you must be alertly on the look-out for a suitable opportunity and use means like cajolery, etc., which are most likely to lead us to what we so heartily desire." (Letter from Right Honourable Henry Dundas to Earl of Mornington, 21st March, 1799).

In reply Wellesley wrote that it was futile to hope for a suitable opportunity so long as the present Nawab lived

> "I am thoroughly convinced", wrote Wellesley, "that no effectual remedy can ever be applied ...... without obtaining from the Nabob powers at least as extensive as those vested in the Company by the late treaty of Tanjore. At the death of the present Nabob, such a treaty might easily be obtained from his successor (if after that event it should be thought advisable to admit any nominal sovereign of the Carnatic, excepting the Company) ...... the whole question of the succession will, therefore, be completely open to the decision of the Company upon the decease of the present Nabob. The inclination of my opinion is that the most advisable settlement would be to place Omdatul Omra's supposed son on the *Musnud,* under a treaty similar to that which was lately concluded with the Raja of Tanjore. It will, however, be expedient that you should immediately consider whether it might not be a more effectual arrangement to provide liberally for every branch of the descendants of Wallajah (the title by which Nawab Mohammad Ali was generally known) and Omdatul Omra, and to vest even the nominal sovereignty of the Carnatic in the Company."

Wellesley "Discovers" Evidence

The reason why Wellesley did not hope that a "suitable opportunity" would present itself during the lifetime of Umdat-ul Umra would seem to be that the latter, like his father, had been paying regularly on due dates the monthly instalments becoming payable to the Company under the "Treaty of Perpetual Friendship". Nor had he infringed or was likely to infringe in any other way the terms of that treaty. But Wellesley's active and fertile brain could not remain idle indefinitely, and he soon "found" a justification for action against Umdat-ul-Umra, and wrote to Henry Dundas:

> "...... the records of the late Tipu Sultan which fell into our hands after the capture of Seringapattam, have furnished me with the most authentic and indisputable evidence that the secret correspondence of a nature the most hostile to the British Power was opened with Tipu Sultan by the late Nabob. Wallajah, towards the close of his life through the agency of Omdatul Omra the present Nabob" (*Wellesley's Despatches*, Vol. II, pp. 244–46).

It will be recalled that by the Treaty of 1792, Tipu had to deliver and send to Madras two of his sons as hostages. Two of Tipu's officials, Ghulam Ali and Ali Raja, were also sent to Madras in attendance on these young princes. It was stated that the correspondence with Tipu was carried on through these two officials of his.

A Commission of Inquiry composed of Englishmen was set up which collected some evidence in support of this accusation. The statements of Ghulam Ali and Ali Raja were recorded. Their written reports from Madras were also brought on record.

Evaluation of the "Evidence"

Major Evans Bell, the author of *The Empire of India* (pp. 107–108) writes:

"We are called upon to believe that the Nawab Wallajah (Mohammad Ali), in his old age, after fifty years of faithful alliance and friendship with the English, and thirty years of almost incessant warfare with Hyder Ali and Tipu Sultan, suddenly took it into his head to conspire against his friends of half a century and to league with his enemies of thirty years ... just when the power of his friends was apparently established without a competitor, and when the power of his old enemy had fallen to nothing, beneath all hope of recovery. Wallajah and Omdatul Omrah are accused of having begun their hostile intrigues with Tipu in 1792 .... And it is with two of Tipu's officials who were sent to Madras in attendance on these young princes, that the Nawabs are accused of having concerted and carried on this desperate conspiracy with their discomfited foe against their triumphant friends and allies."

"Extravagantly improbable as such a tale of conspiracy must appear, we should, of course, be bound to believe it if a sufficiency of evidence were produced. But not only is there no trustworthy evidence brought forward, but every statement made by Ghulam Ali and Ali Raja ...... both in their written reports from Madras found among the records at Seringapattam and in their depositions before the Commission of Enquiry were to be accepted as truth, it would amount to nothing. The proofs of dark designs and hostile intentions on the part of Wallajah and his eldest son, which were collected by the Commission of Enquiry, are really so frivolous, even if considered as true, that but for the strong bias towards any conclusion affording a pretext for assuming the administration of the Carnatic, which we know from his previous endeavours in that direction actuated Lord Wellesley, we should be surprised that he did not throw the whole mass of gossip and guess-work into the waste-paper basket."

James Mill, in his *History of India* (Vol. VI, pp. 217–44), has examined the matter with even greater ability, impartiality and diligence and has conclusively proved that the accusation against the Nawabs of Karnatic was entirely false.

We might also mention the significant fact that Wellesley never faced Umdat-ul-Umra with this accusation of "secret correspondence" and kept the whole proceedings under cover so far at the Nawab himself was concerned.

Death of Umdat-ul-Umra

Early in July 1801, the old Nawab was reported to be dying in his Chipok palace. On 5th July, Col. MacNeill stationed the Company's army which was maintained by the Nawab around the palace under the pretext of preserving the peace which might otherwise be disturbed on the Nawab's death. The Nawab on his death-bed begged the English officers not to disgrace him by bringing the troops into the palace. Ten days later he died surrounded by English officers.

That very day, on 15th July, 1801, the English got hold of Prince Ali Hussain, the son and successor of the deceased Nawab and brought him out of the palace into a tent around which soldiers with drawn swords had been posted. The prince was told that as his father and grandfather had carried on secret correspondence with Tipu which was hostile to the English, the Govemor-General had decided that he (the prince) must sign a treaty similar to the one between Tanjore and the English, and that, instead of ascending his father's *Gadi,* the prince must in future live like an ordinary private citizen. Threats were held out to him but he would not yield. So the English made overtures to Azamuddaula, a very distant relative of the dead Nawab. Azamuddaula agreed to sign any treaty dictated by the English and was installed on the Karnatic *Gadi* on 28th July, 1801. Thereafter, he signed the "treaty" whereby the entire territory of the Nawabs of Karnatic was ceded to the Company, and Azamuddaula's Nawabi was limited to the capital town of Arcot and the Chipok palace where he was lodged.

Prince Ali Hussain's Death

Prince Ali Hussain and his widowed mother were confined to a room of the Chipok palace. He requested more than once that he might be sent to some other distant place as he feared that his life was in danger at the Chipok palace. The requests were unheeded and shortly after the prince was stated to have died of dysentery, the disease of which Najamuddaulah, the Nawab of Murshidabad, was stated to have died 36 years previously during Clive's regime!

Parliament's Commendation

The Karnatic episode was debated by the Parliament in England and some strong speeches exposing the true facts were delivered. One of the Members, Mr. Windham said:

> "...... the policy of the East India Company in India reminded him of the last line of a song written by Dr. Swift for a highwayman, 'every man round may rob if he pleases' ...... the principle by which we were to be guided was that the natives of India had no right, that we had no duties, and that all was to depend upon the decision of our Majesties."

Once again, the English Parliament passed a resolution commending Wellesley for what he had accomplished, even though it was hardly distinguishable from political dacoity.

19

Annexation of Surat

Surat was a Muslim principality ruled by a Nawab under the suzerainty of the Delhi Emperor.

It had the dubious distinction of being the venue of the first English trading centre established on Indian soil. In 1759, there was some dispute between the Nawab and the English and the latter attacked the Nawab's fort at Surat. According to the Dutch traveller, Stevorinus, the English had, before launching the attack, bribed the fort's Indian commandant not to put up any resistance. They had also taken the precaution of bribing the head of the Dutch Commercial House at Surat to prevent his helping the Nawab against the English.

The hostilities speedily ended the same year (1759) in a treaty between the Nawab and the English. Under it, the English traders were given some special concessions and the English undertook to abstain in future from any kind of interference in the administrative or other affairs of the principality. But in actual practice the Nawab was steadily reduced to the position of a mere puppet in the hands of the English. To quote Stevorinus again:

> "The English are the law-makers for everybody. Without their consent neither the Indians nor the Europeans can do anything. In this respect there is no difference or distinction between the Nawab and his humblest subject. Although the English make a show of deference to the Nawab, and would never admit that he was subordinate to them, yet the orders passed by them had to be carried out by the Nawab."

This dual government, nominal by the Nawab and *de facto* by the English, continued till Wellesley took over.

Wellesley Takes Action

Wellesley decided to end the dual government almost as soon as he arrived. The Nawab was asked to "reform" his adminstration, by disbanding his own army, by replacing it with three regiments of the Company's troops and by paying to the Company an annual amount for the regiments' maintenance. The Nawab declined to carry out the "reforms" and pointed out that the English demand for them infringed the treaty of 1759. The refusal led to an increase in the pressure on the Nawab who had ultimately to agree to pay to the Company a lac of rupees every year and in addition to grant some further concessions of the value of Rs. 30,000 to the Company. But before a treaty to that effect could be signed, the Nawab died on 8th January, 1799. He was survived by an infant son who also died a month later. The infant's uncle, Naseeruddin, succeeded to the Surat *Gadi.*

Naseeruddin was immediately faced with a demand by the English for an increase in the agreed amount of one lac of rupees payable to the Company every year. Naseeruddin agreed to pay the amount, but pleaded that he was financially unable to increase it. Wellesley started tightening the screw through Seaton, the head of the English trading centre at Surat. On 18th August, 1799, Seaton wrote to the Governor of Bombay: "I have left no stone unturned and pressed the Nawab to the limit. I am fully convinced that if the Nawab could have afforded it financially, he would have increased the amount." On being informed of this by the Governor of Bombay, Wellesley wrote back on 18th February, 1800:

> "I am fully determined not to acknowledge Naseeruddin as Nawab till he agrees to hand over to the Company the entire civil, criminal and revenue jurisdiction over Surat, in return for an annual maintenance allowance for himself and his family which the Company will pay him out of the collected revenue of Surat." (*Wellesley's Despatches,* Vol. II, pp. 222–23)

Three weeks later, Wellesley sent to the Bombay Governor the draft treaty to the above-mentioned effect which the Governor was ordered to take personally to the Nawab and get him to sign it. The Governor was further directed to dispatch to Surat one company of artillery manned by Europeans, two companies of European infantry and a full regiment of Indian infantry and to see to it that these arrived in Surat before the Governor himself did.

Thus, on 13th May, 1800, Naseeruddin was coerced into signing away his patrimony by executing that "treaty". It was however, considered expedient to continue Naseeruddin as the titular Nawab and, after the treaty was signed by him, Naseeruddin was installed on the *Gadi* with due pomp and acknowledged as the Nawab of Surat by the English. To lend colour to the fiction of Naseeruddin being the ruler of Surat, the preamble of the treaty was worded to the effect that it was entered into by the parties "to confirm and further strengthen the existing friendship between the Honourable East India Company and Nawab Naseeruddin Khan", etc.

The historian Mill has, with remarkable impartiality, admitted the injustice and unscrupulousness of Wellesley's treatment of the helpless Nawab.

20

Schemes Against the Peshwa and Sindhia

We would briefly recapitulate the events narrated in Chapter XII, and follow them up to the time of Wellesley's taking over.

Mahadji Sindhia had died in February 1794, and his grandson Doulatrao Sindhia had succeeded to the *Gadi* at Gwalior.

Peshwa Madhorao Narayan (Madhorao II) had died childless in October 1795, and the English had succeeded in getting Bajirao (a son of Raghoba) installed as the Peshwa.

Tukoji Holkar, who had earlier been instigated by the English to invade Mahadji's territory, had died in 1797, leaving two legitimate and two illegitimate sons. There was an armed clash between the two legitimate sons, Kashirao and Malharrao, and the latter was supported by the two natural sons Jaswantrao and Vithooji. Doulatrao Sindhia sided with Kashirao and militarily helped the latter to victory. Malharrao was killed in action and Jaswantrao and Vithooji fled to Nagpur and Kolhapur, respectively. Kashirao had succeeded to the Holkar *Gadi* and had been thereafter under the influence of Doulatrao Sindhia.

Doulatrao Sindhia was clever and courageous. He had seen in its true colours the background and the implications of the English perfidy towards his grandfather, Mahadji Sindhia. He had also realised the full gravity of the danger to the Maratha Confederacy if it was led by Bajirao alone. He had exchanged views and letters with Nana Fadnavis who was then in jail and had, thereafter himself gone to Poona. Almost the first thing he had done on arriving there was to get Nana Fadnavis released and reinstated as the Peshwa's Prime Minister. Understanding between Nana Fadnavis and Doulatrao Sindhia grew into friendship, and the Peshwa Bajirao speedily came to be guided by both of them. The full control of all the affairs of the Maratha Confederacy had thus passed into the capable hands of Nana Fadnavis and Doulatrao Sindhia. To further strengthen the Maratha Confederacy and lend moral support to the Peshwa, Doulatrao stayed on at Poona with the bulk of his well-equipped and well-trained army.

Wellesley's Plans Go Awry

Wellesley had planned that before Tipu was attacked, the Nizam and the Peshwa were to be effectively paralysed by being pulled into the net of the Subsidiary Alliance. On 8th July, 1798, he wrote to Kirkpatrick, the English Resident at Hyderabad, and to Palmer, the English Resident at Poona, giving them the necessary instructions. We have described (Chapter XIV) the complete success of Wellesley's efforts at Hyderabad but it was an entirely different story at Poona.

Although the Marathas had helped the English to win the 1792 War against Tipu, Wellesley was not by any means sure of the Maratha help if the English attacked Tipu again. The obvious injustice of the planned unprovoked English attack on innocent Tipu might, on the contrary, lead to the Marathas going to Tipu's help with Doulatrao Sindhia's large army at Poona. That Wellesley had apprehensions to that effect is evident from his letter of 8th July, 1798, to Palmer, the English Resident at Poona. "It is likely', wrote Wellesley, "that Tipu would receive full help from Poona, if (Doulatrao) Sindhia continues to stay there. It is, therefore, essential that Sindhia should anyhow be made to leave Poona."

Another reason why Wellesley so badly wanted Doulatrao Sindhia's removal from Poona was that Wellesley was convinced that so long as Bajirao continued to be under the personal influence of Doulatrao Sindhia and Nana Fadnavis, it would be impossible for the English to make a dupe of Bajirao and ensnare him into the Subsidiary Alliance. Consequently, Wellesley's immediate objective was the removal of Doultrao Sindhia from Poona, and the first artifice resorted to for the purpose was the circulation of persistent reports that Zaman Shah, the King of Kabul, was planning an invasion of Northern India close to Sindhia's territory. In the words of Grant Duff (p. 540): "The reported designs of Zaman Shah ... were strongly set forth by the British agents in order to induce Sindhia to return for the protection of his dominions in Hindustan." But Doulatrao Sindhia knew how adept the English were in circulating false reports for their own ends and was not taken in. He did not leave Poona.

Wellesley then sent Col. Collins as the English Resident to Doulatrao Sindhia's capital, Gwalior. It has been stated earlier (Chapter XII) that the English Resident at Gwalior had been recalled and had not been replaced since the Cornwallis regime. The declared object of posting Col. Collins as the English Resident at Gwalior was to strengthen the friendship of the English with the Sindhia *Durbar*. But the real objective would appear to have been to create disaffection against Doulatrao Sindhia in his State and to instigate his tributaries and chiefs to rebel whilst he was away in Poona. Collins succeeded to a certain extent but not enough to compel Doulatrao Sindhia to leave Poona and return to his State. That capable ruler settled each and every trouble thus created in his State, without leaving Poona. So Wellesley failed again.

Wellesley's Dilemma and Decision

Wellesley was now on the horns of a dilemma. Any further delay in launching his planned attack on Tipu was dangerous as it was likely to forewarn Tipu. On the other hand, the attack on Tipu if launched whilst Doulatrao Sindhia and his army were at Poona was almost certain to lead to the Marathas going to the help of Tipu, and if that happened, success against Tipu would become extremely doubtful. Wellesley took the bull by its horns and decided to attack Tipu forthwith. He went to Madras and declared war on Tipu. At the same time he renewed his efforts to immobilise Doulatrao Sindhia and his army. On 3rd of March, 1799, he wrote from Madras to Palmer, the English Resident at Poona, to the effect that he (Wellesley) desired the large English force commanded by Sir James Craig to be stationed on the border of Oudh facing Sindhia's territory on the north-east. Wellesley also expressed the hope that when Sindhia and his Army Chief, Ambaji, learned about the large force on their border, they would abstain from taking any action hostile to the Company's interests.

Wellesley's Plans to Destroy Doulatrao Sindhia

As a matter of fact, Wellesley had realised very much earlier, that if Tipu was overthrown, it would not eliminate all opposition to his (Wellesley's) planned expansion of British rule in India, and that the Marathas would still be stubborn and formidable opponents of the expansion. He also knew that Doulatrao Sindhia, the ablest and strongest of all the Maratha rulers, was the backbone of the Maratha resistance. He had, therefore, finally decided to destroy Doulatrao Sindhia but only after Tipu had been overthrown. In the meantime, he had started making efforts to enlist the support of some Indian rulers, including the Maratha ruler of Berar. Sometime before he wrote the above letter to Palmer, he had posted Colebrooke as the English Resident at the *Durbar* of the Raja of Berar. The following extracts from the Governor-General's letter to Colebrooke (written prior to 3rd March, 1799) quite plainly set forth the work assigned to Colebrooke by Wellesley:

> "The local position of the Raja's territories appears to render him a peculiarly serviceable ally against Daulatrao Sindhia ... it is not prudent to propose to the Raja of Berar, or even to the Peshwa or to Nizam, a treaty of defence nominally against Sindhia. Even the preliminary measures for ascertaining the disposition of the Raja of Berar on this subject must be taken with the greatest caution. The object of our apprehension should appear to be Tipu Sultan; and although 'any other enemy of the contracting powers' may be named in general terms, no suggestion should yet be given by which the name of Sindhia could be brought into question ... A treaty might, therefore, be proposed to the Raja, the immediate and obstensible object of which should be to strengthen and define his defensive engagements against Tipu Sultan, but the terms of which should be such as to admit the insertion of Sindhia's name

> if such a measure should become necessary to the conclusion of the treaty."

We have stated above that Wellesley wrote to Palmer about the stationing of the English force under Sir James Craig on the Oudh border. About a week later on 8th March, 1799 Wellesley wrote to Sir Alured Clarke, the commander-in-chief of the Company's forces at Calcutta, a letter marked "private and secret" to the following effect:

> "In all my private letters to you, I have continuously expressed my wish that a considerable force be stationed on the other border of Sindhia's territory, enough to thwart any move on his part. I would like this force to be re-inforced immediately so that if Sindhia returns to Hindustan with his army, our forces should be enough to cope with his army, in case we have to attack him."

Wellesley further instructed Clarke to prepare the ground for the possible English attack on Sindhia by winning over the Rajput and other Chiefs of Sindhia and enlisting the support of the Rajput rulers of Jaipur and Jodhpur. Clarke was also to try and enlist the help and co-operation of Mahadji Sindhia's widows and other dissident elements in Doulatrao Sindhia's *Durbar,* State and family. Put briefly, Clarke's instructions were to stir up opposition to Doulatrao Sindhia in every possible way and wheresoever feasible. In Wellesley's expressed opinion it was the correct policy to be ready to take advantage of the first suitable opportunity that presented itself for the crushing of Doulatrao Sindhia. But as Wellesley wrote to Clarke, immediate overt hostility against Sindhia would have been inopportune because the English were fighting Tipu in the South, and Sindhia with his army in the South could harass them very much. So Wellesley had decided that the English action against Sindhia must wait till either the latter returned to the North or the English had forced Tipu into a treaty dictated by them.

Doulatrao Sindhia Leaves Poona—English Moves at Poona

In accordance with Wellesley's above instructions, the Company's forces started assembling along the borders of Doulatrao Sindhia's territory, and when the latter learned about it at Poona, he had no doubts left about the English intention to invade his territory during his absence. He had, therefore, to return to the North to defend his territory. He left Poona with his army and Wellesley's long-cherished desire to get Sindhia away from Poona was at last fulfilled.

With Doulatrao's removal from the Poona *Durbar,* it became easier for Wellesley effectively to exert pressure on the Peshwa for roping him into the Subsidiary Alliance, ostensibly as a measure of defence against Tipu. But Nana Fadnavis was at the Poona *Durbar* and succeeded in getting the Peshwa to refuse the Alliance. Wellesley, however, continued to exert pressure on the Peshwa, who promised military help to the English, if the latter asked for it in their fight against Tipu. Wellesley made a second move calculated to lead the Peshwa up the garden path into the snare of the Subsidiary Alliance. On 3rd April 1799, before the fall of Seringapattam, Wellesley wrote to Palmer to convey to the Peshwa an assurance to the following effect:

> "In order to prove the British Government's unselfish love and affection for their friends, the Nizam and the Peshwa, I will see to it that both receive their proper share of Tipu's conquered territory."

Seringapattam fell to the English on 4th May 1799. Wellesley then changed his attitude. On 23rd May 1799, he wrote to Palmer:

> "Before giving to the Peshwa any share of the conquered Tipu's territory, I want to make an all-out effort to get the Peshwa to enter into the Subsidiary Alliance as per draft originally sent to you on 8th July, 1798. I want to know from you as soon as possible whether or not the Poona

Durbar will, in the present changed circumstances, agree to the proposition if it is again put up before them."

Nana Fadnavis's Last Effort Foiled by His Death

Nana Fadnavis was now isolated as the lone opponent of the English designs, which he had clearly seen through during the previous 20 years. The Nizam was now a mere puppet in English hands. Haider and Tipu were dead. Doulatrao Sindhia had to return to the North to his State. But even so, Nana was undismayed. He not only got the Peshwa to refuse to touch the Subsidiary Alliance offered by the English, but demanded from the latter the arrears of the *Chouth* due to the Peshwa under the Delhi Emperor's orders by the Nawab of Surat, the Nizam and the Mysore *Durbar,* all the three of whom were under the full and complete control of the English. Wellesley countered by engineering an armed rebellion by the Peshwa's *Jagirdars* in the South to put down which Nana Fadnavis had to send the Peshwa's army under Parashuram Bhau, which he had got ready to attack the Nizam and the latter's master, the English. He intended to do that after putting down the revolt in the South. But death intervened and before the revolt could finally be quelled, Nana Fadnavis died on 13th February, 1800. His death removed from Wellesley's path the last of the obstacles to his declared aim of heaping in India "kingdoms upon kingdoms" for his "masters".

Ruse to Occupy Strategic Places in Peshwa's Territory

We have mentioned (Chapter XV) Tipu's Chieftain, Malik Jahan Khan, who had refused to surrender to the English and had started raiding the Mysore territory now occupied by the English. His depredations were causing considerable harassment to the English, who sent out a strong force under Col. Wellesley to suppress him. The force had to pass through the Peshwa's territory. Governor-General Wellesley requested the Peshwa, in the name of friendship existing between them, to let the Company's force do so. The weak and short-sighted Peshwa Bajirao committed the mistake of granting the requested permission. Under the guise of operations against Malik Jahan Khan, Col. Wellesley's force quietly entered and occupied, one after another, several places of vital, strategic importance in the Peshwa's territory. The real intention of Wellesley (the Governor-General), who was now back in Calcutta, is expressed in the letter which he wrote on 23rd August, 1800 to Lord Clive (the famous Clive's son), the Governor of Madras. We quote from the letter:

> "... it may become necessary for a large proportion of the troops under the command of Colonel Wellesley to proceed (in concert with those of the Nizam and with a detachment from Bombay) towards Poona. The intermediate motions of Colonel Wellesley must be guided with a view to this probable contirigency ...... it is advisable that Colonel Wellesley should continue to occupy the Maratha territory, ... In either of two possible events, ... first, the flight of Bajirao from Poona; second, the seizure of His Highness' person by Doulatrao Sindhia, in either of these cases Colonel Wellesley's secure establishment, within the Maratha frontier, would facilitate his advance towards Poona ... I, therefore, request your Lordship to inform Colonel Wellesley without delay that on his receiving authentic and unquestionable intelligence either of flight or imprisonment of Bajirao ... the British army is directed and authorized to take immediate possession, in the name and on behalf of the Peshwa, of all the country as far as the bank of the Krishna. Colonel Wellesley will also summon, in the name of the Peshwa, such forts and strong places within the limits described as it shall be judged expedient for the British troops to occupy ... Colonel Wellesley ... will take care to satisfy the inhabitants of the country that the British Government entertain no other view in them than the restoration of the Peshwa's lawful authority."

Wellesley's Plan Faces Difficulty

But neither of the two events mentioned by Wellesley in the above letter materialised. Col. Palmer did indeed try his very best to persuade Bajirao either to go away from Poona or in the alternative to make a request for the Company's troops to arrive for his help because, so at least Bajirao was assured, the threat to the latter's personal safety at the hands of Doulatrao Sindhia was real and imminent. At the same time, efforts were persistently made to provoke hostilities between Bajirao and Doulatrao Sindhia. But all this was of no avail. The Marathas had not yet forgotten the disastrous consequences of Raghoba's flight from Poona 25 years earlier and so Doulatrao Sindhia took every possible care to see that Bajirao did not repeat his father's mistake and leave Poona.

Bajirao's Terms for Subsidiary Alliance

Continued pressure by Wellesley on Bajirao for the latter's entry into the Subsidiary Alliance did however produce some results. According to Mill, Bajirao became agreeable:

(a) to maintain permanently six battalions of the Company's infantry with the requisite artillery, and
(b) to set apart for their maintenance a part of his territory with a net annual income of 25 lacs of rupees.

But this was not all that Wellesley wanted. He was particularly keen on the stationing of the Company's force within the Peshwa's territory. To this Bajirao would not agree. He would not budge from the stand taken by him, namely, that the force should be stationed outside his territory and should enter it only at his (the Peshwa's) request. This obduracy on his part may have been due to the fact that Bajirao had in his mind the case of the Nizam, who was the first Indian ruler to be forced into the Subsidiary Alliance with the English in 1798 (Chapter XIV). In that year the Nizam had to cede a part of his dominion to the English as the price of the latter's friendship. Only two years later in 1800, in contravention of the 1798 treaty, the Nizam was forced to cede to the English an additional and much larger portion of his domain. In return for the military help which the Nizam had given the English in the latter's wars against Tipu, the Nizam had been given a share of Tipu's conquered territory, but it was soon taken away from him in the name of friendship! In addition, the Nizam had completely lost independence and had been reduced to the status of a virtual prisoner in English hands. No wonder even Bajirao was adamant in his attitude to the extent that Col. Palmer had to write to Wellesley:

> "I apprehend that nothing short of imminent and certain destruction will induce him (the Peshwa) to make concession, etc."

Wellesley's Policy and Line of Action

It would appear from the extracts which we would now quote that Wellesley did later on reconcile himself to the acceptance of the limitations upon which Bajirao insisted.

On 23rd June 1802, Wellesley's Secretary, N.B. Edmonstone, wrote confidentially to Lt. Col. Close, who had replaced Col. Palmer as the English Resident at Poona:

> "The measure of subsidizing a British force, even under the limitations which the Peshwa has annexed to that proposal, must immediately place him in some degree in a state of dependence upon the British power, ... *The dependence of a state of any degree upon the power of another naturally tends to increase.* A sense of security, derived from the support of a foreign power, produces a relaxation of vigilance and caution. Augmenting the dependence of the Peshwa on the British power, under the operation of the proposed engagements, would be accelerated by the effect which those engagements would produce by detaching the State of Poona from the other members of the Maratha Empire.

> "The conclusion of such engagements with the Peshwa would preclude the practicability of general confederacy among the Maratha States ... This separate connection with one of the branches of the Maratha Empire would not only contribute to our security, "but would tend to produce a crisis of affairs which may compel the remaining states of the Empire to accede to the alliance" (Secret letter dated 23rd June, 1802 from N. B. Edmonstone, Secretary to Government, to Lt. Close, Resident at Poona).

Mill has quoted (Vol. VI, p. 271) Marquess Wellesley as writing in another letter:

> "Every one of the Maratha States would become dependent upon the English Government; those who accepted the alliance, by the alliance; those who did not accept it, by being deprived of it."

The English intentions as regards (he Indian rulers are clear enough in the light of the above extracts. The sole objective aimed at by the Subsidiary Alliances was to deprive the Indian rulers of their independent sovereignty and to make them entirely dependent on the English Government. This was to be accomplished by playing one ruler against another and roping them into the Subsidiary Alliance one by one.

The immediate objective which Wellesley had in view was to break the Maratha power and he was, therefore, sparing no effort to get any one Maratha ruler into the Alliance. At the Peshwa's *Durbar,* Col. Close was active in leading Bajirao up the garden path, and Col. Collins was similarly engaged at the *Durbar* of Doulatrao Sindhia.

Doulatrao Sindhia Declines Invitation

Col. Collins, however, found Doulatrao Sindhia a hard nut to crack. So, far from accepting the Alliance, Doulatrao Sindhia insisted that as a member of the Maratha Confederacy, he had the unquestionable right to intervene in matters relating to the Peshwa *Durbar* and did exercise that right in preventing the Peshwa from entering into the Alliance. In despair, Col. Collins wrote to Wellesley:

> "Sindhia was anxiously desirous to preserve the relations of friendship at that time subsisting between him and the English Government. At the time, I consider it my indispensable duty to apprise your Excellency that I am firmly persuaded he feels no inclination whatever to improve these relations." Resident Collins' letter to the Governor-General, Mill, Vol, VI, p. 272)

Mill comments on this letter thus:

> "In other words, he (Sindhia) was not yet brought so low, as willingly to descend into that situation in which a participation in the 'system of defensive alliance and mutual guarantee' would of necessity place him." (*ibid*)

Collins therefore emphasised the necessity of first getting or forcing the Peshwa to accede to the Subsidiary Alliance. On the other hand, Col. Close had very definitely asserted that "nothing short of imminent and certain destruction will induce" the Peshwa to do so. Doulatrao Sindhia, too, had fully realised that it would be fatal for the future of the Maratha Confederacy if Bajirao, left to himself, yielded to pressure and acceded to the Alliance. He (Doulatrao Sindhia), therefore, returned to Poona with his army to prevent Bajirao from entering into the Subsidiary Alliance.

Faced with this situation, Wellesley and his colleagues had to plot afresh and change their line of action.

New Moves

We have mentioned earlier that the deceased Tukoji Holkar's natural sons, Jaswantrao Holkar and Vithooji, had been worsted by Kashirao Holkar, with the help of Doulatrao Sindhia in their fight for the Holkar *Gadi* and had run away. Jaswantrao Holkar had sought refuge in Nagpur, the capital of the Raja of Berar, and Vithooji was in Kolhapur. It will be recalled that Wellesley had instructed Colebrooke, the English Resident at Nagpur, to win over the Raja of Berar against Sindhia. Colebrooke had carried out those instructions. In addition, Wellesley had also succeeded to a certain extent in promoting disaffection against Doulatrao Sindhia amongst the latter's Rajput chieftains, and the widows of the late Mahadji Sindhia. They were now willing enough to support Wellesley's action against Doulatrao Sindhia.

The English now provided Jaswantrao Holkar with troops to invade Doulatrao Sindhia's territory whilst the latter was away in Poona. Jaswantrao Holkar left Nagpur and invaded and devastated the nearest territory of Doulatrao Sindhia. The latter had thus to leave Poona once again to defend his invaded territory in Malwa. But this time he left behind at Poona, out of his large army, a contingent of five battalions of infantry and 10,000 cavalry.

There were several battles in Malwa between the armies of Jaswantrao Holkar and Doulatrao Sindhia, in which some advantages were gained by both sides. Sindhia, at last, offered peace to Holkar, but the latter, though willing at first, declined ultimately. The refusal was obviously inspired by the English in whose interests it was necessary that Doulatrao should not be free to return to Poona and interfere with the English plans there.

Revolt Against the Peshwa

As soon as Doulatrao Sindhia had left Poona for Malwa, Jaswantrao Holkar's brother Vithooji raised the banner of revolt against the Peshwa at Kolhapur. The Peshwa's army took Vithooji prisoner. To avenge Vithooji's death, Jaswantrao Holkar advanced on Poona. It suited Wellesley to help Jaswantrao Holkar. By this time, Col. Wellesley, too, had arrived near Poona with his troops, as Wellesley had earlier directed.

The situation in which Bajirao found himself frightened him, and on 11th October 1802, he wrote to the English Resident and agreed:

(i) to cede a fort near the Tungbhadra river, for the permanent stationing of the Subsidiary Army in his territory, and
(ii) to set apart a portion of his territory in Gujarat or Karnatic, with an annual income of Rs. 25 lacs for the Army's maintenance.

But Bajirao's submission to Wellesley's terms did not, by any means, end his troubles. When Jaswantrao Holkar's army arrived and attacked Poona, the English would not help him.

Battle at Poona—Bajirao's Flight

A fierce battle was fought at Poona on 25th October 1802 between Jaswantrao Holkar's army and the Peshwa's army helped by the contingent left at Poona by Doulatrao Sindhia. The Company's army which had by then arrived at Poona and for which Bajirao had agreed to pay did not help the latter. Capt. Filose, the European commander of Sindhia's contingent, betrayed his master and went over to Jaswantrao Holkar, who won the battle. Wellesley thus faced Bajirao with the "imminent and certain destruction" which was what Palmer, the previous English Resident at Poona, had suggested.

Wellesley's letters written at the time clearly show that he was very keen then on forcing Bajirao to run away from Poona and place himself entirely in the hands of the English. After his defeat at the hands of Jaswantrao Holkar, the helpless Bajirao was advised by the English Resident at Poona to run away and he agreed to do so. The Company helped him to flee and provided a ship in which he escaped to Bassein where he arrived on 16th December 1802.

On 24th December 1802, Wellesley wrote to the Court of Directors:

> "The recent distractions in the Maratha Empire have occasioned a combination of the utmost importance to the stability of the British power ... a conjuncture of affairs which appeared to present the utmost advantageous opportunity that has ever occurred of improving the British interests in that quarter on solid and durable foundations ... This crisis of affairs appeared to me to afford the most favourable opportunity for the complete establishment of the interests of the British Empire."

Replacement of Bajirao as Peshwa by Amritrao

Mill has stated that during his fight with Jaswantrao Holkar, Bajirao had offered to the latter peace and friendly relations similar to those between the Peshwa and other Maratha rulers. Jaswantrao Holkar appeared willing and, according to Grant Duff, tried after Bajirao's flight to Bassein, to bring the latter back to Poona as Peshwa. But he was thwarted, because peace between the two would have ended "the distractions in the Marhatta Empire," which Wellesley had deliberately created in "the interests of the British Empire" by playing off one Maratha ruler against another.

Jaswantrao Holkar, having failed to conclude peace with Bajirao and, later, to secure his return from Bassein, had to conclude that Bajirao's flight from Poona was tantamount to abdication by him of the Peshwa's *Gadi.* Consequently, Jaswantrao Holkar and his colleagues decided, with the concurrence of the English Resident in Poona, to instal Amritrao, half-brother of Bajirao, on the Peshwa's *Gadi.*

Bajirao Signs a New Treaty at Bassein

Bajirao was given an assurance at Bassein that if he signed a fresh treaty, he would be re-instated as Peshwa. Bajirao did so on 31st December, 1802. By the new treaty, he implemented the terms already agreed to by him, and ceded to the Company a part of his territory. In addition, he was also made to give an undertaking that in future he would not have any relations with any other Indian ruler without the concurrence of the English Government.

We quote the comments of an English writer on the reasons which forced Bajirao into—

> "... accepting the terms of foreign alliance, which he was aware would lead to a total annihilation of his political independence. The fate of Tipu and the state of humiliating dependence to which the Nizam had been reduced by the acceptance of our subsidiary force were always present to his imagination or sounded in his ears by those who were near him; and we may conclude that it was not without great reluctance that he consented to the treaty of Bassein." (*Origin of the Pindaries*, etc., by an officer in the service of the Honourable East India Company)

Thus, after four years of ceaseless plottings and intrigues, Wellesley at last succeeded in completely destroying the political independence of the Peshwa, the *head* of the Maratha Confederacy and symbol of its solidarity and power. The Confederacy could never recover from the blow. Its total and complete disruption, which the English politicians had been trying to accomplish for about 50 years, was now only a question of time.

21

Reinstatement of Bajirao as Peshwa

After the Treaty of Bassein

With the conclusion of the treaty an all-important stage had been reached in the establishment of the British Empire in India. Mill (Vol. VI, Chap. 2, p. 278) writes:

"Two grand objects now solicited the attention of the British Government. The first was the restoration of the Peshwa, and his elevation to that height of power, which, nominally his, actually that of the British Government, might suffice to control the rest of the Marhatta States. The next was to improve this event for imposing a similar treaty upon others of the more powerful Marhatta princes."

On the other hand, news of the treaty had profoundly dismayed Doulatao Sindhia and other independent Maratha rulers. In Poona itself, there was hardly any sensible politician who liked the return of Bajirao, saddled with the Treaty of Bassein, and his reinstatement as Peshwa by the British. Jaswantrao Holkar and Amritrao, the Peshwa on the *Gadi,* were naturally surely with the English, but both had outlived their usefulness as English tools. Amritrao was a mere figurehead, with Jaswantrao Holkar the real power behind the *Gadi.* In order to counteract Jaswantrao Holkar's influence at the Poona *Durbar* and over Amritrao, bitter quarrels between the two were engineered. Further to increase Jaswantrao Holkar's unpopularity, Col. Close, the English Resident at Poona, instigated and personally helped the former to extort large amounts of money from the citizens of Poona for his own and the Company's benefit.

Col. Close then quietly left Poona and joined Bajirao at Bassein to placate the latter, who was getting restive because the English were delaying the performance of their part of the bargain. The delay was deliberate.

Wellesley's letters disclose the amazing fact that, even at that stage, he was prepared to desert Bajirao if someone else, able to deliver the goods, offered Wellesley a better price for the Peshwa's *Gadi*. Another reason, according to Mill, was that Wellesley was playing on Bajirao's nerves and trying to get from the latter all possible concessions and privileges for the Company, in addition to the treaty. It may, however, be said that Wellesley anticipated armed hostility to Bajirao's reinstatement by Sindhia and other members of the Maratha Confederacy, and so wanted to be fully prepared for war before Bajirao was brought back to Poona.

Wellesley's Plan and Its Execution

A large force was assembled in the South to march on Poona in support of the English plans. It consisted of the Company's Subsidiary contingents stationed at Mysore and Hyderabad, besides the troops sent from Travancore, Karnatic, etc. The contingent from Mysore, which had been joined by the Subsidiary Force intended for Poona under the Treaty, was commanded by Col. Arthur Wellesley, whilst that from Hyderabad by Col. Stevenson, the former being in overall command of both. Col. Arthur Wellesley began his march to Poona and he was instructed to intimidate or buy over the southern Jagirdars, along the line of his march, and generally to create such conditions in and around Poona as would facilitate Bajirao's restoration as Peshwa.

Early in March 1803, the combined forces reached Harihar and Marquess Wellesley himself arrived near Poona at about the same time. His letters disclose that he was still hoping to find someone in Poona who would and could pay a better price than Bajirao for the Peshwa's *Gadi,* or be more useful as an English tool. But apparently he was disappointed. Col. Arthur Wellesley's force advanced from Harihar on 9th March 1803, and crossed the Tungabhadra river on the 12th. The intimidated or bought-over southern *Jagirdars* did nothing to check its advance.

Jaswantrao Holkar Leaves Poona—Amritrao Runs Away

Jaswantrao Holkar had already quarrelled with Amritrao and was induced by the English to quit. He left Amritrao, with a tiny force of 1500 soldiers, to his fate, and started with his entire army for Indore. Incidentally, Wellesley's letters indicate that he had hinted to Jaswantrao Holkar, that if the latter, on his way, plundered not only the Peshwa's territory, but also the territory including the city of Aurangabad belonging to the Nizam, a "friend" of the English, the latter would not mind it! Jaswantrao Holkar took the hint and when the Nizam complained to the English, the latter simply ignored the complaint.

On 20th April 1803, Col. Arthur Wellesley entered Poona with his force. A little earlier, false reports had been circulated by the English that Amritrao was plotting to set fire to Poona. After Col. Arthur Wellesley's entry, it was declared that it was the timely arrival of the English army that had saved the town from being burnt down by Amritrao ! Amritrao ran away, and Col. Arthur Wellesley wrote to his brother, Marquess Wellesley:

> "Matters in general have a good appearance. I think they will end as you wish. The combined chiefs of whom we have heard so much .... have taken not one step to impede our march .... they have not yet made peace among themselves, much less have they agreed to attack, or have any particular plan of attack". (Col. Wellesley's letter to the Governor-General, dated 25th April, 1803)

Bajirao's Re-installation as Peshwa

The stage was now set and everything was ready for Bajirao's re-installation on the *Gadi*. Under instructions issued by Marquess Wellesley, Bajirao left Bassein for Poona on 27th April, 1803. He was accompained by Col. Close, the English Resident, and escorted by over a thousand European and about 1200 Indian soldiers commanded by Col. Murray. He arrived in Poona on 13th May, 1803, and on that very day re-occupied the *Gadi* with the support of his foreign friends. The latter immediately reimbursed themselves for the cost of the expedition by obtaining some additional territory from Bajirao.

The Company's Subsidiary Army was now firmly established in Poona, the capital of the Maratha Empire. But only a few, if any, in the whole of Maharashtra were really enthusiastic about it. The people, by and large, saw in it a humiliation of the Maratha Empire and an evil portent for its future.

We would close this chapter with some quotations from Mill (Vol. VI, Chapter 2, pp. 286–87):

> ".... the most flagitious perhaps of all the crimes which can be committed against human nature, the imposing upon a nation, by force of foreign armies and for the pleasure or interest of foreign rulers, a Government, composed of men, and involving principle, which the people for whom it is destined have either rejected from experience of their *badness*, or, repel from their expectation of better ...
>
> "In his address to the home authorities, dated the 24th of December, 1802, he (Wellesley) declared his conviction, that 'those defensive engagements which he was desirous of concluding with the Marhatta States were essential to the complete consolidation of the British Empire in India and to the future tranquillity of Hindostan ...... Yet the complete consolidation of the British Empire in India, and the future tranquillity of Hindostan .... could never exist till a sufficient bridle was put in the mouth of the Marhatta power."

Need it be mentioned, that ever since Clive's regime, there had been numerous instances of the English imposing on the people of India incapable, unrighteous or unscrupulous rulers at the point of their bayonets or through their intrigues?

22

Origin of the Second Maratha War

The Situation in the Maratha Confederacy

Originally there were five founder-members of the Maratha Confederacy, namely, the Peshwa, Gaikwad, Sindhia, Holkar and Bhonsle (Berar). Each of them had agreed to help one another and not to enter individually into any pact or treaty with any other political power without the concurrence of the others.

Out of the five, Gaikwad had left the Confederacy about the time of the First Maratha War. The Holkar brothers, Kashirao and Jaswantrao, were busy fighting each other for the *Gadi* and the English were keeping them at it by helping each of them alternately. The third, the Peshwa, who was supposed to be the head of the Confederacy, was now as much a prisoner of the English as the Nizam or the Nawab Wazir of Oudh. "The Peshwa" wrote Maria Graham (*Journal of a Residence in India,* p. 84), "... is himself so completely under our dominion that he pays a subsidy to maintain the three thousand troops which surround his palace and keep him a prisoner."

The remaining two, Doulatrao Sindhia and Bhonsle, saw in the submission of the Peshwa to the foreigners' will and dictates, a grave danger to the independence of other Maratha rulers, and to the future existence of the Maratha Empire which, under the circumstances, could not last much longer. Their fears were well founded as is evident from the memorandum later presented to Wellesley by Sir George Barlow, a prominent member of the Governor-General's Council. We quote from it:

> "... No native State should be left to exist in India which is not upheld by the British power, or the political conduct of which is not under its absolute control. The restoration of the head of the Maratha Empire to his Government through the influence of the British power, in fact, has placed all the remaining States of India in this dependent

> relation to the British Government. If the alliance with the Peshwa is maintained, its natural and necessary operations would in the course of time reduce Sindhia ... and the Raja of Berar to a state of dependence upon the Peshwa, and consequently upon the British power, even as if they had acquiesced in the Treaty of Bassein."

Weight and authority are lent to the memorandum by the fact that the Company's Directors had already nominated Sir George Barlow to succeed Wellesley, in case the office of the Governor-General suddenly fell vacant either by Wellesley's death or otherwise.

As stated above, no member of the Maratha Confederacy could even individually conclude a pact or a treaty with any other political power without prior consultation with and the concurrence of the other members. Also, there was a precedent to which the English had been a party. Their Treaty of Salbai with the Peshwa, which ended the First Maratha War, was negotiated through Mahadji Sindhia (Doulatrao Sindhia's predecessor) whom the English had approached and who had presided over the negotiations.

It would appear that after his flight from Poona to Bassein, Bajirao had, before signing the Treaty of Bassein, sent secret agents to Doulatrao Sindhia and Raghoji Bhonsle with appeals to help him in his reinstatement as Peshwa, and had solicited their good offices for a speedy settlement of all the disputes between himself, Doulatrao Sindhia and Jaswantrao Holkar, in order to revive the unity and strength of the Maratha Empire. Thereafter, he, in his utter helplessness, had to sign the Treaty of Bassein on 31st December 1803, and to accept, under duress, terms which he would never have accepted had he been in Poona. The treaty, however, could not be an accomplished legal reality, until it had been ratified, under the Maratha Confederacy convention, by the other members of the Confederacy, Doulatrao Sindhia and Raghoji Bhonsle.

Stand Taken by Doulatrao Sindhia and Raghoji Bhonsle

Wellesley too realised that to make the Treaty of Bassein legally effective and binding, it was essential that it be accepted and ratified by Doulatrao Sindhia and Raghoji Bhonsle. At the same time, Wellesley was also well aware that clauses 3 and 17 of the treaty would be wholly unacceptable to Sindhia. Clause 3 set forth that the Peshwa agreed to the stationing of the Company's Subsidiary Army permanently in his territory and by clause 17 the Peshwa bound himself not to have any relations or communications with any other Indian ruler without prior consultation with the English (Company's) Government. Consequently, when Wellesley approached Doulatrao Sindhia and Raghoji Bhonsle and sought their assent to the Treaty, he took care not to send its copy to either of them. Instead, he conveyed to them verbal assurances that the Treaty did not in any way affect their existing relationship with the Peshwa. Apparently these oral assurances cut no ice with Doulatrao Sindhia or with Raghoji Bhonsle. Wellesley wrote to the Company's Directors:

> "Sindhia has assented to the re-instatement of Bajirao as Peshwa, but he has plainly told Col. Collins that he (Sindhia) will not confirm the Treaty of Bassein until and unless he has before him all the terms of the Treaty and Bajirao's ideas about the same. Raghoji Bhonsle the Raja of Berar has also not agreed to confirm the Treaty."

Wellesley's Real Aim and Objective

Had Doulatrao Sindhia and Raghoji Bhosle ratified the Treaty, it would have meant, *ipso facto,* their assent to clause 17 thereof, which would have led to the final break-up of the Maratha Confederacy and the complete destruction of the Maratha power by isolating the Peshwa from its two most powerful members and ultimately isolating the latter from each other. The total dismemberment of the Maratha Empire was the real aim and objective of Wellesley and its achievement would have been greatly facilitated if Sindhia and Bhonsle had ratified the Treaty of Bassein. But Wellesley had other strings to his bow in anticipation of their opposition to the Treaty and had made his plans accordingly. The plans are set forth in the "most secret and confidential" letter which Wellesley had written to General Lake a week after Bajirao had signed the treaty at Bassein. We quote from it:

> "1 have been desirous for some time past to communicate to you the interesting state of affairs in the Maratha Empire, and the course of policy which I have adopted, with a view to deriving every attainable advantage from this singular crisis.
>
> "The power, whose views might be most apprehended, and whom it is most important to hold in check, is certainly Sindhia. No serious or alarming opposition is to be feared from any other quarter .... Our most effectual mode of controlling Sindhia must be an irruption into his dominions in Hindostan from the ceded provinces of Oudh, and in that case the main and most critical effort must be made from the quarter where you are now present.
>
> "... if any serious contest should arise, ... the most important operations will be directed against Sindhia's possessions to the destruction of his power in Hindostan; and that no probability exists of any important contest in the Deccan.
>
> "... And my plan is, therefore, rather to form such arrangements as may present the most powerful and menacing aspect to every branch of the Maratha Empire on every point on their frontier."

The letter is important and extremely significant because it was addressed to General Lake, whom the rulers of England, impatient to expand their Empire in India, had sent out for helping Wellesley, as the Commander-in-Chief of the Company's armies in India. It may be mentioned that General Lake had been the

Commander-in-Chief of the British Forces operating in Ireland and had helped very materially in depriving that country of its independence. Lord Cornwallis, the Lord Lieutenant of Ireland, has thus characterised General Lake's activities in Ireland: "... the burning of houses and murder of the inhabitants ... the flogging for the purpose of extorting confession; ... universal rape and robbery throughout the country."

General Lake was in the north of India when Wellesley wrote to him the above letter on 7th January 1803 from Barrackpur. It is interesting to recall that some four years earlier, Wellesley had written to Sir Alured Clarke, the then Commander-in-Chief of the Company's forces, chalking out similar plans against Doulatrao Sindhia and had said: "I am equally satisfied of the policy of reducing the power of Sindhia, whenever the opportunity shall appear advantageous" (Governor-General's letter to Sir Alured Clarke, dated 8th March 1799).

Maratha Rulers' Efforts at Self-Preservation

Face to face with the impending calamity of extinction as independent Maratha rulers, the latter now tried frantically to avert it. Bajirao's helpless dependence on the English and his subjection to their will was brought home to him even more forcefully on his return to Poona. He sent special messengers to Sindhia and Bhonsle and pressed them to come to Poona immediately for consultations. The English were not kept in the dark, but were informed about the invitations by the Peshwa, wbowho postponed taking any action under the Treaty, until both Sindhia and Bhonsle had ratified and countersigned it.

Marquess Wellesley's brother, Major-General Wellesley, who as Col. Arthur Wellesley, had on 20th April, 1803 led the English forces into Poona, wrote on 4th June, 1803 (some three weeks after Bajirao's re-installation) to General Stuart, the English Army Commander in Madras to the following effect:

> "Our position in this part of the country is rather unstable ... one of the terms of the treaty provided that Bajirao will place his own army under my command and he had personally promised to me to do so, but he has not done so and violated the treaty and his promise ...... I am afraid that our friendship with him envisaged by the treaty cannot last."

On receipt of Bajirao's invitation, Doulatrao Sindhia decided, before leaving for Poona, to hold consultations with Raghoji Bhonsle and Jaswantrao Holkar, who too wanted to re-unite amongst themselves and with the Peshwa. All the three agreed to meet at Badowli.

The English Reaction

A meeting between Doulatrao Sindhia and the Peshwa was, however, considered by the English as extremely unwholesome for the latter's interests, and the English Residents at the Sindhia and Peshwa *Durbars* did their level best to prevent that meeting. Doulatrao Sindhia was quite openly pressed not to go, whilst Bajirao was pressed to write to the former asking him to come.

Col. Collins had a personal interview with Maharaja Doulatrao Sindhia on 28th May, 1803, which lasted three hours. On the 29th Col. Collins wrote a long letter to the Governor-General about what had taken place at the interview. It was stated therein that in reply to Collins' question, Maharaja Sindhia gave an assurance that the Maharaja did not have any intention of invading the territory of either the Peshwa, the Nizam or of any other ruler. Collins expressed his satisfaction at the assurance and then asked whether or not the correspondence between Maharaja Sindhia, Bhonsle and Holkar aimed at obstructing the implementation of the Treaty of Bassein. Maharaja Sindhia's plain reply was that discussion on the point was not possible for him until he had talked the matter over with the Raja of Berar. Collins pressed Maharaja Sindhia again and again for an indication of the latter's own attitude. Maharaja Sindhia repeated his answer and added that an expression of his own opinion before he had discussed the matter with Raghoji Bhonsle would be a breach of faith with the latter. The Maharaja said that he would be meeting Raghoji Bhonsle within the next few days and that after the meeting he would inform Collins whether the matter would be settled "peacefully or by war".

It is noteworthy that until then, neither Sindhia nor Bhonsle had been given or shown a copy of the Treaty by the English.

On 30th May, 1803, Governor-General Wellesley wrote to Sindhia, who was on his way to Poona and had crossed the river Narmada: "for the preservation of peace, do not proceed any further, but turn back, re-cross the river and return to your capital."

He also wrote to Raghoji Bhonsle, who had started for Poona, and asked him to return to his capital, Nagpur. That very day he wrote to Col. Close, the English Resident at Poona, and directed that even if Sindhia did turn back and went northwards to his capital, the Company's Army in the south was to be kept ready for action to stop Jaswantrao Holkar if he attempted to go to Poona with his army. He also ordered an advance by the Company's troops stationed in the Midnapore Cantonment to the border of Berar's province of Cuttack.

On 3rd June, 1803, Wellesley instructed Col. Collins to tell Sindhia that "he will be risking a fight with the British power, if he went to Poona except with the express permission of the Peshwa endorsed by the English Government". A similar threat of an English invasion of his territory was held out to the Raja of Berar to prevent his going to Poona.

Sindhia and Bhonsle Postpone Their Visit to Poona

Within the next few days, Raja Raghoji Bhonsle arrived to meet Maharaja Sindhia. Collins tried to assure both that it was the Peshwa himself who was against their visit to Poona and that the Treaty of Bassein did not in any way affect either the mutual relations of the Maratha rulers or their relations with the Peshwa. In the name of "peace and amity" he requested both of them to desist from going to Poona and to return to their capitals. The "request" was accompanied by the threat that if they persisted in going to Poona, they would have to take into account the fact that the English armies were already camping on all the frontiers of the entire Maratha Empire. Apparently, neither Sindhia nor Bhonsle wanted war and both agreed to postpone their visit to Poona. They stipulated, however, that they would send their own trusted agents to the Peshwa to get the latter's personal confirmation of the English assurances about the Treaty of Bassein, and that they would return to their capitals if Bajirao's reply proved to be satisfactory. There could be no valid objection to the proposition and so the English were left without even the semblance of an excuse for going to war with the Maratha rulers.

Wellesley's Directions for Declaration of War

But it would appear that Wellesley had not been holding his hand for want of an excuse to go to war with the Maratha rulers. He could always trump up an excuse and actually did do so later. He had been waiting only for the completion of his preparations for war, secretly begun months earlier, and for the rainy season which, experience had proved to be the most suitable time of the year, for warfare against the Marathas. His preparations were now complete and the rains too were not far off. Consequently, on 26th June, 1803 he sent a "secret" despatch to his brother, Major-General Wellesley, who was in command of the English army at Poona, and delegated to him

> "... full powers to conclude upon the spot whatever arrangements may become necessary either for the final settlement of peace, or for the active prosecution of war ..... to vest these important and arduous powers in your hands ... I further empower and direct you to assume and

> exercise the general direction and control of all the political and military affairs of the British Government in the territories of the Nizam, of the Peshwa and of the Maratha States and Chiefs."

Wellesley next day followed up the above despatch by a letter marked "most secret" in which he wrote:

> "On the receipt of this despatch, you will desire Colonel Collins to demand an explicit declaration of the views of Sindhia and of the Raja of Berar within such number of days as shall appear to you to be reasonable, consistently with due attention to the period of the season, and to the facility of moving your army, and of prosecuting hostilities with the advantages which you now possess ... In this event, or in another state of circumstances which appear to you to require hostilities ... I direct you to use your utmost efforts to destroy the military power of either or of both chiefs (Sindhia and Raja of Berar) ... It is particularly desirable that you should destroy Sindhia's artillery, and all arms of European construction, and all military stores which he may possess ...... the actual seizure of the person of Sindhia, or of Raghoji Bhonsla, would be highly desirable ... In the event of hostilities, you will take proper measures for withdrawing the European officers from the service of Sindhia, Holkar and of every other chief opposed to you ... You are at liberty to incur any expense requisite for this service, and to employ such emissaries as may appear most serviceable ... I propose to dispatch proper emissaries to Gohud, and to the Rajput chiefs. You will also employ every endeavour to excite those powers against Sindhia ... You will consider what steps may be taken to excite Kashi Rad Holkar against Jaswant Rao ... the early reduction of Sindhia ... is certain and would prove a fatal blow to the views of France" (Governor-General's letter marked "most secret" dated 27th June 1803, to his brother Major-General Wellesley.)

The reference to the "views of France" indicates that Wellesley had once again trotted out the old bogey of French designs against the English in India as a justification for the political outrage which he was getting his brother to commit. We shall deal with the myth a little later.

On 28th June, 1803, Wellesley wrote to General Lake directing him "to commence the measures for assembling a force with a view to active operations against Sindhia ... You will be able ... to collect forces at the necessary points ... without occasioning any alarm for war" (Marquess Wellesley's letter to General Lake marked "most secret and confidential", dated 28th June 1803).

With this letter, Wellesley enclosed another **giving** detailed instructions about suborning and winning over Sindhia's chief men.

Sindhia and Bhonsle were, of course, unaware of Wellesley's above-mentioned secret preparations for war against them. At an interview with Collins on 4th July, 1803, they expressed their sincere desire to maintain peace and friendly relations with the English and wrote accordingly to Wellesley on 6th July, 1803 personal letters in which they very clearly stated that they did not intend to go to Poona or to obstruct the implementation of the Treaty of Bassein by Bajirao. Wellesley's reply was: "Please return to your capital, otherwise the friendship cannot last." Wellesley did not deliberately mention a time-limit within which Sindhia was to go back. The reason given by Wellesley in his letter to Col. Close reads:

> "I have not fixed when he (Doulatrao Sindhia) should withdraw ... because I wish to keep in my own breast the period at which hostilities will be commenced; by which advantage it becomes more probable that I shall strike the first blow." (Wellesley's letter to Colonel Close dated 17th July 1803)

The next day, Wellesley wrote again to General Lake:

> "You will therefore act confidently and you will use every effort to prepare for the early execution of the very able plan of operations which you have formed." (Marquess

Wellesley's "secret and confidential" letter to General Lake, dated 18th July 1803)

A week later, there was another meeting between Collins and Sindhia, at which the former repeatedly pressed Sindhia to return to his capital. It was, however, pointed out to him:

(a) that the troops of Sindhia and Bhonsle had not moved out of their respective territories,
(b) that both the rulers had solemnly promised that they would neither go up the Ajanti Ghat or proceed towards Poona,
(c) that both had written under their personal seals to the Governor-General assuring him that neither of them would attempt to upset the Treaty of Bassein and the letters were proofs of their friendship for the English,
(d) that both were arranging to send their representatives to the Peshwa to get from the latter the same assurances as had been given to them verbally by the Governor-General, and
(e) that negotiations for peace treaty between Holkar and Sindhia were going on and Sindhia could not return to his capital until these had been finalised.

Wellesley, thereafter, wrote to Col. Collins: "As no peace or pact has yet been concluded between Sindhia and Jaswantrao Holkar, this is the most opportune time to commence hostilities as soon as possible."

MarquEss Wellesley's Most Significant Letter to Lake

In his letter to General Lake dated 27th July 1803, Wellesley wrote:

"Reviewing those statements your Excellency will observe that the most prosperous issue of a war against Sindhia and the Raja of Berar on the North Western Frontier of Hindustan would in my judgment comprise

1st. The destruction of the French State now formed on the banks of the Jumna together with all its military resources,

2nd. The extension of the Company's frontier to the Jumna, with the possession of Agra, Delhi and a sufficient chain of posts on the Western and Southern banks of the Jumna,

3rd. The possession of the nominal authority of the Moghul,

4th. The establishment of an efficient system of alliance with all the petty States to the Southward and Westward of the Jumna from Jayanagar to Bundelkhand,

5th. The annexation of Bundelkhand to the Company's dominions."

The "French State ... formed on the banks of the Jumna" had never been mentioned in any correspondence or negotiations with Sindhia, because it did not exist. Sir Philip Francis, speaking on the Maratha War before the House of Commons, on 14th March, thus dealt with another allegation against the Marathas, particularly against Sindhia:

> "He was aware that the great argument against the Marathas was their harbouring French officers among them, with views evidently hostile to our superiority. It was even asserted that there was an army of 14,000 French troops, under Captain Perron. Of the existence of such a body of troops there was not a single title of evidence before the House ... Indeed, after the minutest investigation, he found that there were not in the whole Maratha army more than twelve French officers; ... as to any wish of Sindhia to admit French troops into his dominions,

> he denied its existence. It was notorious that Sindhia abhorred the idea of foreign troops in any part of his State ..."

The Secretary of State for India at that time wrote to Wellesley twice saying that the English in India had nothing to fear from the French then or in future. The historian, James Mill, has also proved conclusively that the alleged "danger from France" was pure fiction. It will be recalled that this very myth had been resorted to by Wellesley as an excuse for crushing Tipu.

The real aims of the Second Maratha War have been most clearly set forth in sub-paragraphs 2 to 5 of Wellesley's letter to General Lake quoted above. The war was started to appease the empire-hunger of the English and false pretences were pressed into service for camouflaging the naked annexation of the long-coveted fertile and prosperous domains of Sindhia and Bhonsle to the Company's dominions.

Sindhia Furnished with Copy of the Treaty of Bassein—His Reaction

Some seven months after the Treaty of Bassein had been signed by Bajirao, a copy of it was at last furnished to Sindhia in the last days of July 1803. Sindhia immediately wrote the following letter to Marquess Wellesley which the latter received on 31st July, 1803:

> "I have received your Lordship's friendly letter notifying the conclusion of new engagements between His Highness the Peshwa and the English Company at Bassein, together with a copy of the treaty; and I have been fully apprised of its content ...
>
> "Whereas the engagements subsisting between the Peshwa and me are such that the adjustment of all aifairs and of the concerns of his State and Government should be arranged and completed with my advice and

participation ... Notwithstanding this, the engagements which have lately been concluded between that quarter (British Government) and the Peshwa have only now been communicated ... Therefore, it has now been determined with Raja Raghoji Bhonsla, in presence of Colonel Collins, that confidential persons on my part and the Raja's be despatched to the Peshwa for the purpose of ascertaining the circumstances of the (said) engagements. At the same time no intention whatever is entertained on my part to subvert the stipulations of the treaty consisting of 19 articles, which has been concluded at Bassein, between the British Government and the Peshwa, *on condition that there be no design whatever on the part of the English Company and the Peshwa to subvert stipulations of the treaty, which, since a long period of time, has been concluded between the Peshwa's Sircar, me, and the said Raja and the Maratha chiefs."*

On 1st August, 1803, both Sindhia and Bhonsle again wrote a very friendly letter and repeated their request to Wellesley that the matter be kept pending till their confidential agents had reached the Peshwa and returned, and asking further that the matter be settled peacefully by the exercise of patience.

War Declared

But the English were quite ready for war. So, on 1st August, 1803, Col. Collins, the English Resident, left the Sindhia's *Durbar* without giving any formal information to Sindhia and on 6th August, 1803, General Wellesley, on behalf of the Company, declared war against the Marathas. Mahadji Sindhia and Mudaji Bhonsle, the predecessors of Doulatrao Sindhia and Raghoji Bhonsle, respectively, had helped the English at the critical time when the latter were on the point of being uprooted from Indian soil. Their descendants had now to pay for the short-sightedness of their ancestors who had helped the foreigners against their own countrymen.

British Parliament's Verdict on the War

We have quoted above from the speech delivered in the House of Commons on 14th March, 1804 by Sir Philip Francis. The latter was speaking in support of his motion which simply purported to record that the planning of the conquests of territories and of the expansion of their dominion in India was against the wishes of the British nation. The elected representatives of the British nation in the Parliament, however, rejected the motion by an overwhelming majority. We give below some more quotations from the speech delivered by Sir Philip Francis:

> "With regard to the origin of our connection with India, it was hardly necessary for him (Sir Philip) to remind the House that it was originally purely commercial, but it was marked on the part of the native princes with every appearance of good understanding and even kindness. They not only afforded us every facility for carrying on an advantageous trade, but actually conferred on us immunities and exemptions which many of their own subjects did not enjoy. It was, in a mercantile point of view, wise in the native princes to encourage trade with foreign nations. But while their commercial eye was open, their political eye was closed. They did not act on those principles which had so effectually excluded European nations from the dominion of China ...
>
> "... we first had commerce, commerce produced factories, factories produced garrisons, garrisons produced armies, armies produced conquests, and conquests had brought us into our present position." (Hansard's Reports).

23

Intrigues and Machinations

The Situation vis-à-vis the Maratha Rulers

Once a second war against the Marathas had been decided upon, the English resorted to secret intrigues for undermining the Maratha rulers' strength.

The Peshwa was already a virtual prisoner of the English army in his capital and unless some Maratha ruler like Sindhia went with an army to Poona, it was impossible for Bajirao to raise his hand against the English.

A war against the Marathas meant a war against Sindhia and Bhonsle. The English, however, feared a union of Jaswantrao Holkar with Sindhia and Bhonsle in case war was declared against the latter by the English. Jaswantrao was then in his State in the north and had a strong and well-equipped army. The top priority was, therefore, given by Wellesley to the task of minimising the possibility of a reconciliation between Doulatrao Sindhia and Jaswantrao Holkar, efforts for which were still being made in the Maratha camp.

Jaswantrao Holkar Neutralised

All the time that Wellesley had been worrying Sindhia and Bhonsle, he had taken good care to keep on the right side of Jaswantrao Holkar. On the latter's return from Poona, the English had incited and helped him to depose the rightful reiging Maharaja, Kashirao Holkar and seize the Holkar *Gadi* for himself. At that time Wellesley was constantly writing very friendly and flattering letters to Jaswantrao and on 16th July, 1803, sent to him his secret agent, Qadir Nawaz Khan, with a letter in which he said: "Qadir Nawaz Khan is my trusted man and will convey to you verbally the rest of what I want to say." Through Qadir Nawaz Khan, the English succeeded in leading Jaswantrao up the garden path. The latter was taken in, and so there was no reconciliation between him and Sindhia, Even so, the English did not fully trust Jaswantrao's neutrality and took further precautions. They won over his powerful Sirdar, Meer Khan (Amir Khan), who was in command of Jaswantrao's largest detachment, by offers of more lucrative employment in the Nizam's army and by heavy bribes. Meer Khan's disloyalty to Jaswantrao and loyalty to the English were thus secured and to that extent Jaswantrao was weakened. For his firm adherence to the English cause Meer Khan was made the hereditary Nawab of Tonk by the English. Jaswantrao Holkar was thus neutralised at least for the time being. Incidentally, he was completely disillusioned later on, as regards the good faith of the English. But it was too late then.

Intrigues Against Doulatrao Sindhia

As narrated in Chapter XX, Wellesley started secret intrigues against Doulatrao Sindhia, both in and outside his State, in March 1799, and continued them in the years that followed. We have referred to Wellesley's "most secret and confidential" letter to General Lake dated 28th June, 1803, in which detailed instructions about starting and carrying on of further intrigues against Sindhia were given to General Lake. To help the latter in these nefarious activities, an arch-plotter and expert intriguer, Graeme Mercer, was deputed.

On 22nd July, 1803, Wellesley's Secretary, Edmonstone, wrote to Mercer directing him to suborn and conspire with the principal officers, sirdars and tributaries of Sindhia against the latter. Mercer was instructed to promise

> "... the undisturbed possession of their hereditary tenures on the condition of their zealous and ready co-operation with the British Government to the extent of their respective means in expelling the troops of Doulatrao Sindhia from that quarter of Hindostan, and preventing any future attempts on the part of that chieftain, or of any other foreign power, to establish an authority in these provinces". (Letter dated 22nd July, 1803 from Mr. Edmonstone,

Secretary to ihe Governor-General addressed to Mr. G. Mercer, marked "most secret".)

To facilitate the accomplishment of this difficult task, some capable officers were deputed to work under Mercer and the English Collectors at Allahabad, Kanpur and Etawah were instructed to pay to Mercer any amount of money asked for by him for his secret agents and the money so paid was to be debited to the Governor-General.

On 27th July, 1803, Wellesley wrote another "secret letter" to General Lake, listing the names of the Indian rulers and chiefs who were to be won or bought over by General Lake to the English side against Sindhia.

Breach Engineered Between the Emperor Shah Alam and Doulatrao Sindhia

The name of Emperor Shah Alam topped the list sent to General Lake. It may be noted that, as stated earlier, Wellesley in his letter of the same date to General Lake had mentioned, as one of the objects of the contemplated war against Sindhia and Berar, "the possession of the nominal authority of the Moghul". Yet, Wellesley wrote a letter to Emperor Shah Alam to the following effect:

> "The Emperor knows full well the respect in which the British Government hold him as also their devotion to him and his family.
>
> "From the time that the Emperor, unfortunately placed himself under the protection of the Maratha power, the losses and indignities inflicted upon the Emperor and his highly respected family have always deeply pained the Honourable Company and the British Government in India. I am exceedingly sorry that circumstances had so

> far prevented the English from intervening and successfully protecting the Emperor and from ridding him of the tyrannies, the injustice, the inhumanities and the extortions to which he has been subjected, etc."

It will be recalled that it was Warren Hastings who had perfidiously handed over the Emperor to Mahadji Sindhia. The Emperor had never complained against the latter to anybody. On the contrary, in a Persian poem composed by him, in which the Emperor describes his sufferings caused by the treachery of his Mussalman wazirs and courtiers, is a couplet which means:

> "Mahadji Sindhia, my son, dear to my heart, is always busy with efforts to counteract the cruelties to which I am subjected."

But it suited Wellesley to ignore all that. His letter to the Emperor was enclosed with the above-mentioned "secret letter" to General Lake who was instructed to see to its delivery on the following lines:

> "It will be proper to send my letter to the Emperor with the utmost care and secrecy ... Syed Raza Khan is the agent at Delhi of the English Resident at Sindhia's *Durbar* and had been at the Emperor's *Durbar* for a long time. I think he can be fully trusted ... When you give the letter for the Emperor to Syed Raza Khan you will give him such instructions as you think proper. The said agent is to be further instructed to give to you timely and correct information about any developments in Delhi which come to his knowledge."

The English made lavish promises to the Emperor through Syed Raza Khan. They assured him that all his sovereign powers and authority which had been grabbed by the Marathas would be restored to him and he would be reinstated with the help of the English as the *de facto* Emperor of India. On 2nd December, 1803, General Lake presented to the Emperor, under instructions from the Governor-General, a "written agreement" containing all the above promises and assurances. It achieved its purpose of deluding the Emperor with hopes and securing his support for the English against the Marathas.

That the promises and hopes were false was proved when the implementation of the "written agreement" (*Iqrarnama*) was sought. The Chairman of the Court of Directors of the Company, speaking at East India House said: "The Court would be surprised to hear that the document ... called the *Iqrarnama* was nowhere to be found on the records of the Court, or in those of the Supreme Government of India."

This curious statement elicited from Sullivan Rose, a Member of the British Parliament, the following comment:

> "Was it the fault of Shah Alam that this document was not upon record? ... In my judgement, a gross breach of faith has been committed in this case of the Moghul ..."

It will be remembered that it was this very Emperor Shah Alam II, who had granted to the Company the *Dewanee* of the Provinces of Bengal, Bihar and Orissa. But much water had flowed down the Thames since then, and when the Director spoke, almost the the entire dominion of the Moghul Emperor and his centuries-old sovereignty of India had passed into the hands of the Company.

Subornation of Sindhia's Tributaries

Begum Zebunnisan, better known as Begum Sumroo, was a tributary of the Sindhias. She had a sizable Jagir at Sardhana, near Meerut. Wellesley wrote to General Lake:

> "... the local situation of the Begam's *Jageer* renders it desirable that in any engagement concluded with her on the part of the British Government, such conditions should be inserted as may facilitate the introduction of the British regulations into the *Jageer* and I request that Your Excellency's negotiations with the Begam may be directed

> to the accomplishment of this object ... she should be requested to recall her battalions now serving in the army of Doulatrao Sindhia, and to employ whatever influence she may possess over the Zemindars and Chieftains in the Doab, to induce them to place themselves under the authority of the British Government and to employ their resources in assisting the operation of the British arms." (Marquess Wellesley's letter to Lieut. General Lake dated 28th July, 1803, marked "official and secret".

On 30th July, 1803, Wellesley wrote another "secret letter" to General Lake in which he instructed the latter to win or buy over:

> "... the tributaries, principal officers or other subjects of Doulatrao Sindhia exclusively of those described in my General Instructions to Your Excellency and in my instructions to Mr. Mercer (as) may be inclined to place themselves under the protection of the Company ... it (is) both just and expedient that we should avail ourselves, as much as possible, of the discontent and disaffection of his subjects or officers, and I accordingly desire ... you will be pleased to decide on the degree and nature of encouragement proper to be given ... I also authorise Your Excellency to give to all tributaries or others renouncing their allegiance to Sindhia, and acting sincerely in our favour, the most positive assurances of protection in the name of the Company ... It is my ultimate intention to extend the regulations of the British Government throughout the whole of the country, bounded by the rivers Ganges and Jumna, and by the mountains of Kumaon. A part of this territory is possessed by Goojers ... in the vicinity of Sharanpore. "Your Excellency's prudence will dictate the expediency of employing the most efficacious measures for the purpose of conciliating the Goojers, and of inducing them to unite with the British Government for the overthrow of Sindhia's power in the Doab." (Marquess Wellesley's "secret letter" to General Lake dated 30th July, 1803.)

It is worth noting that up to this time war against the Marathas had not been declared and the English were still supposed to be "friends" of the Marathas.

Plan to Conspire with Sikhs Against Doulatrao Sindhia

Sindhia's dominion in the north-west extended up to the Punjab. Several new Sikh principalities had sprung up in the Punjab and in Lahore Ranjit Singh's sun was just rising. Wellesley had reasons to fear that the growing Sikh power might, when the English declared war on the Marathas, join in the latter. He, therefore, tried to secure if not the Sikhs' support, at least their neutrality in the contemplated war. He wrote to General Lake:

> "The chiefs from whose influence or exertions the greatest benefit is to be derived are the Raja of Patiala and those petty chieftains who occupy the territory between Patiala and the Jumna. I understand, however, that Raja Ranjit Singh, the Raja of Lahore, is considered to be the principal among the chiefs of the tribe of Sikhs, and to possess considerable influence over the whole body of the Sikh chiefs.
>
> "I transmit to your Excellency, for the purpose of being forwarded, at such time and in such manner as may appear to Your Excellency to be most proper, letters to those among the Sikh chiefs with whom the agent of the Resident with Doulatrao Sindhia communicated (in the year 1800).
>
> "Adverting to the great distance of Lahore from the scene of intended operations, the only support to be expected from Raja Ranjit Singh is the exertion of his influence with the other Sikh chieftains, to induce them to favour the cause of the British Government.

> "Such of those chieftains as are subject to the control and exactions of the Maratha power may perhaps be detached from the interests of that nation by promises of protection from the British Government, and of exemption from the payment of tribute in future.
>
> "If it should appear impracticable to obtain the co-operation of those chieftains, it would still be an object of importance to secure their neutrality. In your communications to the Sikh chieftains, it may be proper that Your Excellency should suggest to their consideration the danger to which they will hereafter be exposed by any opposition to the interests of the British Government, and the advantages which they may derive from a connection with so powerful a state.
>
> "... require the observance of secrecy and caution in Your Excellency's communications with those chieftains." ("Secret and official" letter of Marquess Wellesley to General Lake, dated 2nd August 1803.)

We might here draw attention to the fact that Wellesley had been deliberately confining to non-Sikh rulers his efforts to drive them into the trap of Subsidiary Alliances and had left the Sikh rulers alone. Sikh power was just then growing and had not attained any solidarity. In 1801 an English freebooter was frequently raiding Sikh territories with a force of Rohilla Pathan horsemen which he had collected. Wellesley's policy in leaving the Sikhs alone now paid dividends. The Sikh rajas and chiefs rendered the desired help to the English in the latter's Second War against the Marathas. Had the Sikhs sided with the Marathas, the English Company would have doubtless been uprooted from Indian soil. As it was, the Sikhs' friendliness towards the English largely contributed to the subsequent growth and progress of Sikh power, particularly of Maharaja Ranjit Singh.

Bribe Offered to Raja of Bharatpur

Raja Ranjit Singh of Bharatpur was one of Sindhia's principal tributaries. In the letter dated 13th August, 1804, written by General Lake to Marquess Wellesley, it was stated that the English had made a promise to the Raja of Bharatpur that if the latter helped the English against the Marathas, then he would be exempted from future payments of tribute and would moreover be granted additional territory as a *Jagir* with an annual income of four lacs of rupees. It is further stated that even the *sanad* granting the *Jagir* was handed over to the Raja of Bharatpur.

Subornation of European Officers in Sindhia's Army

In spite of his success in the above-mentioned intrigues, Wellesley did not think that it would be an easy victory over Sindhia. Consequently he turned to the subornation of the European officers in Sindhia's army.

Mahadji Sindhia had, under the advice and persuasion of Warren Hastings, taken many Europeans, mostly French, into his military service and appointed them to high posts in his army. No deadlier mistake was ever committed by any other Indian ruler and Doulatrao Sindhia had to pay the penalty for his grandfather's blunder. One of the principal commanders in his army was one Capt. Perron, a Frenchman, who had under him a number of other European officers occupying high and responsible posts. All of them worshipped lucre and were mercenaries. Wellesley knew it and issued a proclamation promising huge rewards to the European employees of Doulatrao Sindhia if they deserted or betrayed him. The result was eminently satisfactory to Wellesley. The defection of these Europeans followed and was the severest blow dealt to Doulatrao Sindhia.

Before closing this sordid story, we would emphasise the fact that it is founded on the writings of the English themselves.

24

Empire Expansion

Encirclement of the Dominions of Sindhia and Bhonsle

As many as six large armies occupied strategic positions along the borders of the dominions of Sindhia and Bhonsle. Five of these, including the biggest which was commanded by General Lake, surrounded the former's entire territory, whilst only one was stationed at Ganjam on the border of Bhonsle's province of Cuttack.

The five armies encircling Sindhia's dominion included the Subsidiary Armies of Mysore, the Nizam, the Peshwa, the Nawab of Oudh and the Gaikwad, whilst the sixth was mainly composed of troops from Bengal. Only the officers and a microscopic minority of men in those armies were foreigners. The rest were all Indians. Almost the entire personnel of the huge force was in the service of the Indian rulers, who were further made to provide the sinews of war.

Silver Bullets used for the "Conquest" of Ahmednagar

Ahmednagar, situate between Poona and Aurangabad, had one of the strongest forts of Doulatrao Sindhia. It had been designed and constructed to withstand any siege indefinitely. The English had correctly estimated that the fall of the town and fort at Ahmednagar would completely demoralise the Maratha *Jagirdars* and Sindhia's subjects in the South, and they had planned to make it the first target of their attack. So, some time before the formal declaration of war by the Governor-General (on 6th August, 1803), the latter's brother, General Wellesley, had begun his march on Ahmednagar with his army, of which the Peshwa's Subsidiary Army formed an integral part. Even earlier, the Governor-General had started making secret overtures to Sindhia's officials who were responsible for the defence of Ahmednagar Fort and town.

On 7th August, 1803, General Wellesley arrived close to Ahmednagar and issued a proclamation, in the name of the Governor-General, alleging that war had been declared by the English because of the threatened attack on the English, the Peshwa and Nawab Nizam Ali by Doulatrao Sindhia and the Raja of Berar. The proclamation further assured the citizens and the officials of Ahmednagar of the English friendliness towards them, and, in the name of the Company and the Peshwa, called upon them to deliver the town to the Peshwa's army, which was with General Wellesley. The people and the officials were thus misled into believing the invading army to be their friends and so on 8th August, 1803, General Wellesely occupied the town without any opposition. But the Fort was a different proposition as its commandant hesitated in complying with General Wellesley's summons to surrender. What happened thereafter is thus described in the Ahmednagar Gazetteer, p. 695, edited by Sir James Campbell:

> "When after capturing the town, General Wellesley reconnoitred the fort on 9th August, the complete protection which the glacis afforded to the wall made it difficult to fix on a spot for bombardment. Raghurao Baba, the Deshmukh of Bhingar, received a bribe of four hundred pounds and advised an attack on the east face."

Who knows how many more Raghurao Babas were similarly bribed! There was a show of fighting for two days and on 11th August, 1803, the commandant of the Fort vacated it for the English. It has been recorded that he and his garrison were given safe conduct by the English and were permitted to keep their personal possessions. General Wellesley reported that when he entered the Fort, he found it and its defences in excellent condition and absolutely untouched. Obviously, the Fort had fallen not to steel but to gold and silver bullets. On 13th August, 1803, Wellesley issued a second proclamation appointing Capt.

Graham as the Administrator, on behalf of the Company and the Peshwa, of Ahmednagar and its adjacent regions. After helping Capt. Graham to settle down, General Wellesley marched his army out of Ahmednagar towards Aurangabad on 18th August, 1803.

Wellesley's Indefinite General Assurances to the Peshwa

The Peshwa was the head of the Maratha Confederacy and as such the suzerain of the Sindhias. As Wellesley had taken over the Ahmednagar region in the name of the Peshwa, its administration should have been immediately handed over to the Peshwa exclusively. As it was not done, the Peshwa was naturaly dissatisfied even though he could do nothing about it at the moment. Wellesley was quite aware of the Peshwa's feelings and wanted to assuage them but he also wanted the region to be under the sole and exclusive rule of the English. So he wrote to Col. Close, the English Resident at Poona:

> "I am very anxious that the Peshwa should feel no jealousy about this place (Ahmednagar) ... I wish you would speak ... upon the subject, point out to him how necessary the place is for us ... You may also assure him that a faithful account shall be kept of the revenues, and credit given to the Peshwa for his portion of them." (General Wellesley's letter to Col. Close dated 13th August, 1803).

But Wellesley appears to have had second thoughts, for the very next day he again wrote to Col. Close:

> "Since writing to you yesterday, it has occurred to me that it would be better not to hold out to the Peshwa any promise or prospect of having half the revenue of Ahmednagar, but to tell him generally that the revenues shall be applied to pay the expenses of the war, and that the accounts of them shall be communicated to him. One great object, however, is to reconcile his mind to our keeping possession of the

country, which is absolutely necessary for our communications with Poona; and provided that is effected, I think it immaterial whether he has half the revenue or not ... I beg you to turn this subject over in your mind ... I will delay to write you a public letter till I shall receive your answer." (General Wellesley's letter to Col. Close dated 14th August, 1803).

Three days later, on 17th August, 1803, Wellesley again wrote to Col. Close: "If the Peshwa Bajirao should be satisfied with a general assurance that the conquered territory is to be applied to the benefit of the allies, it will be most convenient.

"But I consider it to be an object of the utmost importance that the Peshwa's mind should be satisfied as far as possible, in order that there may appear no wavering in his intention to adhere to the alliance on which the southern *Jagirdars* might found acts of hostility against the Company."

Wellesley had been fearing for some time, "acts of hostility against the Company", on the part of the Southern Maratha *Jagirdars,* and so to overawe the latter, had posted the army under Gen. Stuart on the border of Mysore. He wanted to keep the Peshwa happy by a vague "general assurance", lest the latter escape from Poona and declare war on the English, in which case the *Jagirdars,* whom the English had duped more than once, might join the Peshwa.

Bribes to Peshwa's Ministers

On 24th August, 1803, Gen. Wellesley wrote to Major Shaw:

"I have no idea that the Peshwa will attempt to fly from Poona; or that if he should be so inclined, he could carry his plan into execution without the knowledge of his ministers. You will have observed from my letter to Col. Close that I have urged him to pay the ministers in order to have accurate information of what passes.

"We cannot contrive to settle the Government at Poona till the conclusion of the war. Bad as the situation of the Government is, it must be allowed to continue. If we were to attempt to alter it now, we should have a contest in our rear, which would be ruinous."

A month later, on 28th September, 1803, General Wellesley wrote to Col. Close, (he English Resident at Poona:

"Lord Wellesley has taken up the question of paying the Peshwa's ministers upon a great scale.

***

"The Peshwa has no ministers. He is everything himself and everything is little. In my opinion, therefore, we ought to pay those who are supposed to be and are called his ministers, not to keep the machine of Government in motion, in consistence with the objects of the alliance as we do at Hyderabad, but to have intelligence of what passes in the Peshwa's secret councils in order that we may check him in time when it may be necessary."

General Wellesley's Opposition

At the conclusion of the war, Gen. Wellesley wrote to the Governor-General on 11th November, 1803, and said quite plainly that no part of the region "conquered by us" should be given to the Peshwa and the Ahmednagar Fort should continue to be occupied by the English. With reference to the territory called "Surat Attavesy" which had belonged to the Peshwa, he said: "... before this territory should be ceded to His Highness the Peshwa, he ought to be required to consent to the improvement of the defensive alliance."

Doulatrao Sindhia at Bay

It will be recalled that Gen. Wellesley left Ahmednagar on 18th August, 1803. On the 24th, he crossed the river Godavari to join forces with the Company's third army commanded by Stevenson which was mainly composed of the Nizam's strong Subsidiary Army and was stationed near Aurangabad in the Nizam's territory.

On the other side, as soon as the news of the fall of Ahmednagar reached them, Doulatrao Sindhia and the Raja of Berar got ready as quickly as possible and invaded the Nizam's territory. Doulatrao Sindhia was only 23 years old then, but the lightning rapidity and the amazing ability with which he marshalled his forces have elicited the admiration even of his enemies.

General Wellesley has recorded the fact that a corps of spies and secret agents had been recruited from amongst the subjects and soldiers of Sindhia and Bhonsle, who from time to time kept the English fully posted about the position and the line of march of the Maratha armies. It was thus easy enough for the English to choose their own time and place for giving battle to the Marathas.

Background of Battle of Assye and of English Success

The battle of Assye is considered to be one of the "decisive" battles fought and won by the English for the expansion of their dominion in India. Its background and salient features are, therefore, of some importance, and may be briefly related.

The locale of the battle was the village of Assye situated on the northern border of the Nizam's territory, and adjoining that of the Raja of Berar. It was fought between Sindhia's infantry and artillery, on the one side, and the English cavalry, infantry and artillery, on the other. Doulatrao Sindhia himself was not present at the battle. Under the misapprehension that the main body of the English army was at Hyderabad, he had rapidly marched towards it with his entire cavalry, outstripping his comparatively slow-moving infantry and artillery. For some reason, the latter stayed on at Assye longer than was necessary. Fodder for the bullocks of the batteries was exhausted and they were taken off and driven to distant pastures for grazing. This happened on 23rd of September, 1803. The English, under Stevenson, attacked immediately. Sindhia's entire artillery was immobilised and the heavy guns could not be moved into position for want of bullocks. Only the Maratha infantry could go into action and it was further handicapped by the absence of their redoubtable leader and, last but not the least, "by the cessation of the British part of their European officers". (*History of the Marathas* by Grant Duff, p. 574.)

Even so, they fought valiantly and according to English records inflicted on the English attackers the loss of 575 English and 1456 Indians killed and wounded in addition to 26 missing, but they had lost the battle before it was begun, and had to retreat. Next day Gen. Wellesley ordered Stevenson to pursue the retreating Marathas but as Mill writes:

> "The enemy (*viz.*, the Marathas) had been so little broken or dispersed by their defeat that they had little to dread from the pursuit of Colonel Stevenson." (Mill, Vol. VI page 358.)

Anyhow Stevenson did not follow in pursuit, because, apparently he did not think it wise to do so.

Some Notable Features of English Preparations for War

We revert to 18th July, 1803, when Gen. Lake, in his memorandum to the Governor-General, wrote:

> "The most essential advantages may be derived from an union With Begum Sumroo ...
>
> "Four of her battalions are now with Sindhia ... means might be contrived to enable those battalions to join General Wellesley."

The Governor-General, in his reply to the memorandum, said:

> "This suggestion is extremely proper, and orders will be immediately sent to Colonel Scott; Mr. Mercer's instructions include this point."

Gen. Wellesley in his letter (dated 26th October, 1803) had stated that with the Maratha infantry was a brigade of four battalions of Begum Sumroo's army and another brigade of about the same size in the Maratha infantry was commanded by Dupont, a European officer. Dupont had been included in the list of 16 officers sent by Gen. Wellesley to the Governor-General and referred to in his letter dated 24th October, 1803, in which he had said:

> "Sixteen officers and sergeants belonging to the Campoos (i.e., Sindhia's camp) have joined Colonel Stevenson under Your Excellency's proclamation of the 29th August. I will hereafter send a list of their names, and an account of the pay each is to receive."

Along with the Governor-General's above-mentioned proclamation to the European officers, a similar proclamation was addressed to the Indian officers too of Sindhia's army, some of whom went over to the English when the battle started, whilst some others remained with the troops under their command to use the same in English interests at a suitable opportunity. The Maratha infantry was thus honey-combed by treasonous cells.

Incidentally, Doulatrao Sindhia's heavy guns and their ammunition were, after the battle, handed over intact to the English by the artillery officers, most of whom were Europeans. General Wellesley found them to be most up-to-date and in excellent condition and freely expressed his admiration.

Offer of Peace Pourparlers

Doulatrao Sindhia was naturally very much distressed by the treachery in his own camp which resulted in the defeat at Assye of his infantry and the capture of his entire artillery by the English.

At that time, he had with him one Balaji Kunjar, a most trusted emissary of the Peshwa. Time and again the English had attempted to bribe and win over Balaji Kunjar, but the latter's loyalty to the Peshwa and his country remained unshaken. He had been sent by the Peshwa to Doulatrao Sindhia for consultations and advice about the Treaty of Bassein and was with Sindhia when the English declared war against the Marathas. A week after the battle of Assye, Balaji Kunjar, at the instance and on behalf of Doulatrao Sindhia, wrote to Gen. Wellesley suggesting a cease-fire and a conference for settling the terms of a peace treaty. The letter does not find a place in the published letters of Gen. Wellesley, but the latter's reply to Balaji Kunjar (dated 5th October, 1803) indicates that Balaji Kunjar had drawn attention to the following facts:

(i) that Doulatrao Sindhia had never had any intention of attacking either the English or anyone else,

(ii) that Doulatrao Sindhia had tried to the very last to settle every dispute through peaceful negotiations, but the English had always evaded negotiations and had never specified their complaints or demands,

(iii) that no formal ultimatum before the declaration of war was given to Doulatrao Sindhia, and his territory was suddenly invaded without warning, and

(iv) that the behaviour of the English Resident Collins towards Doulatrao Sindhia had been objectionable.

The letter concluded with a request that the useless bloodshed might be stopped forthwith and peace negotiations started.

Occupation of Burhanpur and AseerGarh Forts

Gen. Wellesley sent Col. Stevenson northwards to attack and occupy Sindhia's Forts at Burhanpur and Aseergarh. Dupont and the other officers (mentioned before as having been won over by the English) had not yet left Sindhia's army and were in command of the detachments despatched for the defence of these forts. Gen. Wellesley had rightly anticipated that with the connivance of Dupont and the other officers, there would not be any opposition to the occupation of these forts by the English. Stevenson occupied the Burhanpur Fort on 15th October, 1803, and freely looted the prosperous town. Two days later, he advanced towards Aseergarh, attacked the Fort on the 19th and occupied it on the 21st. Dupont and the other 15 European officers having thus betrayed the Forts to the English, now openly deserted Sindhia's army and joined Stevenson's forces.

Scheme to Break-up Sindhia-Bhonsle Combination

After the Battle of Assye, the forces of Sindhia and Bhonsle, mainly consisting of horsemen, retired from the Nizam's territory and moved towards the south after crossing the Tapi river.

Sindhia's Aseergarh Fort was occupied by Stevenson on 21st October, 1803. On the 24th, Gen. Wellesley, in a dispatch to the Governor-General, confessed his "incapability to do Sindhia further injury". Thereafter, he appears to have adopted a deceptively conciliatory attitude towards Sindhia, in a bid to create dissensions between the latter and the Raja of Berar. On the 30th, he wrote to Balaji Kunjar:

> "I have received your letter ... and Col. Stevenson has transmitted to me a Persian letter, in which you have informed him that Mohammed Mir Khan was about to be sent on a mission to me. I shall be happy to see Mir Khan. I will receive him in a manner suitable to his rank, and I will pay every attention to what he may have to communicate."

General Wellesley wrote to Mohammed Mir Khan too: "... I shall be happy to see you, and will receive you with the honours due to your rank and character, and I shall pay every attention to what you may have to communicate."

On 23rd November, 1803, an armistice was signed by the representatives (*Vakils*) of General Wellesley and Sindhia. It provided for an immediate cease-fire in the south, in Gujarat and everywhere else. Its last clause provided that the armistice was to be signed personally by Doulatrao Sindhia and returned to Gen. Wellesley within ten days.

It may be mentioned here that Doulatrao Sindhia's representatives had pressed for the inclusion of the name of the Raja of Berar, too, jointly with that of Sindhia as one of the two parties to the armistice. But the English would not agree on the pretext that the Raja of Berar had no representative at the armistice negotiations. The real reason has, however, been disclosed by Gen. Wellesley himself in his letter dated 23rd November, 1803, to Major Shawe, Private Secretary to the Governor-General, from which we quote:

> "The Raja of Berar's troops are not included in it, and consequently there becomes a division of interest between these two chiefs. AH confidence in Sindhia, if it ever existed must be at an end, and the confederacy is, *ipso facto,* dissolved."

In the same letter, Gen. Wellesley wrote further:

> "I have already apprised the Governor-General that it was not in my power to do anything more against Doulatrao Sindhia ... Sindhia has with him in the field an army of horses only. It is impossible to expect to make any impression upon this army, unless by following it for a great length of time and distance; to do this would remove our troops still farther than they are already from all the sources of supply; and would prevent the operations against the Raja of Berar."

The last sentence of the letter is significant enough as it gives a glimpse of Gen. Wellesley's scheme to divide Sindhia and Bhonsle and then to crush each of them in turn.

The following extract from Gen. Wellesley's letter dated 24th November, 1803, to Col. Close throws further light on the former's plan and his motives for temporarily ceasing hostilities:

> "I have agreed to the cessation of hostilities on the ground of my incapability to do Sindhia further injury, as stated in my dispatch to the Governor-General on the 24th of October; on that of it being impossible to injure his army of horse; on that of the injury he may do me in the operations against Gawilgarh (in Berar) and in Gujarat, to which quarter he has sent Bapuji Sindhia; and on the political ground of dividing his interests from those of the Raja of Berar, and thereby, in fact, dissolving the Confederacy."

On the same day Gen. Wellesley wrote to the Governor-General:

> "If advantage should be taken of the cessation of hostilities to delay the negotiations for peace, Your Excellency will observe that I have the power of putting an end to it when I please; and that, supposing I am obliged to put an end to it, on the day after I shall receive its ratification, I shall at least have gained so much time everywhere for my operations, and shall have succeeded in dividing the enemy entirely."

Apparently, honesty and good faith did not find any place in Gen. Wellesley's diplomatic activities. This was demonstrated within less than a week of the signing of the armistice. He did not wait for the receipt of the ratification of the armistice, but put an end to it even before the stipulated ten days for its ratification by Doulatrao Sindhia had expired.

Surprise Attack on Sindhia's Fort at Argaon

In open violation of the terms of the armistice, Gen. Wellesley suddenly attacked Sindhia's Argaon Fort on 29th November, that is, only six days after the armistice had been agreed to by his representatives and sent to Doulatrao Sindhia for ratification. The Fort fell to the English and the Governor-General wrote to his brother (Gen. Wellesley):

> "... Although I entirely approved of your armistice and thought it a most judicious measure, I confess that I prefer your victory to your armistice; ... I have not yet discovered whether the battle was occasioned by a rupture of the truce on the part of Sindhia; ... or by an accidental encounter of the armies before the truce had commenced; or by a treacherous junction between Sindhia and the Raja of Berar. But, *Qua cunque via,* a battle is a profit with the Native powers."
>
> (Governor-General's letter to General Wellesley, dated 23rd December, 1803).

In his official letters, Gen. Wellesley has given two reasons for the blatant violation of the armistice, but neither of them bears scrutiny. The first reason that Doulatrao Sindhia had not signed and returned the armistice makes no sense, because Argaon was attacked four days before the expiry of the time allowed for the signature and return of the armistice by Sindhia. The second reason was that Doulatrao Sindhia had not complied with the stipulation in the armistice that he would keep his army at least 20 miles distant from the English troops. Gen. Wellesley's letters, however, make it quite plain that as Sindhia's army fell back, the English troops followed it, thus reducing the distance between the two to less than 20 miles.

Occupation of Gawilgarh Fort

The next victim was the Raja of Berar, whose fort at Gawilgarh was similarly taken by a surprise attack treacherously delivered. It lasted three days and its loyal and gallant commander died fighting in its defence.

Gujarat

Some four weeks before the declaration of war, Wellesley had instructed the Governor of Bombay to start preparations for an attack on Sindhia's Fort at Bharoch (Broach) in Gujarat.

It might be mentioned here that Gujarat had been one of the Provinces of the Moghul Empire, till the Nizam had incited and helped the Marathas to invade it and a part of Gujarat had passed under the rule of the Gaikwads. The English had then won over the Gaikwad and had got him to break away from the Maratha Confederacy. Later, the English had got the Gaikwad to cede to Mahadji Sindhia, as a reward for the latter's teachery towards the Maratha Confederacy, the Bharoch Fort and its adjoining territory with an annual income of Rs. 11 lakhs. The Governor-General's instructions to the Governor of Bombay meant that the former had decided to seize by force the Fort and the territory from Mahadji Sindhia's heir and successor, Doulatrao Sindhia.

Most of Sindhia's Gujarat territory was populated by Bhils, ruled by their own petty chiefs who paid tribute to Sindhia. To attack the Bharoch Fort, the English troops had to pass through the Bhil region, and it had, therefore, become essential for them to win or buy over the Bhil chiefs. Some English traders at Surat were pressed into service to do it. General Wellesley's instructions in this behalf are to be found in his letter to the Governor of Bombay dated 2nd August, 1803, from which we quote:

> "... you will urge the gentlemen at Surat to keep on terms with the Bheels ... The number of troops I have above detailed ... *they will not be sufficient for the subjection even of one of their Rajas; ... it* would be better to give up all claims of tribute"

Gaikwad's Subsidiary Army Used to Attack Bharoch Fort

On 6th August, 1803, Gen. Wellesley ordered the Gaikwad's Subsidiary Army to attack the Bharoch Fort immediately.

Anandrao was then the ruling Gaikwad and had very friendly relations with Doulatrao Sindhia. He protested against the use of the Subsidiary Army which was maintained exclusively at his cost and which, according to the terms of the Subsidiary Alliance, could be used only in the service of the Gaikwad and for his help, and not for any other purpose. He also strongly objected to the use of his capital, Baroda, as the base for an invasion of Sindhia's territory. But the Subsidiary Army served under the Company's orders and Gen. Wellesley plainly stated:

> "Although it is not immediately specified ... the Gaikwad should also assist the Company with his forces against the enemies of the British Government" (General Wellesley's letter to the Bombay Government dated 22nd August, 1803).

On 21st August, 1803, an artillery company and two infantry battalions of the Gaikwad's Subsidiary Army marched on Fort Bharoch from Baroda, under the command of Colonel Woodington. The assault was delivered on the 25th and it fell to the English on the 27th. The adjoining territory too was taken over by the English.

In those days, many Arabs had taken military service under several Indian rulers, including Sindhia. They were invariably faithful. Col. Woodington stated to Gen. Wellesley that the Arab contingent in the Fort had put up a very stiff resistance and fought to the last. But it was of no avail as the Fort was attacked before Doulatrao Sindhia could make any adequate arrangements for its defence.

Fall of Sindhia's Pawangarh Fort

Pawangarh was another of Sindhia's Forts in Gujarat. The district of Champaran was under its jurisdiction. After taking Bharoch Fort, Col. Woodington marched towards Pawangarh and attacked it. It fell to him by the evening of 17th September. According to

Col. Woodington, the garrison did not turn out to be loyal to Sindhia and "offered to capitulate". He goes on to say:

> "... To these terms I agreed ... they, however, tacked another stipulation, *viz.,* that I should agree to pay them the arrears due from Sindhia, ... they agreed to the original terms ... Could they have obtained possession of the upper fort, or Bala Killa, at the top of the mountain, I am inclined to think it utterly impregnable." (Colonel Woodington's letter to Colonel Murray dated 21st September, 1803)

Thus, Doulatrao Sindhia lost forever every inch of Gujarat territory which his grandfather Mahadji Sindhia had acquired as the price of his betrayal of the Maratha Confederacy.

Orissa

Most of the Province of Orissa was then ruled by the Bhonsle Rajas of Nagpur and its local chiefs were their tributaries.

The Moghul Emperor's grant of the *Dewanee* of Orissa to the Company covered only that small northern portion of the province which was directly administered by the Emperor's Subedar of Murshidabad. The civil and criminal jurisdiction over the rest of the entire province was exercised by the Marathas. The Company's factory at Baleshwar was also within the Maratha jurisdiction and the Englishmen of the factory carried on their business as the unquestioned subjects of the Marathas. In 1767, when the Marathas demanded from the Company the arrears of the *Chowth,* the Directors were willing to pay up but at the same time urged the Marathas to grant to the Company the *Dewanee* of that part of the province which was under the former's rule. To this the Marathas would not agree. The English intrigues against the Marathas would appear to have been started since then as also the false stories about Maratha atrocities on the people of Orissa.

Instructions to Colonel Campbell

We have stated earlier that one of the six armies detailed for operations against the Marathas was stationed at Ganjam, on the border of Bhonsle's province of Cuttack. It was commanded by Col. Campbell. On 3rd August, 1803, Marquess Wellesley sent detailed instructions to Col. Campbell about spreading disaffection against Raghoji Bhonsle amongst his subjects, the influential priests of Jagannathpuri and the neighbouring *Sardars, Zamindars* and minor chiefs. In compliance with these instructions, a number of people who mattered were won over by bribery and/or threats, so that:

> "... when the English appeared on the scene, the Marathas were left to fight their own battles, quite unsupported by the people ... Had they done so, the turbulent Rajas of the hills and the sea coast might have given us a great deal of trouble." (J. Beams in his "Note on the History of Orissa" published in the *Journal of the Asiatic Society of Bengal* for 1883)

Thus it was that the invading English army from Ganjam did not have to fight at all. Without any bloodshed, it occupied Manikpattan on the 14th and Jagannathpuri on 18th September, 1803.

Occupation of Baleshwar

To the north of Orissa, another detachment of the Company's army led by Capt. Morgan arrived from Calcutta by sea and attacked Baleshwar. The Maratha garrison of the Baleshwar Fort put up a stiff resistance, but the English were helped by Prahlad Nayak, a *Zamindar* of the old town of Baleshwar, and on 21st September, 1803, Baleshwar was occupied by the English who issued a public proclamation that the region had been brought under the rule of the English Company.

Occupation of Barabatti

After taking possession of Jagannathpuri, the army from Ganjam, led by Colonel Harcourt, advanced towards Cuttack. The Fort at Cuttack, called Barabatti, was a very strong one. It had around it a water-filled moat 20 ft. deep and 35 to 135 ft. wide. There was only one narrow bridge over the moat leading into the Fort. Col. Harcourt arrived at Cuttack on 10th October and occupied the town without any opposition at all. Four days later, the Barabatti Fort was also surrendered to them by its treacherous defenders who betrayed their master, Raghoji Bhonsle.

Mayurbhanj and Nilgiri

These were two principalities situate between Baleshwar and Cuttack, and were the next target of the Company's troops from Ganjam and Calcutta, which had joined hands under Col. Harcourt. Sometime earlier, the English had started their machinations against the Rani of Mayurbhanj and the Raja of Nilgiri. According to J. Beams (quoted above), a separate special military detachment had been sent:

> "... to learn the geography of the Mayurbhanj and Nilgiri Hills, especially the passes and to open communications with the Rajas of those two States. Spies were sent into Mayurbhanj and Nilgiri to keep a watch on the chiefs, and passports were to be granted to their vakils or representatives, should they desire to visit Cuttack."

The Rani of Mayurbhanj was at first unwilling to go over to the English. Col. Harcourt wrote to her ingratiating letters but these had little effect. Then the Rani's adopted son, who was the heir-apparent, was won over, and the Rani had to join the English ultimately and to agree to the occupation by the English of a part of Mayurbhanj territory. The English advanced from there and in due course took possession of Sambalpur on 12th January, 1804.

The whole of that portion of Orissa province which had formed a part of the Maratha Empire, was thus annexed by the English Company.

The Reaction of the People of Orissa

J. Beams, in his "Note on the History of Orissa" (referred to above) writes:

> "Well aware of our ignorance of the country, they all with one accord abstained from helping us in any way, no open resistance was ventured upon, but all solidly sat aloof ... papers were hidden, information withheld, boats, bullocks and carts sent out of the way, the *Zamindars* who were ordered to go into Cuttack to settle for their estate did not go, and on searching for them at their homes could not be found, were reported as absent, on a journey, no one knew where. But if from ignorance the English officers committed any mistake, the life suddenly returned to the dull inert mass and complaints were loud and incessant."

The people, doubtless hated and feared the replacement of their own rulers, Marathas and others, by a foreign company. Very soon their fears proved to have been well founded. According to J. Beams, the people had not known want or scarcity of food. Rice was then selling at the rate of about 150 lbs. for a rupee. On the other hand, the English occupation of the region brought in its wake famine. To quote J. Beams again:

> "Cuttack now begins to be noticeable as it is at frequent intervals throughout the early years of British rule as a place in constant want of supplies and always on the verge of famine. On 1st December, 1803, an urgent call is made for fifteen thousand maunds of rice from Balasore. Again on 1st June, 1804, Captain Morgan is ordered to warn all pilgrims of the great scarcity of rice and cowries at Cuttack and to endeavour to induce them to supply themselves with provisions before entering the province."

Acquisition of Bundelkhand

Bundelkhand was under the suzerainty of the Peshwa to whom the local Raja, Shamsher Bahadur, paid tribute. The English got the Peshwa to cede to them the entire Bundelkhand region in exchange for two small areas, one in the south and the other near Surat, which had been earlier ceded to them under the Treaty of Bassein. But Raja Shamsher Bahadur did not agree to the Company becoming his suzerain. The English sent an expedition from Allahabad, under Col. Powell to subdue him. It crossed the Jumna and entered Bundelkhand on 6th September, 1803. Raja Shamsher Bahadur led out his army to fight the English, but his Commander, Gosain Himmat Bahadur, betrayed his master and went over to the English with the large body of troops under his command. On 13th October, there was a battle near the river Kayne between the combined English and Himmat Bahadur's troops and the remnants of Raja Shamsher Bahadur's army under his personal command. The latter was defeated and had to seek refuge in the country beyond the river Betwa. On 16th December, the Treaty of Bassein was modified to regularise the acquisition of Bundelkhand by the English and the Peshwa was made to sign the modified Treaty.

Invasion and Annexation of Koel-Aligarh by General Lake

The region comprising Aligarh, Delhi, Agra and their adjoining areas was, by then, only nominally under the Moghul Emperor's rule. The Sindhias had been for some time its *de facto* rulers. For the defence of the region Mahadji Sindhia had detailed an army under the command of a Frenchman, de Boigne. Later, another Frenchman, M. Perron, had succeeded de Boigne, and was in charge of the defence of the region on behalf of Doulatrao Sindhia.

On 7th August, 1803, General Lake left Cawnpore with an army for the conquest of this region and arrived on its border a fortnight later. The very next day, he very easily "conquered" Doulatrao Sindhia's border fortress of Koel. The ease with which he had taken the fortress was thus explained by Gen. Lake in his "private" letter to Marquess Wellesley, dated 29th August, 1803:

> "... some of his (M. Perron's) confederates left him the moment they heard of our approach, particularly the Jauts, and a few Sikhs ... Six officers of Perron's second brigade are just come in, having resigned service."

General Lake's objective after Koel was Aligarh. But on 1st September, 1803, he wrote to Marquess Wellesley from Koel:

> "I have not yet moved from hence nor am I in possession of the fort of Aligarh; my object is to get the troops out of the fort by bribery, which I flatter myself will be done ... The place is extremely strong, and if regularly besieged, will take a month at least ... Therefore, if by a little money, I can save the lives of these valuable men, Your Lordship will not think I have acted wrong, or been too lavish of cash." (General Lake's letter to Marquess Wellesley marked "private" dated Coel, September 1st, 1803)

It would, however, appear that with the exception of most of the European and some Indian officers, the vast majority of the defenders of the fort did not succumb to Gen. Lake's "bribery". General Lake attacked the fort on 4th September and we quote below from his report to the Governor-General made the same day from Aligarh:

> "As I told Your Lordship in my letter of the 1st instant, I had tried every method to prevail upon these people to give up the fort, and offered a very large sum of money, but they were determined to hold out, which they did most obstinately and, I may say, most gallantly ... I feel I shall be wanting in justice to the merits of Mr. Lucan, an officer, a native of Great Britain who lately quitted the service of Sindhia, to avoid serving against his country, were I not to recommend him to Your Lordship's particular attention.

> He gallantly undertook to ... point out the road through the fort ... received infinite benefit from his service ... it will afford me great satisfaction, if his services are rewarded by Government." (General Lake's letter to Marquess Wellesley, dated 4th September, 1803, from Aligarh)

So, Aligarh Fort fell to General Lake, but not before heavy losses had been inflicted on his army.

M. Perron

We have stated before that M. Perron was in command of the army detailed by Doulatrao Sindhia for the defence of the region which Gen. Lake later invaded. M. Perron's conduct throughout these operations would appear to have been enigmatic. When Gen. Lake started from Cawnpore, M. Perron was at Aligarh with a large army under his command. The Fort, too, was known to be well-nigh unconquerable and impregnable. According to Gen. Lake himself, it was extraordinarily strong. Yet, before Gen. Lake was anywhere near Aligarh, M. Perron left his command to a subordinate officer, M. Padronne, and went away towards Hathras. The historian Mill has stated that Perron could have, had he so desired, obtained from the English a very large sum of money had he handed over to them the large quantity of ammunition, military stores and equipmentwhich he had under his charge. But Perron did not do so. It has also been stated that Perron had lost the confidence of Doulatrao Sindhia, who had appointed and sent another commander to replace him. It is also a fact that most of the French and European officers under Perron had been won over by the English. Marquess Wellesley wrote in one of his letters: "M. Perron also observed that the treachery and ingratitude of his European officers convinced him that further resistance to the British arms was useless."

A hundred years later, on the occasion of the centenary celebrations of the Aligarh Fort, a writer in the *Pioneer* of Allahabad (dated 4th September 1904) stated:

> "It is asserted that he (Perron) had "savings" to a considerable extent invested in the funds of the East India Company."

After the fall of Aligarh Fort, M. Perron left Sindhia's service and went away. We leave it to our readers to judge him.

General Lake's March to Delhi

The Governor-General had written to Gen. Lake to attack after Aligarh, Doulatrao Sindhia's capital, Gwalior. Gen. Lake in his letter dated 12th September, 1803, detailed his reasons for not doing so. One reason apparently was that although secret overtures had been made to Ambajee, Doulatrao Sindhia's Army Commander at Gwalior, Ambajee had not till then agreed to betray his master. Also correspondence was then going on between the Governor-General and the Emperor Shah Alam. On 29th August, General Lake received at Koel a letter from the Moghul Emperor which made him decide to go to Delhi after he had taken Aligarh.

The fort at Kaunga was on his way to Delhi. He attacked and took it on 8th September, 1803. The same day he wrote a letter marked "private" to the Governor-General in which he said:

> "We arrived here (Kaunga) this morning; and found a very strong little fort, which would have caused delay and trouble had not the troops evacuated it the day after the fall of Aligarh ... I think when you hear the 'Secret' manner in which things have been conducted, you will be much pleased; it is quite a new work in the army, and has succeeded wonderfully well. I think to be very near Delhi in three marches."

There can hardly be any doubt that General Lake's "Secret" and "quite new work" which had "succeeded wonderfully well" was nothing else but deliberate subornation by bribery of the officers and men in Sindhia's army.

The Battle on the Bank of the Jumna

A strong force of Doulatrao Sindhia with heavy artillery was then stationed at Delhi. It was commanded by a Frenchman, de Burgoyne, who refused to be bought over. This force gave battle to General Lake's troops when the latter approached the river Jumna. The battle was bloody and fierce and General Lake lost a number of officers and men in action. But ultimately, Lake's "secret" work prevailed. As had happened before, neither steel nor gunpowder but gold and silver won the battle for him and got him the famous artillery of Doulatrao Sindhia. General Lake entered Delhi as a conqueror.

General Lake Takes Over Administration at Delhi

General Lake had an interview with the Emperor Shah Alam on 16th September, 1803. After the interview he took over the entire administration of Delhi that very day. The "Emperor" was deprived of all administrative authority and pensioned off. The Company left him little else but the utterly meaningless title of the "Emperor of India", and that was left only because the aid of the Emperor's name was needed by the Company. But as Major Archer has put it, "it was stealthy duplicity honouring him as long as it was found convenient". We quote Major Archer further:

> "The King has been shorn of his beams of royalty, his revenues have been seized and converted to the use of strangers, his authority everywhere abrogated but in his own immediate family; in short, he has lost all the rights, powers, and privileges, everything but the name of King and King, too, of Hindustan, for the munificent exchange of 12 lacs annually." (*Tours in Upper India* by Major Archer, Vol. I, pp. 126–27)

Colonel Ochterlony was appointed the English Resident at Delhi, as well as the Commander-in-chief of the Company's army there, consisting of a battalion and four companies of Indian and a battalion of Mewati soldiers. Such European officers in Doulatrao Sindhia's army as had deserted and come over to the English were also absorbed in the Company's army at Delhi.

Occupation of the Fort at Agra

On 24th September, General Lake left Delhi for Agra. Thefe were several indecisive skirmishes with Sindhia's garrison at the Fort, but, thanks to General Lake's "secret work", some 2,500 men of the garrison evacuated the Fort and joined his troops. The rest of the garrison surrendered the Fort on 17th October on condition that they and their belongings were given safe conduct out of it, and through the beseigers' camp.

The Battle of Laswari

The last stand by Sindhia's army in the North against General Lake was at Laswari, between Agra and Gwalior. On 27th October, General Lake left Agra on his march to Gwalior. A letter written by him the next day shows that at that time, he had already started his "secret work" in Sindhia's army which barred his way to Gwalior and was a formidable obstacle. It had been reinforced by contingents from the South as also by the Maratha troops defeated at Delhi who had made good their escape. It was also equipped with a number of heavy and most up-to-date pieces of artillery. The two armies joined in a fierce battle at Laswari which was described thus by General Lake:

> "These fellows fought like devils, or rather heroes, and had we not made a disposition for attack in a style that we should have done against the most formidable army we could have been opposed to, I verily believe, from the position they had taken, we might have failed.
>
> ***

> ... "If they had been commanded by French officers, the event would have been, I fear, extremely doubtful. I never was in so severe a business in my life or anything like it, and pray to God I never may be in such a situation again." (General Lake's letter marked "secret", dated 2nd November, to Marquess Wellesley)

Just at the moment when defeat was staring General Lake in the face, the leaders of the Maratha army deserted their posts and went over to the enemy. The "secret work" had once again won for General Lake another of the decisive battles fought by the English in India.

Plans for Conquest of Gwalior

There were, however, two more obstacles to be got over before the English could write "finis" to the power of Doulatrao Sindhia. One was the conquest of the latter's capital, Gwalior, and the other was the defeat and demolition of Sindhia's re-doubtable cavalry, which constituted most of his military strength. Ambajee was in charge of the defence of Gwalior.

After his "victory" at Laswari, General Lake on 2nd November, 1803, wrote to Marquess Wellesley:

> "I feel happy in having accomplished all your wishes, except Gwalior, which I trust we shall get possession of by treaty with Ambajee; the fall of these brigades will bring him to terms immediately."
>
> Next day General Lake wrote again:
>
> "I shall, as soon as I can move my wounded men, begin my march towards that doubtful character, Ambajee, but I shall in the first instance proceed but slowly, as I wish to impress the Raja of Jeypore with an idea, that, if he does not come to terms shortly, I may pay him a visit. All I mean by this is to alarm him into some decisive measure;

> he seems at present to be playing a very suspicious game." (Lake's letter to Governor-General marked "private" dated November 3rd, 1803)

General Lake failed to buy Ambajee but his alarming tactics did succeed with the Maharaja of Jaipur who succumbed to his threats. On 14th November, General Lake wrote a "private and most secret" letter to the Governor-General, in which he said:

> "It (the victory at Laswari) had brought the Raja of Jeypore and all his *wicked and traitorous advisers* to reason, they are now upon their march to my camp." (Italics ours)

We have italicised the terms in which Lake has referred to those whom he had bribed and won, as indicative of his contempt for them. But even after Jaipur had sided with him, General Lake hesitated and did not venture to attack Gwalior.

The English Conclude Peace with Sindhia and Bhonsle

Both sides were now tired of war and wanted peace. Marquess Wellesley wanted to crush completely both Sindhia and Bhonsle. But that appeared impossible. His brother, Major-General Wellseley had already plainly admitted his "incapacity to do Sindhia further injury". Also the English had till then spent quite a fortune in bribes.

Overtures for peace were made and in December, 1803, a peace treaty was entered into by the English with Maharaja Doulatrao Sindhia of Gwalior and Raja Raghoji Bhonsle of Berar, whereby the Company became entitled to annex to its territory the very fertile regions which it had "conquered" from both.

Later, in February, 1804, Doulatrao Sindhia had to enter into the Subsidiary Alliance with the Company, similar to the one between the Peshwa and the Company, against which he had struggled so hard for years. Under it, the Company's Subsidiary

Army, officered by Englishmen in the Company's service and maintained entirely at Sindhia's cost, was stationed in his territory.

Thus ended the first phase of the Second Maratha War. Its achievements exceeded the expectations of Marquess Wellesley, as no other war had till then expanded so much the English Empire in India.

25

Battles Between the English and Jaswantrao Holkar

General Wellesley's Tempting Promises

We have earlier dealt briefly with the mission on which Gen. Wellesley had sent a special emissary, Qadir Nawaz Khan, to Jaswantrao Holkar, with lavish promises made to the latter, by the emissary on behalf of Gen. Wellesley. Thereafter, Gen. Wellesley himself wrote to Jaswantrao Holkar several letters under instructions from the Governor-General in which definite promises were made to the effect that if Jaswantrao Holkar abstained from helping Sindhia and Bhonsle, he would be given 12 districts between the Ganges and the Jumna, Bundelkhand and some districts in the south and regions in the north. The writing of these letters has been admitted in the published letters of the Wellesley brothers. Jaswantrao Holkar trusted the English promises and carried out his part of the bargain. It has been admitted by Gen. Wellesley and Gen. Lake in their letters, that had Jaswantrao Holkar gone to Sindhia's help, it would have been impossible for Gen. Wellesley to win the battles at Assye and Argaon, and for Gen. Lake to have been successful at Agra or victorious at Laswari.

The English Attitude After the War

After the war with Sindhia and Bhonsle, Jaswantrao Holkar sent to Gen. Lake copies of the above-mentioned letters which Gen. Wellesley had written to him and requested performance of the promises made therein. Gen. Lake forwarded these copies to the Governor-General with a covering "private" letter, dated 28th December 1803, and asked for instructions. In reply, Marquess Wellesley on 17th January, 1804 wrote to Gen. Lake a letter marked "secret" from which we quote some extracts:

"The letters of which Jaswantrao Holkar has transmitted copies to Your Excellency must have been forwarded to Holkar by Major-General Wellesley in his own name. I have not addressed any letter to Jaswantrao Holkar, but Major General Wellesley was authorised by my instructions of the 26th June, to open an amicable negotiation with that chieftain.

***

"It is now expedient to decide the course to be pursued with respect to Jaswantrao Holkar ... it is my intention that Your Excellency should immediately open a negotiation with Jaswantrao Holkar.

***

"The authority exercised by Jaswantrao Holkar ... over the possessions of the Holkar family is manifestly an usurpation of the rights of Kashirao Holkar, the legitimate heir and successor of Tukoje Holkar. Consistently, therefore, with the principles of justice, no arrangement can be proposed between the British Government and Jaswantrao Holkar, involving a sanction of the exclusion of Kashirao Holkar from his hereditary dominions.

"Under the sanction of His Highness the Peshwa's authority, the British Government would be justified in adopting measures for the limitation of Jaswantrao Holkar's power, and for the restoration of Kashirao Holkar's rights; either by force or compromise ... it may be expected that His Highness would readily concur in a proposition for the restoration of Kashirao, and for the punishment of Jaswantrao Holkar ...

"The enterprising spirit, military character and ambitious views of Jaswantrao Holkar render the reduction of his power a desirable object with reference to the complete establishment of tranquillity in India.

***

> "An Immediate attempt ... to restore Kashirao Holkar to his hereditary rights would involve more positive and certain difficulty and danger than could be justly apprehended from the continuance of Jaswantrao Holkar in the possession of the territories actually under his authority. A pacific conduct towards Jaswantrao Holkar, in the present moment, will not preclude the future restoration of Kashirao Holkar to the possession of his hereditary rights ... It will be necessary, however, to regulate our proceedings with respect to Jaswantrao Holkar in such a manner as to avoid any acknowledgement and confirmation of the legitimacy of his dominion ... leave Jaswantrao Holkar in the exercise of his present authority ... Your Excellency is authorised to enter into a negotiation with Jaswantrao Holkar ... Jaswantrao Holkar ... will anxiously solicit the countenance and favour of our Government."

What Marquess Wellesley now condemned as "an usurpation" by Jaswantrao Holkar "of the rights of Kashirao Holkar, the legitimate heir and successor of Tukoje Holkar", had been accomplished, it will be recalled, at the instigation and with the active help of the Marquess himself. His solicitude for Kashirao's restoration would, therefore, appear to be nothing more than a pretext for the "punishment" of Jaswantrao Holkar and the "reduction of his power".

It is noteworthy that about a month earlier, General Wellesley had pressed for war against Jaswantrao Holkar. In a letter written by him on 12th December, 1803, from "Camp before Gauregarh" to Major Shawe, the Governor-General's Private Secretary, he had said:

> "... unless we make war upon Holkar, and deprive the Peshwa of his territories, we shall not succeed in driving the Marhattas entirely from these countries, although the Sindhia should cede his rights."

General Lake's Activities

General Lake too had wanted war on Jaswantrao Holkar, but Marquess Wellesley did not consider that the time was yet opportune, and so had instructed Lake to adopt a "pacific attitude" towards Jaswantrao Holkar and "to enter into a negotiation with him". Accordingly Lake desired Jaswantrao Holkar to send his representatives (*Vakils*). The *Vakils* duly arrived and on 18th March, 1804, presented to Lake a list of Jaswantrao Holkar's claims, which contained nothing more than what General Wellesley had promised in his letters.

But Lake had only been marking time and using his "secret" methods. As the historian Grant Duff has stated in his book (page 586), Lake had made secret overtures to three European officers in Jaswantrao Holkar's army, namely, Captains Vickers, Todd and Ryan, who were willing to desert and go over to the English. But before they could do so, their intentions were discovered. They were court-martialled immediately, sentenced to death and executed.

Lake had been busy otherwise too. He had advanced, in February 1804, to the northern border of Jaswantrao Holkar's territory, and barred the only way to and from that direction. Early in April 1804, he had dispatched three battalions towards Jaipur to coerce the Raja of Jaipur into an alliance with the English against Jaswantrao Holkar. He further got hold of some letters stated to have been written by Jaswantrao Holkar to some Hindu and Mussalman princes, in which the former appealed to the latter to combine with him in opposing the English. As borne out by the Indian history of that period, the English were invariably able to produce such "disloyal" letters alleged to have been written by any Indian prince whom they wanted to crush. It would appear to be too much of a coincidence. Anyway, General Lake sent these letters to the Governor-General on 4th April, 1804, and informed the latter that he proposed to post his troops on all the strategic points along Jaswantrao Holkar's northern border.

In the meantime, Jaswantrao Holkar had on 27th March, 1804, written again to Lake politely but firmly pressing for peaceful negotiations for a settlement and asking for Lake's proposals for the same. On 4th April, 1804, Lake sent an arrogant answer asserting that Jaswantrao Holkar's claims were utterly groundless and that the latter should know that even the entertainment of such claims was derogatory to the power and prestige of the British Government. It was manifestly intended to convey to Jaswantrao Holkar that war against him was inevitable.

On 16th April, 1804, Marquess Wellesley replied to Lake's letter of the 4th, saying that he (Marquess Wellesley) had decided on war against Jaswantrao Holkar to be waged "as soon as possible".

General Lake Foiled

General Lake at last got what he had been eagerly waiting for. But he was soon to discover that he had bitten off more than he could chew. For two reasons he had been confident of an easier victory over Jaswantrao Holkar than he had had over Doulatrao Sindhia. One was his "secret" method which he expected to be as successful as ever in winning over officers and men in the enemy camp. But he had not realised that the court-martial and execution of the three European officers in Jaswantrao Holkar's army had made it impossible for him to find potential traitors in that army. The second ground on which his hopes of an easy victory were founded was the projected invasion of Jaswantrao Holkar's territory from the south by General Wellesley.

On 16th April, 1804, Marquess Wellesley instructed General Wellesley to invade from the south the Chandore region in Jaswantrao Holkar's territory. But General Wellesley wrote to Major Malcolm on 20th April, 1804: ... I dare not move my troops from the south." So the second ground, too, on which Lake had founded his hopes, crumbled to dust. The reasons which had led General Wellesley to decide against moving his army from the south were more than one. According to Mill Vol. I p. 401, General Wellesley wrote that it was impossible for him to invade Chandore before the rains set in because there was likely to be an utter lack of supplies of provisions and fodder on the long way to that region and the march of his army would be full of risks. There was another danger, too, to which General Wellesley had drawn attention in his letter dated 17th March, 1804, to General Stuart in which he had stated:

> "Once our army leaves the south for the north, scores of Holkars will be up in arms against us in the territories of the Peshwa and Nizam making it extremely difficult for our army to pass unscathed through the hilly tracts between the rivers Narbada and Tapti."

General Wellesley had, therefore, pressed Lake to start the war himself by attacking Jaswantrao Holkar's territory from the north. But Lake too was faced with similar difficulties and so a stalemate ensued.

Violations of the Treaty with Sindhia

The English had counted on the help of Doulatrao Sindhia and his Subsidiary Army in their projected war against Jaswantrao Holkar. The English intrigues had succeeded, some time earlier, in sowing and nurturing seeds of dissension and distrust between Sindhia and Holkar which they had intended to take advantage of when a suitable opportunity presented itself. Accordingly, on the very day that he conveyed to Lake his decision in favour of war "as soon as possible." Marquess Wellesley also wrote to the British Resident at Sindhia's *Durbar,* and instructed him to prevail upon Sindhia to send his troops in support of the English invasion of Holkar's territory. Doulatrao Sindhia, however, was extremely dissatisfied with the way in which the English were flouting the terms of the Treaty which they had so recently made with him.

Under the Treaty, the Fort at Gwalior and the territory of the Raja of Gohad were to be under the exclusive control and authority of Sindhia. But Marquess Wellesley was keen on keeping the Fort and the Gohad territory in the possession of the Company, and had his eyes on them for a long time. We quote from General Wellesley's letter to Major Malcolm dated 17th March 1804:

> "The fair way of considering this question is, that a treaty broken is in the same state as one never made; and when that principle is applied to this case, it will be found that Sindhia, to whom the possessions belonged before the treaty was made, and by whom they have not been ceded by the treaty of peace, or by any other instrument, ought to have them.
>
> "In respect of the policy of the question ... What brought me through many difficulties in the war and the negotiations for peace? British good faith, and nothing else."

Marquess Wellesley, however, completely ignored the principle of fairplay as also the letter and spirit of the treaty, and directed General Lake to take by force possession of the Fort and the Gohad territory and to hold the same under the Company's authority. General Lake complied and General Wellesley commented on it as follows:

> "I am disgusted beyond measure with the whole concern; ... All parties were delighted with the peace, but the demon of ambition appears now to have pervaded all." (General Wellesley to Major Malcolm, 13th April, 1804)

The reason why Marquess Wellesley could perpetrate this act of high-handedness with impunity may be found in the following extract from General Wellesley's letter dated 26th February, 1804, to Major Shawe (Private Secretary to the Governor-General):

> "... we have got such a hold in his *Darbar* ... that if ever he goes to war with the Company, one half of his chiefs and of his army will be on our side."

Evidently, Sindhia knew this and could do little more than continue to press his just claims.

Doulatrao Sindhia had yet another grievance relating to the violation of the Treaty by the English. Some of his *Purgunnahs,* like Kumargunda, Jamgaon, etc., adjoined Ahmednagar. As mentioned before, the English had possessed themselves of the Ahmednagar Fort. The Treaty provided that Sindhia was to station in these *Purgunnahs* no more than a specified number of his troops. It was also provided that in case the people or the *Zamindars* of these *Purgunnahs* created any trouble against Sindhia or the latter's local *Tehsildars* encountered difficulties in the collection of revenue, then at the request of the *Tehsildars,* the Company's commandant at the Ahmednagar Fort would send out troops to put down the trouble and to help in the collection of Sindhia's revenues. But when serious trouble did break out repeatedly, the English would not give the agreed help when asked for. They even refused to let Sindhia send his own troops to quell the trouble by confronting him with the provision of the Treaty. Sindhia repeatedly complained to the Governor-General and to General Lake but both evaded taking any action.

A Sop to Soothe Sindhia

Marquess Wellesley had realised that in view of the strained relations, Sindhia could hardly be willing to help the English against Holkar. Consequently, when he wrote, on 16th April, 1804 to the British Resident with Sindhia, he instructed the Resident to assure Sindhia that:

> "... It is not his (Marquess Wellesley's) intention, in the event of the reduction of Holkar's power, to take any share of the possessions of the Holkar family for the company. Chandore, and its dependencies and vicinity, will probably be given to the Peshwa; and the other possessions of Holkar situated to the southward of the Godawari to the Subedar of Deccan; all the remainder of the possessions of Holkar will accrue to Sindhia, provided he shall exert himself in the reduction of Jaswantrao Holkar." (Mill, Vol. VI, Chapter XIII)

Readers will no doubt notice the complete absence of Kashirao Holkar's name from amongst the proposed sharers of Jaswantrao Holkar's possessions, although Marquess Wellesley had declared that the restoration of Kashirao's "rights and hereditary possessions" was the chief aim and objective of the projected war against Jaswantrao Holkar.

Ultimately, Sindhia agreed to join the English, either because he could not resist the tempting offer made by the English of "all the remainer of the possessions of Holkar" or because he could see no other safe alternative.

War Started Against Jaswantrao Holkar—English Reverses

Sindhia despatched two expeditions to invade Jaswantrao Holkar's province of Malwa. These were commanded by Bapurao Sindhia and Jean Baptiste Filose. The latter occupied Ashta, Sehore, Bhilsa and other undefended places in Holkar's territory. General Wellesley directed Col. Murray who was then in Gujarat to march with his own and Gaikwad's forces on Holkar's capital of Indore.

General Wellesley himself started from Bombay to invest Chandore, but had to return because of the difficulties he encountered on his line of march.

Col. Murray, too, could not make any headway against Holkar. General Lake had been busy for some months with his old "secret" method. We have mentioned before Holkar's *Pindari* Chief, Ameer (Meer) Khan. On 2nd March, 1804, General Wellesley had written to Major Malcolm from Poona: "Mercer is in treaty with Meerkhan; and if he should draw him off from Holkar, there is an end of the latter."

Ameer Khan's subsequent behaviour had, however, excited the suspicions of the English, and they no longer considered him to be absolutely reliable. Further, Jaswantrao Holkar's alertness leading to the court-martial and execution of the three European would-be deserters from his army had thrown a spanner into the underground machinery of General Lake's "secret" machinations and had thus doomed to failure his future efforts for the subornation of Holkar's officers and men.

The set-back completely disheartened Lake and on 12th May, 1804, he wrote privately to the Governor-General counselling the cessation of the war with Holkar. But the initiative had already passed out of the hands of the English. Some time earlier, Lake had arrogantly informed Jaswantrao Holkar that the British Government and its allies had decided to destroy his power. Jaswantrao Holkar could not possibly ignore the threat. He immediately ordered an attack on the English troops under Col. Fawcett which were then in Bundelkhand. The attack was carried out by some 5,000 of Holkar's *Pindari* horsemen on the night of 21st May, 1804. Col. Fawcett has recorded the fact that the English had been forewarned by their spies of the impending attack, and had stationed a detachment of troops to oppose it at the village of Kooch. What happened there is described in *Wellesley's Despatches* (IV, pp. 72–73):

> "... the detachment in the village, consisting of two companies of sepoys, fifty European artillery, fifty gun luscurs with two 12-pounders, two howitzers, one 6-pounder, and 12 tumbrils, were entirely taken by the enemy, and the men and officers all cut to pieces."

Col. Fawcett was only a short distance from the field of battle and had with him four battalions of sepoys and 450 European soldiers but did not intervene. He was later dismissed for dereliction of duty.

The Governor-General, unaware till then of the English disaster at Kooch, had on 25th May, 1804, acted upon General Lake's advice and instructed Lake and Wellesley as also the Governors of Madras and Bombay, to cease operations against Jaswantrao Holkar. Before receiving these instructions, Lake had written to the Governor-General on 28th May, 1804, informing him of what had happened at Kooch. On 8th June, 1804, the Governer-General replied to General Lake as follows:

> "... the honour of the British arms has been discharged, and the interests of the British Government hazarded ... It is difficult to calculate the extent of the evil consequences which may result from this unparalleled accident ... In consequence of the state of affairs in Bundelkhand, it appears to be necessary to apprise Your Excellency of my opinion that the arrangements stated in my instructions of the 25th May, 1804, must be postponed, and every possible effort and exertion must be made to reduce Jaswantrao Holkar, and the predatory chiefs connected with him."

The cessation of war was thus postponed. About a week earlier, the Governor-General had recalled General Wellesley from the south and replaced him by Col. Wallace as the Commander of the Company's forces in the south.

The English had so far only one small success. General Lake had sent an expedition under Col. Dawn to take Holkar's fort at Tonk Rampura. The fort fell to Col. Dawn on 16th May, 1804, very probably with the connivance of Ameer Khan, who was later made by the English the hereditary Nawab of Tonk.

Fresh Plans for Invasion

It was now planned to invade Holkar's territory from three directions and three forces were assembled for the purpose. The largest was in the north under Lake, the second was in the south under Col. Wallace and the third was in Gujarat under Col. Murray.

Lake despatched an expeditionary force under Col. Monson to invade Holkar's territory from the north. It was composed of five battalions of sepoys, some 3,000 horsemen, artillery and Sindhia's Subsidiary Army. At about the same time, he directed Col. Murray to advance from Gujarat with his and Gaikwad's Subsidiary Army, and invade Holkar's territory from the west. Lake's plan was that the two forces under Col. Monson and Col. Murray were to meet inside Holkar's territory and then jointly to attack and crush Holkar.

Sindhia's Subsidiary Army had joined Col. Monson's force. But Marquess Wellesley did not consider it enough and demanded an additional force from Sindhia to join in the war. Sindhia was by then in financial straits and requested the English for a loan to equip the additional force. The loan was refused and Sindhia had to provide the additional force. It consisted of six or seven battalions of infantry and 10,000 horsemen and was commanded by Bapuji Sindhia and Sadashivrao. It joined Col. Monson's force in due time. Sindhia had naturally expected that thereafter, Col. Monson would arrange for its supplies of provisions, etc., and the English would bear the cost. Accordingly, he requested Lake and Col. Monson, but both ignored the requests. Consequently, when Bapuji Sindhia could not get any help from the English in obtaining supplies, he sent a detachment of his force under Sadashivrao, to get supplies and himself stayed on with Col. Monson with the rest of his force.

Col. Murray's Advance

As directed, Col. Murray marched on Ujjain (Malwa) for the second time. But he encountered insurmountable difficulties in getting any supplies on his way and was, ultimately, left with only two days' provisions in hand. Consequently, he had to turn back towards Gujarat once again.

Col. Monson's March

On 1st July, 1804, Col. Monson entered Holkar's territory at the head of a large force. Then he advanced towards the Chambal river after taking the small fortress at Hinglasgarh. On 7th July, 1804, when he had advanced some 50 miles beyond the Mucundra Pass, he learned that Jaswantrao Holkar had already crossed the Chambal river and was rapidly marching towards him. At the same time, he received news of Col. Murray's return to Gujarat. He had also seen for himself that the people in the countryside along his line of march had been extremely unfriendly to the English and partial to Holkar. He, therefore, hated the march.

The First Encounter

On 8th July, 1804, Monson's and Holkar's forces confronted each other. Monson sent Lt. Lucan with the cavalry to the front line and also sent Bapuji Sindhia with his horsemen in support of Lucan. The two attacked the advancing force of Holkar. A sharp but short clash of arms followed during which some of Lucan's horsemen, it is alleged, went over to Holkar. The rest were wiped off by Holkar's horsemen and Lucan was taken prisoner. Readers will recall Lucan as the Englishman in Sindhia's service who had betrayed his master at Aligarh. Bapuji's horsemen, too, sustained heavy losses and some 700 of them were wounded and disabled. Bapuji lost most of his stores and equipment and retreated to join Monson who had stayed in the rear with his infantry throughout the engagement. He had enough men under him to fight and check the advancing Holkar, but, apparently, lost his nerve completely and beat a hasty retreat, stopping in his headlong flight only when he had reached the border on 9th July, 1804.

Pursuit and Rout of Monson's Force

Jaswantrao Holkar followed in hot pursuit and on 11th July, 1804, caught up with Monson's force on his border. He attacked the latter immediately and Monson had to flee again, leaving behind him numberless dead and wounded. He reached Kotah the next day after a whole night's march. He had hopes of succour from Zalim Singh, Raja of Kotah, but the latter flatly refused to help and Monson was forced to be on the run again. He now proposed to pass through the State of Bundi and cross the river Chambal to reach Rampura, which as stated before, had been occupied by the English on 16th May, 1804. But the Chambal was in high flood and Monson found it extremely difficult to cross over. By 15th July, his artillery had got stuck in the marshy approaches to the river and could not be extricated. His provisions, too, were almost exhausted and he was unable to collect any supplies from the neighbouring villages. In utter despair, he blew up his ammunition and after putting his guns out of action he left them with the Raja of Bundi, who though not unfriendly, was yet unable to render much help. Anyhow Monson managed to cross the Chambal and reached another river the Chameli on 17th July. The Chameli was also in flood and it took ten days' time to get his force across it. Throughout the retreat, some of Holkar's horsemen, who had arrived in Kotah, continuously harassed his force by sporadic attacks in which hundreds of his men were killed. Many more were drowned or died of an epidemic. Had Jaswantrao Holkar caught up with Monson at that stage, he could have easily wiped off his entire force, but luck seemed to have favoured Monson in the form of continuous heavy rains, which apparently hampered Holkar's movements, and thus Monson was able to reach Rampura with the exhausted fragments of his army on 29th July.

General Lake, in his letter of 21st July has stated that so far as numbers were concerned there was not much difference between the forces of Col. Monson and Jaswantrao Holkar. He has indicated in that letter that he (Gen. Lake) was still busy with his "secret" methods in Jaswantrao Holkar's army.

The reaction of the Governor-General to Col. Monson's failure is set forth in the following extracts from his "most secret and confidential" Notes to Lake dated 28th July, 1804.

> "By a letter just received (half past 4 o'clock p.m.) from Lieut. Colonel Lake to Captain Armstrong, dated 20th July, it appears that Colonel Monson's detachment was retreating before Holkar, and had quitted the Mucundra Pass.
>
> "This is a most painful state of affairs. Nothing can retrieve our character but the most vigorous effort. I fear that all our exertions will now be too late to recover all we have lost.
>
> "The despatches received today seem to leave no hope of success unless the Commander-in-Chief can again take the field in person, and attack Holkar with vigour ...".

We also quote from a subsequent "private" letter written by Marquess Wellesley to General Lake dated 17th August, 1804:

> "Since the date of my last notes, it appears that Colonel Monson's detachment has retired altogether from Malwah with loss of guns, camp equipage, etc., and in great distress."

Bapuji Sindhia's Defection

We have mentioned before that Bapuji Sindhia was in the forefront and had suffered heavy losses in the two engagements with Holkar on the 8th and 11th July. He was still with Monson when the latter reached the Chambal river from Kotah on the 14th July. When Monson had started sending his men across the river in boats, Bapuji Sindhia had asked him to send back the boats to enable him (Bapuji Sindhia) and his force also to get across. For some reason, Col. Monson did not send back the boats and Bapuji Sindhia's force was stranded.

Monson's failure to send back the boats was of a piece with his earlier behaviour towards Bapuji Sindhia throughout the campaign. Bapuji Sindhia had no other alternative but to turn back to Kotah. Near Kotah he was surrounded by Holkar's force. Bapuji Sindhia was now entirely at Holkar's mercy. His men had not been paid for a very long time and were seething with discontent, the more so, because of the shortage of rations. They and Raja Zalim Singh of Kotah prevailed upon him to go over to Holkar. This he did, with the force under his command.

General Lake's Help to Col. Monson

Col. Monson had reached Rampura on 29th July, 1804. Lake immediately sent him reinforcements and directed him to sally forth from Rampura and attack Holkar. But Monson did not venture to advance from Rampura for about a month and when he did leave, he went towards Kushalgarh (in Jaipur State), instead of going forward to attack Holkar. The reason may have been that another commander of Sindhia, Sadashivraobhau Bhaskar was at Kushalgarh, with six battalions and 21 guns and Monson hoped to get substantial help from him.

Col. Monson Defeated Again

But Jaswantrao Holkar had not given up his pursuit of Monson. The day after the latter left Rampura, Jaswantrao Holkar came up with his cavalry and encamped near the river Bannas. Monson sent a part of his force and some equipment across the river Bannas and himself stayed behind to give battle to Jaswantrao Holkar. In the engagement that followed, he appeared to be winning in its initial stages, but was, eventually, defeated and made good his escape to Kushalgarh, where he arrived on the night of 25th August.

Col. Monson's Flight to Agra

Col. Monson had hoped that Sadashivraobhau Bhaskar would side with the English and give him substantial help. Sadashivraobhau Bhaskar, however, took his cue from Sindhia and his Commanders, who were, by then quite fed up with the English. Monson did not find Kushalgarh safe enough and left the very next day for Agra. Holkar's horsemen harassed him on the way and there were several skirmishes, but he succeeded in reaching Agra on 31st August.

Failure of Plan to Check Jaswantrao Holkar

Jaswantrao Holkar had driven out of his territory in the north the Company's invading army. The English had, thereafter, feared an invasion of their territory by him. Preparations were immediately made to check him. The Company's detachments stationed at Delhi, Agra and Muttra were considerably re-inforced and all the ways leading to these places were heavily guarded. In addition, three other detachments, one in Bundelkhand, another (Sindhia's Subsidiary Army) at Ujjain and the third on Gujarat's border under Col. Murray were alerted to be ready to invade Holkar's territory on that side. Marquess Wellesley felt quite confident that his plan would make it impossible for Jaswantrao Holkar to invade the Company's territory anywhere. But the plan failed in the north.

After Col. Monson's flight to Agra, Jaswantrao Holkar broke through the cordon flung round him and attacked the Company's territory of Muttra. He defeated the Company's defending force which beat a hasty retreat and took possession of the territory. He was in a position to march on to Delhi, but serious difficulties, which will be related later, prevented him until it was too late.

Consequences of Col. Monson's Retreats

Never before had "the honour of the British arms been disgraced" to such an extent except perhaps in the First Maratha War. The invincibility of the British arms was now an exploded myth in the whole of India. It was demonstrated, too, that the military successes of the English till then had not been due to their superior equipment, valour or expert knowledge of warfare as compared with those of the Indians, but to the "secret" methods of intrigue, bribery and corruption resorted to by them. These had been successful so far as Sindhia and Bhonsle were concerned, but had failed miserably in the case of Holkar whose men could not be bought over at any price and whose people refused to co-operate with the English in any shape or form.

The heavy losses inflicted on the English in the repeated reverses and retreats which marked the seven weeks of Monson's march from Mucundra Pass to Agra have thus been described by Gen. Lake:

"I will not at present say anything more upon this disgraceful and disastrous event, as my feelings are for many reasons too much agitated to enter into the misfortunes and causes of them. A finer detachment never marched, and sorry I am to say, that if this account of Lieutenant Anderson is correct, I have lost five battalions and six companies, the flower of the army, and how they are to be replaced at this day, God only knows. I have to lament also the loss of some of the finest young men and most promising in the army." (Gen. Lake's "private" letter to the Governor-General dated 2nd September, 1804)

General Wellesley's comment was: "I tremble at the political consequences of that event."

The Governor-General wrote back to Lake on 11th September, 1804:

"We must endeavour rather to retrieve than to blame what is past, and under your auspices. I entertain no doubt of success. Time, however, is the main consideration. Every hour that shall be left to this plunderer will be marked by some calamity; we must expect a general defection of the allies, and even confusion in our own territories, unless we attack Holkar's main force immediately with decisive success ... I perfectly agree with you that the first object must be the defeat of Holkar's infantry in the field, and to take his guns; ... Holkar defeated, all alarm and danger will instantly vanish. You will also take every step for confirming our allies, and for encouraging desertion from Holkar by renewing the proclamation of last year; or by other encouragements."

Jaswantrao Holkar had by now developed into as much of a "terror" for the English as Haider Ali or Tipu Sultan had been. "Plunderer" was not the only epithet by which they referred to him. "Monster", "murderer", "devil" and "robber" were some of the others by which Lake and the Governor-General often referred to him in their letters to each other. Not much water had flowed down the Hooghly since the Governor-General used to write complimentary and even flattering letters to Jaswantrao Holkar and had made lavish promises to him in return for his help against Sindhia which the Governor-General solicited and Holkar gave. These promises had been, as stated before, repudiated, and Jaswantrao Holkar's defeat and destruction had now become the Governor-General's "first object".

With reference to the last paragraph of the above-quoted letter of the Governor-General, Lake on 22nd September, 1804, reported to the following effect:

> "The men in Holkar's forces are strange. Some of them express their willingness to come over to us and they will be taken in if they do. But I can put very little trust in what they say. If disaffection against Holkar can anyhow be created amongst them, it could be useful to us. Efforts will, therefore, be made to incite them against Holkar."

The Governor-General had good reasons to fear "a general defection of the allies", namely, the Indian rulers who had till then helped the English. Besides Sindhia, other Indian rulers, too, no longer trusted "British good faith" or British promises.

Efforts to Win Over Raja of Bharatpur

The Raja of Bharatpur was one of the principal tributaries of Sindhia. It will be recalled that in 1803, the neutrality of Raja Ranjit Singh of Bharatpur in the war against Sindhia and Bhonsle had been secured by the English by a treaty, whereby, in return for the help to the English, the latter had promised to exempt the Raja from all future payments of the tribute. The Raja had, therefore, abstained from giving any help to Sindhia and Bhonsle, when the English attacked them.

This time, too, the Governor-General tried to enlist the Raja of Bharatpur's support against Jaswantrao Holkar, and on 22nd August, 1804, wrote to Lake to the following effect:

"I hereby authorise and direct you to assure the Raja of Bharatpur in the clearest possible terms that the British Government had decided to observe and carry out, at the specified time, all the terms of their existing treaty with him. You are further to assure him that the accusations against the British Government about the latter's intentions to interfere in the internal administration of his state, or to bring under the civil or criminal jurisdiction of the Company's courts, any part of his territory, or his army, or to violate any of the terms of the treaty, were utterly groundless and had been manufactured by villains."

But it was difficult to dupe the Raja, as according to Mill, the accusations against the English were not entirely groundless (Mill, Vol. VI, p. 420).

The Raja saw through the assurances given to him. He considered them to be a mere eye-wash calculated to enlist his help against Jaswantrao Holkar or, at least, to secure his neutrality. Also he was aware of the underground intrigues carried on by the English in his own state to overthrow his rule and establish their own over his state and people. The deciding factor which led to his joining Holkar was, however, the number of the English atrocities to which the people of the Doab region had been subjected ever since the English had seized that region from Sindhia about a year or so earlier.

The region was situated between the Ganges and the Jumna, and was near the Bharatpur territory. Its population was almost entirely Hindu. After seizing it, the Governor-General had placed it under the direct civil and revenue administration of General Lake.

Lake's Administration of the Doab

Doab was a fertile and prosperous region, populated by flourishing agriculturists. Lake started fleecing them and even extorting money from them in every possible way and under any pretext that served. The land revenue and taxes were increased to such an extent that the farmers and cultivators were left with even less than what they needed for they barest necessities. They were already groaning under the intolerable burden of exactions and levies, when their religious susceptibilities were grossly wounded by the wholesale slaughter of cows to provide beef for the English soldiers of the Company. Even the holy Mathura was not spared that ignominious sacrilege. The Hindu Jat Raja of Bharatpur was shocked beyond measure and was furiously indignant. The people of Doab elected and appointed him as their leader and protector against the English atrocities. They also extended their whole-hearted support to Jaswantrao Holkar. Negotiations were started for a United Front of the people of Doab with the Raja of Bharatpur and Jaswantrao Holkar against the English.

Lake came to know of the situation as it had developed and the knowledge made him keener than ever to destroy the independence of the Raja of Bharatpur, so that the Doab people may be left without an able and honest leader, thereby reducing the chances of any help to Jaswantrao Holkar by the Raja of Bharatpur or by the people of Doab.

Holkar Loses Malwa and the Southern Regions

Whilst Jaswantrao Holkar was continuing his triumphant march in the north, his Malwa and southern territories were invaded by the Company's forces under Col. Murray and Col. Wallace, respectively.

Ever since he had been given the assignment to march on Jaswantrao Holkar's capital, Indore, Col. Murray had been busy with Lake's "secret" methods. He had solicited instructions from the Governor-General "relative to the extent to which he might be permitted to encourage desertion among the adherents of Jaswantrao Holkar, and to offer them employment in the service of the allies." (Despatch of the Governor-General-in-Council to the Secret Committee, dated 24th March, 1805.) It will be recalled that Murray had to stop his march to Indore twice before, and to turn back towards Gujarat. By the time he made his third attempt, his "secret" methods had succeeded and so he reached and occupied Ujjain within three days "without any resistance" (*ibid*). He established his headquarters at Ujjain from where he raided and occupied the entire Malwa province as also Jaswantrao Holkar's capital Indore.

In the south, Wallace, who flad succeeded General Wellesley, started from Poona to invade Jaswantrao Holkar's southern territory and crossed the Godavri river on 18th Septemttor, 1804. Ten or twelve days later, he received reinforcements. In the beginning of October, the Peshwa's own army joined him. Within a month Wallace seized Chandore and a number of Jaswantrao Holkar's forts to the south of the Tapi river.

News of these losses reached Jaswantrao Holkar at Mathura so he gave top priority to the adoption of ways and means of regaining what he had lost.

General Lake Reaches Muttra

Lake left Cawnpore and reached Agra on 22nd September. After assembling his forces at Sikandra, he began his march on Mathura (1st October, 1804). In the meantime, Jaswantrao had left Mathura for Delhi, in a bid to establish his authority there and to win over the Delhi Emperor. Lake followed him.

Jaswantrao Holkar's Failures and Retreat Towards Bharatpur

Jaswantrao failed at Delhi. The Fort was strongly garrisoned by troops under Col. Ochterlony, who was also the British Resident at the Emperor's Court, and had acquired full and complete confidence of the Emperor by giving him false hopes and promises. The Emperor exercised his influence entirely in favour of the English. Jaswantrao Holkar failed in his objectives and learning that Lake was following him in hot pursuit from Mathura, left Delhi hurriedly two days before Lake's arrival.

Jaswantrao then proceeded towards Saharanpur, as he hoped to get assistance in that area from the Sikh Sardar, Dolcha Singh, Bamboo Khan and Begum Sumroo. He was, however, disappointed. As related earlier, Bamboo Khan and Begum Sumroo had already gone over to the English. As regards Dolcha Singh, Marquess Wellesly had taken steps to win him over and written to Lake in his "official and secret" letter dated 10th September: "It is possible that the services of this chieftain may eventually be employed with effect ... when the river Jumna shall become fordable. I deem it advisable, therefore, to authorise Your Excellency, if you should think proper to subsidize Dolcha Singh during the war ..."

It may be mentioned that the Sikhs had invariably helped the English to Establish their dominion over India. Dolcha Singh refused to help Jaswantrao, who retreated towards Bharatpur, a sadly disappointed and disillusioned man.

26

Siege of Bharatpur

Jaswantrao Holkar Pursued on Way to Bharatpur

When he left Saharanpur for Bharatpur, Jaswantrao divided his army into two portions. He first despatched his infantry and artillery by one route and then followed with his cavalry by another. Lake decided to intercept both on their way to Bharatpur. He left Delhi on 31st October in pursuit of Jaswantrao with a force composed of three regiments of European and three of Indian cavalry and some heavy guns. At the same time, he ordered Major-General Fraser to follow in pursuit of Jaswantrao Holkar's infantry and artillery. Major-General Fraser left Delhi on 8th November, with a large detachment of Indian infantry, two regiments of Indian cavalry and some artillery.

Lake followed Jaswantrao to Shamli but when he got there, Jaswantrao Holkar had already left the place. He resumed his pursuit and at Farrukhabad got within striking distance of Jaswantrao Holkar on 17th November, but did not engage him in battle. Jaswantrao continued his journey undisturbed till he entered Bharatpur territory. The GovernorGeneral wrote about this futile pursuit to Lake.

> "It is unfortunate that Holkar's person should have escaped you. You are equally impressed with me by the absolute necessity of seizing or destroying him. Until his person be either destroyed or imprisoned, we shall have no rest. I, therefore, rely on you to permit no circumstance to divert you from pursuing him to the utmost extremity."

Major-General Fraser did better than Lake. He caught up with Holkar's infantry and artillery near the fort of Dig in Bharatpur territory on 12th November, and engaged them in battle just outside the fort. According to the English account, he lost 643 men, including 22 English officers Major-General Fraser himself was killed in action. The losses on the other side were reported to number about 2,000 killed and wounded in addition to the 87 heavy guns seized by the English. Jaswantrao Holkar's infantry retreated and took refuge in the Dig fort, where later on, Jaswantrao Holkar joined them with his cavalry. The event was acclaimed and celebrated as a "victory" by the Governor-General and Gen. Lake. The latter wrote to the Governor-General on 19th November, that is, a week after the engagement: "The rapidity of my march has astonished all the natives beyond imagination."

He did have some reason to claim credit for the "rapidity". From 31st October to 17th November, he had covered, on an average, 23 miles per day.

Raja Ranjit Singh of BharatPur Declares for Jaswantrao Holkar

In spite of overtures from the English, the Raja of Bharatpur had been undecided. Then something happened which left him no other alternative except to join Jaswantrao Holkar against the English. Mar Wellesley accused some prominent and respectable Bharatpur citizens of carrying on secret correspondence with Jaswantrao Holkar and of hatching with him a conspiracy against the English. At first, the Raja was ordered to arrest and hand over to the English all such persons as may be named by Lake. The order was followed almost immediately by the Governor General's authorization of Lake to arrest and shoot such persons without making any reference to the Raja at all. No self- respecting independent ruler could put up with such an affront to his prestige and authority. Added to this was the fact that Jaswantrao Holkar had taken refuge with Raja Ranjit Singh and the latter was bound by tradition to protect him. The Raja made common cause with Jaswantrao Holkar against the English, and Lake was happy about it. He wrote to Mar Wellesley on 27th November: "... it will not be in my power to avoid attacking and reducing his forts without delay."

The English Take Dig Fort

Lake reached Dig with his force on 8th December and laid siege to the fort. He began bombarding it on the 13th when heavy guns and ammunition had arrived from Agra. After ten days of shelling, a portion of one of the walls was breached. But by that time, the entire force inside the fort had been evacuated and had gone to Bharatpur. When the Company's troops entered the fort through the breach at midnight on 23rd December, they found it deserted and took possession of the empty shell after having lost in the siege 227 men killed. The town of Dig was occupied by them the next day.

The Governor-General had earlier written to Gen. Lake:

> "The entire reduction of the power and resources of the Raja of Bharatpur, however, has now become indispensably necessary and I accordingly authorise and direct Your Excellency to adopt immediate arrangements for the attainment of that desirable object, and for the annexation to the British power, in such manner as Your Excellency may deem most consistent with the public interests, of all the forts, territories and possessions belonging to the Raja of Bharatpur." (Governor-General's letter to General Lake, dated 20th December, 1804, marked "secret and official")

After occupying the Dig fort and town, the English lost no time in taking possession of the surrounding countryside till, it has been stated, only the capital town of Bharatpur was left with Raja Ranjit Singh. The latter was then asked by the English to surrender Jaswantrao Holkar to them but he disdainfully refused to do so. Lake marched on from Dig and laid siege to Bharatpur on 3rd January, 1805.

First English Assault Repulsed

Bharatpur was a walled city about eight miles long. The mud wall enclosing it was very thick and high, and was flanked on the outside by a wide, deep water-filled moat. The fort was located on the eastern corner of the city, and cannons had been mounted on the city-wall. Raja Ranjit Singh's entire army as also Jaswantrao Holkar's infantry were encamped inside the city. Jaswantrao Holkar's cavalry had stayed out at some distance from the city to harass the rear of the Company's army and to prevent supplies and provisions from reaching it.

The besiegers began to shell the city on 7th January. Two days later a portion of the city-wall was breached. A column managed to cross the moat and attempted to enter the city through the breach. But "... the column after making several attempts, with heavy loss, was obliged to retire." (General Lake to Mar Wellesley, 10th January, 1805.)

English Assaults Fail Again

The shelling of Bharatpur was resumed and continued for two days by its besiegers. On 21st January, 1803, they made a determined effort to enter the city but failed for the second time. Lake reported to Mar Wellesley:

> "... I am sorry to add that the ditch was found so broad and deep, that every attempt to pass it proved unsuccessful, and the party was obliged to return to the trenches, without effecting their object.
>
> "The troops behaved with their usual steadiness, but I fear, from the heavy fire they were unavoidably exposed to for a considerable time, that our loss has been severe."

The failure of his second attempt disheartened Lake so much that he did not venture to make another till he had received reinforcements, and so the besieging army was idle for a whole month.

Murray had, in the meanwhile, returned to Gujarat after annexing to the Company Jaswantrao Holkar's possessions in Central India. His entire force was sent under Major-General Jones to help Lake. It reached Bharatpur on 12th February, 1805.

Fresh military stores and ammunition as also a number of new extraheavy guns were obtained from Agra and other places. The place at which the city wall appeared to be narrowest was chosen as the target for shelling which had been resumed. On 20th February, the Company's army made its third attempt to take the city. But the defenders took that very way to sally forth in a sortie against the besiegers, and drove the latter back across the moat. European soldiers had been leading the assault, but when they were ordered to counter-attack, they held back. We quote from Mill (Vol. p. 426):

> "The Europeans, however, of His Majesty's 75th and 76th, who were at the head of the column, refused to advance ... The entreaties and expostulations of their officers failing to produce any effect, two regiments of Native Infantry, the 12th and 15th, were summoned to the front and they gallantly advanced."

The Indian soldiers fought the Bharatpur column that had come out in the sortie and pushed them back into the city.

Bribe to Raja of Bharatpur Suggested

The repeated failures utterly confounded Mar Wellesley and he appears to have decided to bribe the Raja of Bharatpur and so induce him to desert Jaswantrao Holkar. On 5th March, 1805, he wrote:

> "While the Commander-in-Chief is preparing for the siege of Bharatpur, or actually engaged in it, might it not be advisable to endeavour to detach Ranjit Singh from Holkar? Although Bharatpur has not fallen, ... Holkar would be hopeless if abandoned by Ranjit Singh."

The inducement suggested by Mar Wellesley was that should Ranjit Singh "renounce Holkar altogether," he would be "restored to his possessions." (*ibid*)

Lake accepted the suggestion and wrote to the Governor-General:

"Every endeavour is being and will be made to detach Ranjit Singh from Holkar ... Holkar and his followers would have little hope if abandoned by Ranjit Singh ... A correspondence is now going on between me and Ranjit Singh, which 1 am in hopes will lead to an accommodation sufficiently favourable to the British Government and prevent any future union of interests between that chief and Jaswantrao Holkar."

Lake Averts Threat to His Rear

Having failed to take Bharatpur in a fair fight, Gen. Lake centred his hopes on his "secret" methods, to which he resorted as suggested by the Governor-General. The latter had in his letter also made the suggestion that:

"Mr. Seton and General Smith should be authorised to offer a settlement of land to such of Amir Khan's followers as would quit him. Even Amir Khan himself might be offered a Jagheer, if he will quit Holkar's cause, submit to the British Government, and come into General Smith's camp."

Amir Khan, one of Jaswantrao Holkar's noted Sirdars, valued money more than his loyalty to his master. He was in command of Holkar's cavalry which had been harassing Gen. Lake's rear and preventing provisions and supplies from reaching him. Amir Khan had been carrying out his assignment with zest so that he could coerce the English into accepting the terms on which he expressed his willingness to desert Jaswantrao Holkar. Lake wrote to the Governor-General with reference to the latter's above suggestion:

"A settlement of land should certainly be offered to Amir Khan's followers. Amir Khan is most exorbitant in his demands. He asks thirty-three lacs of rupees in the first instance and Jagheer for 10,000 horse. This was his

> proposal in Rohilkhund, and I doubt much if he would now be more moderate ..."

Lake was, however, in an alarmingly weak position. The morale of his men was at a very low ebb, and his stores and provisions were running out as Amir Khan was effectively preventing their replenishment. Then there was the risk of Amir Khan attacking his rear, in which case Lake's force would have been caught between two fires and practically annihilated. So, a bargain was struck with Amir Khan through Gen. Smith, who had been sent out with a cavalry ostensibly to attack Amir Khan. The latter was "attacked" as arranged, and "defeated" at Afzalgarh. Amir Khan beat a retreat and joined Jaswantrao Holkar at Bharatpur. On 23rd March the "victorious" Smith Joined Lake who was still "besieging" Bharatpur. The "secret" method of Lake had succeeded in averting the grave danger to his rear.

Mar Wellesley Anxious for Peace

On 9th March, Mar Wellesley wrote to Lake:

> "... I feel too strong a desire for the early termination of the war, even on any terms ... I request Your Lordship not to attempt to renew the siege without full and ample means for its prosecution; nor to attempt any assault while the least doubt exists of success. I fear that we have despised the place enemy so much as to render both formidable."

Raja Ranjit Singh's Reactions to Offers of peace

Lake offered peace to Raja Ranjit Singh repeatedly. The latter summarily declined each time even to consider the terms offered. Correspondence between them was nevertheless continued.

Apparently, Raja Ranjit Singh was hoping that Doulatrao Sindhia would come to the aid of Jaswantrao Holkar. He was also expecting Amir Khan to attack the rear of the besiegers. When he was disappointed by both, he began to pay more attention to the offers of peace which were still being kept open by Lake for his acceptance. But he would on no account agree to deliver the person of Jaswantrao Holkar to the English. Evidently, the English saw no point in insisting on it and lifted the siege. About the end of March 1805, Raja Ranjit Singh quite openly helped Jaswantrao Holkar and his force to leave Bharatpur and go on their way to Sabalgarh without any obstruction and in perfect safety.

Peace Treaty Between the English and the Raja of Bharatpur

In the beginning of April 1805, a peace treaty was concluded by the English with Raja Ranjit Singh, whereby all the possessions of the latter including the Dig fort, which the English had seized and occupied during the hostilities, were given back to him and the *status quo* restored in toto. Doulatrao Sindhia's cavalry did come to the rescue but only after the peace treaty had been finalised.

The Legend of Bharatpur

The mud-walls of Bharatpur had humbled to the dust the pride of English military might. The invulnerability of the Bharatpur fort and the superb courage and determination of its defenders became legendary throughout the country, and the hypnotism produced on the Indian mind by the bogey of English superiority was dispelled for a considerable time to come.

The devout among defenders and besiegers alike ascribed the former's success to direct divine help. Thornton has recorded in his *Gazetteer of India:*

> "In 1805, during the first siege, some of the native soldiers in the British service declared that they distinctly saw the town defended by that divinity dressed in yellow garments and armed with his peculiar weapons, the bow, maco, conch and pipe."

Doulatrao Sindhia's Lost Opportunity

We have mentioned that Sindhia's cavalry arrived at Bharatpur in aid of Jaswantrao Holkar and Raja Ranjit Singh, after the latter had concluded peace with the English. The question arises, how did it happen? We shall attempt to answer it by narrating what had taken place between the English and Sindhia since their treaty of November 1803. We have already mentioned the flagrant violations of the treaty by the English, violations which "disgusted beyond measure" even Gen. Wellesley. (General Wellesley to Major Malcolm, 17th March, 1804.) We have also mentioned that the Governor-General promised to Sindhia large portions of Jaswantrao Holkar's territory, if the former joined the English against Jaswantrao Holkar, and that Sindhia had agreed to help them and did so at first. But before long, reasons for Sindhia's mistrust of the English and their promises grew and multiplied to such an extent that, on 18th October, 1804, he had to write plainly to Mar Wellesley. He specified the parts of his territory which the English, in clear violation of the treaty, had seized either for themselves or for giving them away to others. He concluded the letter by declaring that he could not reconcile himself to these losses of his territory and so had decided to marshal his forces and, if necessary, to enlist a new army and use them for regaining what had been taken away from him by force. Thus there were substantial grounds for the English to fear Sindhia's making common cause with Jaswantrao Holkar as also for the latter's hopes of aid from Sindhia, hopes which were shared by the Raja of Bharatpur, too. There can hardly be any doubt that had Sindhia attacked Lake's force in the rear, it would have been a major disaster for the siege of Bharatpur. Sindhia saw a golden opportunity not only of regaining what he had lost in territory, power and prestige but also of reviving the moribund Maratha Confederacy and restoring to it the status it had before the beginning of the Second Maratha War. Consequently he lost no time in taking advantage of it. He was at Burhanpur when he came to know that Bharatpur had been besieged by the English. He immediately despatched the entire body of his *Pindari* horsemen to Bharatpur and himself followed with the rest of his army. He was, however, frustrated and lost the opportunity because of traitors in his own camp. One such was Jean Baptiste, a high officer in his army. It would appear that Lake's "secret" method had, sometime earlier, succeeded with Jean Baptiste. On 22nd September, 1804, Gen. Lake had written to Mar Wellesley in a "private" letter from Agra:

> "Jean Baptiste ... is desirous of coming to me but requires a lac and a half of rupees to pay his troops. He is reported to be a good and fair man, and by what I have seen of him lately from his correspondence, has every appearance of being so; but I must be more convinced that he is so before I give him money, at any rate not to that extent; if he does anything worth notice, it will be time enough to pay him."

Jean Baptiste was controlling the movements of Sindhia's army and he saw to it that the *Pindari* horsemen which Sindhia sent to Bharatpur in advance did *not* arrive there in time. His task was probably made easier by the fact that most of the *Pindari* horsemen had earlier been in Amir Khan's service and were still under his influence.

Another person in Sindhia's *Durbar* on whom the English had acquired a hold was Sindhia's Chief Adviser, Munshi Kamalnain, who had signed in Sindhia's name the 1803 treaty with the English. According to James Mill, Kamalnain was in the pay of the English and watched over and safeguarded their interests whole-heartedly.

Apparently unaware that Jean Baptiste had prevented his *Pindari* horsemen from reaching Bharatpur, Sindhia continued to advance with the rest of his army and reached the river Chambal. When the English came to know of it, they immediately conveyed to Sindhia, through Munshi Kamalnain, a tempting offer. It was to the effect that if Sindhia went back and attacked and seized any districts in Holkar's Malwa territory (which had formerly belonged to Sindhia), then all the districts seized by him together with a large amount of money in cash would be presented to him by the Company. Sindhia did not succumb to the temptation and did not go back to invade Malwa. But somehow he was prevailed upon, either by Munshi Kamalnain or otherwise, to go back eight miles from the Chambal river and encamp at Sabalgarh.

Later, when Jaswantrao Holkar joined Sindhia at Sabalgarh, the latter came to know of Jean Baptiste's treachery and put him under arrest. But by that time Jean Baptiste had done something "worth notice" and had earned the payment promised by the English.

The Raja of Berar Soothed and Threatened

The Raja had refused point-blank to endorse the annexation by the Company of several of his most fertile provinces and "still considered the alienation of the provinces in question to be an act of injustice and a violation of faith on the part of the British Government".

The English came to know that Jaswantrao Holkar had been making efforts from Mathura to win over the Raja. So the Resident at the latter's capital (Nagpur) was "instructed to assure the Raja of the most amicable disposition of the British Government towards him". At the same time, the Resident was directed:

> "to take a proper opportunity of apprising the Raja of Berar in the most public manner of the information which the British Government had received with regard to his proceeding, in connection with Jaswantrao Holkar, and to inform him that "the Governor-General had deemed it necessary, without awaiting any explanation, to make preparatory arrangement for the eventual purpose of ...

punishing treachery on the part of the Raja". The Resident, however, was directed to "suspend these representations until he should have learnt the result of the Commander-in-Chief's first operations against Holkar, unless circumstances should render an immediate statement of them useful and necessary."
(Note—All quotations in this paragraph are from the despatch of the Governor-General to the Company's Directors dated 9th March, 1805).

Raja Raghoji Bhonsle did not go to the aid of Jaswantrao Holkar at Bharatpur.

ABOUT THE AUTHOR

Pandit Sunderlal was an eminent Gandhian and freedom fighter. He was originally a revolutionary and belonged to the famous Ghadar party. After coming in close contact with Mahatma Gandhi in the early 1920s, Pandit Sunderlal became a Gandhian and a practitioner of non-violence and Ahimsa. He represented the holistic evolution of a revolutionary to a Gandhian believing in non-violence and worked closely with Mahatma Gandhi in Sevagram Ashram, Wardha. He was imprisoned seven times for participating in the Indian freedom movement.

Pandit Sunderlal founded the Hindustani Culture Society in 1941. He was part of a goodwill mission to the erstwhile Hyderabad state in 1948. He was President of the All India Peace Council during 1950–62 and President of the India–China Friendship Association. He pursued three key missions throughout his life—promoting the essential unity of all religions, promoting communal harmony between Hindus and Muslims, and promoting and practising the composite culture of India.

Pandit Sunderlal's original work in four volumes, entitled *Bharat Mein Angrezi Raj*, was published in 1929, banned by the British, and republished when the ban on the book was lifted. In 1941, he published *Geeta aur Quran* simultaneously in Hindi and Urdu. This book has been translated into many languages. He authored more than 40 books. Pandit Sunderlal launched *Karmayogi* in 1909. He was editor of *Swarajya*, a Hindi weekly in the early part of the 20th century.